Raúl Eduardo Chao

Cuba in 1933
A chronicle of the 1933 Cuban Revolution:
the perspective from Washington.

From the same author:

HISTORIA DE LA QUÍMICA INDUSTRIAL
TOTAL QUALITY AND PRODUCTIVITY MANAGEMENT
PERFORMANCE MANAGEMENT
STRATEGIC PLANNING
MANAGEMENT DEVELOPMENT
PROCESS IMPROVEMENT TEAMS
QUALITY STRATEGIES
GESTIÓN DE FUTURO

CONTRAMAESTRE
BARAGUÁ
POEMAS Y MEMORIAS DE CUBA
JIMAGUAYÚ
GUÁIMARO
FREEDOM EMBATTLED
COLONIAL CUBA
REPUBLICAN CUBA
EXILED CUBA
THREE DAYS IN MARCH
RAÍCES CUBANAS
ÁLBUM DE CUBA
RESCATANDO A MARTÍ
UN FESTÍN DE PALABRAS
DAMN THE REVOLUTION
MADAME SECRETARY
LA GRAN ESTAFA
LA MEMORIAS DEL ALMIRANTE CERVERA
MATANZAS EN LA INDEPENDENCIA DE CUBA
LA GUERRA DEL 1868
LA TREGUA FECUNDA
LA GUERRA DEL 95
OUR CONSUL IN HAVANA
EL DIARIO DE GUERRA DE MÁXIMO GÓMEZ
CUBA BAJO LA BANDERA NORTEAMERICANA
CUBA EN 1958
CUBA EN 1959
CATACLYSM OR HOAX
MARXISTS AT THE GATE
MARXISTAS EN LAS PUERTAS
CROWDS
¡VIVA ESPAÑA!
CUBA IN 1933

Dedication

To Maggie and Bertie Bustamante,
creators and the soul of
Herencia Cultural Cubana
and *Herencia magazine,*
and, through them, to all
Cuban exiles
that have been
for over a half century
committed to the liberty
and sovereignty of
our Republic of Cuba.

A picture that appeared in the front page of **The Mid-Week Pictorial**, published by **The New York Times** in August 26, 1933. It shows the young soldier who assassinated Antonio Jiménez, Chief of Gerardo Machado's Secret Police, as he is raised with acclaim by the public in Cuba, on August 12, 1933.

Raúl Eduardo Chao

Cuba in 1933
A chronicle of the 1933 Cuban Revolution:
the perspective from Washington.

DUPONT CIRCLE EDITIONS

WASHINGTON, D.C.   LONDON   SYDNEY

Copyright © 2019 by Raúl Eduardo Chao

All rights reserved Under International and Pan American Copyright Conventions. Published in the United States.
Dupont Circle Editions

Library of Congress Catalog Card pending

Chao, Raúl Eduardo, 1939-
CUBA IN 1933 / Raúl Chao

ISBN- 978-1-79488- 418-2
Printed in the United States of America

FRONT COVER:
HAVANA IN 1933. THE CENTRO GALLEGO

BACK COVER:
PARQUE DE LA LIBERTAD
MATANZAS, CUBA

No part of this publication may be reproduced, stored or introduced into a retrieval system, or transmitted, in any form, or by any means, without the prior written permission of both the copyright owner and the above publisher of this book. The scanning, uploading, selling and/or distribution of this book, by any means, including the Internet, without the permission of the publisher is illegal and punishable by law.

Table of Contents

Introduction	8
Cuba in the early 1930s	9
A prelude to the 1933 Revolution in Cuba	10
A chronicle of the Years before The 1933 Cuban Revolution	14
Cuba in 1933	24
Imminent conflicts in Cuba	29
January	27
February	30
March	34
April	35
May	41
June	68
July	93
August	112
September	175
October	272
November	322
December	391
Aftermath	372
Appendices	373
The Crimes of Machado	374
US Warships in Cuban Waters	388
Gerardo Machado & Communism	390
Index	394

Introduction

The 1930s saw major attempts at revolution in Cuba. Prompted by a cruel dictatorship, the economic hardships of a world depression, and the growing control of their economy by Spaniards and North Americans, a group of Cubans led by students and intellectuals sought radical reforms and a profound transformation of Cuban society. In January 1934, after the overthrow of the regime of Gerardo Machado y Morales (President, 1925-33) and the short-lived first presidency of Ramón Grau San Martin (President, 1933-34, 1944-48), they were catapulted into power. Their revolution failed, however. Despite the rise of militarism, the opposition of the United States, and the many divisions among Cuban political elites and within the revolutionary ranks, Cuba returned to less turbulent times. Fulgencio Batista (President, 1940-44; Dictator, 1952-59) and the military emerged as the arbiters of Cuba's politics, first through de facto ruling and finally with the legal election of Batista to the presidency in 1940.

The end of World War II and the end of the early Batista era brought to power the offspring of the 1933 Revolution. With the election in 1944 of Grau San Martin and, four years later, his successor, Carlos Prío Socarrás (president, 1948-52), an era of democratic government, respect for human rights, and accelerated prosperity ensued. Yet political violence and corruption increased. Many saw these Auténtico administrations, belonging to the Cuban Revolutionary Party (*Partido Revolucionario Cubano-PRC)*, more commonly known as the Authentic Party (Partido Auténtico), as having failed to live up to the ideals of the revolution. Others still supported the Auténticos and hoped for new leadership that could correct the vices of the past. A few conspired to take power by force.

This book looks at all these events from the perspective of the United States. It is based on telegrams, Telex conversations, memoranda and inquiries from Washington to and from Havana, recently declassified by the American government. These are complemented with chronological listings of events in Cuba and Washington.

RAÚL EDUARDO CHAO
LAKELAND, FLORIDA

Cuba in the early 1930s

A prelude to the 1933 Revolution in Cuba

The story of the events in Cuba in the early 1930s, is naturally a consequence of the uncertainties and anxieties created by the serious economic downturns and a severe economic crisis in the long years of the previous decade. In 1920, there was a sharp drop in the price of sugar that resulted in financial chaos and social misery. Searching for a culprit, various groups blamed Cuba's economic dependence on the United States. For intellectuals and politicians, the crisis quickened the need for change of the existing societal order. Many Cubans were barred from becoming productive members of society. Decision making was basically in the hands of the United Sates from abroad, and wealthy industrialists, Spaniards and Americans, from inside. The economic crisis led to a resurgence of economic nationalism, a demand for protective legislation to Cuban interests, and a reassessment of the close economic ties that had been forged between the United States and Cuba. A main concern, of course, was the repeated interventions of the United States government in Cuba's internal affairs, allowed and permitted by the Platt Amendment.

A strong Anti-United States mood, xenophobia, and reclamation of people's destinies became the main themes of a budding nationalism. As Cubans entered the 1930s, the list of concerns was expanded to include demands for social justice, for the end of political corruption and the end of economic dependence on a single crop.

Alfredo Zayas Alonso, president from 1921 to 1924, made good use of this clamor for nationalism and the reaffirmation of Cuba's sovereignty by confronting the American special envoy, **Enoch Crowder**. Unfortunately, his administration was overshadowed by graft, mismanagement, and plain and simple corruption. He nevertheless was able to retrieve Cuba's credit, avert intervention, and secure long overdue title to **Isla de Pinos** after a two-decade imposition by the **Platt Amendment**.

In the 1920s and early 1930s, young Cuban University graduates had difficulties finding jobs due to the country's economic environment and the structure of the financial, commercial and industrial sectors. This, naturally, increased the frustrations of an entire generation that could not enjoy the well-deserved returns of their efforts, nor apply their acquired knowledge. Full of frustrations and deter-mined to take action, the students from the **University of Havana** organized themselves as the **Federation of University Students** (*Federación Estudiantil Universitaria-FEU)*, occupied university buildings, and orchestrated short-lived student strikes. They got a series of academic and administrative reforms, larger government subsidies, and the establishment of a **University Reform Commission** composed of professors, students, and alumni. Unfortunately, this university reform movement, which had started as a crusade for academic reform, developed political overtones when they began to protest the decision of President Gerardo Machado to reelect himself and remain in power for longer than he had been elected to serve.

After Machado announced his decision, in April 1928, he set up a packed **Constitutional Convention** that granted him a new six-year period of power without reelection and abolished the vice presidency. In November, through a fake election in which he was the only candidate, Machado was given a new term, to run from May 20, 1929, to May 20, 1935.

When **Tomás Estrada Palma**, Cuba's first elected president in 1902, was persuaded to re-elect himself and remain in power in 1905, he was confronted with a rebellion organized by **José Miguel Gómez**, the charismatic veteran leader from Santa Clara, and the Liberal Party. His critics accused him of ignoring the 1901 Constitution. The opposition led by regional leaders rose up in rebellion in what became the **August Little War** or *Guerrita de Agosto*. The small rural guard force was incapable of suppressing the uprising, and Estrada Palma requested US military intervention.

Machado's situation was different. His decision, at first only brought about a wave of national indignation against the violation of the Constitution, but his regime still enjoyed the support of the business and conservative sectors of society. Increased revenues had begun to bring prosperity, and Machado's improved administration, especially in the field of public works, had gained him a strong following. The Cuban armed forces, organized two decades earlier during Gómez's administration, also strongly backed the regime. Only a few officers were discontented with Machado's reelection, but they were powerless and ineffective in their opposition. The US was having domestic and international problems of its own and looked with indifference at events in Cuba. The times were not ripe to become involved in Cuban affairs if the Machado administration-maintained order and stability and a friendly posture toward Washington.

Machado impeded the growth of political opposition by winning control of the **Conservative Party** (*Partido Conservador*) and forging an alliance with both the **Liberal Party** and the small **Popular Party** (*Partido Popular*). He was also able to control Congress and the Judiciary and submit them to his executive's will.

It was different with the University students. There was a formidable and uncompromising student opposition to his decision to do away with the 1901 Constitution and prolong his presidency. The students, from University of Havana and from many of the island High Schools, rioted and demonstrated in numerous towns throughout Cuba. Machado took urgent measures to thwart any opposition, and closed the University, dissolved the FEU, and abolished the *University Reform Commission*. He also expelled from Cuba various Spanish and European labor leaders as undesirable aliens. Antigovernment newspapers were closed, and, on his orders, the military began to survey and police any dissenters. He vowed to keep peace and order at any price. The students, however, were adamant. A group of the more bellicose launched the **University Students Directorate** (*Directorio Estudiantil Universitario-DEU*, the *Directorio*) to battle the system. It issued a Manifesto upholding the students' rights to participate in Cuba's political life and reject Machado's illegal reelection travesty.

Machado retaliated when students tried to take over the University. The **University Council**, composed of faculty and administrative officials, formed disciplinary tribunals and expelled most of the *Directorio* leaders. Cubans began to view with admiration and respect the fearless student generation that was ready to battle Machado's police. Besieged by shock waves of a world-wide depression and oppressed by an increasingly ruthless dictator, many Cubans, especially those among the less favored sectors of society, turned their alliances to these young people instead of traditional politicians. It became the **"generation of 1930."** History has yet to form a definitive decision on the worth of these belligerent and confrontational youngsters. To some, they were irresponsible and undisciplined; to others they were big-hearted idealists. Regardless to either interpretation, the *"generation of 1930"* opened a new style of politics in Cuba. Violence was now compatible with the sacred right to vote and make decisions about the common future.

Cuba was overwhelmed in the early 1930s by a catastrophic spiral of conflicts and bloodshed. Violence among men has proven to bring unexpected consequences... collateral damage in military lingo. While the leadership of the *Directorio* were in jail in 1931, a rather small group of students formed a splinter organization, the **Student Left Wing** (*Ala Izquierda Estudiantil-AIE*). It was simply a tool of the **Cuban Communist Party** (*Partido Comunista de Cuba-PCC*), founded in 1925 by **Rubén Martínez Villena**, a popular poet and intellectual who would later fight in the Spanish Civil War (1936-1939) on the Communist side.

Cuba became a turmoil of strikes, appeals to the *proletariat* and internal struggles within the armed forces. A democratic group also surfaced: the **Nationalist Union** (*Unión Nacionalista*), headed by a War of Independence colonel, **Carlos Mendieta**. In 1931 Mendieta and Menocal, the former president, organized a short-lived uprising in Pinar del Rio Province. That same year, a group led by engineer **Carlos Hevia** and journalist **Sergio Carbó** equipped an expedition in the US and landed in Oriente province, only to be crushed by Machado's army. Most prominent, perhaps, of these anti-Machado groups was established in 1930, the **ABC**, a clandestine extremist organization composed of intellectuals, students, and the middle sectors of society. None of this proved to be positive for Cuba. And so on... and on.

For Cubans, when it comes to the accomplishments of the **1933 Revolution**... as *Ho Chi Ming* responded when asked if the *French Revolution had been good for France...*

"...it is too early to tell..."
1871-

Gerardo Machado Morales,
(1871-1939)
5th President of Cuba.

A Chronicle of the years before the 1933 Cuban Revolution

1925

May 20 *Gerardo Machado Morales* of the Liberal Party takes possession of the presidency of Cuba. He declares publicly against reelection.

August 2 The *III World National Workers Congress* in Havana recognizes the *National Confederation of Workers of Cuba (CNOC)*. Anarcho-syndicalist *Alfredo López* is elected general secretary.

August 16 Foundation of the *Communist Party of Cuba* in Havana, a merger of several socialist organizations.

Jean-Claude Forestier
(1861-1930)

November 19 Anarchist *José Cuixart* was murdered in La Cabaña. One more among the numerous political murders in prisons.

November 23 *Julio Antonio Mella* is arrested and accused with possession of explosives and having placed a bomb in the *Payret Theater*.

Gerardo Machado
(1871-1939)

December 16 A new electoral law prevents the formation of new parties.

December 23 *Mella* ends her hunger strike after his 30-day prison sentence.

December 26 A presidential decree dissolves the *University Assembly* and prohibits any non-cultural student associations. A plan for urbanization Havana during 1925-1930, is drawn up by the French architect **Jean-Claude Nicolas Forestier** (1861-1930).

Julio Antonio Mella
(1903-1929)

1926

January 27 The Cuban Senate rejects the *Lombard Law*, sanctioned by the representatives, which would force companies to hire 75% of Cuban workers.

April 14 A strike by the *Railway Brotherhood* begins, especially in the eastern part. It ends on May 30.

May 10 The construction of the **Cuban Central Highway**, which will cross the island, at the cost of $ 56 million is approved.

June 15 The Spanish delegation to Cuba is raised to the category of Embassy.

Cuban Central Highway
In 1925

The **Lombard Law** was a proposal approved by the Cuban Congress in 1925, providing that 75% of employment in companies in Cuba, with 75 % of salaries, would be paid to Cuban workers.

August 11 The FEU sends a telegram to **General Plutarco Elías Calles**, president of Mexico, in solidarity with his anti-clerical policy.

August 26 The Dean of London's *St. Paul's Cathedral* states in the British press that Cuba's per capita income is higher than the English.

September 7 President *Machado* imposes military instruction in all *Secondary Education Institutes*.

Miguel Mariano Gómez
(1889-1950)

October 20 The *1926 Hurricane* hits the island with enormous violence.

November 19 *Miguel Mariano Gómez* is elected mayor of Havana.

November 12 *Machado* speaks for the first time of dictatorship in public.

December 21 *Orestes Ferrara* is appointed Cuban Ambassador to Washington.

Plutarco Elias Calles
1925 Mexico President

December 31 The financing of the new *Cuban Central Highway* 1939 goes to the *Chase National Bank*.

Col. Orestes Ferrara
(1876-1972)

1927

January 6 The Ministry of Interior (Interior) gathers the entire circulation of the newspaper *El Heraldo de Cuba*, well known as contrary to the government of *Machado*.

January 17 A *Manifesto of Protest* of a group of Cubans headed by *Enrique José Varona* against the *Platt Amendment* is published in Havana.

February 6 The *Machado* pro-reelection campaign begins.

March 2 The works of the *Cuban Central Highway* reaches San Francisco de Paula, near Havana.

March 15 The first issue of the *Advance* magazine is published. It will continue until 1930. It is considered a milestone in avant-garde culture with *Francisco Ichaso* and **Jorge Mañach** as editors.

March 28 President *Machado* asks the House of Representatives to increase his term from four to seven years with the possibility of re-election; all of this is prohibited by the 1901 Constitution.

March 29 The House of Representatives approves the bill to modify the Constitution and extend the elective mandate of presidents, which are extended 4 years.

Path of the 1926 Hurricane, affecting Havana and Miami

March 30 Student protests shake the island. The police invade the University campus as the students go to the house of **Enrique José Varona**.

April 7 Creation of the *University Student Directory* founded by **Antonio Guiteras Holmes** and **Eduardo Chibás**.

April 13 *José E. Obregón*, son-in-law of *Machado*, is appointed representative of the *Chase National Bank*.

Antonio Guiteras
(1906-1935)

Cuba in 1933   16

April 20 *Machado* departs on an official visit to the US. There he makes an appeal to review the *Platt Amendment*, for attracting *US capital* to Cuba and for lowering tariffs on Cuban sugar.

May 6 The *Grupo de Detallistas* (Retailers' Group) publishes a manifesto with its ideals and condemns the government.

May 8 *Machado* returns from the US and receives a great welcome.

May 11 The President partially suspends the *University Statutes* and declares the end of classes on the following 28th of the month.

June 21 The *Constitutional Reform Project* is published in *Cuba's Official Gazette* and a *National Assembly* is called to modify the Constitution.

Eduardo Chibás
(1907-1951)

October 13 Public meeting places are restricted. The right to assembly is also limited, taking another step towards the dictatorship.

November 11 Classes are suspended again at the *University of Havana* under the pretext of the need to complete the preparatory works of the *VI Pan American Conference* to be held in Havana.

November 20 The **Woman's Right to Vote** is finally approved. *Bohemia* magazine becomes a weekly magazine.

Enrique José Varona
(1848-1933)

Issue of Bohemia
with Women's Vote

1928

January 16 The president of Cuba, *Machado*, and **Calvin Coolidge**, from the US, inaugurate the *VI Pan American Conference* in the *National Theater* in Havana before a group of Latin American delegates.

Cuban Stamp commemorating the VI International American Conference in

January 25 The construction of the University of Havana *monumental staircase* is finished.

February 11 The *Juventud Católica Cubana* (Cuban Catholic Youth) is founded.

February 12 *Machado* travels with the pilot *Charles Lindbergh* over Havana as part of the celebrations of the *VI Conference*.

February 20 Cuba signs the *Right of Asylum* with other Latin American nations during the *VI Pan American Conference*.

March 5 Elections to the *Constitutional Convention*.

April 11 The University of Havana is occupied militarily.

April 14 The first meeting of the *Constitutional Convention* takes place.

US President Calvin Coolidge with Cuban President Machado

May 9 The Constitutional Convention (violating Art. 1 15 of the Constitution of 1901) approves the extension of powers for two years. *Machado* can be re-elected for a period of six. The vice presidency disappears.

May 10 , Secretary of the Interior, resigns from office.

May 11 Machado promulgates the *Constitutional Convention* reforms in the *Official Gazette*.

July 19 The Liberal, Conservative and Popular Parties proclaim *Machado* the only

Fundación de la Juventud Católica Febrero 11. 1928

candidate for the next elections.

September 28 Five prisoners are killed in *Isla de Pinos*. It is estimated that about 195 were killed there.

November 19 Elections are held in Cuba with *Machado* as the only candidate.

Cuban National Capitol

1929

January 10 *Julio Antonio Mella*, a fanatical Communist leader, is murdered in Mexico by Mexican Communists.

Jorge Mañach
(1898-1961)

April 30 The *Cuban Congress* proclaims *Machado* president for a period of six years, until May 20, 1935.

October 24 The Worldwide Financial and Stock Market Crisis starts today, *Black Thursday*, at the *New York Stock Exchange*.

November 21 The brand new *Cuban National Capitol*, headquarters of the *House of Representatives* and the *Senate*, is inaugurated in Havana. A huge statue of the Republic is placed inside, the work of the Italian sculptor *Angelo Zellelli*.

1930

January 8 The government lowers the salaries of public officials by 10% and 15%.

January 14 *Machado* issues a Presidential Decree prohibiting any demonstration, meeting or political rally during the harvest, except for members of the Liberal, Conservative and Popular Parties.

March 7 *Federico García Lorca* arrives in Havana. He leaves on June 12.

April 19 The air postal service between New York and Havana begins. The Supreme Court declares the ban on meetings issued by *Machado* unconstitution-

Federico García Lorca
(1898-1936)

al. Great anti-Machado demonstrations in the Havana's Central Park.

May 18 A political rally in Artemisa, Pinar del Río, ends violently with six dead and multiple wounded. Ten days later, *Juan Gualberto Gómez, Roberto Méndez Peñate, Carlos Mendieta* and other leaders of the *Nationalist Union* are prosecuted for these events.

September 28 The University Student Directory (DEU), is organized by students, with the leadership of *Carlos Prío, Antonio Varona, Justo Carrillo, Felipe Pazos, Rubén de León, Mario Labourdette, Ramiro Valdés Daussá, Raúl Roa, Inés Segura, Silvia Martel, Salvador Vilaseca, Rafael García Bárcena, Rubio Padilla, Rafael Trejo* and others.

Miguel de Unamuno
(1864-1936)

September 30 *Rafael Trejo* a DEU student is injured in a demonstration was headed to the home of the patrician Enrique José Varona but does not reach its destination, during a police charge. A rogue policeman wounded Trejo causing his death the next day.

October 3 The government suspends Constitutional Guarantees.

October 10 Lunch-tribute to dictator Machado by sergeants and army classes organized by Sgt. Pablo Rodríguez Silverio. Attending, among others, were *Sergeant Fulgencio Batista*, the first Sergeant *José Eleuterio Pedraza* and Sergeants *Pedro and Otilio Rojas*.

October 15 A series of *Tánganas* (scandalous daily student rallies) are directed against the government.

October 21 Frequent bomb explosions are a daily occurrence.

November 19 Partial elections throughout the country. Liberals triumph overwhelmingly.

November 11 Several Anti-Machadist student disorders.

Arsenio Ortiz
El Chacal de Oriente

November 17 Students in secondary schools refuse to attend classes.

December 10 The Machado government restores Constitutional guarantees.

December 11 A new Decree suspending constitutional guarantees.

December 15 A new Decree closes the University of Havana, which is occupied by the army.

December 27 Classes are closed at all Normal Teacher's Schools.

December 30 A *Message of the Spanish Intellectuals* is signed among others by **Miguel de Unamuno**, Ortega, Jiménez de Asúa, Marañón, Azorín, Valle Inclán, Pitaluga. It prognosticates a Civil War in Spain.

1931

January 3 The *Cuban Student Left Wing*, a communist tendency group, emerges in Havana.

February 2 Classes are closed at 6 High School (Institutes) along several provinces in Cuba.

Carlos Mendieta
(1873-1960)

February 14 Almost 100 University professors are detained and processed.

February 15 *"La Porra,"* a repression group against anti-Machado, appears.

February 23 A bomb explodes in the Presidential Palace. *Miguel Mariano Gómez*, elected mayor of Havana, and by order of Machado, is soon replaced (impeached) after criticizing the government.

February 24 Inauguration of the *Cuban Central Highway*.

February 25 Beginning of a massive and systematic search for bombs, chemical material and weapons.

April 19 The Machado government recognizes the Spanish Republic.

Mario García Menocal
(1866-1941)

April 25 **Arsenio Ortiz** and his henchmen are accused of crimes before the investigating judge Balmaseda. The trial is diluted by the accused having the backing of the government.

July 1 A presidential Decree maintains closed the University of Havana, the Institutes and the Normal Teacher's Schools.

July 30 A streetcar strike begins that, after two days, becomes a general strike against *Machado*.

August 7 The landing of a rebel ship, the *"Río Verde,"* fails. On board are **Mario García-Menocal** and *Carlos Mendieta*, conspiring against the regime.

August 16 *Menocal* and *Mendieta* are arrested by Navy units and taken to *La Cabaña*.

August 17 A successful landing of an expedition in Gibara, where **Carlos Hevia** and the journalist **Sergio Carbó** participate.

August 19 Gibara is *bombed* to subdue the insurgents.

September 21 The population census is Cuba shows 3,962,344 inhabitants.

October 31 Foundation of the *ABC Movement* by the young lawyer Joaquín Martínez Sáenz.

December 19 Colonel *Cosme de la Torriente*, a member of the *Revolutionary Board* in exile in New York, arrives in Havana trying to gain understanding and secure a peace agreement between the dictatorship and the opposition.

Carlos Hevia
(1900-1964)

1932

January 13 Machado proclaims an amnesty in favor of the August rebels in *"Rio Verde"*. In a few days he releases 400 political prisoners. The *ABC* prepares a terrorist campaign against the dictatorship.

May 19 23rd Street of El Vedado is baptized as *Avenida General Machado*.

May 21 Bomb packages sent by mail become frequent.

June 1 *Orestes Ferrara* is appointed *Secretary of State* (Foreign) and Oscar B. Cintas, Ambassador to Washington.

Joaquín Martínez Sáenz
(1900-1970)

September 27 **Clemente Vázquez Bello**, president of the *Senate* and the *Liberal Party* is killed by shots in the *Country Club of Havana*. In revenge, the police murders that night several members of the *Freyre de Andrade family*: Guillermo, Leopoldo and Gonzalo.

September 28 Sixty kg of dynamite are discovered in the *Cemetery of Colón*, near the pantheon of the *Vázquez Bello family*.

Sergio Carbó
(1892-1971)

Attendance by the dictator's funeral was expected, but at the last minute, the wife of the murdered man arranged for his funeral at Las Villas. The murder plot is attributed to the ABC movement.

October 13 Constitutional guarantees are restored with a view to the next elections to Congress.

November 19 Partial elections to Congress, provincial councils and municipalities, with participation by the *Conservative, Liberal* (Machado's) *and Popular parties*. Liberals win in five provinces but not in Pinar del Río, which is considered conservative territory.

November 8 *Franklin D. Roosevelt* is elected president of the US. A possible American mediation between opposition and government in Cuba begins to take shape.

November 9 A deadly *tsunami* sweeps and completely wipes out the town of *Santa Cruz del Sur* in Camagüey. It would be the biggest natural catastrophe in the history of Cuba.

November 10 Premiere at the *Teatro Martí* of the Cuban zarzuela *Cecilia Valdés*, music by *Gonzalo Roig*. The *López Serrano* building is built in Deco style.

December 31, 1932
Cubans believe that next year, 1933, will be consumed by a brutal and deadly revolution.

Clemente Vázquez Bello
(1887-1932)

The 1932 devastating tsunami
in Santa Cruz del Sur

Cuba in 1933

Imminent Conflicts in Cuba

As the year 1933 started, Cuba was in an unusual situation. The country was at a significant period of prosperity and President Machado had the support of almost every sector of the business and traditional communities. National revenues were higher than ever, the government administration was showing signs of improvement, prosperity had reached Cuba like never before and the President had realistic and viable plans that would bring the country to sustainable growth, partially due to massive projects in public works. The Cuban armed forces strongly backed the regime and, in terms of foreign relations, the United States had so many domestic and international problems that was viewing Cuba with indifference and was disinclined to become involved in Cuban affairs, as long as the Cuban administration kept order and stability and a friendly attitude toward Washington.

Yet most Cubans sensed that the country was quickly approaching difficult times politically. Starting back in 1928, students began to aggressively protest the decision of President Machado to remain in power for another term. Machado was claiming that his economic program could not be completed within his four-year term and that only he could carry it out if his presidency was extended. In 1928, he called for a Constitutional *Convention* that granted him a six-year new period of power without reelection and abolished the vice presidency. After the Convention, he presided over a fake election in which only he ran as candidate. That brought about a popular wave of national indignation that debilitated his presidency.

His response was to increasingly militarize the country making use of the military in a variety of civilian posts, both at the national and local levels. Additionally, he firmed his control over the *Partido Conservador* (Conservative Party) and lined it up with his own *Partido Liberal* and with the small *Partido Popular* (Popular Party). The result was his absolute control of Congress and the Judiciary, and their complete subservience to his Executive will. Finally, he temporarily closed the university, abolished the *University Reform Commission*, expelled several Spanish and European labor leaders from the country as undesirable aliens, closed antigovernment newspapers and gave the military an even wider role in surveilling and policing the population.

The University students responded by setting aside their crusade for academic reform and turning their efforts into the defense of democracy in the country. To openly confront and oppose the regime, a small but determined group organized what they called the *Directorio Estudiantil Universitario-DEU* (the University Students Directorate). Its first act was to issue a Political Manifesto attacking Machado's abuses. When they protested in front of the University, Machado rapidly stroked back. Upon his orders, the University's *Faculty and Administrative Council* expelled most of the Directorio leaders. At a clash with police, a student leader, Rafael Trejo was killed; it became the turning point in the struggle against the regime. Many Cubans thought the students had been irresponsible and undisciplined; for others they became the best exponents of patriotic idealism.

By 1931, the main leaders of the *Directorio* were in jail, as well as a small group from a splinter organization, the *Ala Izquierda Estudiantil, AIE* (the Student Left Wing). The AIE, as most people suspected, was nothing but a tool of the *Partido Comunista de Cuba, PCC*, (the Cuban Communist Party). In addition to the AIE and the PCC, a smaller group, the *Partido Unión Nacionalista, PUN*, (the Nationalist Union Party) participated in strikes and anti-Machado propaganda. Very prominent among these anti-Machado groups was the ABC, a covert extremist organization organized by academics, lawyers, students, and professors, all from the middle class, calling for the expropriation of large landholdings, nationalization of health, power, transportation and public services, restrictions on land acquisitions by US companies, and political liberty and social justice. Abroad, particularly in New York City, several of these organizations formed the *Junta Revolucionaria*, who also participated on demonstrations and sabotage actions.

Few Cubans noticed that, while this was happening in their midst, the rest of the world was experiencing the first shock waves of a devastating world depression. Worst of all, in Germany and Italy the ferments of world totalitarism was taking hold. The Italians were the targets of Fascism indoctrination by Benito Mussolini while in Germany, *German National Socialists* were heeding to the words of Adolph Hitler.

What follows are some noteworthy events occurring in Cuba and the perspective of American diplomats as they found out, observed, analyzed and took actions as they dealt with these events.

JANUARY OF 1933

Events in Cuba

January 7 *Carlos Mendieta, Méndez Peñate* and *Aurelio Hevia* seek asylum in the Mexican embassy. A month later they receive authorization to travel to Miami.

Washington Telex

HARRY HANK GUGGENHEIM, US AMBASSADOR IN CUBA, WRITES TO US SECRETARY OF STATE **HENRY L. STIMSON.**

HAVANA, January 5, 1933-noon.

My dispatch 1472, December 31. Killing of González Rubiera was followed by murder on January 3 of ex-policeman Manuel Cepero who warned Major Arsenio Ortiz *(see dispatch No. 1441, December 8)*. Police yesterday arrested several oppositionists, among them a member of student directorate known as Dr. Hernández whose real name was Alvarez.

The Embassy received numerous requests to ensure safety of person[s] in hands of the police. Without making official representations, in each case brought to my attention I informally conferred with Government officials expressing hope that lives would be respected.

Last night I personally called on the Secretary of State in regard to Hernández and was assured there was no cause for apprehension in this or other cases. Hernández or Alvarez died shortly after midnight in a hospital to which he had been brought with a bullet in his head. Orestes Ferrara this morning explained that he had ascertained last night that no person named Hernández was under arrest.

These killings of prisoners have deeply stirred public opinion and have strengthened belief that no person under arrest is safe from official vengeance. I have asked for an appointment with the President and shall endeavor to use my personal influence to discourage further acts of this kind.

(Signed) Harry F. Guggenheim

--◇◇◇--0--◇◇◇--

HARRY HANK GUGGENHEIM, US AMBASSADOR IN CUBA, WRITES TO
US SECRETARY OF STATE **HENRY L. STIMSON.**
Havana, January 9, 1933-4:00 PM

My telegram No.1, January 5, noon. I saw President Machado this morning. He did not attempt to disclaim Government's responsibility for recent murders of students which he characterized as a stupid mistake. He said that in future the lives of prisoners would be respected. His attitude during our conversation was most cordial and he reiterated his willingness to follow any suggestions that I might care to make at any time. I stressed the imperative need of measures designed to restore public confidence which he has repeatedly promised to take but has not carried out.
(signed) Harry F. Guggenheim

--◊◊◊--O--◊◊◊--

FRANCIS WHITE, US ASSISTANT SECRETARY OF STATE, WRITES TO
US SECRETARY OF STATE **HENRY L. STIMSON.**
Washington, January 10, 1933

The Cuban Chargé d'Affaires, Dr. José T. Barón, called and after first discussing briefly the Chaco matter said that he had a letter from Sr. Orestes Ferrara directing him to discuss with me the events that took place in Cuba last week. He said that the Government regretted very much the bloodshed that had occurred and then Dr. Barón gave a somewhat involved description of what took place when the students were killed. One student pulled out a gun and the police, as well as the terrorists, he said, are jumpy on account of what has taken place; each side is looking out to save itself and when the student pulled out his pistol the police shot him. With regard to Alvarez, he said that the police had found that this man was the one who had participated in the assassination, if he had not indeed been the principal assassin, of Vásquez Bello.[5] The police found that this man was being hidden in a certain house belonging to a Sr. Cuervo and had gone there to get him. Dr. Barón was not clear as to what happened from that point on except that Alvarez was finally shot. Dr. Barón then said that he had made an *aide-mémoire* for himself to remember what Ferrara's letter contained. He said that this memorandum contained the main points in Mr. Ferrara's letter although the wording was somewhat different, and he left it with me. It is attached hereto.

I told Dr. Barón that I had been much shocked by the news that came from Cuba last week and that this sort of thing was doing Cuba and President Machado's government a great deal of harm. Dr. Barón said that he agreed, and he thought it most unfortunate.

I told him that having known Ferrara for some time I had great hopes when he went down to Cuba that this sort of thing would cease. I said I realized the difficulties the Government is having with the Opposition but that nevertheless I could see no excuse for this sort of thing and that these continual assassinations, the closing of universities, muzzling of the press, et cetera, were certainly doing Cuba a great deal of harm in the outside world. Dr. Barón said he agreed but that the situation was very difficult; that the Opposition were without leaders and could not be dealt with. I said I realized the difficulty of dealing with some of the opponents of the Machado Administration, but I thought it incumbent upon the Government, as its first task, to try by some means to reestablish confidence in Cuba. I said that from this distance it was not possible to indicate the means by which this could be done; that that was something which the Cuban Government would have to study over and find out for itself. I said I thought they should direct their attention primarily to this matter. I said that of course Ambassador Guggenheim had taken an interest in this matter, but he was only interpreting the general public sentiment in this country in counselling the Cuban Government as I was doing, to do something to better conditions.

Dr. Barón said he realized the bad effect that this was having and referred to the attacks that came out in *La Prensa* of New York against Cuba. I told him that it was not just *La Prensa* but American papers as well. Dr. Barón said yes, that he had seen several articles recently in the *New York Times* which were not favorable to Cuba. I told Dr. Barón that they would have to expect this same sort of thing if present conditions prevail in Cuba.

(Signed) Francis White

--◊◊◊--O--◊◊◊--

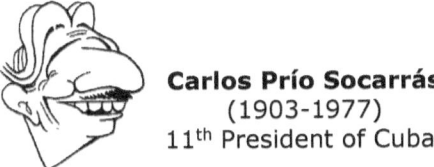

Carlos Prío Socarrás
(1903-1977)
11th President of Cuba.

FEBRUARY OF 1933

 Events in Cuba

February 13 Lawyer *Joaquín Martínez Sáenz* is arrested; the police declared he is the chief of the **ABC**, the anti-Machado action organization.

February 20 Increasing number of fires in cane fields and uprisings in Matanzas, Las Villas and Camagüey provinces, apparently intending to encourage an American intervention that would overthrow Machado.

 Washington Telex

HARRY HANK GUGGENHEIM, US AMBASSADOR IN CUBA, WRITES TO US SECRETARY OF STATE **HENRY L. STIMSON.**

Havana, February 28, 1933

Sir: I have the honor to report that there have been several occurrences during the past fortnight which may be regarded as symptomatic of the increasing state of unrest prevailing in Cuba.

Beginning on February 13, when the police arrested two lawyers and three other employees of the firm of Rosales and Lavedan, attorneys for the National City Bank of New York and other American enterprises, and a group of seven young men alleged to have been surprised at a secret meeting in a down town office building, the authorities have shown increased diligence in the apprehension of persons suspected of conspiring against the Government.

February 24th being a national holiday, the customary precautions were observed from the 23rd to the 25th for the maintenance of order, and with the exception of eight bomb explosions on the night of the 23rd, the seizure of supplies of arms and am- munition in the building formerly occupied by the local YMCA and numerous arrests of alleged conspirators, the day passed off quietly in Havana. It is understood that the ABC or the left-wing student's organization, or possibly both, had announced their intention of creating disturbances in various parts of the city, but with the exceptions mentioned above, their plans failed to materialize. It was also reported that the same groups had called upon all opponents of the

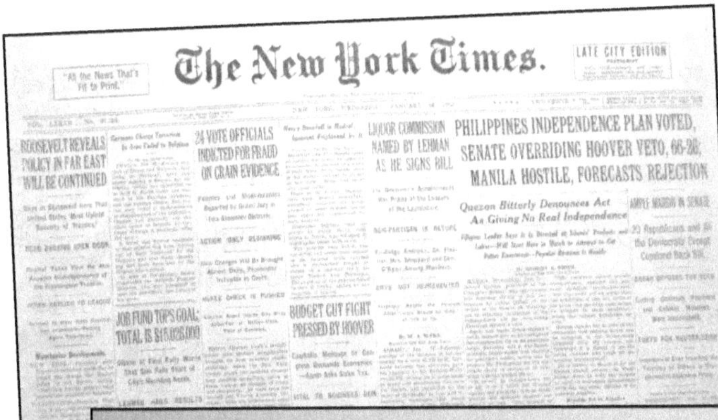

"All the News That's Fit to Print."

The New York Times.

LATE CITY EDITION

ROOSEVELT REVEALS POLICY IN FAR EAST WILL BE CONTINUED

24 VOTE OFFICIALS INDICTED FOR FRAUD ON GRAIN EVIDENCE

LIQUOR COMMISSION NAMED BY LEHMAN AS HE SIGNS BILL

PHILIPPINES INDEPENDENCE PLAN VOTED, SENATE OVERRIDING HOOVER VETO, 66-26; MANILA HOSTILE, FORECASTS REJECTION

Quezon Bitterly Denounces Act As Giving No Real Independence

AMPLE MARGIN IN SENATE

JOB FUND TOPS GOAL; TOTAL IS $15,026,000

BUDGET CUT FIGHT PRESSED BY HOOVER

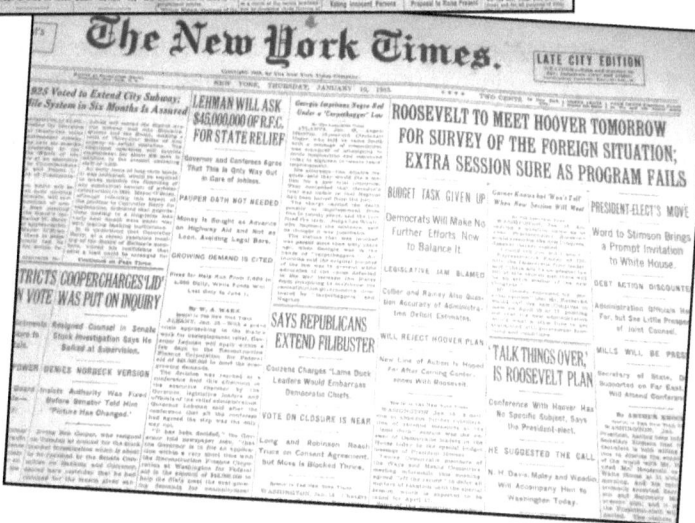

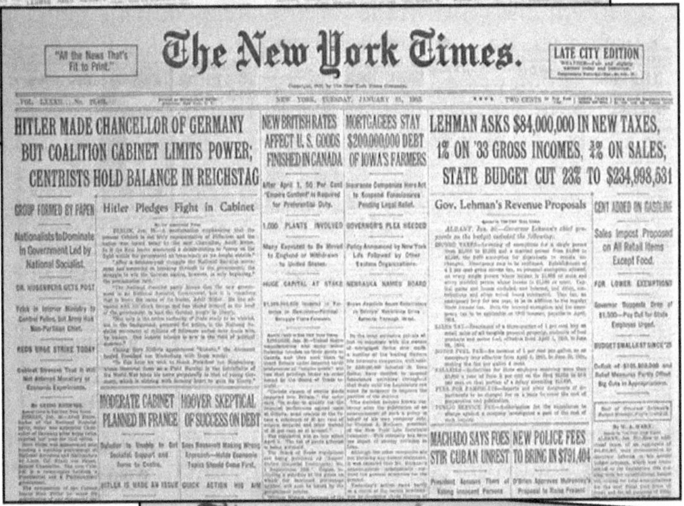

"All the News That's Fit to Print."

The New York Times.

LATE CITY EDITION

NEW YORK, TUESDAY, JANUARY 31, 1933.

HITLER MADE CHANCELLOR OF GERMANY BUT COALITION CABINET LIMITS POWER; CENTRISTS HOLD BALANCE IN REICHSTAG

GROUP FORMED BY PAPEN

Nationalists to Dominate in Government Led by National Socialist.

Hitler Pledges Fight in Cabinet

NEW BRITISH RATES AFFECT U. S. GOODS FINISHED IN CANADA

MORTGAGEES STAY $200,000,000 DEBT OF IOWA'S FARMERS

LEHMAN ASKS $84,000,000 IN NEW TAXES, 1% ON '33 GROSS INCOMES, 1/2% ON SALES; STATE BUDGET CUT 23% TO $234,998,531

Gov. Lehman's Revenue Proposals

CENT ADDED ON GASOLINE

Sales Impost Proposed on All Retail Items Except Food.

MODERATE CABINET PLANNED IN FRANCE

HOOVER SKEPTICAL OF SUCCESS ON DEBT

MACHADO SAYS FOES STIR CUBAN UNREST

NEW POLICE FEES TO BRING IN $791,404

The New York Times.

LATE CITY EDITION

LEHMAN WILL ASK $45,000,000 OF R.F.C. FOR STATE RELIEF

ROOSEVELT TO MEET HOOVER TOMORROW FOR SURVEY OF THE FOREIGN SITUATION; EXTRA SESSION SURE AS PROGRAM FAILS

BUDGET TASK GIVEN UP

Democrats Will Make No Further Efforts Now to Balance It.

PRESIDENT-ELECT'S MOVE

Word to Stimson Brings a Prompt Invitation to White House.

COOPER CHARGES 'LID' WAS PUT ON INQUIRY

SAYS REPUBLICANS EXTEND FILIBUSTER

'TALK THINGS OVER,' IS ROOSEVELT PLAN

As the year 1933 starts, **Hitler, Roosevelt,** the **Philippines, budgets and Gerardo Machado** are on the front pages of important US papers.

Government to restrict their expenditures, beginning February 24, to the necessities of life and specially to refrain from purchasing gasoline, thus depriving the Government of essential revenues. There is no sign that this appeal has met with any response, nor is it reasonable to suppose that it could have been otherwise in view of the well-recognized fact that the impoverished condition of the Cuban people has long since forced them to adapt their lives to the most stringent economies.

Reports from the interior are somewhat less reassuring. Disregarding rumors, of which there have been some of a disquieting nature, mention may be made of the following incidents the authenticity of which has been confirmed by official sources.

During the past week four trains were derailed in different parts of the island, two on the lines of the British-owned United Railways of Havana and two on those of the American-controlled Consolidated Railways of Cuba.

On the night of February 23, a switch and a culvert at Colorado, a small town in Camaguey Province, were destroyed and a train was derailed. On the same night a train was derailed between Puerto Tarafa and Ciego de Avila, also in Camaguey Province. Two nights later a bomb caused the derailment of a train in Matanzas Province. In none of these cases was anyone injured. However, on the night of February 26, the engineer and fireman of a United Railways freight train were killed when their locomotive and five cars were derailed when passing over a switch that had been torn up.

On February 23 and 24 telephone and telegraph wires were cut in several places, principally in Camaguey Province, but the Embassy is informed that this damage has since been repaired.

The Embassy's Military Attaché has been able to obtain confirmation of a report that on February 23 a group of about 7 men attacked the Rural Guard post at Central San Antonio, Oriente Province. Only two of the guards were in the barracks at the time. One of them jumped out of the window and succeeded in driving off the attacking party, wounding at least one of them. These men came from the city of Guantanamo and are known to the authorities who are now endeavoring to round them up.

A party of about 20 men, described by the General Staff as a marauding band, is operating near the boundary line between the provinces of Santa Clara and Camagüey, with headquarters apparently at Guadalupe. These men have been burning cane fields and destroying other property. Detachments of the Army are said to be closing in on them and their capture is expected within a few days.

(signed) Harry F. Guggenheim

In Miami, an assassin tried but failed to take **President Roosevelt's** life and New Yorkers panicked when a sad **Babe Ruth** commented that he might have to leave the Yankees. Of course, he immediately got a raise in salary.

MARCH OF 1933

Events in Cuba

March 4 *Franklyn D. Roosevelt* assumes the presidency in the US. In Cuba, there are increasing attacks on American

March 5 Juan *Gualberto Gómez* (1854-1933) died. He was a friend and collaborator of *José Martí*, a liberal militant and a man of prestige. Although born of slave parents, he was trilingual and possessor of a great culture.

March 9 Bank panic on the US after it leaves the gold standard.

March 22 A Revolutionary Board is created in Miami, composed of delegates of the Student Directory, Revolutionary Action, professors of the University of Havana, the Cuban Revolutionary Ensemble, the Nationalists and the ABC. The Board is chaired by naturalist *Carlos de la Torre and Huerta*. A founding declaration is signed by García-Menocal, Santiago Verdeja, Colonels Mendieta, Aurelio Hevia, Méndez Peñate, Miguel Mariano Gómez, Dr. Grau San Martín, Ricardo Dolz, Carlos Saladrigas, Carlos Hevia and others.

March 27 Publication in Miami of the first joined statement of Revolutionary Board members with a group of traditional politicians in Cuba. The *DEU* is pronounced against the so-called *Mediation*.

Washington Telex

HARRY HANK GUGGENHEIM, US AMBASSADOR IN CUBA, WRITES TO US SECRETARY OF STATE **HENRY L. STIMSON**.

Havana, March 9, 1933

I am reliably informed that the various groups of Cuban Oppositionists in Miami are completing plans for the formation of one united committee of the Opposition under the presidency of Carlos Mendieta. Those joining in this movement include Menocal and his lieutenant, Fraga; Hevía and Méndez Peñate of the Unión Nacional-

ista; Gómez who has gone to Miami from New York and his supporters, Tapia and Espinosa, and also Méndez Capote and San Martín. Negotiations are now being carried on including in this committee representatives of the ABC and of the students in Havana.
(signed) Harry F. Guggenheim

--◊◊◊--0--◊◊◊--

APRIL OF 1933

 Events in Cuba

April 3 The government declares a *moratorium on debts*, given the deep financial crisis.

April 14 Machado police apply the escape law to assassinate *Raimundo* and *José Antonio Valdés Daussá*, children of Cuba's Central Treasury. The murder is witnessed by *James D. Phillips* of *The New York Times* in Havana, who will report on the event.

April 18 Appointment of *Benjamin Sumner Welles*, as personal representative of Roosevelt and *Mediator* of the crisis. Roosevelt confers with the Cuban Ambassador *Oscar Cintas* about the depth of the Cuban crisis.

April 28 *Antonio Guiteras* leads an attack on the military headquarters in San Luis, Oriente; he is a member of the *Directorio of 1927*.

 Washington Telex

EDWARD L. REED, US CHARGÉ D'AFFAIRS IN CUBA, WRITES TO US SECRETARY OF STATE **HENRY L. STIMSON.**

Havana, April 8, 1933

I have the honor to report that, according to information furnished the Embassy from sources believed to be reliable, there were several killings in and near Havana on the night of April 6.

Lieutenant Pau, Military Supervisor of Guanabacoa, was shot and mortally wounded while returning from Havana by unidentified persons in an automobile. Rural guards arriving on the scene are said to have fired indiscriminately at the first group of persons they encountered, seriously wounding or killing three villagers whose curiosity had been attracted by the shots. Policemen along the road into Havana unsuccessfully endeavored to stop an automobile believed to have been the car used by Pau's assassins. One policeman is reported to have been killed and another wounded by the occupants of this automobile.

In the meantime, according to Embassy's informants, the secret police arrested a young man named Carlos Manuel Fuertes outside of the Payret Theatre in Havana. Fuertes is said to have been a member of the student directorate and to have been in hiding in the theatre for several months past. Later in the night his body was found near the *Ermita de los Catalanes* on Ayestarán Street. I am also informed that the police arrested one Charles Pemberton, believed to be an American citizen, son of the owner of the Payret Theatre. Pemberton is accused of having sheltered Fuertes, who was wanted in connection with the murder of Vázquez Bello, and another youth named Ildefonso or Mario Alvarez. He was "released" for two days, which means that he has been given an opportunity to leave the country.

There were bomb explosions in Havana and Santa Clara on the night of April 6. In the former city three persons were injured. At Santa Clara, the bomb did considerable damage to the principal hotel and killed one person.

None of the above incidents has been reported in the local press.

(signed) Edward L. Reed

--◇◇◇--0--◇◇◇---

EDWARD L. REED, US CHARGÉ D'AFFAIRS IN CUBA, WRITES TO US SECRETARY OF STATE **HENRY L. STIMSON.**

Havana, April 15, 1933

I have the honor to report that a bomb exploded close to the residence of Dr. Orestes Ferrara, Secretary of State, on the morning of April 13, killing a small boy aged 3 and seriously wounding a man. This bomb was hidden in an abandoned pushcart and was probably intended for Dr. Ferrara's new and very ostentatious house near the University.

On the night of April 13 there were numerous bomb explosions, variously estimated at from 11 to 17, in different parts of the city, including 2 churches, a theatre and several schools. A few persons are reported to have been injured but information regarding their number and the extent of their injuries is not available.

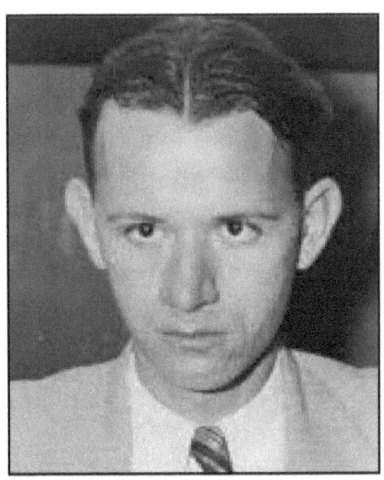

The exequias for Professor **Valdés Daussá** at the University in 1933; **Dr. Ramón Grau San Martín** in 1933 and **Antonio Guiteras**, future Minister of Gobernación (the interior).

According to the local correspondent of the *New York Times*, who claims to have been an eyewitness, the *ley de fuga* was applied by the police yesterday afternoon to two young men, named Valdez Daussá who, he states, were shot down at 29th and "G" Streets in the Vedado.

(signed) Edward L. Reed

--◊◊◊--0--◊◊◊---

EDWARD L. REED, US CHARGÉ D'AFFAIRS IN CUBA, WRITES TO US SECRETARY OF STATE **HENRY L. STIMSON.**

Havana, April 17, 1933

I have the honor to supplement with the following details my dispatch of April 15, 1933, in which I cited the local correspondent of the *New York Times* as authority for the report that two brothers named Valdés had been shot and killed in Havana by persons in the employ of the Government.

Following the large number of bombings on the night of April 13, the investigations of the police led them to suspect the activities of certain persons residing in a house at Campanarío No. 103. This house was raided by the police on the afternoon of the 14th and in it were found several bombs like those which had been distributed the preceding night. Among the inmates of the house were the Valdés brothers, one of whom, it is said, threw a bomb at the police. The bomb failed to explode, and the brothers were taken into custody.

These young men, one of whom was a lawyer and the other a physician, appear to have been closely identified with the more radical opposition element. A third brother was sentenced some time ago to serve eight years in jail after having been found guilty of participation in a plot to kill the President by means of a mined automobile.

Versions differ as to what happened following their arrest. According to the *New York Times* correspondent, who says he saw one of them killed, they were taken in an automobile to 29th and G Streets in the Vedado, told to get out and run for their lives and shot down as they fled by marksmen in civilian clothes who were posted at the top of a high bank overlooking the street intersection at that point.

The police tell a different story. As related to me by Secretary of State Ferrara, who had it from the Chief of the National Police, this version is that the brothers were taken to police headquarters where they broke down and offered to lead the police to a place frequented by their fellow conspirators. The police accepted their offer, placed them in an automobile under guard and set out in accordance with their directions. When the top of "G" Street had been reached, the prisoners endeavored to escape and were shot when they refused to obey the order to halt. This story is so thin that I doubt very much whether Dr. Orestes Ferrara himself believes it.

What probably occurred was that the police, feeling certain that they had captured two of the persons principally responsible for recent bomb outrages in Havana, took the law into their own hands and executed their captives. The alternative would have been to subject the prisoners to a protracted legal procedure in the military tribunals and subsequently in the Supreme Court, with the probability that any sentence commensurate with their offense would have been commuted by the next Administration. While this does not, of course, extenuate the reprehensible practice of the Cuban police in applying the so-called *ley de fuga* to their captives, it may at least offer a partial explanation of their conduct. It should also be borne in mind that a good many members of the police force have been murdered, that the police are working under considerable nervous tension and that they are exasperated because popular sympathy is alienated from them to the degree that criminal attacks against them arouse no indignation in the minds of the public.

It is persistently rumored that several other members of the ABC or of the student left wing organization were also killed on Good Friday, but it has not proved possible to confirm these reports.

The Embassy has, however, obtained official confirmation of a story current last week that one private soldier had been fatally shot and another severely wounded when they resisted arrest at the barracks of Battery No. 5 in the Vedado. It appears that the communists had succeeded in establishing there a "cell" composed of a few members of the battery; that this was discovered by the commanding officer who ordered their arrest and that two of them refused to submit.

(signed) Edward L. Reed

--◊◊◊--0--◊◊◊---

 **Fulgencio Batista y Zaldivar**,
(1901-1973)
9th President of Cuba.

CORDELL HULL, US SECRETARY OF STATE, WRITES TO
EDWARD L. REED, US CHARGÉ D'AFFAIRS IN CUBA

Washington, April 20, 1933

The President desires to appoint Benjamin Sumner Welles, at present Assistant Secretary of State, as Ambassador Extraordinary and Plenipotentiary of the United States to Cuba.

A full biography of Mr. Welles may be found in the Department's Circular Instruction of April 6, 1933, to American Diplomatic and Consular Officers, notifying them of the appointment of Mr. Welles as Assistant Secretary.

Ascertain whether the appointment of Mr. Welles would be agreeable to the Cuban Government and cable reply.

(signed) Cordell Hull

--◊◊◊--0--◊◊◊--

EDWARD L. REED, US CHARGÉ D'AFFAIRS IN CUBA, WRITES TO
CORDELL HULL, US SECRETARY OF STATE.

Washington, April 20, 1933

The Secretary of State of Cuba informs me that the appointment of Mr. Welles is agreeable to his Government.

(signed) Edward L. Reed

--◊◊◊--0--◊◊◊--

STATEMENT BY
BENJAMIN SUMNER WELLES, ASSISTANT US SECRETARY OF STATE.

Washington, April 24, 1933

If, and when, my nomination is confirmed by the US Senate, I shall go to Cuba, not as a Special Envoy of the President, but as his permanent Ambassador Extraordinary and Plenipotentiary accredited to the Cuban Government presided over by President Gerardo Machado Morales.

I am a convinced believer in the policy of the "good neighbor" proclaimed by the President in his inaugural address and emphatically reiterated in the address delivered on the celebration of Pan American Day. There is no country of the Western Hemisphere with which our relations should be closer or more friendly than with Cuba; or one, in our dealings with which, the policy of the "*good neighbor*" is more essential. Our historic participation in Cuba's war of independence; our treaty relations; our geographical proximity; and finally, the very practical fact that Cuba is potentially one of the greatest customers of the American Continent for United States goods, and that she herself depends upon fair and generous treatment from the United States for her economic life, all combine to demand today, more than ever before, that the two nations join as equal, sovereign and independent partners in the consideration of those measures best adapted to further the economic and commercial interests of each one of them and of the world at large. It is almost needless to add that such consideration would serve no useful purpose were it not undertaken upon a basis of mutual respect, mutual tolerance, and common advantage.

In accordance with the policy of the Administration of encouraging reciprocal trade agreements, I look forward to undertaking detailed consideration of this vital problem at as early a date as may prove feasible to both Governments.

It will be in that spirit that I shall undertake my official duties. I go to Cuba animated by a peculiar sympathy, which I have held for many years, for the Republic of Cuba and for every element of the Cuban people; welcomed by a generous message from the President of Cuba; and determined, in accordance with my instructions, to further, in every way possible, the joint interests of our two countries.

(signed) Benjamin Sumner Welles

--◊◊◊--0--◊◊◊--

MAY OF 1933

 Events in Cuba

May 7 Arrival in Havana of *Sumner Welles* aboard the cargo ship "Petén," property of the United Fruit.

May 17 More uprisings against Machado across the island. Several murders are presumably committed by Commander *Arsenio Ortiz* in Las Villas and Camagüey.

May 19 *Rubén Martínez Villena* returns from Moscow mortally sick, ready to organize workers against Machado.

May 26 At the request of Ambassador Welles, *Arsenio Ortiz* is prosecuted and expelled from the country with discretion.

--◊◊◊--0--◊◊◊--

 Washington
Telex

CORDELL HULL, US SECRETARY OF STATE, WRITES TO
BENJAMIN SUMNER WELLES, APPOINTED US AMBASSADOR IN CUBA

Washington, May 1, 1933

The policy to be pursued by this Government in its relations with the Republic of Cuba must be determined primarily by its rights and obligations as set forth in the first five articles of the treaty between the United States and Cuba signed at Havana May 22, 1903, which articles likewise form a portion of the Cuban Constitution first promulgated on May 20, 1902. These articles are as follows:

1. That the government of Cuba shall never enter into any treaty or other compact with any foreign power or powers which will impair or tend to impair the independence of Cuba, nor in any manner authorize or permit any foreign power or powers to obtain by colonization or for military or naval purposes or otherwise, lodgment in or control over any portion of said island.

2. That said government shall not assume or contract any public debt, to pay the interest upon which, and to make reasonable sinking fund provision for the ultimate discharge of which, the ordinary revenues of the island, after defraying the current expenses of government shall be inadequate.

3. That the government of Cuba consents that the United States may exercise the right to intervene for the preservation of Cuban independence, the maintenance of a government adequate for the protection of life, property, and individual liberty, and for discharging the obligations with respect to Cuba imposed by the treaty of Paris on the United States, now to be assumed and undertaken by the government of Cuba.

4. That all Acts of the United States in Cuba during its military occupancy thereof are ratified and validated, and all lawful rights acquired thereunder shall be maintained and protected.
>

Ramón Grau San Martín,
(1887-1969)
10th President of Cuba.

The **economic news** in the United States and the **famine in Russia** are the big news in the papers in the mid-1930s.

5. That the government of Cuba will execute, and as far as necessary extend, the plans already devised or other plans to be mutually agreed upon, for the sanitation of the cities of. the island, to the end that a recurrence of epidemic and infectious diseases may be prevented thereby assuring protection to the people and commerce of Cuba, as well as to the commerce of the southern ports of the United States and the people residing therein.

Now, the Government of the United States is forced to view with the gravest concern the situation now existing in Cuba. You are familiar with the developments which have taken place since President Machado first assumed office in 1925.

While the President at first repeatedly asserted his intention of serving but one constitutional term of four years as President, he nevertheless approved the passage, in the Spring of 1927, of an act by the Cuban House of Representatives, providing, among other things, for the proroguing of his own term for a period of four years. It is reported that President Machado, during the course of his visit to Washington, which took place after the passage of this legislation by the Cuban House of Representatives, obtained the tacit approval of the American Government to the general principles embodied in this act. Subsequent to President Machado's return to Cuba, the Congress passed the Constitutional Reform Bill with the provision that the President's term should be prorogued for a period of two years.

Under the terms of the Cuban Constitution, as promulgated in 1902, amendments to the Constitution proposed by the Congress did not become effective until approved by a constituent assembly specifically elected for that purpose. Consequently, after the project for constitutional reform had been enacted by the Cuban Congress, elections were held for delegates to the constituent assembly and these delegates were elected under a revised form of the so-called *"Crowder Electoral Code"*, the revisions in the code making possible the election of delegates individually selected, in their great majority, by members of the existing House and Senate, and in most instances the Senators and Representatives themselves served as delegates to the constituent assembly. It is obvious that the revision of the Electoral Code made possible at this time the election of delegates favorable to the proroguing of the terms of the President, of the members of the Senate and of the members of the House of Representatives, and that such delegates were by no means elected through the untrammeled vote of the Cuban people themselves.

The constituent assembly so selected convened in the month of April 1928. Under the terms of the then-existing Constitution, the duties of the constituent assembly were *"limited either to approving or rejecting the amendment voted by the co-legislative bodies"*. Notwithstanding this clear provision and the clear intent thereof, the constituent assembly revised completely several of the provisions of the project submitted by the Cuban Congress. There was a reasonable measure of doubt that the constituent assembly acted "ultra vires". The Supreme Court of Cuba has, however, consistently refrained from rendering a decision upon this question.

Among the more important provisions of the amendments made to the former Constitution were the following:

By the terms of Article 66, the Presidential term was extended from four to six years and the President prohibited from serving in that office for two consecutive terms. Whereas the reforms as voted by the Cuban Congress had prorogued for a period of two years the term of office of President Machado, the constituent assembly redrafted this provision by providing for a call for elections in the year 1928, specifying, however, that the first Presidential term to which the provisions of Article 66 above referred to would be regarded as being applicable, would not commence until May 20, 1929. President Machado was thereby rendered eligible for re-election in the year 1928.

Among the other measures provided by the reforms to the Constitution enacted at this time, the tenure of office of Senators was increased from eight to nine years and the total number of all Senators increased from twenty-four to thirty-six; the term of Representatives in Congress was increased from four to six years and the term of both Senators and Representatives actually in office at the time was extended for a period of two years; the office of Vice-President was abolished, and provision was later made in the so-called Emergency Electoral Law of July 11, 1928, that in the event of a vacancy occurring in the Presidential office, the vacancy should be filled from among the members of the Cabinet, the Secretary of State, because of his ranking position therein, to be the First Substitute, the election of a permanent successor to be held within a period of sixty days thereafter. Furthermore, in general, all elective provincial and municipal authorities were to be retained in office for an additional two-year term.

In the elections held under the Emergency Electoral Law which took place in November 1928, President Machado was the sole candidate and was re-elected for a term of six years, his present term being due to expire May 20, 1935. Due to the pressure of public opinion as expressed through the increasing political opposition to his Administration and, in part, presumably, for purposes of political strategy, President Machado, in December 1930, agreed to the restoration by the Cuban Congress of the original Crowder Electoral Code without the inclusion of amendments of significance.

There exists, consequently, in Cuba, at the present time, an electoral code which can guarantee fair elections to the Cuban people, provided, of course, that the Cuban Government and the Cuban people themselves desire free and fair elections.

Opposition to the Administration of President Machado had already gathered force by the Autumn of 1927, when it became apparent that the President was anxious to extend the term of office for which he had been originally elected. The speculative period, however, and the carrying out of the Government's Public Works Program, resulted, for a brief period, in economic improvement in Cuba.

The climax of this period was very nearly coincident with the time when President Machado became a candidate for re-election, and the attention of the Cuban people was consequently diverted from political issues, and opposition to the President and to his Administration was temporarily allayed.

With the beginning of the period of depression and with rapidly increasing economic distress, opposition not only became active again, but gradually increased to a degree of bitterness and of animosity to the President's person hitherto unknown in Cuba. Political opposition has degenerated into a ruthless campaign of violence against the President and against the members of the Administration. Repressive measures enacted by the Machado Administration; the suspension of constitutional guarantees; the declaration of martial law with attendant resort to the use of military tribunals in lieu of civil courts; the imposition of strict censorship; the brutal assassination or imprisonment of the President's political opponents, have failed to curb the campaign of terrorism resorted to by President Machado's opponents, Not only all of the political leaders of importance, but a great majority of the intellectual leaders of Cuba as well, have been forced to leave the Republic and most of them have taken refuge in the United States. Due to the unwillingness of the student bodies to endure silently the measures of repression undertaken by the Cuban Executive the University of Havana and the secondary schools throughout the Island have been closed by Governmental Decree for nearly three years, and while some of the students have taken refuge in Europe and in the United States to complete their education, a very large percentage of them are actively engaged in subversive activities, notably

US Ambassador **Benjamin Sumner Welles** was, by and large, the US decision maker in Cuba during the crisis of 1933. On the photos, with **Churchill, Joseph Kennedy, Cordell Hull** and **Batista**. On the right his best-seller after he left office.

through such organizations as the ABC. Many of them have been assassinated by the police authorities and many of them have been imprisoned. It is apparent that under conditions such as these, those groups among the younger generation from whom the leaders of Cuba of tomorrow must spring, are being brought by experience to the conviction that changes in government in Cuba must be effected not by the orderly processes of constitutional government, but by the resort to measures of violence and revolution.

The propaganda of those opposed to the Machado Administration has for many months been very much in evidence in the United States. The American press has given pre-eminence to the Cuban situation. Leading members of the Congress of the United States have very naturally interested themselves in the domestic concerns of Cuba.

It cannot be denied that the existence of such a as that existing in Cuba is necessarily a matter which must rightly give the Government of the United States deep anxiety. Its rights and obligations under its treaty relations with Cuba; the close geographical proximity of Cuba to the United States; its desire to enter into negotiations with the Cuban Government looking toward a reciprocal trade agreement which in its judgment would be of the utmost benefit both to the Cuban people and to the people of the United States and which cannot be undertaken so long as this situation of political unrest in Cuba continues, all jointly force it to the belief that its friendly assistance must be tendered to the Cuban people in their effort to see an adjustment of what are fast becoming intolerable conditions.

Under the terms of Article III of its Treaty of 1903 with Cuba,

"the Government of Cuba consents that the United States may exercise the right to intervene for the preservation of Cuban independence, the maintenance of a government adequate for the protection of life, property, and individual liberty..."

The Government of the United States now reiterates the interpretation given to that provision by the Honorable Elihu Root, then Secretary of War, on April 2, 1901:

"The intervention described in the third clause of the Piatt Amendment is not synonymous with intermeddling or interference with the affairs of the Cuban Government but the formal action of the Government of the United States, based upon just and substantial grounds, for the preservation of Cuban independence arid the maintenance of a government adequate for the protection of life, property, and individual liberty."

Under this interpretation, it will be evident to you that conditions in Cuba, highly unsatisfactory and even alarming as they may be, do not constitute a just basis for the formal action of the Government of the United States looking towards intervention. On the other hand, the Government of the United States cannot, in the interest of its own citizens, and because of its interest in the welfare of the Cuban people, assume that this interpretation of Article 5 of its treaty with Cuba can prevent it from experiencing grave disquiet while it sees a situation developing in the Republic of Cuba which would appear, perhaps, to result at some time either in the remote or in the near future in open rebellion against a Cuban Government, with consequent destruction of human life and property, and with the probability that there might then well be no government existing in Cuba adequate to preserve life, property, and individual liberty. This Government, on the content feels it obligatory upon it to offer its friendly advice for the purpose of correcting and stemming that course of events and the potential dangers resulting therefrom.

It must be clearly understood, however, that any efforts of the Government of the United States exerted in this direction are not to be construed as measures of intervention. They are, on the contrary, measures intended to prevent the necessity of intervention. They are measures to be taken in view of the responsibilities assumed by the United States under its treaty relations with Cuba, as Cuba's nearest friend, and for the purpose of assuring the maintenance of Cuban independence and Cuban sovereignty.

 I. You will therefore express to President Machado the belief of the Government of the United States that the measures it is now suggesting to him are to be considered by the Cuban Government solely as the representations of Cuba's closest friend among nations, for the purpose of facilitating an adjustment of the various problems with which the Cuban Government is now confronted, which constitute in themselves, necessarily, a matter of intimate concern to the Government of the United States because of the provisions of the Treaty existing between the two nations.

 II. You will point out to President Machado, in the most forcible terms, that in the opinion of your Government, there can be expected no general amelioration of conditions in Cuba until there is a definite cessation of that state of terrorism which has existed for so long a period throughout Cuba, and particularly in Havana. You will explain to him that the continuing reports of the murder of Cubans in all ranks of life by members of the armed forces of the Cuban Government have profoundly stirred public opinion in this country; that public feeling in the

United States is in danger of becoming gravely prejudiced against the Cuban Government, with resultant impairment of the high regard which the American people should rightly hold for the people of the neighboring Republic. You should state that this Government makes all due allowance for the need of the Cuban Government to undertake measures of control in view of the nature of the campaign which the opposition factions are waging against it. You will, however, express the earnest hope of this Government that the President will, at the earliest moment, enforce the strictest discipline among the members of the armed forces of Cuba so as to prevent a continuation of such atrocities as those which have so frequently been countenanced in recent months under the provisions of the "Ley de Fuga", and that the Cuban Government will, in. so far as may be possible, prevent the incarceration, much more the execution, of political or press offenders.

III. In concluding your representations upon this matter, you will state that it is the very definite belief of your Government that the essential prerequisite to any basic improvement in Cuba is the speedy cessation both of overt acts against the Government and of extreme measures of repression by the Government.

IV. You will express to the President the desire of the United States to offer, in any form deemed most suitable by both Governments, the friendly mediation of the Government of the United States between President Machado and the members of the political factions and other elements opposed to the Cuban Government. The nature of such mediation and the form in which it may be exercised must, necessarily, be left to your discretion. You will, however, regard as your chief objective the negotiation of a definite, detailed, and binding understanding between the present Cuban Government and the responsible leaders of the factions opposed to it, which will lead to a truce in the present dangerous political agitation to continue until such time as national elections can be held in Cuba and the responsible officials of a new constitutional government can be elected under reasonable guaranties of popular suffrage without fraud, without intimidation, and without violence.

V. Coincident with your discussion with the President of Cuba of the questions above set forth, you should express to President Machado the earnest desire of the Government of the United States to assist the Cuban Government in every feasible manner in the consideration of measures intended to ameliorate the distressing economic situation now existing in the

Republic of Cuba. You will state that this Government, as a portion of its general policy of negotiating reciprocal trade agreements with other nations of the world, is particularly desirous of considering the bases of a reciprocal trade agreement between the United States and Cuba, which, in its belief, would redound to the advantage of both nations. You may say that this Government is strongly inclined to the view that a speedy improvement in economic and commercial conditions in Cuba would result in an immediate allaying of popular unrest and of political agitation, and that the Government of the United States hopes that the Cuban Government will be disposed to give the consideration of this problem preferential attention. You may likewise point out that the Government of the United States is favorably disposed to receive any suggestions from the Cuban Government as to any other manner in which the friendly cooperation of this Government might be effectively exercised in assisting the Cuban Government in its desire to bring about general commercial and economic improvement.

In conclusion, you will always bear in mind that the relations between the Government of the United States and the Cuban Government are those existing between sovereign, independent, and equal powers; and that no step should be taken which would tend to render more likely the need of the Government of the United States to resort to that right of formal intervention granted to the United States by the existing treaty between the two nations.

(signed) Cordell Hull

--◊◊◊--O--◊◊◊--

CORDELL HULL, US SECRETARY OF STATE, WRITES TO JEFFERSON THOMAS CAFFERY, US AMBASSADOR IN COLOMBIA

Washington, May 6, 1933

For Jefferson Thomas Caffery from William Phillips, Under Secretary of State. The President has in mind appointing you Ambassador to Cuba on the termination of Benjamin Sumner Welles' period of ambassadorship there, which may be in about 3 months' time. Welles will then return to the State Department and resume his position of Assistant Secretary. Meanwhile, we should like to have you fill the vacancy here of Assistant Secretary. In this way you can become conversant with Cuban affairs and be of general assistance to the Department. Please let me know whether this arrangement is agreeable to you.

(signed) Cordell Hull

--◊◊◊--O--◊◊◊--

JEFFERSON THOMAS CAFFERY, US AMBASSADOR IN COLOMBIA, WRITES TO
CORDELL HULL, US SECRETARY OF STATE

Bogotá, May 7, 1933

For Phillips from Caffery. I should be happy to be appointed Ambassador to Cuba on the termination of Sumner Welles' period and in the meantime fill the vacancy of Assistant Secretary of State. Thank you.
(signed) Jefferson Thomas Caffery

--◊◊◊--0--◊◊◊--

EDWARD L. REED, US CHARGÉ D'AFFAIRS IN CUBA, WRITES TO
CORDELL HULL, US SECRETARY OF STATE

Havana, May 8, 1933

Ambassador Benjamin Sumner Welles arrived yesterday.
(signed) Edward L. Reed

--◊◊◊--0--◊◊◊--

BENJAMIN SUMNER WELLES, US AMBASSADOR IN CUBA, WRITES TO
CORDELL HULL, US SECRETARY OF STATE

Havana, May 11, 1933

Presented letter of credence this morning.
(signed) Benjamin Sumner Welles

--◊◊◊--0--◊◊◊--

BENJAMIN SUMNER WELLES, US AMBASSADOR IN CUBA, WRITES TO
CORDELL HULL, US SECRETARY OF STATE

Havana, May 13, 1933   [Received May 14 – 5:35 p.m.]

I had yesterday 2-hour conversation with the Secretary of State and this morning a conversation of equal length with the President of the Republic.

At the outset of my conversation with the President I indicated in general terms the policy of the Government of the United States towards Cuba. I stated that my Government reiterated the interpretation of its responsibilities under the Piatt Amendment in the sense laid down by Secretary Root in 1901, namely that the right of intervention was not construed as being synonymous with intermeddling in the domestic or political concerns of Cuba. I further stated that my Government believed that the prime requisite to ensure the permanent welfare of Cuba was the maintenance of constitutional government and the fortification of the tradition of orderly procedure in constitutional government; and that to secure those

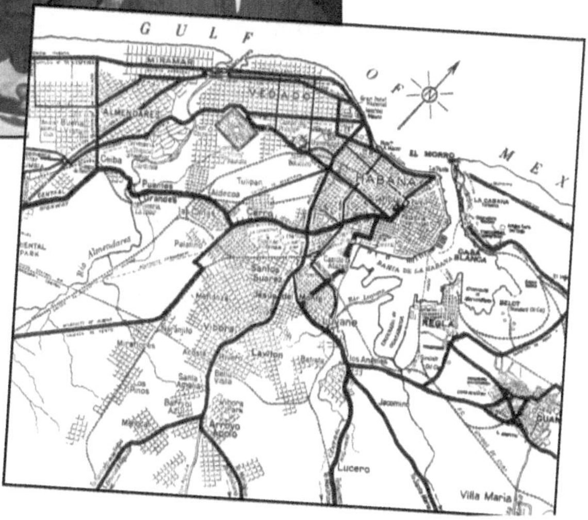

Key US diplomats participating in Cuba during the 1933 events. *Top, left to right*: **Hugh Simons Gibson**, Ambassador to Brazil, **Henry L. Stimson,** 46th US Secretary of State, **Josephus Daniels,** US Ambassador to Mexico. *Center*, **Jefferson Caffery** Ambassador to France in 1945, sitting on the left, with **Georges Bidault**, French *Ministre des Affaires Etrangères*, and **René Mayer**, *Ministre des Finances* at the signing of the **Plan Marshall** at the Quai d'Orsay; bottom, a map of Havana in the 1930s.

ends the Government of Cuba could count on the friendly cooperation of the United States in every appropriate manner.

I stated that my Government had been caused very grave disquiet by the long-continued political agitation which had existed in Cuba and that public opinion in the United States had been very frequently shocked by acts of terrorism committed by the opponents of the administration of President Machado and as deeply shocked by acts of cruelty and oppression on the part of the military authorities of the Cuban Government. I said that it was our desire to offer our unofficial good offices for the purpose of putting an end as soon as possible to this state of political agitation with all of its inherent evils both because of our abiding interest in and sympathy with the people of Cuba as well as because of our well-founded belief that steps toward any permanent basic economic improvement in the Republic of Cuba could not be taken with complete success until political quiet once more existed.

I continued by saying that it was my hope that President Machado would find it possible to carry out a program of conciliation leading towards the holding of absolutely fair and uncontrolled national elections in the autumn of 1934 and that for this reason it seemed to me highly desirable that the Cuban Government adopt, at as early a moment as the President deemed appropriate, certain measures providing for the gradual return to the Cuban people of their constitutional guarantees. I said that to my mind an essential prerequisite to this would be a decree by the President imposing penalties in the future, to be determined by a special tribunal, for any illegal acts committed by military or police, whether of killing by *ley de fuga* procedure, of torture or of unlawful [apparent omission]; the gradual relaxation of censorship and of the prohibition of free speech; and the raising of martial law as soon as possible.

In concluding this summary I said that my Government was disposed to enter into the consideration of the bases for a reciprocal trade agreement with the Cuban Republic and that I was under the very positive impression that not only the eventual benefits to be derived from such agreement but also the turning of the attention of the general public from political agitation to questions of economic interest to every Cuban citizen would have a markedly beneficial psychological effect.

The President was very obviously impressed with the declarations which I made to him. He said that he found himself not only in full accord with the suggestions I had offered but deeply appreciative of the attitude taken by the United States Government. In considerable detail he went into the nature of the political agitation against his administration. He said that the leaders of the Opposition had neither a constructive program to present nor any recommendations to offer other than the overthrow of the constituted Government of Cuba. He said that it was his most earnest desire to take with the utmost rapidity every measure tending towards a return to normal constitutional procedure. In this connection he referred to the fact that military censorship of the press had been lifted 2 days ago and that the very great majority of political offenders had been freed from imprisonment during the past week. He emphasized the fact that not only all of the political leaders who had previously been arrested but the individuals as well who had attempted to assassinate him had been released from prison and were now at liberty either in the United States or in the Republic. He said that not only would he accept but that he welcomed as the only sure help in the crisis through which Cuba was now passing the unofficial good offices of the Government of the United States for the purpose of providing a political truce in Cuba which would make it possible for all parties to go to the next national elections with complete assurance that the candidate desired by the majority of the Cuban people would be the next President of the Republic. He declared emphatically that not only would he not under any conditions whatsoever be a candidate himself for a future term, and what to my mind was perhaps the most striking of the assurances given me was the definite intimation that in order to assure the Cuban people of all factions that the coming national elections would not be controlled, the President himself would not be averse at an appropriate moment before the electoral period began to resign his office either temporarily for the duration of the electoral period or permanently until the next constitutional term commenced.

I seized the opportunity of discussing in some detail the various plans which had been under consideration in Washington before my own departure providing for an improvement of our commercial relations' with Cuba; I stated that at the present time it was impossible to give any definite assurances as to what form these plans would eventually take but that I felt able to say that my Government would be prepared to consider a fixed allotment for Cuban sugars; an increase in the existing preferential [tariff?] covering such allotment; and that it held the belief that under such conditions the anticipated stabilization of the price of sugar in the American market at a fair figure would be of the utmost benefit to the Cuban people as a whole. I was given the positive assurances that were the United States to negotiate on such a basis a reciprocal trade agreement with the Cuban Government, the Cuban Government in turn would grant us a practical monopoly of the Cuban market for American imports, the sole reservation being that in view of the fact that Great Britain was Cuba's chief customer for that portion of sugar exports which did not go to the United States the Cuban Government would desire to concede certain advantages to a limited category of imports from Great Britain. The Secretary of State was particularly emphatic in amplifying this statement by declaring that the Government would be willing to agree to abolish, as regards American imports, those consumption and other taxes which have in so many instances seriously restricted American importations during the past few years.

Photos, top to bottom: May 27, 1933, the ship **St. Louis,** full of refugees from Germany's Hitler, arrives at Havana but is denied disembarking passengers. Eligio Sadiñas (**Kid Chocolate**) is at the peak of his career as World Featherweight Champ. The Nazi party tightened its grip on the German people. In the photo the **burning of books** in May of 1933.

I hold the very strong belief that the policy to be pursued in Cuba under present conditions should be as follows:

The economic benefits to be derived from a fair commercial agreement between the United States and Cuba and even the negotiations' leading towards such an agreement will assist in part in distracting public attention from politics.

By acting through and with the present Cuban Government, which is well aware of the fact that it could not for long remain in power were the support of the United States to be even negatively withdrawn from it, it may be possible to carry out a program of constitutional and electoral reform which will make it possible for fair national elections to be held in 1934.

If the present acute bitterness of feeling against the President and the members of his Government persists or becomes intensified during the coming year it would in all probability be highly desirable that the present chief executive be replaced at least during the electoral period by some impartial citizen in whom all factions have confidence. I do not feel, however, as a practical question that any attempt should be made to anticipate such a change. President Machado can preserve order joined with unquestioned loyalty and discipline of the Cuban Army. If some other individual replaced him the loyalty of the Army would be questionable; the Opposition would be as it is now, divided into factions which have absolutely no common ground other than that of desiring the removal of the President. Under such conditions general chaos might well result during the course of which the first objective on the part of malcontents would be the desire to bring about intervention by the United States through the destruction of American property.

I am hopeful that by a series of concessions which the President may make to public opinion and by the continuance of negotiations for commercial agreement agitation may be kept relatively quiet until such time as the Cuban Congress can make essential amendments to the electoral code and approve the needed reforms to the existing constitution, which would be later voted by a freely elected constituent assembly.

Finally, the negotiation at this time of a reciprocal trade agreement with Cuba along the lines above-indicated, will not only revivify Cuba but will give us practical control of a market we have been steadily losing for the past 10 years not only for our manufactured products but for our agricultural exports as well notably in such categories as wheat, animal fats, meat products, rice and potatoes.

It will be this policy that I shall attempt to carry out unless I am instructed to the contrary.

I beg to request that a copy of this telegram be sent to the President for his information.

(signed) Benjamin Sumner Welles

--◊◊◊--0--◊◊◊--

BENJAMIN SUMNER WELLES, US AMBASSADOR IN CUBA, WRITES TO
CORDELL HULL, US SECRETARY OF STATE

Havana, May 13, 1933   [Received May 14 - 8:23 p.m.]

I was advised this morning by President Machado that you are to have a conference with the Cuban Ambassador in Washington next Monday to discuss commercial problems of interest to both Governments. Since I understood from my last conversation with you that the discussions you will undertake with the Cuban representative in Washington will envisage only a general survey of economic questions, I should appreciate it, provided you see no objection, if the Cuban Ambassador were informed that, after the conclusion of your conversation with him, I am authorized to enter into a preliminary and tentative consideration of the bases for a reciprocal trade agreement between the United States and Cuba. I would naturally in any conversations held here make no commitments whatever, since in any event under present conditions it would be impossible to do so. For the reasons expressed in my previous telegram, May 13, 6 p.m., my position will be materially strengthened with the Government here if conversations relating to this matter are undertaken by me coincident with any representations I may make to the Cuban Government on other topics. Furthermore, I feel confident that a preliminary discussion in general terms of our future commercial relations with Cuba will, as those held now, serve a very useful purpose in view of the stated desire of the Cuban Government to offer us any advantages which our Government deems desirable.

(signed) Benjamin Sumner Welles

--◊◊◊--0--◊◊◊--

BENJAMIN SUMNER WELLES, US AMBASSADOR IN CUBA, WRITES TO
CORDELL HULL, US SECRETARY OF STATE

Havana, May 16, 1933

Referring to the Embassy's May 13, 4 p.m., I intend within the next 2 or 3 days to commence informal conversations with Secretary of State Dr. Orestes Ferrara covering possible bases for the future negotiation of a new commercial agreement between the United States and Cuba. I beg to request that you advise me if there is any reason why conversations of this character should not be initiated at the present moment and, should there be no objection, if there are any particular points that you would desire me to emphasize.

Dr. Ferrara has informed me confidentially that while he has not yet approached President Machado in the matter, he desires to head the Cuban delegation to the World Economic Conference. It is his desire to have as fellow delegates:

In March and April of 1933, the **economic recovery** across the world filled the papers, **Roosevelt** is busy implementing the policy of the **New Deal** and Cubans, for the first time, go into **exile in Miami**, Florida.

Ambassador Oscar Cintas and Sr. Manuel Portuondo, the latter specifically as an expert on sugar questions.

(signed) Benjamin Sumner Welles

--◊◊◊--0--◊◊◊--

BENJAMIN SUMNER WELLES, US AMBASSADOR IN CUBA, WRITES TO
CORDELL HULL, US SECRETARY OF STATE

Havana, May 22, 1933   [Received 8:02 p.m.]

For the President. The Associated Press publishes a report that you intend during the coming week to make a statement regarding the situation in Cuba. The intimation is given that your statement will bear upon the political situation.

I am endeavoring to persuade opposition leaders, through means of communication which I have established, to give their cooperation towards an arrangement fair to all concerned. I now am led to believe the cooperation of most of them will be forthcoming. I shall, of course, keep you closely advised as to what progress is being made. Should it later develop that a few of the important leaders of the opposition remain obdurate, a statement by you, insisting upon cooperation of the leaders of all Cuban factions in the determination of a solution of the Cuban problem for the ultimate benefit of the Cuban people as a whole, would presumably have overwhelming and probably deciding effect. I suggest, consequently, that if you intend issuing such a statement as that reported, it would probably be more beneficial later than at this juncture.

(signed) Benjamin Sumner Welles

--◊◊◊--0--◊◊◊--

BENJAMIN SUMNER WELLES, US AMBASSADOR IN CUBA, WRITES TO
CORDELL HULL, US SECRETARY OF STATE

Havana, May 22, 1933   [Received 11:50 p.m.]

Mr. F. Adair Monroe, Junior, President of the Cuba Company, accompanied by Mr. Schreiber, Manager of the Sugar Central owned by that company at Jatibonico, called on May 19. They reported that three of their guards who had been in their employ for some 8 years and who served likewise as deputy police under the control of the local police authorities had been seized by a detachment of the Guardia Rural under the personal command of Major Arsenio Ortiz on May 16th merely on suspicion of having aided revolutionary activities and had been summarily shot without due investigation and without any trial.

The Cuba Company has been on particularly friendly terms with the Machado administration and there is consequently no reason to believe that the report made to me has been colored by any opposition on the part of the company's officials to the Cuban Government.

I took up the matter immediately with the Secretary of State. I impressed upon him in the most serious manner that if atrocities of this kind continued, not only would any policy of conciliation in Cuba be utterly impossible but I was very certain as well that public opinion in the United States would not tolerate such a situation any more than it had been willing to countenance a similar situation in the years preceding the Spanish-American War. I stated that this occurrence was aggravated by the fact that the individuals murdered were the employees of an American company.

Dr. Ferrara told me that he not only understood my viewpoint but was in absolute accord with me. He said that the only reason that Ortiz had been sent to Santa Clara Province was because of the President's fear that one or two of the chief Cuban officers in command in that region were not loyal to the Cuban Government. He told me that he would urge the President immediately to have a full investigation made and, in any event, recall Major Ortiz without further delay.

Dr. Ferrara called to see me May 20th. He told me the President had ordered Colonel Delgado to proceed immediately to Santa Clara to make a full investigation and that due punishment would be given to Ortiz or to any other officers responsible for the atrocity should the facts be determined to be as reported to me. He further told me that the President would recall Major Ortiz to Havana not later than May 23.

I shall report by telegraph the result of the official investigation as well as the action which the President may take.

(signed) Benjamin Sumner Welles

--◊◊◊--O--◊◊◊--

BENJAMIN SUMNER WELLES, US AMBASSADOR IN CUBA, WRITES TO **CORDELL HULL**, US SECRETARY OF STATE

Havana, May 25, 1933   [Received 2:30 p.m.]

I have had two conferences with the Secretary of State, the Secretary of the Treasury and the Secretary of Agriculture regarding the concessions which the Cuban Government would be willing to make to the United States in a reciprocal trade agreement provided that the United States Government were able to make the concessions to Cuban sugar discussed in a general way before my departure for Washington. I have found a general disposition to grant to the United States, those advantages to our agricultural exports and our principal manufactures which we consider necessary. There is a natural desire to afford protection to legitimate Cuban industries and further the desire as already reported to the Department not to impair the advantages now possessed in Cuba by Great Britain for her textiles and certain other categories of imports, the latter of which do not compete materially with American products.

The general theory maintained by the Cuban Government is that of making such concessions to us as will balance whatever advantages we may be willing to concede them.

I shall hold the last of these conferences tomorrow since Dr. Ferrara's departure for London makes it impossible to continue them for the time being. I shall, in full, detail to the Department the results of my three conferences on this topic early next week.

I have emphasized repeatedly to the Cuban Government that these conversations were solely for the purpose of exchanging views and of ascertaining in general what the Cuban Government would be prepared to do for us were the Government of the United States willing and able to enter into a new commercial agreement with Cuba. I have reiterated that we could not under present conditions make any definite proposals and that in consequence we did not ask any positive commitments at this juncture from the Cuban Government.

(signed) Benjamin Sumner Welles

--◊◊◊--0--◊◊◊--

BENJAMIN SUMNER WELLES, US AMBASSADOR IN CUBA, WRITES TO **CORDELL HULL,** US SECRETARY OF STATE

Havana, May 25, 1933   [Received 7:05 p.m.]

President Machado has this morning sent word to me through Dr. Ferrara that the official investigation made by Colonel Delgado of the atrocities in Santa Clara Province attributed to Major Arsenio Ortiz has confirmed in detail the report of the facts as communicated by me to the Cuban Government and as reported in my telegram under reference.

A further investigation is now in process in order to verify the report that a 15-year-old boy who was an involuntary eyewitness of the murder of the three guards was hanged by Major Ortiz at the spot where the murders took place. The President requested Dr. Ferrara to assure me positively that if this latter atrocity was confirmed Major Ortiz would be publicly court-martialed; the further statement was made by the President that Major Ortiz would in any event be immediately removed from the Army and that while the precise nature of his punishment had not yet been determined upon, the least punishment that would be meted out to him would be immediate exile from Cuba.

(signed) Benjamin Sumner Welles

--◊◊◊--0--◊◊◊--

Images, top to bottom: the press reports the attempt on the life of **Dr. Grau San Martín;** End of the year photo of a **Cuban primary public school**, as in all schools in Cuba, fully integrated; a political cartoon in the US criticizing **Roosevelt's New Deal program.**

BENJAMIN SUMNER WELLES, **US AMBASSADOR IN CUBA**, WRITES TO
CORDELL HULL, US SECRETARY OF STATE

Havana, May 25, 1933   [Received 9:40 p.m.]

Yesterday I had my second long conference with Dr. Cosme de la Torriente, former Ambassador in Washington, former President of the Assembly of the League of Nations and prominent member of the group of leaders opposing the Machado administration.

I discussed in general terms with Dr. de la Torriente the possibility of a solution of the Cuban political problem. I told him that in my judgment any solution must be based upon the preservation of the structure of constitutional government and upon the utilization of the existing Congress as the means of carrying out such reforms as might be agreed upon in a conciliation program. I told him that I was positively opposed to the proposal publicly announced by the members of the revolutionary junta in New York providing for the installation of a provisional and unconstitutional government in Cuba.

I found Dr. de la Torriente in entire accord with the point of view above-expressed. He declared himself as positively opposed to revolution, equally opposed to American intervention and strongly desirous of American mediation to accomplish the ends set forth in my telegram number 43 of May 13.

He showed me letters he had received yesterday from Mendieta and Méndez Peñate (the former, the most influential leader in the New York junta) stating that they would join with him in supporting a program of solution, fair both to the existing Government and to persevering opposition factions. He likewise assured me that the same support would be given him by Miguel Maríano to dispose Gómez and by Carlos Hevía who are likewise members of the New York junta. Dr. de la Torriente further asserted within the past 2 days since the time of my first interview with him he had received assurances from the leaders of the two dissident factions of the Conservative Party that they would support a peaceful adjustment of the present difficulties through the unofficial mediation of the United States Government. I was likewise assured that the members of the Popular Party, the least important of the three Cuban parties, would coincide in any arrangements of the type proposed.

This tentative understanding does not yet include agreement on the part of General Menocal nor of his followers now refugees in Florida. I have hopes of obtaining their assent to a program of conciliation through Méndez Capote who is now with General Menocal in Florida.

The attitude of the opposition leaders with few exceptions appears to be far more reasonable than the attitude they announced publicly in New York some weeks ago. I shall continue to discuss bases of adjustment with Dr. de la Torriente until all essential details are agreed upon in principle and until the latter has received

Top to bottom: Cuban diplomats in Washington DC, the second from the left is **Orestes Ferrara**, the Ambasador, stock certificates of The **Cuba Company**, **Don Cosme de la Toirriente** in 1933, **public transportation** in La Havana in 1933.

the written assent of the leaders mentioned to these bases. I shall then initiate discussions of these bases with the President. It is obvious to my mind that no accommodations or concessions, financial or economic, should be made to the Cuban Government until a positive understanding is had as to the course the President will be willing to pursue with regard to the solution above proposed.

I beg to request that this telegram be sent to the President for his information.

(signed) Benjamin Sumner Welles

--◊◊◊--O--◊◊◊--

BENJAMIN SUMNER WELLES, US AMBASSADOR IN CUBA, WRITES TO **CORDELL HULL**, US SECRETARY OF STATE

Havana, May 29, 1933 [Received 8:46 p.m.]

Dr. Ferrara leaves today for London as Chairman of the Cuban Delegation to the World Economic Conference. During his absence the Secretary of State ad interim will be General Alberto Herrera until recently Chief of the General Staff of the Cuban Army and last week appointed Secretary of War and Marine in President Machado's Cabinet.

President Machado at present favors General Herrera as the candidate of the Liberal Party for the Presidency in the next national elections. Dr. Ferrara has assured me that he himself will return to resume the Secretary ship of State not later than the first week in July and that the President has no intention of appointing General Herrera to replace him permanently in that office.

(signed) Benjamin Sumner Welles

--◊◊◊--O--◊◊◊--

BENJAMIN SUMNER WELLES, US AMBASSADOR IN CUBA, WRITES TO CORDELL HULL, US SECRETARY OF STATE

Havana, May 29, 1933 [Received May 30, 12:27 a.m.]

On May 27 the *Diario de la Marina* published an officially inspired interview with President Machado. Among the significant statements made by the President were the following:

"A little generosity and good faith on the part of my opponents would be sufficient to enable Cuba to recover moral peace.

I wish my political opponents would be willing like good Cubans to discuss without prejudice the problems at issue with me around a table. If they convince me I am wrong, they will save themselves from the hardships of exile and they would save the country the effects of the prolonged agitation from which it is suffering I would go to my home with my conscience clear of all blame." The interview contains no definite commitments on the part of the President but the intimation that the President is willing to reach a compromise by negotiation is made emphatically plain.

In a conference with Ferrara yesterday afternoon I expressed to him my gratification at the initiative taken by the President. I remarked that it might well be considered as a fair approach towards a solution of the political problem. Dr. Ferrara said that that was in fact the President's desire. I was likewise assured that the President would welcome my mediation.

I had immediately afterwards a conference with Dr. de la Torriente. The latter told me that since my last interview with him he had received additional assurances from important opposition leaders that they would support him in negotiations through me providing for an adjustment of the political situation through compromise. He further stated that he had received positive assurances from leaders of the two secret societies known as the ABC and the OCRR that these organizations would refrain from further violence in the hope that a peaceful settlement with the Government could be reached. Dr. de la Torriente has requested General Menocal's brother to proceed to Miami to endeavor to persuade General Menocal to give his formal consent to the negotiations which it is desired to initiate. Dr. de la Torriente hopes by the end of the present week to have received authorization from the great majority of the political leaders and the non-political Opposition groups to represent them in this effort at mediation.

The principal danger in the present situation lies in the fact that while President Machado is now inclined to follow a policy of conciliation which has been made evident by his removal of Major Ortiz from military command, by the continuing release of political prisoners and by the gradual relaxation of police and censorship regulations, and while the principal elements of the Opposition, both political leaders and secret societies, are making, I believe, a sincere effort to prevent for the time being any resort to open violence and terrorism, the directors of the Opposition activities are very far from possessing a complete control over all the organizations in the Opposition. Any return to violence on the part of a dissident group will bring about prompt action necessary by the Government and should this then provoke counter-reprisals, negotiations might break down at any time.

Furthermore, while the political leaders are secretly only too anxious to obtain our mediation they are at the moment jockeying for political advantage in the next national elections and in some instances this advantage will be sought through an appeal to the more radical element of the population by public announcements that they will not countenance diplomatic intervention in any guise by the United States.

Since I have now received assurances both from the President and from a leading representative of the Opposition in the person of Dr. de la Torriente that my mediation is desired I shall discuss the general bases of an agreement as of my own initiative both with the President and with Dr. de la Torriente as soon as I am confident that the latter is in fact backed by a sufficient number of Opposition groups to make these discussions of positive value.

I beg to request that a copy of this telegram be sent to the President for his information.

(signed) Benjamin Sumner Welles

--◊◊◊--0--◊◊◊--

JUNE OF 1933

 Events in Cuba

- **June 11** The Spanish pilots *Mariano Barberán* and *Joaquín Collar* arrive at Camagüey airport from Seville. They had traveled on the plane "*Cuatro Vientos*," beating several records. The next day they are enthusiastically received in Havana.
- **June12** Ambassador Welles offers to mediate between the government and its opponents. ABC accepts it on June 14; the DRE rejects it.
- **June 22** *Dr. Carlos de la Torre* and the *Revolutionary Board* adhere to Welles Mediation.
- **June 28** The Cuban government deferred until 1945 the payment of 20 million dollars owed to the *Chase National Bank*.

 Washington Telex

BENJAMIN SUMNER WELLES, US AMBASSADOR IN CUBA, WRITES TO **WILLIAM PHILLIPS** , US UNDER SECRETARY OF STATE

Havana, June 2, 1933   [Received 2:45 p.m.]

A major problem in the present situation in Cuba is the fact that the university is closed owing to the unwillingness of both professors and students to permit any continuation of university activities under present conditions.

In discussing this condition yesterday with the President we came to the conclusion that the attempt should be made to change the institution from a government-controlled university to an independent organization operating under the control of a self-perpetuating board of trustees entirely removed from governmental influence, the Government merely contributing in the annual budget the amount necessary to make possible the carrying on of the university work.

The President advised me that he was very anxious to obtain the services of some competent American authority who could come to Havana to study the situation and draw up for the benefit of the Government a charter comprising the essential points above indicated.

I beg to request that the Department endeavor to obtain the services of an American expert along these lines. I have reason to believe that the Government would not only be willing to enact immediately whatever legislation were to be recommended by him but also that this particular solution would eliminate to a great extent the unrest which now exists to such an extreme degree among the student groups in Cuba.

(signed) Benjamin Sumner Welles

--◇◇◇--0--◇◇◇--

BENJAMIN SUMNER WELLES, US AMBASSADOR IN CUBA, WRITES TO **WILLIAM PHILLIPS**, US UNDER SECRETARY OF STATE

Havana, June 2, 1933   [Received 8:45 p.m.]

I had a long interview with Machado in this matter yesterday afternoon. I told the President that the time had now come when I felt it possible for me to offer my friendly and unofficial mediation between the political groups supporting his administration and the political groups and independent factions comprising the Opposition. I said that this offer was conditional on my services being welcomed by him and by most of the Opposition leaders.

The President assured me that not only were my services in this capacity welcome to him but that he felt confident that in no other manner could any adjustment of the political problem be brought about.

I told the President that in my judgment there was only one satisfactory manner of solving the present political situation and that was through compromise on the part of all concerned. I felt that such compromise must be worked out in accordance with the structure of the existing constitution and through the existing Congress. I said that the solution proposed by the Opposition which called for the immediate resignation of the President and his substitution by an impartial Secretary of State was not satisfactory to me; that if this were done under the present constitution, national elections would have to be called within a period of 60 days to elect a successor to the President to fill out the latter's unexpired term; that under present conditions only one party was organized and that was the President's own, the Liberal Party, and the result would necessarily be that any candidate of that Party would be elected and so far as the Opposition was concerned the situation would remain exactly the same as at present save for the fact that there undoubtedly would be so much unrest and agitation in the country that it is doubtful whether the same control could be exercised by the next executive as was now exercised by the President himself.

I said that to my own mind the proper solution was an immediate reform of the electoral code based upon the recommendations

Cuba during the first election of Gerardo Machado to the Presidency: news of the victory of Hoover in the US elections of 1928; a political rally in Nuevitas, Camaguey, and LIFE, a popular English language magazine Published briefly in Havana.

Photos, top to bottom: The studios of **CMQ, the radio and TV station** founded on March 12, 1933 by **Miguel Gabriel** and **Angel Cambó**, later bought by the **Mestre** brothers; Cuba remembers the extraordinary feat of pilots **Barberán and Collar**, flying from Sevilla to Camagüey in June of 1933.

of the electoral expert whom we would obtain for the Government; that such reform must envisage complete liberty for reorganization immediately of the existing political parties and for the organization as political entities of modulate groups or factions so that public opinion could make itself felt in every proper manner in the next national election and need not attempt to express itself solely through the existing political parties which are under the complete domination of old-time political leaders. As a subsequent step I proposed the reform of the constitution to comprise the election of a Vice-President who must be an individual of outstanding reputation and regarded by all important factions or groups as absolutely impartial; the limitation of the term of the next President to a term of 5 years with no immediate reelection; a decrease in the existing number of Congressmen and a shortening of the terms of such Senators and Congressmen as have had extended the terms for which they were originally elected. All these steps could be taken under the present constitution within 6 months.

The President agreed with these suggestions. He then told me of his own initiative that he would be willing as a patriotic gesture to retire from the Presidency after the election of a Vice-President who possessed the qualifications above indicated as he stated he would have been willing to do at any time these past 3 years if there had been a Vice-President.

Should this program be carried out it would be possible for the President to retire in favor of the new Vice-President at any time after the selection of the latter. I did not indicate in my conversation with the President the time when I thought such retirement on his part would be desirable but limited myself to saying that I did feel that it was essential that the Vice-President should be in control of the Government during the next national electoral period. To this the President agreed.

In concluding my conversation with the President I told him that I did not feel that any one phase of the existing Cuban problem could be dealt with separately but I thought on the contrary that the political, the economic and the financial aspects of the situation should be dealt with as parts of a whole. To this view the President gave his complete assent.

I believe that a solution along the lines above proposed is the only proper solution. It would safeguard the Government of the United States from the obligation to undertake any direct official intervention in Cuban affairs. It avoids a bad precedent for Cuba in that no provisional nor unconstitutional form of government is set up. Finally, it provides a hope for the future in the reforms to be made both in the electoral code and in the constitution.

I shall today continue my conversations with prominent members of the Opposition, and I am hopeful that during the coming week I may receive more ample and definite assurances of their support in these negotiations than I have yet secured.

In order to maintain his control of the situation and in order to refrain from appearing to concede to the Opposition any right to demand his resignation, the President will continue until a definite agreement has been reached in all public statements to insist upon his determination to remain in office throughout his term. I am in entire accord with his belief that this attitude on his part is desirable under present conditions.

I beg to request that a copy of the above be sent to the President for his information.

(signed) Benjamin Sumner Welles

--◊◊◊--0--◊◊◊--

BENJAMIN SUMNER WELLES, US AMBASSADOR IN CUBA, WRITES TO **WILLIAM PHILLIPS** , US UNDER SECRETARY OF STATE

Havana, June 6, 1933   [Received 2:10 p.m.]

President Machado requests me to extend to Professor McBain his official invitation to come to Cuba to formulate recommendations for amendments to the electoral code.

The President likewise invites Professor McBain to undertake for the Cuban Government the drafting of a charter for an independent university and extends his invitation as well to any expert assistant such as the member of the faculty of the Columbia University suggested by Professor McBain whom Professor McBain may indicate.

President Machado has likewise requested me to ascertain the remuneration desired by Professor McBain and his assistant. I suggest that if it is possible for Professor McBain to accept the position under such conditions he should not ask for remuneration in excess of $230 a month which is the amount now being paid to the members of the Cabinet. He should, of course, request in addition to such compensation all travelling and subsistence expenses. The remuneration of his assistant should be proportionate. The President will be willing to pay any remuneration desired by Professor McBain, but should the salary given him be in excess of that of the members of the Cuban Cabinet it would unquestionably give rise to considerable popular opposition which it is desirable to avoid at this time.

I beg to request that I be advised of the approximate date of Professor McBain's arrival. The latter should cable his formal acceptance of the invitation directly to President Machado.

(signed) Benjamin Sumner Welles

--◊◊◊--0--◊◊◊--

BENJAMIN SUMNER WELLES, US AMBASSADOR IN CUBA, WRITES TO
WILLIAM PHILLIPS, US UNDER SECRETARY OF STATE

Havana, June 6, 1933   [Received 9:30 p.m.]

I had a further interview with the President last night.

I told the President quite frankly that I felt it was a mistaken policy on his part to reiterate in public statements his determination not to leave the Presidency until 1935 and particularly to allege in such statements that the Opposition is inconsiderable and that an overwhelming majority of the Cuban people support him and his followers. I remarked that while I was entirely in accord as I had previously stated to him with belief that he should not at the present time give any indication that he would consider retiring from the Presidency before the expiration of his term of office inasmuch as such indication would weaken his control over the Congress and over the Army yet I did not feel that it was in accord with his determination to pursue a conciliatory policy for him to continue to provoke by intemperate statements the hostility of the Opposition factions. I told him that after his last public interview it had caused me the greatest personal effort to prevent certain of the Opposition factions from a further resort to terrorism and violence and that I had no confidence whatever that I could prevent a recurrence of open hostilities if he persisted in such provocation.

I stated that three of his foremost political opponents, the directors of the student and professorial groups and the directors of the ABC organization, now supported my mediation and that if we were to have any useful results therefrom it was, in my judgment, essential for the President not only to determine, as he has, upon a policy of conciliation but also to make known to the public that such is his intent.

I suggested therefore, that he advise the Cuban people within the next few days that he had reached a decision on the following three points:

1. That he considered the basis of an adjustment of the political situation could be reached through a reform of the existing constitution which reform should be taken with a minimum of delay and in the drafting of which all shades of public opinion should have full representation in order that the new constitution should favor no individual and no political party but should be of benefit both immediate as well as future to the Cuban people as a whole.
2. That in his opinion the suppression of the Vice-Presidency by the last constitution had been a fundamental error and that the Vice-Presidency should be restored not only for the constitutional term commencing in 1935 but through a transitory provision in the new constitution for the remainder of the existing Presidential term as well.

3. That in his judgment, in view of the present political situation, the individual to hold the office of Vice-President during the remainder of the present Presidential term should be a citizen of outstanding reputation who had not taken an active part in political strife and who should be recognized as impartial by all groups and by all parties.

The President told me that he would comply with my suggestion and that he would make such public declaration on Thursday of this week. He further stated that before making such public statement he would submit a draft of it to me for any amendment that I might desire to suggest.

I further requested the President now to relax the censorship on the representative newspapers of the Republic in such a manner as to permit reasoned declarations to be made by members of the Opposition. I said that I was anxious that Dr. de la Torriente, for example, be given full liberty to make statements of this character through the press. I told him that Dr. de la Torriente had already prepared a statement urging the acceptance of mediation on the Government of the United States in order that an adjustment of the political situation here might be found and that I felt the publication of such a statement would be highly useful at this juncture. The President gave orders in my presence that this be done. I believe that with the publication of the President's declaration above referred to there will be a very distinct change for the better in public sentiment here. The revulsion caused by the President's last public statement was extremely violent and during the whole day of last Saturday I was very fearful that the situation could not be controlled. Both former Chief Justice Gutierrez Veneos and Dr. de la Torriente, as well as the leaders of the student and of the so-called intellectual groups, have, however, been extremely helpful and it was due in great part to their cooperation that the situation improved.

Notwithstanding the statements made yesterday by Dr. de la Torriente I am positively advised that Mendieta, Méndez Peñate, and Gómez will join in the mediation negotiations. Menocal, however, is still recalcitrant and insists that the only sortition he will accept is one to be obtained through revolution. In this connection I beg to inquire whether the Secretary before his departure from Washington requested, as I had asked, that the Department of Justice take immediate steps to prevent the shipment of arms and ammunition from Florida to Cuba as well as the sending of any expeditionary forces from there. It is imperative, as I indicated in my personal letter to the Secretary of May 20th,[23] that local authorities in Florida be prevented from assisting General Menocal and his followers in Miami to violate the neutrality laws of the United States and by so doing jeopardize my present hope of succeeding in finding a peaceful and constitutional solution for the Cuban problem.

Gerardo Machado was President of Cuba from May 20, 1925 to August 12, 1933. His Vice President was **Carlos de la Rosa.** He was preceded by **Alfredo Zayas** and succeeded by **Carlos Manuel de Céspedes and Quesada**. He was born September 28, 1871 in Camajuaní, Cuba and died March 29, 1939 (aged 67) in Miami Beach, Florida. He was married to Elvira Machado Nodal, his cousin, with whom he had three children, Laudelina (Babe), Angela Elvira, Berta. He also had two children out of wedlock, Leonor and Heriberto. Before he was was President of Cuba (1925–1933) he was a general of the Cuban War of Independence in 1895. He was born in a poor background. In his youth, his enemies said he have been a cattle rustler before he joined the fight for independence. He was one of the youngest Cuban generals of the 1895 to 1898 Cuban War of Independence. Only two other War of Independence generals were younger: Calixto Enamorado (1874–1951) and Enrique Loynaz del Castillo (1871–1963). In the war he fought in Cuba's middle provinces, along with José Miguel Gómez (1858–1921), who also was president on the Liberal Party ticket, and José de Jesús Monteagudo.

Photos, top to bottom: his **Cabinet** in 1933, when he was deposed; in a group with **Elvira, his wife, his children and grandchildren**, in Miami in 1937.

I beg to request that a copy of this telegram be sent to the President for his information.

(signed) Benjamin Sumner Welles

--◊◊◊--0--◊◊◊--

BENJAMIN SUMNER WELLES, US AMBASSADOR IN CUBA, WRITES TO
WILLIAM PHILLIPS, US UNDER SECRETARY OF STATE

Havana, June 8, 1933   [Received 1:45 p.m.]

Referring to our telephone conversation yesterday the newspapers here this morning announce that the President has positively abandoned his intention of requesting authorization of Congress in this session to undertake the negotiation of reciprocal trade agreements in the form originally proposed.

It is highly desirable that I be instructed to announce at the first possible moment that I am authorized to undertake the negotiation of a revision of the existing commercial convention between Cuba and the United States or else that the Department announce that such negotiations will be undertaken by the Department with the Cuban Embassy at Washington.

If no announcement is made and the impression is given that there is no hope of economic improvement in Cuba through a revision of the commercial convention until sometime in the indefinite future, the reaction here will be extremely prejudicial. If the negotiation of the revised convention is undertaken without delay not only will the psychological effect be good but the new convention could be presented for ratification to our Senate in the next regular session with the probability that ratification would be obtained and consequently that shortly thereafter the resulting change in conditions would operate not only in benefit of Cuba but also of our own exporters.

(signed) Benjamin Sumner Welles

--◊◊◊--0--◊◊◊--

BENJAMIN SUMNER WELLES, US AMBASSADOR IN CUBA, WRITES TO
WILLIAM PHILLIPS, US UNDER SECRETARY OF STATE

Havana, June 8, 1933   [Received 5:40 p.m.]

My telegram No. 72, June 6, 1 p.m. In accordance with his promise to me, the President last night gave to the press an official declaration covering precisely the points I had suggested. I was afforded the opportunity of revising the text before issuance in order to avoid any possible confusion as to the President's intent.

In the first section of this declaration the President urged the creation of the position of Vice-President at the earliest possible moment through a transitory reform of the constitution. He declared his determination that the individual to hold this office should be "of high character and impartial" unconnected with political activity and should not be a candidate for any office in the general elections of 1934. In the second section the President stated that it was his determination that in the task of constitutional reform every political party and every independent faction should be given free and ample opportunity to cooperate. In the third and concluding section [of] his declaration the President stated that as soon as Congress has passed the new version of the electoral code which will be drafted by the Supreme Electoral Tribunal upon the recommendations of Professor McBain full and absolute guarantees will be offered so that in accordance with the provisions of that code the existing political parties can reorganize freely and so that "the new political forces representing groups of voters who are not members of the existing political parties" can organize. In this manner the political parties and independent groups will be given the opportunity to present candidates not only in the national elections of 1934 but also in the election of delegates to the Constitutional Convention which will have to approve the reforms of the constitution which are now to be undertaken by the Congress.

A full text of President Machado's declaration will be sent by mail. The reaction has been unexpectedly favorable both in the ABC and in the student and intellectual organizations.

I beg to request that a copy of this telegram be sent to the President for his information.

(signed) Benjamin Sumner Welles

--◊◊◊--0--◊◊◊--

WILLIAM PHILLIPS, US UNDER SECRETARY OF STATE, , WRITES TO
BENJAMIN SUMNER WELLES, US AMBASSADOR IN CUBA

Washington, June 8, 1933

You are instructed to proceed with negotiations for the revision of the commercial treaty with Cuba in connection with the Administration's policy of obtaining reciprocal trade agreements with other countries. The treaty will be submitted to the Senate at the next session of Congress. Public announcement that these instructions have been sent you will be made by the Department probably tomorrow.

(signed) William Phillips

--◊◊◊--0--◊◊◊--

BENJAMIN SUMNER WELLES, US AMBASSADOR IN CUBA, WRITES TO
WILLIAM PHILLIPS, US UNDER SECRETARY OF STATE

Havana, June 10, 1933

Dr. de la Torriente's statement was published in the local press this morning as previously agreed. The major portion of the statem-

The Cuban embassy buildings in Washington.
Photo, top: the brownstone mansion at **1529 18th Street NW**, bought by Cuba upon recommendation of Gonzalo de Quesada in 1914. It later became the residence of US Secretary of State Charles Evans Hughes.
Photo bottom: The lavish mansion at **2630 16th Street NW**, in the exclusive Meridian Hill neighborhood, bought by President Alfredo Zayas in 1923, during the US presidency of Warren G. Harding. During the years of prohibition. Federal agents accused Cuban diplomats of distributing alcohol from this embassy building. This building is now the Cuban Embassy once again. Finally, a photo of the embassy's reception area.

ent is devoted to a vigorous but nevertheless constructive and temperate attack on the policies of the Machado administration. In the concluding paragraphs he refers to the recent invitation of President Machado to his opponents to discuss the solution of the existing political problem with him as "good Cubans" and reiterates his own opinion as previously expressed that a satisfactory solution can only come through a discussion by representatives of the Government and of the factions comprising the opposition to the Government—such representatives to be necessarily individuals who are free from passion and who have not undergone personal loss or suffering from the events of the past few years. In conclusion Dr. de la Torriente states that in his judgment, such a discussion, even with the restrictions indicated, would be useless unless both sides previously agree upon "an individual in whom both sides have confidence who would be willing through his mediation and advice to bring them to a definite agreement".

The opinion thus expressed by Dr. de la Torriente in which he expresses his desire that my mediation be accepted by all the opposition factions, as it has already been accepted by the Government, will be supported in additional statements to be made in the press today and tomorrow by outstanding citizens of the opposition factions including Dr. Varona who has very great influence among the elements composing the so-called intellectual groups.

Dr. de la Torriente has now succeeded in uniting here a group comprising outstanding members of every one of the opposition groups. They are almost all in accord with the program determined upon and are necessarily far better aware of the favorable reaction created opposition sectors by the events of the past few days than are the other representatives on these same groups composing the junta in New York. Yesterday they agreed to send to the United States today Dr. Albanés who is a leading figure in the opposition section of the Conservative Party in Congress; and Dr. Roberto Méndez Peñate brother of Colonel Méndez Peñate of the New York junta. These two representatives will first visit General Menocal in Miami and then proceed to New York to confer with the members of the junta there. They will insist through instructions given to them by the newly-formed group in Havana that the leaders in the United States either agree to come to Cuba and cooperate or else remain in the United States and enter into a commitment to refrain from urging or from directing any further acts of violence in Cuba. They will inform General Menocal that there is no popular support in Cuba today for his revolutionary program.

I am hopeful owing to the importance of these emissaries and owing to the definite decision to cooperate reached by the Havana group that the New York junta will soon disintegrate. With regard to General Menocal I strongly recommend that at an early date some proper representative of our Department of Justice see him in Miami and advise him that because of the consideration which the Government of the United States wishes to show him as a former

President of Cuba and as a friend of the United States he should realize that he and his friends are under strict surveillance and it is hoped that he will not lend himself to any infraction of the neutrality laws of the United States. A warning couched in these terms would have a very decisive effect upon General Menocal under present conditions.

I beg to request that a copy of this telegram be sent to the President for his information.

(signed) Benjamin Sumner Welles

--◊◊◊--0--◊◊◊--

BENJAMIN SUMNER WELLES, US AMBASSADOR IN CUBA, WRITES TO **WILLIAM PHILLIPS**, US UNDER SECRETARY OF STATE

Havana, June 14, 1933

General Menocal's son-in-law Dr. Sardiñas and the General's confidential adviser Dr. Martínez Zaldo leave this afternoon for Miami to interview Menocal and to insist on it that he abandon any revolutionary activity and agree to appoint a representative to cooperate in the plan I had indicated. They advise me that from information they received yesterday they understand Menocal will agree to their representations.

Miguel Mariano Gómez of the New York junta has expressed to me today through a friend who received a message from him this morning that he desires to return to Cuba likewise for the purpose of cooperating.

The ABC directors have advised me that positive assurances will be given me by the association tomorrow welcoming my unofficial mediation and committing the organization to refrain from any terrorist activity pending favorable solution. The attitude taken by this organization will be followed by the other two principal secret societies.

The leaders of the Opposition sectors here are becoming increasingly indignant at the public declarations which are being made in New York by members of the junta who at the same time are sending them confidential messages to the effect that my mediation is the only method by which a satisfactory adjustment can be obtained. I have reason to believe that if by the end of this week the New York junta does not refrain from publishing statements of this character the newly formed junta in Havana will declare itself in control of negotiations on behalf of the Opposition factions. I intend to wait for a few more days in the hope that the New York junta will agree to cooperate and to come to Havana for this purpose. I am not willing however to wait longer than Monday of next week before commencing with representatives of the Government and with the duly selected representatives of the Opposition here the consideration of the essential reforms to the constitution in order that we can commence the program indicated in President Machado's last public statement.

(signed) Benjamin Sumner Welles

--◊◊◊--0--◊◊◊--

BENJAMIN SUMNER WELLES, US AMBASSADOR IN CUBA, WRITES TO **WILLIAM PHILLIPS**, US UNDER SECRETARY OF STATE

Havana, June 16, 1933   [Received 6:08 p.m.]

I was handed yesterday a written memorandum by the directors of the ABC accepting my friendly mediation between the Government and the opposition factions. Their acceptance was based upon the understanding that my mediation had no aspect of intervention but was to be interpreted I as the friendly effort of the representative of a friendly government to reestablish peace in the Republic and that such mediation would be carried out loyally and "with a view to the ideals and real interest of the Cuban people". The additional statement was made that while my mediation was accepted unconditionally the association would feel itself free to withdraw should the negotiations be unduly protracted, should they take a form contrary to the interests and ideals of the Cuban people or should they have to be undertaken *"under oppressive circumstances which would plainly demonstrate bad faith on the part of the Cuban Government."*

Finally, the ABC from the date upon which this memorandum was handed to me *"enters into a formal obligation to refrain from all forms of agitation directed against the constituted authorities in Cuba".*

I have given to the press by agreement with President Machado the essential points contained in this memorandum. I have felt it desirable to regard as strictly confidential that portion of the memorandum which is couched in terms which are offensive to the members of the Government.

The immediate reaction to the announcement that the ABC has accepted my mediation has been as was to be expected highly favorable. The representative of the ABC in the New York junta has been ordered to withdraw from the same and it is the expectation on the part of all the representatives of the other opposition factions that the initiative taken by the ABC will at once create a break-up of the New York junta and insure the acceptance of my mediation by all of the other factions involved.

I have yet no direct information from General Menocal.

(signed) Benjamin Sumner Welles

--◊◊◊--0--◊◊◊--

The extraordinary public works done by Machado during his first presidential term (1925–1929), which were a period of great prosperity in Cuba.

Top photos: the **Cuban National Capitol Building** under construction in 1928. It was commissioned by Machado and built from 1926 to 1929 under the direction of *Eugenio Rayneri Piedra*. *Bottom photos*, the works on the monumental stairways at the entrance of the **University of Havana**.

BENJAMIN SUMNER WELLES, US AMBASSADOR IN CUBA, WRITES TO
WILLIAM PHILLIPS, US UNDER SECRETARY OF STATE

Havana, June 16, 1933   [Received 9:05 p.m.]

I have now received the formal acceptance of my mediation by the directors of the OCRR and of the organization composed of the high-school professors. The university professors have sent me word that a similar reply is to be expected tomorrow from the university group.

I have had a conference with Dr. Albanés, Dr. Martínez Zaldo and Dr. Sardiñas who returned yesterday evening from Miami where they interviewed General Menocal who advises that while he is now entirely willing to accept my mediation he is unable to send me official word to that effect owing to his commitment to the New York junta until the junta has either officially accepted my mediation or else has been disbanded.

In replies to inquiries I have stated that I was unwilling to make any direct representations to the New York junta or to receive any representative from the junta. It appears to me desirable that the junta disband at the earliest possible moment and that whatever discussions take place prior to mediation should take place in Havana directly between the various opposition factions and myself. I have every reason to believe that this solution is now only a question of days.

(signed) Benjamin Sumner Welles

--◊◊◊--O--◊◊◊--

WILLIAM PHILLIPS, US UNDER SECRETARY OF STATE, , WRITES TO
FRANKLYN D. ROOSEVELT, PRESIDENT OF THE US, AT SEA

Washington, June 20, 1933

Ambassador Welles reports the probability that he will receive in the very near future the agreement of all the various opposition factions to accept his mediation in their controversy with the Cuban Government. You may recall that President Machado has already made known his willingness to confer with the opposition leaders to work out a satisfactory solution of the present political difficulties. Welles is of the opinion that the great mass of the Cuban people desires that these discussions, which should begin shortly, produce a settlement.

Welles believes that a message from you, delivered propitiously, at the outset of these discussions, would be of the utmost value for the success of the negotiations, and would have a most helpful effect on public opinion. I have drafted the following as a suggestion for such a message for Welles:

"It is very heartening and the source of much satisfaction to me to know that the Cuban people now believe that a

peaceful discussion of their country's problems is the most satisfactory means of determining their country's destinies, and that the best way of reconciling their political difficulties is to be found in the peaceable and orderly process of frank but constructive discussions. I wish the Cuban people every success in these discussions for I am convinced that the restoration of political peace is a necessary and essential preliminary step on the way to Cuba's economic recovery. The representatives of all factions may rest assured that the moral support of the American people will be behind these attempts at the peaceable adjustment of Cuban problems through the orderly procedure of Constitutional Government."

(signed) William Phillips

--◊◊◊--O--◊◊◊--

WILLIAM PHILLIPS, US UNDER SECRETARY OF STATE, , WRITES TO BENJAMIN SUMNER WELLES, US AMBASSADOR IN CUBA

Washington, June 21, 1933

President authorizes following message:

"It is very heartening and the source of much satisfaction to me to know that the Cuban people now believe that a peaceful discussion of their country's problem is the most satisfactory means of determining their country's destinies, and that the best way of reconciling their political difficulties is to be found in the peaceable and orderly process of frank but constructive discussions. I wish the Cuban people every success in these discussions for I am convinced that the restoration of political peace is a necessary and essential preliminary step on the way to Cuba's economic recovery. The representatives of all factions may rest assured that the moral support of the American people will be behind these attempts at the peaceable adjustment of Cuban problems through the orderly procedure of Constitutional Government."

He adds however,

"it should of course be made clear that request for any assistance from Welles originates from Cuban Government and people and is not suggested in first instance by Washington."

(signed) William Phillips

--◊◊◊--O--◊◊◊--

BENJAMIN SUMNER WELLES, US AMBASSADOR IN CUBA, WRITES TO
WILLIAM PHILLIPS, US UNDER SECRETARY OF STATE

Havana, June 21, 1933   [Received 9:00 p.m.]

I was handed this afternoon by the duly accredited delegates of the University their formal acceptance of my tender of good offices. The memorandum contains the following three points as those upon which the acceptance of the University is based.

> *(1) Because the tender of good offices as a procedure recognized in international law does not imply any infringement whatever of the sovereignty or of the independence of Cuba and because from the moment in which these negotiations do not follow the course indicated to that end which is shown below, all of those who had accepted the offer would be at liberty to withdraw from the negotiations.*
>
> *(2) Because this tender of good offices has been made by the Ambassador of a government which at the present time is carrying out an anti-imperialistic policy based upon its desire of furthering more cordial relations between the nations of America upon a foundation of absolute respect for the rights of all and, furthermore, because of the outstanding qualities of the person of the mediator.*
>
> *(3) Because the professors hold the firm conviction, and that has been their basic motive in accepting the offer, that those negotiations will lead in a short space of time and effort to the solution of our problems making an end to present conditions in Cuba and reestablishing the rule of law which is today unknown and because through these negotiations there can be obtained the realization of the most earnest desires of the Cuban people. The professors desire likewise to emphasize that throughout the course of their deliberations and at the moment of reaching this decision they have not forgotten for a single moment the students of our University who form an essential part of the same and who have acted in so virile, self-sacrificing and generous a fashion that it could never be forgotten by any of the professors who are obligated both morally and as citizens to remember always their sacrifice and their noble idealism and above all the martyrdom of those who have fallen in a heroic struggle for right and justice.*

The formal acceptance on the part of the University was adopted unanimously and notwithstanding the protest of the three professors who have formed part of the revolutionary junta in New York. The I influence of this decision on the part of the University will be very great because the University carries far greater weight with public opinion in Cuba than can be realized outside of the Republic.

Miguel Mariano, Gómez's representative, will visit me tomorrow morning to advise me of his acceptance of my offer on behalf of his political party.

In order to avoid any misapprehension by the American press as to the nature of the offer which I have made both to the Government and to representatives of the opposition factions I wish to emphasize that I have repeatedly stated to all elements that this offer has been limited to my "tender of good offices" with the hope that its acceptance might serve to bring about conversations in Cuba between representatives of the Government and representatives of the opposition factions in order that the Cuban people themselves might solve their domestic political problems through a program fair and satisfactory to all concerned. I have furthermore repeatedly stated that this offer not only involved no intervention on our part in Cuban domestic affairs but was made on the contrary for the specific purpose of avoiding the creation of a situation which might force the Government pf the United States to consider its responsibilities and obligations under the permanent treaty. Finally I have stated that any solution of the Cuban political problem which might be freely agreed upon as the result of the tender of my good offices by representatives of all factions of Cuban public opinion and which provided for the maintenance of the forms of constitutional government must be a solution which would be favorably regarded by the Government of the United States.

The terms "arbitration", "mediation" and "good offices" are used here almost interchangeably and without any very clear realization of the distinction between these respective words. I have consistently made it plain that my offer was merely a friendly demonstration of the desire of the President of the United States to further a pacific and constitutional settlement of the policy of chaos which has continued with such tragic consequences during the past 3 years and could necessarily therefore not imply in any sense the incurring of any contractual obligation on the part of the United States.

I have obtained the publication recently of certain leading articles and editorials which make the nature of my offer very clear and I think that public opinion in Cuba now realizes the precise nature of the step I have taken. It would be helpful however if the American press also made these facts as above-indicated entirely plain.

(signed) Benjamin Sumner Welles

A word about the ABC revolutionary organization.
The ABC was founded in October of 1931 in opposition to the government of Gerardo Machado. It used a hierarchy of clandestine cells, in which each member would oversee a cell on the next level. The first cell was labeled A; the next tier B; then C, and so forth. It gained prominence not so much for its ideology, as for its tactics, such as acts of terrorism, targeting police officers and soldiers, and high-profile individuals like Senate President **Clemente Vázquez Bello**. The group's most prominent members were **Dr. Joaquín Martínez Sáenz**, **Jorge Mañach** and **Francisco Ichaso**. The membership was predominantly students and professionals. It maintained close contact with Cuba's radical student groups, such as the **Directorio Estudiantil Universitario**, led at the time by student leader **Eduardo Chibás** Such groups carried out bombing missions, with the ABC providing funding and equipment. Interestingly, Batista's unique position as a stenographer made him valuable to the cause and he agreed to be an informant for the ABC for several months in 1932.
Aside from its activities against Machado, the ABC called for a range of reforms, including women's suffrage, worker's rights (legalization of unions, eight-hour day, right to strike, pensions), the elimination of latifundios through taxation, and the creation of cooperatives, as well as the creation of a Cuban National Bank. Its ideology was contrary to both communism and fascism, firmly based on Cuba's national capitalist development. According to US Ambassador Benjamín Sumner Welles, *"the ABC members are both intelligent and well-disposed..."* After the fall of Machado, Martínez Sáenz served as Secretary of the Treasury, and
Carlos Saladrigas as Secretary of Justice.

Photos above, top to bottom, left to right:
1933 Cuban Senate President **Andrés Vázquez Bello**, the ABC Manifesto of 1933, **Eduardo Chibás**, **Francisco Ichaso**, **Joaquín Martínez Sáenz**,
and **Jorge Mañach**.

BENJAMIN SUMNER WELLES, US AMBASSADOR IN CUBA, WRITES TO
WILLIAM PHILLIPS, US UNDER SECRETARY OF STATE

Havana, June 22, 1933

I had this morning my first interview with the President in 2 weeks. General Machado has been seriously ill and is still unable to transact official business.

I advised the President in detailed fashion of the conversations I had had with representatives of the opposition factions and of my opinion that within a few days all of the important elements in the opposition with the possible exception of the Menocal group would have accepted my tender of good offices. The President elaborated at great length upon his desire to meet the opposition halfway although he consistently maintained that no confidence whatever was to be placed in any promises which might be forthcoming from General Menocal and that the student organizations would undoubtedly promote disturbances during the time that conversations were continuing here.

The President informed me that he would select immediately three delegates to represent the Government in the mediation negotiations. I expressed my earnest hope that the individuals to be selected by him would be of conciliatory character and it; is my present impression that the delegates whom the President will select will be Barreras, the President of the Senate; Averhoff, the Secretary of the Treasury; and Herrera, the Acting Secretary of State.

The President informed me that he himself has dictated the outlines of the editorial appearing yesterday in the *Heraldo de Cuba*, the Government paper, which was entitled *"The Good Offices of Ambassador Welles"*.

This editorial called attention to the fact that the President himself had taken the initiative in the conciliation policy and that the Government of General Machado strongly supported the utilization of my good offices "because the Ambassador does not prejudice our Sovereignty; does not affect in the slightest degree our rights as an independent people; and because he is carrying out the points of the good neighbor of President Roosevelt." The editorial continues by declaring that the utilization of my good offices will make it possible for the Cuban people "to reach an agreement through serene, reasonable and thoughtful discussion, the only manner in which law, justice and respect for individual rights can prevail, even in the most bloody conflicts, and through which men who do not permit themselves to be blinded by the dictates of hate nor the savage impulse of barbarism can make themselves heard".

The editorial concludes with the statement that...

> *"... the tender of the good offices of the Ambassador is the offer of a loyal friend in a destructive and tragic family quarrel, extended with the hope that it may be solved*

through the channels of civic action and of civilization. No good Cuban should therefore withhold from him his sympathy, create difficulties in his task, nor close his heart beforehand to the sentiments of gratitude which so lofty a policy should necessarily make grow in every worthy soul, whether this effort meets with success or not".

The President desires me to express to the Department that this editorial is the expression of his own attitude about the utilization of the good offices which I extended.

(signed) Benjamin Sumner Welles

--◊◊◊--0--◊◊◊--

BENJAMIN SUMNER WELLES, US AMBASSADOR IN CUBA, WRITES TO **WILLIAM PHILLIPS**, US UNDER SECRETARY OF STATE

Havana, June 23, 1933

I am informed that within the next few days certain of the opposition factions will publish in the United States declarations of the reasons which have caused them to accept my tender of good offices. Probably a good many of these declarations which will be intended to appeal to the most radical of the members of the opposition, will either misconstrue or exaggerate the essential character of my services. It will be helpful if the Department would refuse to issue any opinion regarding such declarations and merely limit itself to stating that the official interpretation given by the Cuban Government to my tender of good offices is clearly defined in the editorial in the Government organ *Heraldo de Cuba* of June 22 of which portions were quoted in my telegram under reference and full copy and translation of which are being sent to the Department today by air mail.

(signed) Benjamin Sumner Welles

--◊◊◊--0--◊◊◊--

BENJAMIN SUMNER WELLES, US AMBASSADOR IN CUBA, WRITES TO **WILLIAM PHILLIPS**, US UNDER SECRETARY OF STATE

Havana, June 26, 1933

I have been confidentially advised that the Council of the University Student Group is planning to send a delegation to visit me to inform me that the group wishes to accept my good offices provided that representatives of two Latin American Republics join with me in the mediation proceedings. Should this develop I shall state that I should be extremely glad to have representatives of two Latin American Republics join with me in the effort to promote a peaceful solution of Cuba's political problem but that of course it must be understood that the initiative in this regard cannot come from me; that it must on the contrary be a suggestion acceptable both to the Government and to all of the other factions in the opposition who have accepted my good offices and furthermore that the Latin American Governments selected must likewise express their willingness to have their representatives act in such capacity.

I see no theoretical objections to the proposal. While it is possible that the need for the United States to consider its responsibilities and obligations under the permanent treaty may be contingent on the success or failure of these present negotiations such a decision must necessarily rest on the United States Government itself. In other words should the present efforts at mediation break down and a revolutionary condition obtain in Cuba to such a degree as to make it necessary for the United States to intervene, such decision cannot be influenced by the cooperation at the present juncture with me of the representatives of other American Republics. The objections that I foresee are entirely practical in their nature. Many of the opposition factions would be unwilling to agree to the proposal to be made by the University Student Council because of their realization that other Latin American Governments have no influence whatever with President Machado while he, on the contrary, would only be willing to agree to the tender of good offices by the representatives of Latin American Governments such as those of Venezuela or the Dominican Republic which are dictatorial in their nature like his own. Consequently, I believe that the possibility of the suggestion being adopted is remote, but I think it is wiser for me to take the position that I would welcome such cooperation should it be agreeable to all concerned.

(signed) Benjamin Sumner Welles

--◊◊◊--O--◊◊◊--

Benjamin Sumner Welles, US Ambassador in Cuba, writes to **William Phillips**, US Under Secretary of State

Havana, June 30, 1933

The President has appointed today as his personal representatives in the mediation proceedings General Herrera, Acting Secretary of State, Dr. Averhoff, Secretary of the Treasury, and Dr. Ruiz Mesa, former Secretary of Justice and now a member of the House of Representatives.

The opposition factions which have accepted my tender of good; offices have today appointed the following delegates: Dr. Cosme de la Torriente for the Unión Nacionalista; Dr. Martínez Sáenz for the ABC; Dr. Wilfredo Albans, representative from Oriente for the Conservative opposition party; Dr. Santos Jiménez for the Liberal opposition party headed by Dr. Miguel Mariano Gómez; Dr. Dorta Duque for the University; Dr. Aragon for the professors of the normal and high schools; Dr. Silverio for the OCRR; and Sarita Lamar for all of the women's organizations. I shall formally commence

The news of the day in mid-1933 includes a lot of weather, sports and the inauguration of **Franklyn Delano Roosevelt** as President of the US on March of 1933.

mediation proceedings tomorrow morning, receiving first the delegates of President Machado and subsequently

in a separate interview the delegates of the opposition. I shall read to each group the message from the President and make a brief statement myself outlining the nature of my own participation in the negotiations.

I had this morning an interview with President Machado in which I explained to him the manner in which I intended to conduct the mediation proceedings. He gave me again very clearly to understand that he would be willing to leave the government in the hands of a vice-president throughout the electoral period but that if he were to maintain his present control of affairs such determination by him must not now be publicly announced nor must it be made the subject of any condition to be imposed by the opposition. I stated to him that I was in full accord and that such action on his part must be understood when the time came as coming freely as of his own initiative.

(signed) Benjamin Sumner Welles

--◊◊◊--0--◊◊◊--

JULY OF 1933

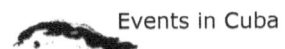 Events in Cuba

July 1 An important government-opposition meeting is hosted by Welles as part of his Mediation in the premises of the US embassy. The meeting is boycotted by the Directorio, the Communists, General *Mario García-Menocal*, the Student Left Wing, several High School student organizations and the radical ABC. The participation is limited to the Nationalists of *Cosme de la Torriente*, the ABC, the OCRR, the cloister of university professors and secondary school teachers, the Conservatives, a group of women oppositionist and the Revolutionary Union.

July 4 A United Front is created, chaired by *Dr. Martínez Sáenz*, of the ABC organization, who requests a Constituent Assembly.

July 15 Press censorship is lifted. By tacit agreement, no cartoons or fierce articles would be published.

July 23 A strike of Havana buses drivers is declared, which tends to complicate the situation. Days later the strikers throw "Molotov" cocktails against strikebreakers.

July 26 An amnesty is declared for political and terrorism crimes. Constitutional guarantees are restored, and many prisoners of political crimes of rebellion and even blood are released from prison.

July 29 A meeting of teachers in Santa Clara is dissolved by the police. The teachers send a complain to Ambassador Welles.

July 31 Numerous merchants in Santa Clara close their businesses in solidarity with the teachers attacked by the public force.

Washington Telex

BENJAMIN SUMNER WELLES, US AMBASSADOR IN CUBA, WRITES TO **WILLIAM PHILLIPS**, US UNDER SECRETARY OF STATE

Havana, July 1, 1933

I formally declared mediation proceedings commenced this morning. I received in the Embassy the delegates of the Government at 10 a.m. and the delegates of the opposition at 11 a.m. I read the President's message to both groups. It was received with the most enthusiastic approval. The declaration of the President is of peculiar value in that it makes definitively clear the President's personal interest in the success of these negotiations.

I subsequently read a statement emphasizing the fact that my tender of good offices would not have been made if I had not previously clearly understood that my services were desired by both sides in the controversy. A copy in full of my statement will be sent by mail.

On Monday I shall hold a meeting of the delegates of the opposition to determine the agenda and to exchange preliminary views. I have arranged for a meeting of the governmental delegates on Tuesday for the same general purpose. I am happy to state that there is very evident on both sides not only a conciliatory disposition but an apparent feeling of expectancy that these negotiations will have a successful outcome.

The opposition factions are already splitting into two groups, one extremely radical: and the other, the larger group, decidedly conservative. In the former category is of course the A B C which is composed very largely of radicals. Fortunately, however the representatives of that organization are both intelligent and well-disposed and I am hopeful that for some weeks at least the organization can be kept in line.

(signed) Benjamin Sumner Welles

--◊◊◊--O--◊◊◊--

WILLIAM PHILLIPS, US UNDER SECRETARY OF STATE, , WRITES TO
BENJAMIN SUMNER WELLES, US AMBASSADOR IN CUBA

Washington, July 7, 1933

Personal for the Ambassador. Could you give me any idea how much longer you feel that, in justice to the work which you are now doing, you should remain in Havana? I realize, of course, that there is still much to be done in the political field, as well as in the negotiations for the revision of the commercial treaty. With me it is a question of considering whether it would be worthwhile to appoint Caffery Assistant Secretary of State pending your return.
(signed) William Phillips

--◇◇◇--O--◇◇◇--

BENJAMIN SUMNER WELLES, US AMBASSADOR IN CUBA, WRITES TO
WILLIAM PHILLIPS, US UNDER SECRETARY OF STATE

Havana, July 7, 1933

Negotiations between the Government and the opposition delegates have until now progressed very favorably. All measures providing personal guarantees for the members of the opposition parties which have accepted mediation as requested by them have been granted by the Government and will be made public this afternoon.

After considerable difficulty I succeeded in convincing the President of the necessity of raising martial law and of the reestablishment of constitutional guarantees in the province of Havana, the only province of the Republic in which martial law exists at the present time. The President through his representatives has informed me this morning that he will reestablish constitutional guarantees here as soon as a law governing the press which has been drafted has been passed by the Congress and as soon as a special law vesting exclusive jurisdiction in the Supreme Court of the Republic of all cases covering the illegal use of explosives has been passed. I am in accord with the President that before a return to normal constitutional procedure in the province of Havana can be effected the authorities of the Government should be provided with the security entailed in these laws. The President assures me that these two laws will be passed before July 15th. The reaction to the reestablishment of constitutional guarantees will, of course, be overwhelmingly favorable.

Negotiations are now in progress whereby all the small remaining groups of revolutionary outlaws in the interior of the Republic can give themselves up to the authorities under full

Some of the participants in the process of **Political Mediation** in mid-1933. *From top to bottom, left to right:* **General Alberto Herrera Franchi**, **Manuel Dorta Duque**, **Fulgencio Batista** (at the center) with a group of 1933 generals that include **Francisco Tabernilla** and **Eleuterio Pedraza**, **Ambassador Sumner Welles** with **Carlos Manuel de Céspedes Jr.** and, finally, **Batista** in plain officer's uniform, with only one medal and the rank of Colonel.

guarantee of liberty and personal safety. I believe that all these remaining groups will return to their own homes within the coming week.

Early next week the opposition delegation will present to me a draft project of constitutional reform for transmission to the President's representatives. In the study which these latter will make of the opposition's proposals they will be assisted by a parliamentary commission which the President will appoint tomorrow consisting of three members of each House.

(signed) Benjamin Sumner Welles

--◇◇◇--0--◇◇◇--

BENJAMIN SUMNER WELLES, US AMBASSADOR IN CUBA, WRITES TO **WILLIAM PHILLIPS**, US UNDER SECRETARY OF STATE

Havana, July 8, 1933

It is almost impossible at this juncture to reply with any certainty. Any change at this stage in the political negotiations no matter who replaced me would almost inevitably create a complete breakdown. The mediation negotiations will probably come to a crisis in about 2 to 3 weeks' time. If the outcome is successful, I should unquestionably remain here until the constitutional reforms to be agreed upon and the new electoral code have been passed by Congress. If the negotiations fail it would probably be wise to make the change at that time since a radically different policy would then have to be inaugurated.

The purely political work may be divided into three steps: (1st) getting the opposing factions to consent to try to find an agreement; (2nd) the negotiation of such agreement; (3rd) the carrying out of the agreement which is a process which must continue until November 1934. The first step only is accomplished while the second is underway. I feel that I should be replaced only when a definite decision is reached by me as to whether the second step can or cannot be taken.

About the commercial treaty the groundwork is practically completed. I expect to commence final negotiations myself about the end of this month. I do not anticipate protracted delay in reaching an agreement on the treaty unless the Department has views other than those which I myself have in mind.

My hope is that I may be relieved not later than the end of September. I am particularly anxious as you know to undertake the preparatory work for the Inter-American Conference at Montevideo next December and 2 months at least I have this morning been informed by General Herrera that 45 political prisoners will be released before the middle of next week. In general, the conciliatory disposition shown by the Government in the negotiations has caused a very speedy return to more normal conditions. The declaration opposing the mediation proceedings made public by General

Menocal in Miami yesterday and republished here has created very little impression. Menocal has been consistently losing prestige during the past 3 weeks and even the closest members of his family here in Cuba are openly supporting the mediation proceedings. Practically all his political followers of importance have joined the opposition wing of the conservatives in supporting the mediation proceedings and are represented in the proceedings' through their delegate, Dr. Albanés.

would be required for this task which I consider of fundamental importance.

In view of the above I should think therefore that it would be preferable to appoint Caffery Assistant Secretary of State until it is possible for me to leave Havana.

(signed) Benjamin Sumner Welles

--◇◇◇--O--◇◇◇--

BENJAMIN SUMNER WELLES, US AMBASSADOR IN CUBA, WRITES TO **WILLIAM PHILLIPS**, US UNDER SECRETARY OF STATE

Havana, July 12, 1933   [Received 12:41 p.m.]

A bomb was placed in the doorway of the American Club yesterday which exploded without causing any serious injury or any material damage.

Upon their own initiative all the delegates of the opposition represented in the mediation proceedings made public immediately a joint declaration condemning in the strongest words this action. As an indication of the change in public opinion this declaration is significant inasmuch as three of the sectors signing this declaration, namely, the ABC, the OCRR and the UR had until 5 or 6 weeks ago been pursuing exactly the same terrorist activities which they now strongly condemn.

The secret organizations of the opposition are making an immediate investigation to try and ascertain the individual responsible for the placing of this bomb. I anticipate having a report both from the Government and from the opposition within the next 48 hours. I have reason to believe that the bomb was placed either by a member of the Government secret police which is bitterly opposed to the mediation proceedings or by a member of the local Menocalista group which I have verified was directly responsible for the placing of the bomb in Dr. de la Torriente's house last week.

(signed) Benjamin Sumner Welles

--◇◇◇--O--◇◇◇--

BENJAMIN SUMNER WELLES, US AMBASSADOR IN CUBA, WRITES TO **WILLIAM PHILLIPS**, US UNDER SECRETARY OF STATE

Havana, July 12, 1933   [Received 4:00 p.m.]

The last 4 days of the mediation proceedings have been somewhat critical due to the irritation caused the ABC by the refusal of the authorities to release Dr. Castellanos and a group of the members of that organization who had been seized shortly before commencement of proceedings in possession of a considerable quantity of arms and explosives. This feeling was intensified because the arms had been placed in Dr. Castellanos' house in order to prevent less responsible members of the organization from having control of them. Last Sunday the delegate of the ABC informed me that he was instructed to abstain from further meetings of the opposition delegates until the Government demonstrated a more concrete desire to furnish the guarantee asked by the opposition members. The professors of the university and in fact all the opposition delegates took the same ground but did not refuse to attend such meetings as I might desire to have with the opposition delegates.

The President at my instance yesterday afternoon decreed the immediate freedom of those members of the ABC above-mentioned and likewise authorized me to state that essential guarantees desired by the opposition were granted *in toto.*

The delegate of the ABC consequently returned to the mediation conferences yesterday and at a full conference of all of the opposition delegates held at the Embassy in the afternoon complete satisfaction was expressed by all of the opposition groups with the existing situation. On Thursday therefore the opposition delegates will hand to me the first draft of constitutional reform for transmission to the Government's representatives.

The President informed me yesterday that in order to expedite negotiations he had caused the Liberal Party, the Popular Party and that portion of the Conservative Party which has been cooperating with the administration each to appoint a committee of five members to represent their respective parties before me in the mediation proceedings. The President stated that he felt that this was a more practical plan than his original intention of appointing a congressional committee inasmuch as all the political parties would now be on record as supporting the utilization of my tender of good offices. This action on the part of the President is distinctly beneficial in the sense that through the control of the rank and file of each party which these committees' will have due to the appointment on them of the most important leaders of each party it will make much less likely any breakdown in the mediation proceedings since even if later on some of the opposition factions break away the organized political strength of the country will be thrown behind the negotiations. The Popular Party while it has been assumed to have been entirely under the control of the President during the past 4 years has now commenced to adopt an independent attitude and many of its members are in fact leaders in the opposition as for example Dr. Silverio who is the delegate of the OCRR in the mediation proceedings. The Conservative Party likewise has within the past week taken an open attitude of opposition to the Government in opposing recent tax legislation sought by the President in Congress and I consider it not at all unlikely that before very long the Congressmen belonging to the orthodox wing of the Conservative Party who have heretofore refrained from appearing in the House of Representatives will once more attend sessions and after reorganization of the leadership of the party amalgamate the hitherto dissident wings of the Conservative organization. In other words, the Popular and Conservative Parties will likely soon return to a normal condition of opposition to the Government and will be prepared to avail themselves of the opportunities for party reorganization which the new electoral code will furnish.

The disadvantages of the representation in the mediation proceedings of political party committees lie primarily in the fact that since I will now have to deal with 15 additional individuals in the sessions which may be held the opportunities for interminable discussion and protracted delay are greatly enhanced.

Professor McBain is proceeding very rapidly with the formulation of his recommendations for revision of the electoral code. He has conferred frequently with experts connected both with the Government and with the opposition and he finds that these representatives of both sides are in very material accord with the nature of the recommendations which he is prepared to submit. He has not yet commenced his study of the university problem.

(signed) Benjamin Sumner Welles

--◊◊◊--0--◊◊◊--

BENJAMIN SUMNER WELLES, US AMBASSADOR IN CUBA, WRITES TO **WILLIAM PHILLIPS**, US UNDER SECRETARY OF STATE

Havana, July 17, 1933   [Received 12:50 p.m.]

The President at my request late Saturday evening decreed the abolition of the censorship of the press. Of their own initiative the editors and proprietors of every newspaper and magazine published in Havana had previously given me their written assurance that until such time as a press law which is now pending in Congress is passed, their publications would not publish any material which might tend to disturb public order or interfere with the successful course of the mediation negotiations. The press law referred to has been drafted with a view to the suggestions made by the opposition delegates.

The one obstacle that prevents the immediate reestablishment of full constitutional guarantees lies in the fear of the President that once the guarantees are reestablished members of the opposition will at once bring suits in the civil courts against the members of his administration based upon occurrences which have taken place

A Quick Summary of the organized opposition to Machado...

The Opposition to Machado were:

The **ABC**, a secret society of intellectuals willing to oppose Machado through terrorism and sabotage; it called for changes in Cuban society and its economy and the furtherance of social justice, including the elimination of large land holdings, public ownership of public services and the promotion of cooperatives. The ABC sought to prohibit the acquisition of Cuban land by American interests.

Several **Student groups**, particularly the **Directorio Estudiantil Universitario (DEU)** (University Student Directorate, generally known as the **Directorio**).

Carlos Mendieta, a former colonel in the War of Independence, organized the Partido Unión Nacionalista (Nationalist Union) to oppose Machado.

Labor Unions. Often led by Spaniards and other immigrants from Europe.

The **Partido Comunista de Cuba (PCC)** (Communist Party of Cuba), one branch of which, mostly students, called itself the **Ala Izquierda Estudiantil (AIE)** (the Student Left).

Supporting Machado were:

The **Cuban Army**. It had been purged of officers who might oppose Machado; many army officers filled civilian administrative positions, increasing the power and prestige of the army.

Business interests. The times were prosperous, and businesses wanted stability to enjoy that prosperity; that included a vigorous program of public works projects.

The **organized political parties**. Machado was from the Liberal Party, but he controlled also of the Conservative Party and the small Partido Popular (Popular Party).

Manufacturers. Machado's Liberal Party moved toward protectionism and Cuban manufacturers liked that.

The Hoover administration in Washington, D.C.

Machado fought his opposition ruthlessly. He closed *Havana University*, abolished the student organization (*FEU*) and the *University Reform Commission*, had the *University Council* expel the student leaders. To counter the opposition of the labor unions, he had the *non-Cuban leaders deported back to Europe*.

here since the winter of March 1931 when martial law was first declared. There appears to be no way this danger can be
eliminated except through the immediate passage of a general amnesty bill which would necessarily have to include all members of the Government as well as those members of the opposition who have been found guilty of offenses against the authorities and who have not been pardoned. There will be necessarily violent objection on the part of some of the opposition factions to such whitewashing of officials of the Government but all of the more moderate members of the opposition are in favor of such a measure as the easiest way out of the difficulty in view of their realization that an amnesty bill of this character will in any event inevitably be passed sooner or later.

(signed) Benjamin Sumner Welles

--◇◇◇--O--◇◇◇--

BENJAMIN SUMNER WELLES, US AMBASSADOR IN CUBA, WRITES TO **FRANKLYN D. ROOSEVELT** , PRESIDENT OF THE US

Havana, July 17, 1933   [Received 3:50 p.m.]

MY DEAR MR. PRESIDENT: Your letter of June 24th made me very happy. I appreciate deeply what you were good enough to write. I am more than satisfied if what I have been attempting to accomplish here in Cuba merits your approval.

The situation in general is distinctly encouraging, far more so than I had hoped six weeks ago. President Machado and the three organized political parties of the Republic have formally accepted my tender of good offices, and every important faction in the opposition has taken the same action with the exception of the small and constantly diminishing group which surrounds General Menocal. I am unable to attach very much importance to the student groups. While they have not expressed their approval of what we are trying to do, they at least have declared that they will suspend all terroristic activities. It is now twelve days since we commenced negotiations and I am happy to say that the various delegates are concentrating upon questions of principle, upon the need for changing the system rather than the individuals and have modified very distinctly the uncompromising and unreasoning attitude which many at first maintained.

I think there is now a good chance that through a reform of the Constitution and through the utilization of the new electoral code which Professor McBain is helping to draft, we can work out a fair and just solution of the political problem strictly within the lines of constitutional procedure. In this connection, I feel that I must have specific and personal instructions from you. At sometime within the next two or three weeks, the suggestion will be made that after a Vice President satisfactory to all parties has been selected and has taken office, the President resign and make it thus possible for the Vice President to remain in entire control of the Government until a new Constitutional Government has been elected in November 1934. This means that President Machado will have to permit the Vice President to take control about May 1934. The term which he now is filling would normally expire in May of 1935. The reason for this suggestion, which to my mind must necessarily be acceded to by President Machado, is that no opposition party will go to the national elections in November 1934 if President Machado remains in control of the Government. They are confident that fair elections cannot be held so long as he remains in the Presidency. As I have reported several times to the Department, I have every reason to believe that President Machado will agree to take this action should he be permitted to take it of his own initiative, and should it not be forced upon him as a condition by the opposition. The solution in my mind, furthermore, is fair to all concerned, inasmuch as the President's own party will have just as many guaranties in the person of the Vice President, in the new constitutional reforms, and in the new electoral code as the opposition parties will have. It is perfectly possible, in fact, as I now sum up the situation, that the candidate of the President's, the Liberal, party will be elected in 1934. Consequently, the only sacrifice that the President will have to make will be to shorten his term by one year, and you will recall that the last constitutional reform which made the President's reelection possible was accomplished in such a manner as to leave very grave doubt as to its legality and as to its conformity with the articles of the preceding Constitution.

In the same last constitutional reform—that of 1928—the Senators and Congressmen extended their own terms of office. No more striking blow at the principle of representative government can be conceived. These extended terms must, of course, all be cut in the new reform so that the entire Senate and House will be renewed in the general elections of 1934.

Moreover, if the opposition parties do not go to the elections of 1934, whoever is elected in those elections will have bitter opposition to him throughout the term for which he is elected, and, in all likelihood, we will again be confronted with a situation in Cuba identical with that through which we have just been passing.

I consider the plan suggested both reasonable and eminently fair to all concerned, and I wish to urge it upon President Machado as a patriotic solution of Cuba's problem when the time comes. I wish, however, to have your specific authorization to do this and I wish, further, to be authorized to tell him that such oral representations as I make to him in this sense are being made with your full knowledge and approval.

The ground is very well cleared now for me to commence immediately the negotiations for the revision of the commercial treaty. Cuban public opinion is, in general, thoroughly well satisfied with the treatment accorded Cuba in Washington in the Sugar Conferences. If, when consumption of sugar in the United States once

Cubans had no time to think about important or interesting world events in *July of 1933*. Such things as **Babe Ruth** hitting a Home Run and wining the First All Star Game for the American League; the opening banquet for the **London Economic Conference**, where Roosevelt, represented by **Cordell Hull**, reiterates that the US will not restore the gold standard; and Cardinal Secretary of State **Eugenio Pacelli**, who later became **Pope Pius XII**, signing a pact with Nazi Germany's **Von Papen** guaranteeing the rights of the Roman Catholic Church in Germany.

more returns to normal, Cuba is permitted to export into the United States 2,000,000 tons of sugar at a stabilized price, and with the

added preferential advantage which I hope we will be authorized to give Cuba in the new commercial treaty, she will definitely be set upon her feet again, because her exports of sugar to the world market and local consumption of sugar total another million tons, and with a production of 3,000,000 tons of sugar annually, there is no reason why social conditions in Cuba should not improve materially, providing the next Government undertakes the passage of much needed social and economic legislation. We will likewise regain an exceedingly important market for our exports. I am, of course, keeping the negotiation of the commercial treaty as a leverage until I know where I stand on the political solution.

I cabled Bill Phillips the other day that I hoped very much that I could consider my portion of the Cuban task accomplished by the end of September and then return to the Department. I am particularly anxious to take up the preliminary work for the inter-American Conference at Montevideo in December, which, in my judgment, if properly handled, can result in the greatest benefit to the United States.

The overwhelming success of the Administration during these four months has given me greater satisfaction than I can express.

Faithfully yours,
(signed) Benjamin Sumner Welles

--◇◇◇--0--◇◇◇--

BENJAMIN SUMNER WELLES, US AMBASSADOR IN CUBA, WRITES TO **WILLIAM PHILLIPS,** US UNDER SECRETARY OF STATE

Havana, July 19, 1933   [Received 3:55 p.m.]

As indicated in recent cables to the Department, I consider it indispensable that constitutional guarantees in Havana be restored immediately by President Machado in order that the members of the opposition especially and the citizens of this province in general may no longer be subject to the arbitrary rule of the military and may be afforded the opportunity within customary legal limitations both of meeting and of expressing their opinion without being liable at any given moment to a jail sentence. It is impossible to conceive of a successful outcome of the present negotiations unless this step is taken in the immediate future.

A general amnesty is presumably necessary as a preliminary step in order that members of the Government may be protected against suits brought in the civil courts for acts committed during the past two and one-half years which suits could be undertaken when martial law is raised. Such amnesty must of course in my judgment include all political offenders.

The President of his own accord declared to me that constitutional guarantees would be reestablished before July 16th. No steps have yet been taken towards the drafting or passage of the general amnesty required and I have good reason to believe that certain members of the President's Cabinet have advised him to delay as long as may be possible. If martial law continues none of the delegates of the opposition will continue negotiations and none of the prominent leaders of the opposition will return from the United States in view of their well-founded fear that they would be subject at any moment to being thrown into prison.

The President is absent from the capital and is expected to return tomorrow. I shall see him immediately upon his return and state to him that I am not willing to continue negotiations unless he will comply with the assurances which he gave me more than a week ago. I should like to have immediate authorization from the Department to state that the Department is fully in accord with the statement which I will make to the President in this sense. All the factions of the opposition have kept their promise to me to refrain from any acts of violence or attacks upon any of the authorities of the Government. Whatever acts of violence have taken place, and there have only been four during the past 6 weeks, have been committed by individuals not connected with any of the important opposition groups, and the armed forces at the command of the President are more than sufficient to preserve order in any emergency. There is consequently no justification for further procrastination in restoring normal guarantees to the people of Havana and I cannot emphasize too strongly that a continuation of these negotiations will be impossible unless this measure is taken in the immediate future. I beg to request a reply from the Department by cable at the earliest possible moment.

(signed) Benjamin Sumner Welles

--◊◊◊--O--◊◊◊--

WILLIAM PHILLIPS, US UNDER SECRETARY OF STATE, , WRITES TO **BENJAMIN SUMNER WELLES,** US AMBASSADOR IN CUBA

Washington, July 7, 1933

You are authorized to state that the Department is fully in accord with the statement you intend to make to President Machado, as set out by you.

(signed) William Phillips

--◊◊◊--O--◊◊◊--

BENJAMIN SUMNER WELLES, US AMBASSADOR IN CUBA, WRITES TO
WILLIAM PHILLIPS, US UNDER SECRETARY OF STATE

Havana, July 26, 1933   [Received 3:20 p.m.]

The general amnesty bill has now passed both houses of Congress and will be promulgated by the President this morning. It will take effect upon publication. The law as finally passed contains all the amendments suggested by opposition leaders and is all-embracing. As a result, all political offenders, whether those convicted or those awaiting trial, will be immediately released from prison and their civil rights restored. Furthermore, all political offenders in exile abroad may return since any charges that might lie against them are automatically quashed. The terms of the amnesty bill, of course, likewise whitewash all officials of the Government responsible for crimes committed in the political turmoil of the past 6 years. Certain non-political sectors of the opposition have protested publicly against the passage of this bill but have confidentially informed me that they favor it because of the benefits accruing to the members of the opposition and because of the fact that it made immediately possible a return to more normal conditions.

The President assured me last night that simultaneously with the promulgation of the amnesty bill he would proclaim the reestablishment of constitutional guarantees which latter measure consequently should become effective tomorrow. The resulting abolition of martial law, the elimination of courts martial and military tribunals and the placing of the responsibility for the maintenance of order in the hands of the police and of the civil courts will necessarily tend immediately to create a favorable atmosphere for the successful outcome of the mediation negotiations. It is, of course, highly probable that the sudden change from military repression to constitutional liberty will result in sporadic attacks upon the authorities but I am personally confident that every important faction of the opposition is making a sincere and determined effort to prevent disorder and to maintain discipline within their ranks. The gravest element of danger in my judgment lies in the utterly irresponsible attitude pursued by portion of the press. The editors and proprietors of all the Havana newspapers of their own initiative assured me that they would refrain from the publication of inflammatory or seditious material during the mediation proceedings. This voluntary obligation has, however, been broken by one or two of the newspapers and while a severe press law will be passed within the next 48 hours it is very probable that this portion of the press will succeed in stirring up public opinion to an altogether unwise extent against the Government and the existing Congress.

Immediately after the definite reestablishment of constitutional guarantees I shall call the first meeting of the Mixed Commission, composed of members of all of the existing political parties represented in Congress and all representatives of the opposition sectors, to reach an agreement upon the constitutional reforms

Two photos of Machado a few days before his losing the presidency of Cuba.
On top: with a group of his **bodyguards**.
On the bottom: **signing a decree** promulgating a **general amnesty** promised to US Ambassador Sumner Wells, as well as proclaim the reestablishment of **Constitutional guarantees**. It was too little and too late for the opposition.

proposed by the opposition. The project of reform proposed by the latter embraces permanent reforms and, on this basis, I anticipate a very speedy agreement on both sides.

Once an agreement is reached, I shall try to obtain an agreement on the so-called transitory reforms which, of course, involve the solution of the existing political problem. The present tendency on the part of the opposition, although opinion has not as yet crystallized, is to suggest that inasmuch as the 4-year Presidential term is to be reestablished in the new constitution and the Vice-Presidency reestablished President Machado agree to shorten his existing term so that the Vice-President now to be selected will replace him until the end of the present Presidential term of office and further to suggest that the existing Congress consent to shorten its term to the period ending May 1934. The exact way these suggestions will be proffered, however, remains to be determined and I have stated that I was not willing to discuss the transitory reforms until a final agreement had been reached on the permanent reforms.

(signed) Benjamin Sumner Welles

--◇◇◇--0--◇◇◇--

BENJAMIN SUMNER WELLES, US AMBASSADOR IN CUBA, WRITES TO **WILLIAM PHILLIPS** , US UNDER SECRETARY OF STATE

Havana, July 26, 1933   [Received 6:40 p.m.]

I had an interview with the President this morning in the course of which he informed me that he had already promulgated the amnesty bill and the decree reestablishing constitutional guarantees referred to in my telegram 115, July 26, 11 a.m.

The President emphatically assured me that the success of the mediation negotiations was his own success and that inasmuch as that was the case he would at all times and in every way facilitate the reaching of a fair agreement. He urged me to do what I could to expedite the return to Cuba of Colonel Mendieta and of Colonel Méndez Peñate. He expressed the belief that it was essential for them to lose no time in organizing their political strength and that in such effort now that constitutional guarantees had been reestablished, no hindrance of any kind would be put in their way for the issuance of political propaganda, for the holding of political meetings, and for any other legal form of activity desired by them. He likewise assured me that Miguel Mariano Gómez would be offered exactly the same facilities although for personal reasons (the President being convinced that Dr. Gómez was directly involved in an attempt to assassinate himself and his family) he would decline to have any personal relations with him which attitude he will likewise adopt with regard to General Menocal should the latter return.

Finally the President emphatically stated that once the permanent reforms to the constitution had been agreed upon the leaders of the opposition should agree upon five or six essential points comprising the transitory reforms and reach an agreement through me with the leaders of the political parties upon them and that once such agreement should be reached he himself would interpose no obstacle to the carrying out of such agreement.

I have obtained the impression in conversations with leaders of the Liberal Party, the President's Party, that they are looking to the future rather than to the present and that should they find a candidate who had strength among the opposition factions they would agree to almost any compromise. A portion of the party is considering the possibility of supporting the candidacy for the Presidency of Miguel Mariano Gómez and there is very considerable sentiment among the rank and file of the party in support of the candidacy of Colonel Mendieta.

If the President's frame of mind as made evident today in my conversation with him were to continue unchanged there would be no possibility of an unsuccessful outcome of the present negotiations. The chief difficulty is, however, that the President changes his mind with the utmost frequency, and it is impossible to foretell what his opinion may be when the transitory reforms are brought up for discussion.

(signed) Benjamin Sumner Welles

--◊◊◊--0--◊◊◊--

BENJAMIN SUMNER WELLES, US AMBASSADOR IN CUBA, WRITES TO **WILLIAM PHILLIPS**, US UNDER SECRETARY OF STATE

Havana, July 27, 1933   [Received 1:00 p.m.]

Four hours after the termination of my interview with the President, General Machado made an entirely unexpected visit to the Senate and to the House. In the rambling and at times almost incoherent speeches which he made, the President asked the support of all of the political parties until 1935 and stated that my own mediation here had already been gladly accepted by him because it was *"spontaneously offered by a friend of Cuba"* and was not undertaken *"upon the instruction of the United States Government"*. The obvious intention of the President was to make clear that my mediation did not imply any infringement of the sovereignty of Cuba nor impair the authority of the Cuban Government. His visit to the Congress was due to the fact that it was reported to him early in the afternoon that a debate would probably take place in which the charge would be made that the reestablishment of constitutional guarantees and the passage of the amnesty bill had been impressed upon the President and that the leaders of the Conservative Party particularly and some of the members of the Liberal Party would take the lead in urging that the parties take steps to conserve their own interests and sever existing connections with the Machado administration.

The President's speeches were delivered at a singularly inopportune moment and were in many passages most unfortunately worded. They will unquestionably create a very great measure of disquiet among the opposition circles and will necessarily hinder materially the rapid progress of the mediation negotiations which I had anticipated yesterday morning. The President's action yesterday afternoon confirms more than ever the opinion expressed in the last paragraph of my telegram number 117 above referred to.

If an appropriate opportunity is presented to comment on President Machado's speeches it would be helpful if the Department would state that while of course my tender of good offices has been made spontaneously as stated by President Machado, it could not have been made other than with full authorization of my Government.

(signed) Benjamin Sumner Welles

--◊◊◊--0--◊◊◊--

BENJAMIN SUMNER WELLES, US AMBASSADOR IN CUBA, WRITES TO **WILLIAM PHILLIPS**, US UNDER SECRETARY OF STATE

Havana, July 27, 1933   [Received 9:30 p.m.]

The first meeting of the Mixed Commission composed of delegates of the opposition and delegates of the three political parties took place this afternoon. I commenced the proceedings with a brief address emphasizing again the salient features of President Roosevelt's message to the Cuban people as made public on July 1st. The meeting was significant in that for the first time in 3 years constructive discussion between members of the opposition and of the Government's adherents took place. A distinctly patriotic and satisfactory spirit was shown by both sides and agreement was reached on several important features of the constitutional reform as proposed. The next meeting of this Commission will be held tomorrow and every day subsequently under my chairmanship until a final agreement is reached.

(signed) Benjamin Sumner Welles

AUGUST OF 1933

 Events in Cuba

August 1 The government occupies Santa Clara. The unease is extended to Havana and Santiago de Cuba.

August 2 Railroads go on strike for 24 hours, in solidarity with bus employees, also on strike.

August 3 *Martínez Villena* extends the strike to port dockers, linotype workers and barbers. The ideological and historical separation between ABC and DEU is made public.

August 5 A general political strike against the dictatorship of Machado begins. The whole country is paralyzed. Machado desperately tries to approach the Communist Party, offering them legalization, an offer that is not rejected.

August 7 People go on the streets after a rumor that Machado has left the country. People are shot by the police in the streets. The rumor had been spread by a pirate radio station.

August 8 Ambassador Welles delivers an ultimatum to Machado to appoint a new Secretary of State and a Vice President to take office at once. Welles demands Machado to leave.

August 9 Roosevelt asks Cuban Ambassador *Oscar Cintas* to resign.

August 10 Machado reaches a desperate agreement with the opposition, particularly the sectors controlled by the communists, to whom he grants their request for legalization of the Communist Party. The party tries to revoke the strike order but most of the country refuses to do so.

August 11 The Army revolts against the government at the La Fuerza fortress. The rebels are joined by Aviation and the Navy, as well as the headquarters of Columbia and La Cabaña. Only the forces at the Atarés fortress in Havana remain loyal.

August 12 Machado finally presents his resignation and leaves *General Alberto Herrera Franchi* in the presidency. Herrera designates as Secretary of State, *Carlos Manuel de Céspedes*. Machado flees to

Nassau. Orestes Ferrara and other senior officials flee by plane to the US. The people, excited, throw themselves into the streets. Revenge against the *"cheerleaders, torturers and experts"* of the police. Some soldiers are dragged through the streets. The residences of the high ranking *Machadistas* are sacked. Violent death of *Colonel José A. Jiménez*, head of the *"porra"*. The Army joins the people.

August 13 *Carlos Manuel de Céspedes*, son of the leader of the 1868 War of Independence, takes possession of the provisional presidency of the Republic. Roosevelt declares that the transmission has been legal and that it is not necessary to recognize him. *Carlos de la Torre*, president of the Revolutionary Board in Exile, supports him. Machado states in Nassau, Bahamas: *"History will prove that my work has been good."*

August 14 *Rafael Montoro Valdés* (1852-1933) died; he was an illustrious autonomist and deputy for Cuba in the Spanish Courts, as well as Secretary in the governments of Mario García-Menocal and Alfredo Zayas.

August 14 Céspedes appoints a mediation-friendly concentration cabinet, composed of various opposition groups, such as the OCRR and ABC. Colonel *Julio Sanguily, Jr.*, assumes the leadership of the Army General Staff but, having his health broken, he must be hospitalized. Two US destroyers dock in Havana. No troops disembark. Welles telegraphs to President Roosevelt that the cabinet is consistent with the policy of the New Deal, is capable and composed of integral people. The Student Directory, opposed to the Céspedes government, calls for the dissolution of Congress, the removal of governors and mayors, full punishment of torturers and accomplices of the dictatorship and the removal of the president and the prosecutor of the Supreme Court.

August 15 Traitor José Soler, a former anti-Machado militant, is put on trial by the DEL and executed days later for espionage in favor of Machado during his imprisonment in the Isla de Pinos prison. Knowing very well the communists, he also reported on the militants J. Ordoqui, Chelala, Vivó and Sandalio Junco. He was responsible for the betrayal of DEU student Carlos M. Fuertes, killed by the sadistic brigadier Antonio Ainciart and his "experts."

August 16 Roosevelt announces Welles-Céspedes talks to rehabilitate the country's economy.

August 17 Manuel Márquez Sterling is appointed ambassador to Washington; *Carlos García Vélez*, son of Calixto García, to Spain. The anarcho-syndicalist leader *Margarito Iglesias* is exhumed from a moat in the Castle of Atarés.

August 18 Sumner Welles replaced by *Jefferson Cafferty*. Massive reception to *Dr. Gran San Martín*, who returns from exile. Sergeant-stenographer *Fulgencio Batista* talks at the funeral of Sergeant *Miguel Ángel Hernández*, killed in the Castle of Atarés by the Machadista police. It asks for a "true revolution."

August 19 Massive burial of three victims of the Machadista police, whose remains were exhumed from the foothills of the Castle of Atarés. They were *Félix E. Alpizar*, student of the DEU, *Margarito Iglesias*, anarcho-syndicalist worker, and an engineer sergeant, *Miguel A. Hernández*.

August 20 *Juan F. Edelman* appointed president of the Supreme Court. Return of *General Mario García-Menocal*, who declares himself against Mediation, complains to Roosevelt and establishes contacts with the officers, all of which annoys Welles.

August 22 A Manifesto of the Student Directory is published; it has an ideological approach and a political program, rejecting Mediation but assuming some of Céspedes approaches. The government expects changes in the sugar quota and tariff. Various meetings in the second half of August of leaders of the DEL at *Gustavo Cuervo Rubio's* house with the honest and genuine part of the Cuban army, where stand out captains Carlos Montero and Enrique Varona, as well as Lieutenants Carlos Valdés Fauli, Manuel F. Goudie, Pedro Morfi Linares, Ricardo Adam Silva, Rafael Galeano Herrera and others. Several leaders of the DEU also meet with sergeants and soldiers.

August 24 The Céspedes government proclaims Presidential Decree No. 1298 whereby it reestablishes the Constitution of 1901, repeals the 1928 Machado Constitution, dissolves the Congress and leaves vacant the Supreme Court positions approved after May 1929, summons general elections for February 24, 1934 and recognizes all the country's international obligations. Welles telegrams Roosevelt, expressing that... "Cuba is in the process of disintegration."

August 25 Desiderio Arnaz, father, former mayor of Santiago de Cuba, was arrested at the Hotel Saratoga. The *"Junta de los Ocho"* or *"Revolutionary Board,"* composed by Sergeants Fulgencio Batista, Pablo Rodríguez, José Eleuterio Pedraza, Manuel López Migoya and others, begins to meet at the Enlisted Club of Columbia Military Camp.

August 26 The newspaper *La Semana*, published by *Sergio Carbó* reappears.

August 28 Two members of the Martínez Sáenz cabinet, *Carlos Saladrigas* and *Eduardo Chibás*, threaten to leave the cabinet for not calling the government a Constituent Assembly.

August 29   Retired general *Armando Montes*, Zayas secretary in 1921-1925, infamous among the troops for cutting places and salaries, returned as Secretary of War. This worries the troops, and it could perhaps trigger a rebellion.

August 30 The magazine Social stops publication. It was an illustrated monthly magazine, dedicated to art, letters, theater, sports and fashion, founded in 1916 by cartoonist *Conrado W. Massaguer*. It reappeared again from 1935 to 1938.

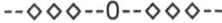

 Washington Telex

Memorandum by
William Phillips , US Under Secretary of State
Washington, August 2, 1933

The Cuban Ambassador called to my attention the press reports which were appearing in the United States and in Cuba to the effect that Ambassador Welles had announced that there will be no progress in the commercial treaty negotiations until the political conferences had reached a satisfactory conclusion. In other words, said Mr. Cintas, Mr. Welles is using the economic distress in Cuba, which can only be cured by a new commercial treaty, to bring pressure to bear upon President Machado to carry out Mr. Welles' wishes; the Ambassador gave vent to his feelings on this subject and to the improper course which Mr. Welles was pursuing, which he said led

Three photos of **Miguel Mariano Gómez**, a prospective future President of Cuba.
On top: Former president (1906-1910) **José Miguel Gómez** with his **wife
América Arias** and, behind Gómez, his son **Miguel Mariano Gómez**.
On the center: **Cordell Hull** shaking hands with **Miguel Mariano Gómez** in 1932.
On the bottom, left to right: **Gerardo Machado**, Orestes Ferrara,
Charles Lindbergh and **Miguel Mariano Gómez** on February 9, 1928.

to certain disaster, one or two alternatives would result—either President Machado would be shot, or American Marines would be landed; he saw no other way out of the impasse which was rapidly approaching.

I told Ambassador Cintas that at this morning's press conference I had been asked to explain the press statements to which the Ambassador had just referred; I had said in reply to these inquiries that informal conversations were proceeding between the Embassy and the Cuban Government in preparation of the more formal treaty negotiations; that Ambassador Welles was so preoccupied with his political conferences that he had not had time up to the present to take up seriously formal treaty negotiations, but that undoubtedly he would do so as soon as he had the opportunity; that I had denied, I said, that the United States was holding up commercial treaty negotiations until President Machado had come to terms.

The Ambassador talked at length in his usual strain of the iniquities of the present situation and of the false position which Mr. Welles was taking in dictating a policy to President Machado; he warned me that such a policy was doomed to failure and that any such failure would be a great blow to the prestige of the United States.

(signed) William Phillips

--◇◇◇--0--◇◇◇--

BENJAMIN SUMNER WELLES, US AMBASSADOR IN CUBA, WRITES TO **WILLIAM PHILLIPS**, US UNDER SECRETARY OF STATE

Havana, August 2, 1933   [Received 6:45 p.m.]

Professor McBain yesterday handed his completed report for electoral reform to President Machado. In my judgment the recommendations are admirable in every way and if carried out will eliminate a very material percentage of fraud and of motives for corruption in future elections.

The President has requested me to obtain the confidential approval of the opposition leaders to the report and as soon as that is obtained he will send the report, together with the draft of the required changes in the existing law, with a special message to Congress in which he will urge the immediate passage of the necessary legislation.

A copy of the report in English is being transmitted immediately to the Department by mail.

(signed) Benjamin Sumner Welles

--◇◇   ◇--0--◇◇◇--

BENJAMIN SUMNER WELLES, US AMBASSADOR IN CUBA, WRITES TO
WILLIAM PHILLIPS, US UNDER SECRETARY OF STATE

Havana, August 2, 1933   [Received 7:48 p.m.]

I had a private interview with the President yesterday afternoon. The President commenced his conversation by referring to his addresses to the Senate and to the House of last week and expressed his regret for certain portions of them. He stated that almost invariably when he spoke in public, he made statements which he did not intend. Since the truth of this assertion on the part of the President is very obvious and since it was evidently his desire to terminate the incident with this expression of regret I made no reference thereto beyond expressing my appreciation of the fact that he had referred to me as "a friend of the Cuban people".

President Machado voiced his concern over the disorder which was occurring in so many parts of the Republic and expressed his deep appreciation of the fact that I had succeeded in having the leaders of all of the opposition factions issue a joint manifesto urging the groups which they represented to hold no public meetings or parades under present conditions in order to avoid disturbances. I told the President that I felt it would be easier to maintain tranquility and to avoid regrettable incidents like those which occurred during the preceding 2 days such as the death of a woman Communist demonstrator and the ill treatment of school teachers by the police, if the police were given the most stringent orders not to interfere with public demonstrations unless the demonstrators were injuring private property or assaulting the authorities. There are a great many rumors to the effect that certain members of the Government who are bitterly opposed to the mediation proceedings, notably Dr. Zubizarreta, the Secretary of Gobernación, are utilizing the secret police to stir up these popular demonstrations and are trying to obtain a general strike throughout the Republic which would presumably result in such disorder that the Government would once more be obliged to declare a state of martial law. I have yet however absolutely no evidence to confirm these rumors.

In my conference with the President and in an earlier conference which I had yesterday with the Speaker of the House of Representatives, who is the leader of libels [*Liberal?*] Party in the lower House, both of them stated that the Congress would unquestionably ratify any agreement which was entered into under my auspices by the Government, the political parties and the opposition leaders provided such agreement made it possible for the President to resign his office in a *"decorous"* manner such as the institution of a Vice-Presidency would be. Both stated unequivocally that they realized that the President would have to resign his office immediately after the Vice-President was inaugurated. The Speaker of the House furthermore stated that he would be the first to declare publicly that if the agreement which was to be entered into provided for the shortening of the terms of all of the present members of the Senate and House to the date of the next national elections he would be willing to make such a sacrifice but he stated very positively that he felt it would be extremely difficult to obtain the consent of all of his colleagues in the House of Representatives to the same action and said that he hoped for a compromise on this point.

The meetings of the Mixed Commission composed of the members of the political parties and the delegates of the opposition are proceeding in a highly satisfactory and expeditious manner. The delegates are at present discussing the advisability of limiting materially the powers of the executive and are agreed unanimously upon the prohibition of reelection of all executive officials.

(signed) Benjamin Sumner Welles

--◊◊◊--0--◊◊◊--

BENJAMIN SUMNER WELLES, US AMBASSADOR IN CUBA, WRITES TO **WILLIAM PHILLIPS**, US UNDER SECRETARY OF STATE

Havana, August 4, 1933

The first definite proof I have received of probable governmental complicity in the general strike threat was the visit a few minutes ago of the delegates of the Liberal Party requesting me in view of the seriousness of the situation in the Republic to suspend the mediation negotiations. My reply to them was as emphatic as I could make it. I stated that if mediation proceedings broke down, I could assure them that the opposition factions would immediately return to terrorism and to revolution and that in my judgment in view of the unrest which now exists the Government could not possibly withstand the assault which would be made immediately upon its authority. I told them that if they persisted in their intention, they themselves would be directly responsible for the downfall of the Government and for disaster to the Republic of Cuba.

The delegates told me at the termination of the interview that they withdrew their suggestion and would continue in the mediation negotiations with the utmost sincerity and unimpaired spirit of cooperation.

I will see the President at 1 o'clock today and shall request a definite statement from him as to whether this suggestion by the representatives of his party is to be interpreted as an expression of his own opinion.

(signed) Benjamin Sumner Welles

--◊◊◊--0--◊◊◊--

BENJAMIN SUMNER WELLES, US AMBASSADOR IN CUBA, WRITES TO
WILLIAM PHILLIPS, US UNDER SECRETARY OF STATE

Havana, August 5, 1933

After their interview with me the directors of the Liberal Party went immediately to see the President and told him that the Liberal Party felt that the only possible salvation for Cuba lay in the agreement which they believed could be reached through the mediation negotiations and that under no consideration would the Liberal Party withdraw from the proceedings.

I had lunch yesterday with President Machado. He was in a highly nervous and excitable condition but in his conversation with me both courteous and entirely reasonable. He told me that the mediation had weakened the authority of his Government but that he himself believed that the only possible solution lay in the agreement which could be reached through the mediation negotiations. He said that he was willing to agree to any fair solution proposed but that he was not willing to agree to be "thrown into the street". I agreed to certain minor requests which he made of me, namely, that the opposition be prevented from publishing in the newspapers complaints which they made to me as mediator of action taken against them by subordinate authorities of the Government. He admitted that the visit to me earlier in the morning by the directors of the Liberal Party had been made at his instigation and likewise frankly admitted that his party had differed with him in the matter. I am under the very distinct impression that for the first time since he was elected the Liberal Party have summoned up enough courage to dictate to the President and are not being dictated to by him. In a private conversation which I had last night with one of the directors of the Liberal Party he told me that in their interview with the President early yesterday morning the President was utterly uncontrolled and gave the impression of a man who was unbalanced mentally. He told me that it was impossible to argue or reason with the President at that time but that he felt the attitude taken by the directors of the party in the second interview would prevent any further insistence by the President that the Liberals withdraw from the mediation negotiations.

The Mixed Commission stayed in session for 10 hours yesterday and I shall keep the Commission in permanent session today and tomorrow Sunday until a final agreement is reached on the permanent reforms to the constitution. Practically all-important points have already been agreed to other than the length of the Presidential term and the independence of the judiciary. On the latter point an agreement can readily be reached. On the former point a compromise will probably be necessary. The agreement already arrived at includes a modified parliamentary system which limits materially the powers of the executive and which I have every reason to >

One of the most rabid and permanent adversaries of Gerardo Machado was a young Cuban Communist called **Rubén Martínez Villena** (1899-1934), who since his death has become a patriotic martyr for leftists and anarchists throughout Hispanic America.

In the 1930s, Martínez Villena organized general strikes against Machado, wrote letters of protest him, and served as legal advisor to the **Workers' Federation of Havana** and the **National Workers Commission of Cuba**.

Machado and Martínez Villena had a legendary personal encounter at the home of a Cuban government minister, who introduced them. Almost immediately, there was a discussion between Machado and Villena, in the middle of which Machado told Villena:

«*You are right, young man. I don't know what Communism is, nor Anarchism, nor Socialism. But I am not tainted by students, or workers, or veterans, or patriots, or you or Mella.*»

Martínez Villena allegedly responded:

«*I had never seen, nor I had ever known you; I have heard you are a brute, a savage! You are a beast, an ass with claws.*»

Martínez Villena was a car carrying member of the PSP, the Cuban Communist Party, a dear friend and personal attorney of Julio Antonio Mella and Juan Marinello, a sick man with tuberculosis that went to the Caucasus Mountains in the Soviet Union for treatment, knowing that the most advanced medical techniques were closer, in the United States.

He named his only child **Rusela**, in honor of the USSR, and always called her «*his wife's little ruso-cubana.*» With the support of Cuba's Communist government, Martínez Villena's biography has been written by Raúl Roa and Roberto Fernández Retamar and published by the Cuban government in 1964 and 1982.

believe will prove highly beneficial to Cuba if finally enacted.

(signed) Benjamin Sumner Welles

--◊◊◊--0--◊◊◊--

BENJAMIN SUMNER WELLES, US AMBASSADOR IN CUBA, WRITES TO **WILLIAM PHILLIPS,** US UNDER SECRETARY OF STATE

Havana, August 7, 1933   [Received 12:20 p.m.]

In view of the extreme gravity of the situation here it would be of the utmost usefulness to me to have a reply to the inquiry contained in my letter to the President of July 17 of which you have a copy.

(signed) Benjamin Sumner Welles

--◊◊◊--0--◊◊◊--

BENJAMIN SUMNER WELLES, US AMBASSADOR IN CUBA, WRITES TO **WILLIAM PHILLIPS,** US UNDER SECRETARY OF STATE

Havana, August 7, 1933   [Received 4:15 p.m.]

The general strike has now spread throughout the Republic. Every form of transportation is tied up. The Government employees of the Departments of Sanitation, Communications, and of the Treasury, have declared themselves on a strike and consequently no telegraphs are functioning, and the ordinary sanitary requirements of the city will no longer be complied with. All the provision merchants, restaurants, and even the hotels, are closed and there will be a state of near starvation within the next 24 hours. While some of the police in the capital have been guilty of the same tactics pursued during the past months which have resulted in the injury of a score of people in the city yesterday, the strike up to the present time has been absolutely peaceful in character and so far as I am informed there has been no aggression against the authorities nor damage to private property except on a very inconsiderable scale in the interior.

Saturday night and yesterday morning I had continuous interviews with the official representatives of the three political parties and of the members of the opposition. I have decided that the only possible solution to prevent a state of utter chaos in the Republic soon is the following:

1. Appointment by the President of an impartial Secretary of State acceptable to all elements.
2. The request by the President of the [Congress] for leave of absence and authorization by him of the new Secretary of State to reorganize the Cabinet giving representation to all important political elements.

3. The immediate passage by the Congress of the constitutional reforms which have been elaborated by the Mixed Commission as the result of which the members of House of Representatives will agree to shorten their terms so that half of the House will be renewed in the national elections of 1934 and those representatives remaining in the House to shorten their terms to a corresponding extent as those who will vacate in that year.
4. Half of the Senate is renewed in 1934 and the remaining Senators to agree to shorten their terms to a total period of 6 years.
5. The creation of the Vice-Presidency said Vice-President to assume the Presidency upon his inauguration.

I had an interview with President Machado yesterday afternoon. I communicated to him my views and I impressed upon him that if he did not accept this entirely constitutional and dignified solution as an act of patriotism and sacrifice on the part of all concerned I believed that the situation here would very rapidly degenerate into a condition of absolute anarchy which would result in the loss of innumerable lives and destruction of property. I reminded him of the obligations of the United States under the permanent treaty, but I told him that the whole purpose of my mission here was to avoid the United States Government having to consider the carrying out of such obligations. The President expressed his entire willingness to resign as soon as the Vice-Presidency was created but stated that in his judgment for him to ask for leave of absence and to allow a Secretary of State to carry on until the Vice-President was inaugurated would be disastrous in its consequences. I told him that I could see no reason for such belief on his part and that I thought the disaster would arise from his not being willing to adopt such a measure. He referred to the fact that the Congress as a measure of precaution desired to suspend constitutional guarantees today and I said that in view of the gravity of the situation I had no objection to offer thereto provided that the guarantees were suspended for a limited and fixed period, which he agreed to.

I have had this morning an interview with the leaders of the Liberal Party. They are now in session with the President and will tell him that in their judgment, for the benefit of the country, for the benefit of the Liberal Party, and for his own reputation, the President must adopt the measures indicated above. Both the Conservative and Popular Parties are absolutely in accord with the solution proposed and they will, before evening, as will the directors of the Liberal Party, obtain the consent of the members of House and of the Senate to the steps indicated.

Most of the factions of the opposition will agree to this compromise although certain of the more radical elements will probably demur.

If this agreement can be reached within the next 48 hours and made public, I am very confident that the strike will immediately cease and that the state of the country will rapidly become normal once more. If an agreement is not reached through the unwillingness of the President to take the action necessary, I foresee the gravest consequences.

(signed) Benjamin Sumner Welles

--◇◇◇--0--◇◇◇--

BENJAMIN SUMNER WELLES, US AMBASSADOR IN CUBA, WRITES TO **WILLIAM PHILLIPS** US UNDER SECRETARY OF STATE

Havana, August 7, 1933   [Received 7:13 p.m.]

The President has not yet reached any decision as to his course. I have just been advised by General Herrera that he has removed the former Chief of Police of Havana who is execrated by the public and replaced him with an officer in whom the public will have confidence. Meetings of the members of Congress of both the Liberal and Conservative Parties are now in session and I shall be advised by the leaders of the parties as soon as a decision is reached.

The streets are filled this afternoon with almost unmanageable crowds and the police have been firing upon them to prevent them from congregating around the capitol and around the President's palace. The President himself is at his country place outside the city.   (signed) Benjamin Sumner Welles

--◇◇◇--0--◇◇◇--

WILLIAM PHILLIPS, US SECRETARY OF STATE, WRITES TO **BENJAMIN SUMNER WELLES,** US AMBASSADOR IN CUBA

Washington, August 7, 1933

Referring to the Under-Secretary's telephone conversation with you this afternoon the President authorizes me to say that he approves the plan as outlined in your last telex of August 7.

(signed) William Phillips

--◇◇◇--0--◇◇◇--

A cartoon published by the Magazine **La Semana**. It pokes fun at the U.S. decision to surround Cuba with warships after the overthrow of the Céspedes government on September 4, 1933.

BENJAMIN SUMNER WELLES, US AMBASSADOR IN CUBA, WRITES TO
CORDELL HULL, US SECRETARY OF STATE

Havana, August 7, 1933

I requested an immediate interview with President Machado. General Herrera informed me that the President was indisposed and consequently unable to receive me although the Liberal Party leaders inform me, he is receiving them tonight. I shall endeavor to obtain an interview tomorrow morning. I think it would be helpful if the Cuban Ambassador in Washington were informed by the Department tomorrow of the President's authorization and approval as conveyed to me and of the very grave consequences which may ensue if President Machado refuses to agree to an eminently fair and patriotic Cuban solution of the political problem which every faction has agreed to including the President's own party.

The killed this afternoon in Havana alone total 17 and the wounded over 100. I feel it obligatory to emphasize the extreme seriousness of the situation.

(signed) Benjamin Sumner Welles

--◊◊◊--0--◊◊◊--

MEMORANDUM BY
WILLIAM PHILLIPS, US UNDER SECRETARY OF STATE

Washington, August 8, 1933

The Cuban Ambassador called me on the phone to say that he had been talking with President Machado this afternoon, that there had been a meeting of the workers at the Palace and that the strike had been called off; all the workers, he said, had agreed to go back to work and complete tranquility existed throughout Cuba; President Machado told Ambassador Cintas that Mr. Welles had presented this morning, in writing, a communication which, in fact, meant the overthrow of the Government; President Machado said that he could not and would not be *"pushed out by the United States".* Ambassador Cintas said that, although he knew Mr. Welles had this in mind for a long time, this was the first proposal he had made of it directly to the President; the Ambassador repeated that Machado had said to Mr. Welles that he would not accept the plan suggested of the substitution of the Secretary of State and the ultimate election of a Vice-President.

(signed) William Phillips

--◊◊◊--0--◊◊◊--

BENJAMIN SUMNER WELLES, US AMBASSADOR IN CUBA, WRITES TO
CORDELL HULL, US SECRETARY OF STATE

Havana, August 8, 1933   [Received 10:35 p.m.]

To be delivered immediately to the President at Hyde Park. I have just sent to the Department a full report upon the situation here and my recommendations of policy in connection therewith which I have requested be communicated to you immediately.

President Machado has this afternoon informed the Senators and Representatives that my statement to him that the solution presented by me was offered with your full approval and was presented with your authorization is false and that no such approval has been given me by you. I am informed that Cintas has cabled him to that effect. I understand that you are seeing Cintas at noon tomorrow. I beg that you inform him that I am acting in every detail with your fullest authorization and approval. I also beg to request that you inform Cintas that while the purpose of my mission here is to avoid the existence of a situation which would give rise to intervention by the United States if a situation of anarchy exists and there is no government in Cuba capable of protecting *"life, property and individual liberty"* as provided in the third article of the permanent treaty the United States will not evade its obligations under that provision. Both Cintas and President Machado have repeatedly given important leaders here the belief that I am not authorized by you to act and that the attitude I have adopted is one of bluff. I feel that it is essential if I am to succeed in procuring a solution of this very grave situation that Cintas be told by you to inform President Machado immediately that absolutely no act of mine has been taken except with your full approval and authorization.

(signed) Benjamin Sumner Welles

--◊◊◊--0--◊◊◊--

BENJAMIN SUMNER WELLES, US AMBASSADOR IN CUBA, WRITES TO **CORDELL HULL,** US SECRETARY OF STATE

Havana, August 8, 1933   [Received August 9 at 4:48 a.m.]

I had an interview with President Machado this morning. I told the President that in accordance with my conversation with him of last Sunday afternoon, I handed him as mediator a solution of the Cuban political problem which represented a compromise accepted by the sectors of the opposition, by the directors of the Popular and Conservative Parties and by seven leaders of the President's own party, the Liberal Party, including the president of that party, and which compromise would permit the Cuban people to return immediately to a state of peace and tranquility, and be enabled as a result thereof to devote themselves to the restoration of Cuba's economic prosperity. I told President Machado further that I was specifically authorized to state that the solution as proposed by me met with the full approbation of the President of the United >

Late in the summer of 1933, the government cannot suppress the strikes and outrage of people. *Photos from top to bottom:* **Col. Juan Blass Hernández**, an ABC militant known as *El Sandino Cubano*, was murdered after surrendering at **Atarés** fortress; there are incidents of **looting and arson** in Havana; in Santiago de Cuba, a mob kills **Corporal Ismael Heredia** in retribution for the government's cruelties. By the end of July, the crowds and the bloodshed cannot be controlled.

States.

The President immediately stated that he would not accept this solution as proposed and that I could inform the President of the United States that he would prefer armed intervention to the acceptance of any such proposal. It was obvious that he was in a state of mental disturbance bordering on hysteria which, however, later changed into a more reasonable attitude. He stated that he was as much in favor of my mediation as he had ever been and that no one could have carried out their official duties in a more friendly spirit and in a manner less calculated to injure the susceptibilities, either of the Republic or of any individual, than I had. I pointed out to him, that notwithstanding his assertions in a radio address which he had broadcast last night, the solution as proposed, represented neither imposition nor interference by the Government of the United States, but was a solution which had been drafted as the result of conferences between the representatives of every part of Cuban public opinion. I stated that the solution in no wise impaired the sovereignty of the Republic and was furthermore entirely in accord with existing constitutional procedure in Cuba; that it must be obvious to him that rightly or wrongly the refusal to the Cuban people to return to a state of political tranquility was due to the fact that the existing Cuban Government was charged with all of the tragedies and economic disasters which had taken place during the past 3 years; that it had been my earnest hope that the President as a patriotic gesture would agree through the solution proposed to make it possible for a rapid return to normal conditions here and that it was my firm belief that unless the solution proposed or one similar to it was carried into effect, no such betterment could be possible.

The President informed me that he accepted the last three points of the solution proposed but would never accept the first two. I inquired whether this was intended to mean that he would refuse to consider any counterproposition and he told me that on the contrary he would consider the desirability of formulating a counterproposition. To this I replied that in view of the extreme gravity of the situation here I felt that I was entitled to receive a reply from him within a very brief period.

The Presidents of the Conservative and Popular Parties have been to see me today to assure me of their unfaltering support in view of their belief as stated in a formal resolution of the Conservative Party *"That Mr. Welles be advised in his character as mediator, as likewise all those who compose the mediation commission of the fervent desire of the Conservative Party for a solution of the domestic political problems which now confront the Republic and of the hope which inspires the Conservative Party that with a high spirit of patriotic sacrifice there will be established shortly peace and relief to the Cubans".*

The President has appealed to the cupidity of many of the members of the Liberal Party in Congress in order to stir up opposition to the solution proposed, owing to the fact that necessarily the representatives who agree to shorten their terms will have to give up the lucrative privileges to which they are now entitled.

I trust that through the joint influence of the political leaders in Congress and of certain of the higher-minded members of the Cabinet such as General Herrera, the President will reconsider the attitude which he has taken. I am, however, by no means hopeful of the outcome.

I think the situation demands forceful and positive action by the Government of the United States in order that our prestige both here and in the rest of the continent may not be seriously prejudiced. If President Machado remains in power he can only continue through the exercise of the most brutal methods of repression, which will culminate time and again in such tragedies as that which took place in Havana yesterday. It will be impossible for him to govern without a continuance of martial law and the suspension of all constitutional guarantees, which condition makes it possible, of course, for the President and the military authorities to assassinate, to throw into prison, and to deprive of *"life, property and individual liberty"*, any citizen in the Republic.

The Government of the United States has clearly demonstrated its intention to use every possible means at its disposal to further and to support a peaceful and constitutional adjustment by the Cuban people of their problem. The realization of that end is made impossible solely by the unwillingness of one man, President Machado, to retire from the office which he holds through a reelection which in its genesis is unquestionably unconstitutional. Throughout the course of my mission here, I have exerted every possible effort to avoid the creation of a situation which might result in intervention by the United States. If the present condition is permitted to continue much longer, I am positive that a state of complete anarchy will result which might force the Government of the United States, against its will, to intervene in compliance with its obligations under the permanent treaty.

I should like further to emphasize the fact that in my own judgment the permanent treaty imposes upon us responsibilities as regards the Cuban people. I do not see how the Government of the United States can, in view of its treaty obligations, continue its formal support of a Cuban Government which has consistently deprived the Cuban people of their constitutional rights, which has been guilty of atrocities which have shocked the entire continent, and which refuses to consider the acceptance of a fair and Cuban solution of this disastrous situation. I believe that intervention should be avoided at any cost except that of failing to comply with our treaty responsibilities, but on the other hand I believe that should President Machado positively refuse to agree to the solution proposed, or to one similar in character, the Government of the

United States should no longer accord its moral support to the Government of Cuba and should withdraw recognition.

I do not believe that the withdrawal of recognition would in all probability force us to intervene; I think that if the President himself was advised that we would withdraw recognition unless he accepted a fair solution of the problem, he would be obliged to accept such solution by most of the members of his Cabinet, by the Army and by the great majority of Congress. If, however, he persists in refusing to accept any compromise after notification that recognition would be withdrawn, in such event, I do not believe that his Government would be able to maintain itself for more than an exceedingly brief period and should steps be taken by me in advance in accordance with the leaders of the political parties and with the important leaders of the opposition to provide for the installation of a stable government immediately upon President Machado's forced resignation, I have every reason to believe that the situation here would continue sufficiently within control to make it unnecessary for the United States Government to undertake even a brief armed intervention.

The Department will understand that I have for many weeks' past been giving the possibilities which have now arisen the most serious consideration, and it is in view of the considerations set forth above that I make the following recommendations:

1. That if at the end of a reasonable period President Machado has given me no indication that he will either accept the solution proposed by me as mediator or adopt some other solution equally satisfactory, I be authorized to inform him that the United States Government will withdraw recognition of the Cuban Government within a stated time unless the President consents to a solution of the character proposed and that I be instructed to declare that the action would be based upon the unwillingness of my Government to continue to lend its moral support to a government in Cuba which is maintaining itself in power by martial law and through the exercise of brutal methods of repression, and which is unwilling to agree to a compromise acceptable to every element of public opinion in Cuba existing at the present moment.
2. That I finally be instructed, upon the expiration of the period indicated in the preceding paragraph, should President Machado still refuse, formally to withdraw recognition of the Cuban Government after having agreed with the political leaders and with the leaders of the opposition upon means of installation of a stable government, and to leave the Republic.

In order that I may be guided by a thorough knowledge of the instructions of the President and of the Department, I beg to request that this recommendation of policy by me be placed in the President's hands at the earliest possible moment and in any event before he sees Cintas tomorrow and that I be advised of the course I am to pursue at the earliest moment that such instructions can be cabled to me.

(signed) Benjamin Sumner Welles

--◊◊◊--O--◊◊◊--

BENJAMIN SUMNER WELLES, US AMBASSADOR IN CUBA, WRITES TO **CORDELL HULL,** US SECRETARY OF STATE

Havana, August 9, 1933   [Received 2:05 p.m.]

In summarizing the views expressed in my telegram of August 8, 9 p.m., I feel it desirable to emphasize the following points as the result of the intensive study I have made here during the past 3 months:

1. There is absolutely no hope of a return to normal conditions in Cuba if President Machado remains in office. No one other than the exceedingly small clique of officeholders surrounding him has any trust or confidence in him and he represents in his person to every other Cuban the cause of economic distress and personal suffering which has existed during the past 3 years.
2. So long as this condition continues there is no possible chance of improving economic conditions in Cuba, and there will be immense loss to the Cuban people themselves and as a natural corollary to all the American interests doing business in or with Cuba.
3. The solution proposed by me as mediator represents a compromise framed by the representatives of all Cuban factions both of the opposition and of those which have in the past been cooperating with the Government and if such solution could be carried into effect I have the utmost confidence that peace and tranquility would be restored to Cuba within a week.
4. If my recommendations are adopted and recognition is withdrawn from the Machado Government I believe that the President would be forced to resign his office within a very limited period and that a stable government could be installed in strict accordance with the provisions of the existing constitution within a period of hours thereafter provided arrangements to that end are made by me before recognition is withdrawn.
5. If recognition is withdrawn there will likely be for a brief period of disturbances in the city of Havana. If my recommendations are adopted and this eventuality takes place, I feel that two American warships should be in Havana harbor with instructions not to land a man except in the gravest emergency the terms of which should be defined beforehand.

Backtracking in his promises of granting concessions to the opposition and to the request for an affirmation of restituting the Constitutional guarantees, **Machado** responded in a stern tone: «*The re-establishment of the guarantees is a prerogative of the President of Cuba and will be done when the President considers it necessary.*» Hours later he added: «*The mediation of Mr. Welles cannot damage our sovereignty, because it is a result of his spontaneous desire and not of any instructions received from the government of the United States.*» Bus drivers and streetcar workers went on **strike**, while crowds marching in support of the strike spreaded throughout the island.

The ultimate objective, in addition to the immediate objectives above-mentioned, of the recommendations which I formulated, is to permit the Cuban people to hold free and constitutional elections for a new government in accordance with the existing constitution in November 1934. If President Machado remains in power even until February of next year no political parties can reorganize and none of the opposition parties will organize, with the consequence that the elections due to be held in November 1934 would once more result in the election of a government which did not come into power with the free consent of all of the Cuban people.

You will understand, I am sure, that the recommendations I have made have been offered with reluctance and only after the most careful consideration. I can frankly state, however, that I see no other solution.

(signed) Benjamin Sumner Welles

--◊◊◊--0--◊◊◊--

BENJAMIN SUMNER WELLES, US AMBASSADOR IN CUBA, WRITES TO
CORDELL HULL, US SECRETARY OF STATE

Havana, August 9, 1933   [Received 2:40 p.m.]

The Spanish Ambassador has complained to me of the treatment to which Spanish citizens have been subjected during the past 3 days by the authorities of the Government. Three Spaniards have been killed by the police, two of them without having given the slightest motive for such action, and some 60 in the city of Havana have been arrested on the pretext that they have refused to open the stores of which they are the owners. The Ambassador has protested vainly to the authorities and although he has succeeded in obtaining the release of some, many are still in prison. He wishes to cooperate with me in every possible manner but necessarily feels that the Spanish Government cannot permit such a to continue indefinitely without taking very strong measures.

The British Minister has been to see me this morning. He spoke to me of damage done to British property in the interior and of a report which he had received through Reuters that a British cruiser was being sent to Cuba. He told me however that he did not believe the report as he had had no official word.

(signed) Benjamin Sumner Welles

--◊◊◊--0--◊◊◊--

BENJAMIN SUMNER WELLES, US AMBASSADOR IN CUBA, WRITES TO
CORDELL HULL, US SECRETARY OF STATE

Havana, August 9, 1933   [Received 3:32 p.m.]

Personal for the Under Secretary. I have received confirmation this morning from two reliable sources of the fact that yesterday at a secret meeting at which were present Ainciart, until recently Chief of Police, and four other police captains, a plan was decided upon should President Machado be forced to resign to assassinate me in order to provoke immediate American intervention. Countless reports of a similar character have come to me during the past 10 days to which I have paid no attention. In this instance the information comes directly from one of those present when the plan was concerted who is a member of one of the secret organizations. It has furthermore a creditable basis inasmuch as I was directly responsible for the removal of Ainciart from his position and since he is fully aware that should a change in government take place, he would be immediately subject to trial and punishment for the innumerable crimes of which he is personally guilty. By forcing, as he thinks, an American intervention he would be guaranteed by the intervening power against aggression from Cubans and against punishment inasmuch as the blame for such action would be attributed immediately by the authorities to one of the secret societies and if there were no witnesses present the conspirators would naturally escape scot-free.

I shall naturally not change in the least my mode of existence nor take other than ordinary precautions, but I think the information will give you an indication of the now existing here.

(signed) Benjamin Sumner Welles

--◇◇◇--O--◇◇◇--

BENJAMIN SUMNER WELLES, US AMBASSADOR IN CUBA, WRITES TO **CORDELL HULL,** US SECRETARY OF STATE

Havana, August 9, 1933   [Received 8:20 p.m.]

As the result of the intensified propaganda of President Machado yesterday evening and throughout this morning it is possible that a resolution will be adopted by the Cuban House of Representatives tonight attacking my course here. I have been handed by a member of the House a copy of a draft prepared by a violent supporter of the administration which contains among others the following declarations:

"That the activities of His Excellency the Ambassador of the United States to Cuba interfering in the interior problems of the Government have caused a deep perturbation of public order and the threat embodied in his insinuations of possible intervention in our country are a violation upon our rights as a free and independent people and an aggression upon the sovereignty of small nationalities."

Inasmuch as the proposal handed by me to President Machado was headed "proposal of the mediator for a just and fair solution of the Cuban political problem" and the proposal contained exactly the points enumerated in my telegram 129, August 7, noon, to the Department and inasmuch as I have never discussed the possibility of intervention with any political leader or with anyone other than President Machado and in that, case in the precise terms communicated to the Department in my cable above referred to it is obvious that the proposed resolution is solely predicated upon the continued allegations by President Machado that I was acting without the authority of my Government and had attempted to force the acceptance of a solution without authorization.

Referring to my personal telegram to the President of last night and to my conversation by telephone with the Under Secretary this morning, if President Machado is permitted to believe as he apparently does that the United States will under no conditions and under no circumstances comply with its treaty obligations, I have every reason to believe that he will not give in until the very last possible moment. If on the other hand it is emphatically made clear to him that while the whole object of my mission has been to avoid intervention and that the United States will only consider intervention if it is forced to do so by the clear requirements of its treaty obligations as contained in article 3 of the permanent treaty it is much more probable that he will finally agree to the solution proposed, I cannot help but feel that it is an infinitely wiser policy on our part to state very clearly at this juncture that we will not evade our treaty obligations if we are obliged to comply with them, rather than to evade the issue and let matters slide into a state of affairs where we will have to take the only action which we desire to avoid. The President himself and those around him are confident that because of the prejudice to our own interests the United States Government will not intervene now under any conditions whatsoever. If they can be dissuaded from that belief a peaceful solution will be far more probable.

(signed) Benjamin Sumner Welles

--◊◊◊--O--◊◊◊--

CORDELL HULL, US SECRETARY OF STATE, , WRITES TO
BENJAMIN SUMNER WELLES, US AMBASSADOR IN CUBA

Washington, June 9, 1933

At Ambassador Cintas' request, the President received him this afternoon.

The President reminded the Ambassador that the eyes of the world are centered upon President Machado, not to see how he can extricate himself out of the present political difficulties, but to see whether he will act as a truly great man, who has the interests of his entire people at heart. He added that President Machado can go down in history as a great man, a great leader and a great patriot if he will take the step recommended by the representatives of all the Cuban political parties and so avoid what might easily develop into bloodshed and anarchy. The President appealed to President Machado, through Ambassador Cintas, to prove to the world his high purpose in this crisis.

The President informed Ambassador Cintas that you are and had been acting at Havana with his fullest authorization and approval. He added that he had no desire to intervene but that it was our duty to do what we could so that there should be no starvation and chaos among the Cuban people.

Ambassador Cintas then pointed out the difficulties surrounding President Machado's position and that he could not allow himself to be forced out of the presidency. The Ambassador agreed that, if means could be found by which President Machado could act as of his own initiative, there was still hope that he could be persuaded to do so. He agreed that a face-saving device was necessary. The President suggested that the economic situation should be utilized for this purpose rather than the political crisis, that if President Machado could step out in order to save the Cuban people from starvation, he would not only be saving his "face" but would be performing a noble act. The President suggested that, in this event, a shipload of food supplies could be sent from this country to Havana for the benefit of the Cuban people.

Ambassador Cintas promised to call up President Machado on the telephone as soon as he had reached New York, would report his conversation and would thereupon call up the Secretary of State or the Under Secretary and give us the reaction of President Machado.

At the conclusion of the interview the President gave out the following statement:

> "The President and Ambassador Cintas discussed the Cuban situation, especially in its economic aspects. They feel that the problems of starvation and of depression are of such immediate importance that every political problem should be met in the most patriotic spirit, in order to improve conditions at the earliest possible moment. The Ambassador is communicating with his Government."

Inasmuch as Ambassador Cintas has expressed the hope that President Machado may be willing to make some counterproposal tomorrow or the next day, we think it would be desirable for you not to press him further at the moment.

(signed) Cordell Hull

--◊◊◊--0--◊◊◊--

BENJAMIN SUMNER WELLES, US AMBASSADOR IN CUBA, WRITES TO
CORDELL HULL, US SECRETARY OF STATE

Havana, August 9, 1933   [Received 10:30 p.m.]

I have just been handed the official resolution of the Popular Party in which is contained the following declaration:

"The Popular Party in order to bring about concord, reestablish moral peace among Cubans and to maintain and fortify the independence of the Republic against every risk, hereby express their absolute identification with the procedure of the representatives of the Popular Party, all of the agreements reached as to constitutional reform, as to the establishment of the parliamentary system of government, as to the enforcing of the rights of individuals and likewise as to the shortening of the terms of office enjoyed by the members of this party in the national Congress".

The decision reached by the Popular Party in its National Assembly which met this afternoon thus confirms the declarations previously made to me by the chiefs of that party. The Conservative Party which has already taken similar attitude as the Department was advised together with the Popular Party comprise a little less than half of the membership of both Houses.

(signed) Benjamin Sumner Welles

--◊◊◊--0--◊◊◊--

BENJAMIN SUMNER WELLES, US AMBASSADOR IN CUBA, WRITES TO
CORDELL HULL, US SECRETARY OF STATE

Havana, August 10, 1933   [Received 7:04 p.m.]

President Machado this morning with the help of Ferrara succeeded in forcing the executive committee of the Liberal Party to pass a resolution rejecting the solution presented by me as mediator. The President attempted to persuade the Conservative and Popular Parties to take the same action. The President of the Conservative Party refused and in the letter sent by him to President Machado at noon today of which he sent me a copy he stated that while his party had not requested the President to retire he invited him *"in the name of the Conservative Party to make the gesture as an act of the highest nobility which would add luster to his name together with his titles of General and President of the Republic."* The heads of the Popular Party have stated that the resolution of the party communicated by me to the Department in my 141, August 9, 8 p.m., is all-inclusive and was clearly intended by them to

In August of 1933, there were **protests** and **demonstrations** across almost every city in Cuba. Machado, nevertheless, refused to be forced out of the presidency. Cuba was fast developing into a very poor country, due to political unrest and the world economic depression. On the lower photo, a view of **Llega y Pon**, where more than 1,500 Cubans were living in 1933 in the most abject of conditions. In 1933, it competed in misery and deprivation with other slums habaneros like **Las Yaguas**, la **Cueva el Humo** y **El Fanguito**.

express their approval of the solution presented to President Machado. They advised me they will refuse the President's request.

It is obvious that the leaders of the Liberal Party are doubtful which way to jump. Both Senator Barreras, President of the Senate, and Governor Barceló, the President of the Liberal Party, told me in unmistakable terms that they felt that the solution proposed was the only one that would save the country and that it must consequently be accepted by the President. Ferrara told me this morning however that both of these individuals had stated to him not only that they were not in accord with the President's retirement but that I had told them in my conversation with them that the President's decision must be reached within 48 hours. Needless to state I never made any such assertion to either of these two Liberal leaders and the allegation is false as are all the others which the President's supporters are attributing to me. I am advising the Department of these facts in view of my belief that the attempt will very soon be made, if it has not already been made, by the Government to try and show that I have exceeded my instructions and my faculties as mediator.

(signed) Cordell Hull

--◇◇◇--0--◇◇◇--

Josephus Daniels, US Ambassador to Mexico, writes to Cordell Hull, US Secretary of State

Mexico, August 10, 1933   [Received 9:45 p.m.]

In a talk with Dr. Puig today he said that Mexico thought most Cubans wished Machado's removal or abdication but felt that intervention by the United States alone would not be approved by Latin American countries. It might indeed militate against agreements by the Montevideo Conference in the success of which he is deeply interested. He pointed out that Machado following the plan of Huerta would appeal to Cubans against intervention by *"the Colossus of the North"* stimulating the natural opposition to outside dictation. This would strengthen his position with Cubans. However, if the United States should say in effect that whereas the Piatt Amendment imposed upon it a right and a duty but that it generously proposed to act in cooperation with other countries on this continent, this joint action, such as Wilson's belated confidential conference in the Huerta situation would be wise. I know it would be hailed with approval in Latin America. Puig believes it would result in the ousting of Machado. If Mexico was represented on such a body this country would cooperate in securing for Cuba a government which would ensure peace and bring prosperity. Just before I called on Dr. Puig the Japanese Minister was there. He had said to Dr. Puig that it looked like the United States was about to do in Cuba what Mexico and our country had condemned Japan for doing in Manchuria. Puig answered that there was no such analogy because under the

Platt Amendment and the Cuban Constitution the United States had both a right and duty to intervene to end Cuban revolution.

I hope Pan American participation in reaching settlement in Cuba may be invoked and Mexico invited to take part. Memorandum of conversation being sent by air mail.

(signed) Josephus Daniels

--◊◊◊--0--◊◊◊--

BENJAMIN SUMNER WELLES, US AMBASSADOR IN CUBA, WRITES TO **CORDELL HULL,** US SECRETARY OF STATE

Havana, August 10, 1933   [Received 8:18 p.m.]

For the President. I am deeply grateful for the statements you made concerning me to the Cuban Ambassador yesterday. They have been of the utmost help. Every possible effort is being made by the Government supporters to convince the members of Congress and the members of the opposition that I am acting without your approval and at the same time to attribute statements to me which I have never made. I believe that the suggestion you made through Cintas to President Machado should be acceptable. I further believe that your idea of a gesture of generosity towards the Cuban people in this critical moment will be helpful. The situation is increasingly disquieting but I can assure you that I shall exert every effort of which I am capable to try and promote a solution by the Cubans themselves. The chief difficulty of the moment is to enable the political leaders to obtain correct information.

(signed) Benjamin Sumner Welles

--◊◊◊--0--◊◊◊--

BENJAMIN SUMNER WELLES, US AMBASSADOR IN CUBA, WRITES TO **CORDELL HULL,** US SECRETARY OF STATE

Havana, August 10, 1933   [Received 8:42 p.m.]

I had this morning a very long conversation with Ferrara. I read to him a paraphrase of the Department's Telex of August 9, 6 p.m. In accordance with the authorization given me over the telephone later I am sending Ferrara a written copy of such paraphrase. It was perfectly obvious that Cintas had not reported correctly to Ferrara his conversation with President Roosevelt.

The bases of Ferrara's' arguments were: an indefinite extension of time before reaching any decision; acquiescence on our part for the Government to put down the general strike by any means necessary as a method of insuring public order in the future; and finally that the solution proposed by me as mediator should have been proposed some 6 or 7 months from now during which time I should have permitted negotiations to drag on.

After a protracted discussion Ferrara stated that President Roosevelt's suggestion that food supplies be sent here to alleviate distress was a futile gesture and that if possible bases for agreement could be reached upon a liberal loan to be made by the United States Government to the Machado administration without interest for a stated period together with the immediate negotiation of a new commercial treaty which would grant Cuba material advantages he would advise President Machado to resign sometime later after the effects of the action taken by the United States Government had permitted President Machado to regain his lost popularity.

I replied to the Secretary of State that I could not convey any such bargain to my Government predicated on a continuance of power of the Machado administration; that I had reached the conclusion that normal conditions in Cuba could not exist so long as the present administration continued and that I believed any counterproposal advanced by President Machado should be based upon patriotism and the needs of the Cuban people and the interests of the Cuban Republic rather than upon any idea of the United States making loans to Cuba over which the existing Machado administration would have control. I stated that while I was without authority to say so it was my personal belief that as soon as there existed in Cuba a constitutional government which merited the confidence of all of the Cuban people the Government of the United States would be disposed to consider favorably any reasonable requests for economic assistance which might be advanced.

Ferrara told me that he would like to think matters over; that he would confer with President Machado tomorrow morning and that he would then, tomorrow afternoon, talk again with me and give me some indication in a definite way of what President Machado intended to do.

(signed) Benjamin Sumner Welles

--◇◇◇--0--◇◇◇--

CORDELL HULL, US SECRETARY OF STATE, , WRITES TO
BENJAMIN SUMNER WELLES, US AMBASSADOR IN CUBA

Washington, August 10, 1933

Ambassador Cintas called at the Department this morning and had an interview of nearly 2 hours with the Secretary and Under Secretary. He went over the whole situation and insisted that our method of approach had been wholly wrong and was decidedly pessimistic as to the outcome. The Secretary said that he hoped General Machado would agree to cooperate in the endeavors that are being made to prevent a situation of anarchy and chaos in Cuba.

He said that the chief purpose of Ambassador Welles' mission to Cuba is to avoid a condition which would call for our responsibilities under the Permanent Treaty. In reply to the Secretary's query as to what suggestion he had to offer in the circumstances, the Ambassador said that it would be helpful if the Department would ask you to come to Washington for consultation; the Ambassador felt that in this way President Machado would be freer to make concessions which it was impossible for him to make while he was in the position of being pressed to do so through you by the United States Government.

Later in the day Ambassador Cintas asked the Under Secretary to transmit this suggestion to the President, which the Under Secretary felt obliged to do this afternoon by telephone. With the President's authority the Under Secretary conveyed the following reply to Ambassador Cintas:

> "That the President had received the message and had given it consideration, but that he was not disposed to ask Ambassador Welles to come to Washington for consultation, that once more he desired it to be understood that he had the utmost confidence in Ambassador Welles and felt sure that the Ambassador was doing everything possible to be helpful in the circumstances; furthermore the Under Secretary conveyed, at the President's request, the message that obviously the next move was up to President Machado and that that move was a simple one, that certain suggestions had been presented to President Machado by representatives of the various political groups, that President Machado had turned down two of the five suggestions and that it was, therefore, now up to him to offer some counterproposal in place of these two, that the President was waiting for action by President Machado and that time was the essence of the whole problem."

Ambassador Cintas told the Under Secretary, on receiving this message, that he was leaving for Cuba this evening and that he desired to be helpful. The Under Secretary assured him that he had an opportunity to be of immense help and that he was counting upon him for such assistance.

(signed) Cordell Hull

--◇◇◇--0--◇◇◇--

BENJAMIN SUMNER WELLES, US AMBASSADOR IN CUBA, WRITES TO
CORDELL HULL, US SECRETARY OF STATE

Havana, August 11, 1933   [Received 12:10 p.m.]

As a decided rebuff to the attempt made throughout the clay of yesterday by President Machado to force the Conservative Party to reject the mediation negotiations and the solution proposed by me to President Machado the Senators and Representatives of the Conservative Party in Congress last night passed the following official resolution:

"That the party has always been contrary to foreign intervention since it is its supreme ideal to maintain unimpaired the national sovereignty in accordance with the point of view invariably maintained by the Conservative Party, neither this parliamentary committee nor the party has at any time requested the President to shorten his term. But that this parliamentary committee in accordance with the instructions of the party has accepted without any mental reservations whatsoever the mediation of the Ambassador of the United States and is disposed to support any sacrifices whatsoever as may be necessary in order to reestablish normality in Cuba and cordiality in the Cuban family within the respect of the sovereignty of the Republic."

(signed) Benjamin Sumner Welles

--◊◊◊--0--◊◊◊--

CORDELL HULL, US SECRETARY OF STATE, , WRITES TO
BENJAMIN SUMNER WELLES, US AMBASSADOR IN CUBA

Washington, August 11, 1933

Personal from the Secretary to the Ambassador. Both the President and I appreciate the trying difficulties with which you are faced in Cuba and have repeatedly informed Ambassador Cintas that we have the utmost confidence in you and what you are doing to be helpful.

Out of the mass of information which has been sent to the United States from Cuba some misapprehension has arisen as to what you are doing, and there has been some adverse comment, both here and in Latin America, that the United States is attempting to coerce rather than to persuade. I of course understand the difficulties you are facing and place no reliance whatsoever on these reports; however, I trust you will bear them in mind and do what you can to correct them.

At the Press Conference this morning I intend to reiterate that Ambassador Cintas was informed prior to his departure to Havana that you have the entire confidence of the President and myself. At the same time, I shall repeat that you are using your good offices in an endeavor to help the Cubans find a Cuban solution for their difficulties; that it is a mistake to speak of a "Welles' plan" as the only plan under discussion is a Cuban plan, agreed upon by Cubans and put forward by yourself on their behalf; and that it is important to bear in mind that you are acting as a mediator making a friendly

By early **August of 1933**, it was evident that normal conditions in Cuba could not exist so long as the Machado administration continued to rule. In the photos above, **Antonio Jiménez**, Chief of Police, was murdered by unknown assailants, people took to the streets to talk and express their anger, and President **Roosevelt** ordered the **destroyers CLAXTON** and **TAYLOR** to sail from Key West for Cuba. CLAXTON stayed only 24 hours in Havana and TAYLOR sailed to Guantanamo Bay.

effort to assist the Cubans to find a satisfactory solution for their problems.

(signed) Cordell Hull

--◊◊◊--0--◊◊◊--

BENJAMIN SUMNER WELLES, US AMBASSADOR IN CUBA, WRITES TO
CORDELL HULL, US SECRETARY OF STATE

Havana, August 11, 1933   [Received 8:35 p.m.]

After conferences last night and this morning with political leaders of all parties and with the most prominent members of the opposition I have determined in an interview which I shall hold with Ferrara this afternoon to state to him that if President Machado declares that he will not accept the first two points in the solution proposed by me but offers as of his own initiative as a counter-proposition a request for leave of absence until a Vice-President is inaugurated and the immediate resignation of all of the members of his Cabinet with the exception of General Herrera, the latter then to become acting head of the Government until a Vice-President is inaugurated, I will personally accept such a solution; recommend it to my Government for its approval; and recommend it to the leaders of the opposition as a solution of the immediate political crisis. General Herrera is Secretary of War and until Ferrara's return was Acting Secretary of State. I had a confidential talk with General Herrera late last night in which he gave me his formal commitment that in the event that the President suggested an arrangement of the character above-indicated he would accept the responsibility and would obligate himself to appoint a national Cabinet composed of those representative men of all political groups whom the leaders of such groups indicated. If the constitutional reforms are immediately passed the Vice-President will be inaugurated not later than next February and General Herrera would then retire from office turning over the Government to a new and impartial individual as Vice-President agreed upon by all elements, who would hold the national elections of 1934 and govern the country until the next constitutional period, 1935.

This suggestion should in every sense of the word be acceptable to President Machado for the following reasons:

1. It permits him to save his face by declaring that he has not accepted the solution proposed by me but of his own initiative appointed one of the members of his Cabinet as head of the ad interim Government to hold office until the Vice-President takes over.
2. It offers security to President Machado for the lives and property of himself and of the members of his present Government as well as of the members of his family. The fear of assassination

is in my judgment the fundamental obstacle to President Machado's refusal to relinquish office under the solution originally proposed.
3. It offers absolute guarantees to all the members of the Liberal Party who are afraid of reprisals by the opposition.
4. It ensures the loyal support of the Cuban Army which is unanimously devoted to General Herrera although he is now retired from the Army and thus assures the maintenance of public order during the period entailed.
5. Some of the opposition factions will protest but the retirement of President Machado and the formation of a national Cabinet giving representation to every element will in a very short period bring acquiescence. The principal leaders of the opposition have unanimously decided to accept this proposal since in their belief it is the only method of obtaining Machado's resignation and of avoiding American intervention which in their opinion Machado is at present determined to force.
6. From the point of view of the United States Government it seems to me a thoroughly satisfactory solution inasmuch as it would be a solution undertaken upon the initiative of the President of Cuba and agreed to by the political parties and the main leaders of the opposition. It is essentially a Cuban solution of the Cuban problem.

I may say that General Herrera is the only member of the present Government who has unswervingly supported my efforts to bring about a peaceful solution of the political problem and that he has invariably maintained faith with me. His entire life has been spent in the Army and he has to my knowledge upon two occasions refused to permit the Army to be used for political purposes. He is exceedingly amenable to suggestions which represent the interest of the United States Government. While he has been chief of the Cuban Army since the beginning of the term of President Zayas 12 years ago until the month of May when he retired, he has not in any sense been responsible personally for the atrocities which have been committed by certain Army officers during the past few years.

In accordance with President Roosevelt's message to the Ambassador I shall insist upon prompt action. While the situation remains in general quiet it cannot remain quiet much longer. Any incident might provoke a general explosion.

I shall cable the Department further as soon as I have had my conference with Ferrara at 4 o'clock this afternoon.

(signed) Benjamin Sumner Wells

--◇◇◇--0--◇◇◇--

BENJAMIN SUMNER WELLES, US AMBASSADOR IN CUBA, WRITES TO
CORDELL HULL, US SECRETARY OF STATE

Havana, August 11, 1933   [Received 11:40 p.m.]

Dr. Ferrara, the Secretary of State, has just informed me that President Machado has instructed him that in view of the serious crisis of the moment he will be willing to ask leave of absence from the Congress not later than Wednesday of next week; request the immediate resignation of his Cabinet with the exception of General Herrera permitting the latter full authority to form a national Cabinet composed of representatives of all sectors of Cuban public opinion. Machado will present his resignation to the Congress to become effective immediately after the Vice-President, who is to be impartial, not connected with active party politics, and acceptable to all elements, is inaugurated.

The President, nevertheless, intends to send to me tomorrow *"for the record"* a counterproposal to the solution presented to him by me as mediator. This counterproposition I understand will contain a request for the United States Government to give the new temporary Cuban Government both economic and financial assistance immediately. It likewise declares for a new version of the Piatt Amendment and for an indefinite continuation of the existing administration. At the close the statement is made, however, that if this counterproposition is found unacceptable by the mediator the President will consider any other solution. The President has instructed Ferrara to state to me that as soon as this first counterproposition is declared by me not to represent the desires of the representatives of the Cuban political organizations, he will then of his own initiative take the action described in the first paragraph of this telegram.

The maintenance of public order during the next few days until the final step is taken will be exceedingly difficult. It is for that reason that it is essential that no indication be given by the Department of the President's intention to leave his office immediately until further arrangements for publication of such intention are determined upon here.

I am advised that the decision of the President to take action immediately was due to the fact that all of the ranking officers of the Army throughout the Republic had notified him that the Cuban Army would not support him further.

The rumors concerning General Herrera have been circulating continuously this afternoon. Some of the more violent members of the opposition are bitterly opposed to this solution. The more responsible leaders of the opposition, however, have determined to accept this solution as a patriotic necessity in order to insure protection of the elements which have been supporting the present Government and they are confident that the control which can be exerted through a National Cabinet will be sufficient to insure the success of the interim Government until the new Vice-President takes office.

The principal danger in the present situation lies in the fact that President Machado has postponed taking this action for a week beyond the time when it should have been taken. Unless the strike can be broken within the next few days before notification of a change in administration, disorders may very likely occur.

(signed) Benjamin Sumner Wells

--◊◊◊--0--◊◊◊--

BENJAMIN SUMNER WELLES, US AMBASSADOR IN CUBA, WRITES TO
CORDELL HULL, US SECRETARY OF STATE

Havana, August 12, 1933   [Received 5:22 a.m.]

Since the abortive revolt of the first battalion of artillery yesterday afternoon there have been several threatened revolts in diverse portions of the Army insisting upon the immediate resignation of President Machado. Ferrara, who impresses me as temporarily mentally unbalanced, without authorization of President Machado announced the latter's resignation and his substitution by General Herrera by telegraph to all the local commanders. Certain of these discovered the fact that the announcement was untrue, and a far more serious revolt was at once imminent. I think the situation is now in control. If General Herrera is enabled by this afternoon to announce that he will appoint a Cabinet consisting of representative members of all parties and giving their names I am hopeful the effect of Ferrara's imprudence may be overcome.

The President apparently intends to hasten his resignation to Saturday or Sunday at the latest.

(signed) Benjamin Sumner Wells

--◊◊◊--0--◊◊◊--

BENJAMIN SUMNER WELLES, US AMBASSADOR IN CUBA, WRITES TO
CORDELL HULL, US SECRETARY OF STATE

Havana, August 12, 1933   [Received 5:40 a.m.]

After the promise of certain of the Army leaders at 4 o'clock this morning that they would agree to the ad interim Presidency of any Cuban provided President Machado would retire from the office, I was advised at 7 that they had again changed their minds and would accept anyone other than General Herrera to whom they were personally devoted but whom they feared the great mass of the opposition would not accept on account of his past intimate connection with President Machado. As a consequence of this in a very high spirit of patriotism General Herrera assured me at 8 o'clock this morning that since it is necessary to follow constitutional procedure he would accept the ad interim Presidency as soon as the Congress had agreed to the legal absence requested early this morning in the special message sent by President Machado since under the existing constitution the Presidency ad interim can only be entrusted to one of the members of the Cabinet; that immediately after taking over the Presidency ad interim here he would appoint Dr. Carlos Manuel de Céspedes, former Secretary of State and former Minister at Washington, Secretary of State of the Republic and would immediately thereafter entrust the Presidency of the Republic to Dr. Céspedes. Dr. Céspedes has accepted the offer and will retain General Herrera in his Cabinet as Secretary of War with which step all the ranking officers of the Army are in entire accord. Dr. Céspedes has the great advantage of being regarded as thoroughly impartial by everybody in Cuba. He is likewise popular with the Liberal Party which at present controls the majority of the House and of the Senate and he is furthermore a most sincere friend of the United States. Dr. Céspedes will try to form his Cabinet during the remainder of the morning and early this afternoon and will inform me late this afternoon what appointments he has determined to make.

The procedure which is being followed consequently is strictly constitutional and in accordance with my telephone conversation with Assistant Secretary Caffery this morning. I understand that no official act of recognition by the United States is required. In accordance with our understanding I will first advise the Department of the constitution of the Cabinet and I beg to request immediate authorization to enter official relations with the new government immediately afterwards.

President Machado after sending his messages requesting leave of absence and entrusting the Government of the Republic to General Herrera left the city for his country place where he is amply protected by two companies of troops in whom he has confidence. Most of the members of the former Government, all of whom have handed in their resignations which have been accepted, are in concealment fearing reprisals by the populace. Up to the present, however, while the city is filled with cheering crowds, I have had no report of serious disorder except around the capitol where troops have now been sent to maintain order in order that the deliberations of Congress may not be interfered with.

The determination of President Machado to act with this patriotism is due to the fact that he was finally and definitely informed last night that all of the ranking officers of the Army were unanimous in demanding that he leave the Presidency during the course of today. His action cannot therefore in any sense of the word be described either as to the result of pressure by the United States nor as the result of a patriotic gesture on his part.

Fortunately the solution which has now been elaborated and which I have every confidence will be acceptable to the enormous majority of the Cuban people has been worked out solely by the Cubans themselves and represents in my judgment the expression of the volition of very nearly the totality of the Cuban people. The next few days will probably be difficult, but I now have confidence that the situation has been saved and that no further action on the part of the United States Government will be necessary.
(signed) Benjamin Sumner Welles

--◊◊◊--0--◊◊◊--

JEFFERSON THOMAS CAFFERY, US UNDER SECRETARY OF STATE, , WRITES TO
BENJAMIN SUMNER WELLES, US AMBASSADOR IN CUBA

Washington, August 12, 1933

The President and Secretary have asked me to express their warm congratulations to you and their appreciation of what you have done.
(signed) Jefferson Thomas Caffery

--◊◊◊--0--◊◊◊--

JOHN P. HURLEY, US AMBASSADOR IN NASSAU, WRITES TO
CORDELL HULL, US SECRETARY OF STATE

Nassau, August 13, 1933   [Received 9:50 a.m.]

Ex-President Machado arrived here at daylight this morning.
(signed) John P. Hurley

--◊◊◊--0--◊◊◊--

BENJAMIN SUMNER WELLES, US AMBASSADOR IN CUBA, WRITES TO
JEFFERSON THOMAS CAFFERY, US UNDER SECRETARY OF STATE

Havana, August 12, 1933   [Received 5:40 a.m.]

Please express to the Secretary my deep appreciation of his generous message.
(signed) Benjamin Sumner Welles

--◊◊◊--0--◊◊◊--

Photos above.
1- Members of the Directorio jailed in the **Isle of Pines prison**:
Standing, left to right, Ramiro Valdés Daussá, Rubén León, Carlos Guerrero and Fernando López. Seated: Rafael Escalona, Juan Febles, Roberto Lago, Carlos M. Fuertes Blandino and Félix E. Alpizar.
2- Members of other organizations jailed at the **Castillo del Príncipe prison**:
Standing, left to right: Julio César Fernández, Ismael "El Chino" Seijas, Emilio Laurent, Justo Carrillo and Fernando Leyva. *Crouching*: Carlos Prío Socarrás and Casimiro Menéndez.
Below, right, the US press reporting on **violence in Cuba**.

BENJAMIN SUMNER WELLES, US AMBASSADOR IN CUBA, WRITES TO
CORDELL HULL, US SECRETARY OF STATE

Havana, August 13, 1933   [Received 4:25 p.m.]

For the President. I deeply appreciate your message. Without the unfailing support you have given me this solution, now promising to make possible a period of peaceful reconstruction in Cuba, would never have been obtained.

I feel we should determine at the earliest possible moment what if anything we can do to tide the new Government over financially. As you know, the Government is bankrupt and Government employees are practically starving as the result of non-payment of the salaries for months past. I shall formulate my recommendations within the next 2 or 3 days but it looks to me now as if the only two possible alternatives were,

1. A small loan to make possible the payment of arrears in salaries, or,
2. Our consent and the consent of the American bankers to a limited moratorium on the service of the foreign debt.

Conditions this morning have improved very materially. The Army appears completely loyal to the new Government and the situation in all the larger cities including Havana very well under control.

Thank you again for your message.

(signed) Benjamin Sumner Welles

--◊◊◊--0--◊◊◊--

BENJAMIN SUMNER WELLES, US AMBASSADOR IN CUBA, WRITES TO
CORDELL HULL, US SECRETARY OF STATE

Havana, August 13, 1933   [Received 6:15 p.m.]

Dr. Céspedes, after the passage by the Congress last night of the necessary legislation in accordance with the existing constitution, this morning formally took the oath of office as President ad interim before the Supreme Court of the Republic. His Cabinet yet but partially decided upon will contain the following:

Secretary of the Treasury, Senator Daniel Compte, Conservative, who has the reputation of having an excellent practical knowledge of governmental finance;

Secretary of War and Marine, Captain Demetrio Castillo Pokorny, non-partisan. Captain Castillo is a graduate of West Point, was at one time General Crowder's aide, is half-American, was Secretary of Public Works in the "Honest Cabinet" of the Zayas Government and merits the entire confidence of Dr. Céspedes;

Secretary of Sanitation, Dr. Presno, one of the outstanding people of the country and a professor of the university;

Secretary of Public Instruction, Dr. Dihigo, likewise an outstanding professor of the university.

Dr. Torriente was urged to accept any Cabinet post he desired but refused on the ground that his prominence in the mediation activities made it undesirable for him to accept public office at this time. Dr. Martínez Sáenz of the ABC has been invited to accept the position of Secretary of Justice but has not yet reached a decision. The other posts will be filled before tomorrow morning.

The situation in the cities is in general much more satisfactory. Martial law has been declared effective throughout the Republic and the military have taken a very determined attitude which has had a salutary effect. The crowds are still hunting down the hated members of Machado's secret police.

Most of the members of the Machado Government have left the country by airplane but General Herrera, who came to the conclusion yesterday that, while the Army had formally accepted him as Secretary of War, public opinion would not tolerate him in that capacity and consequently handed in his resignation to Dr. Céspedes, is still here hidden with his family on the top floor of the National Hotel. I have taken every possible precaution to ensure his safety and I have requested guarantees of the Government for him and for those members of the Senate and of the House who are the most unpopular. General Herrera expects to sail on the *Santa Ana* tomorrow night for New York with his family and I shall go with him personally to the steamer.

The telegraph operators voted last night to go back immediately to work and the newspapers were published this morning for the first time in a week. Dr. Céspedes will see representatives of the other striking unions during the day and urge them as a patriotic gesture to return to work tomorrow morning.

In view of the fact that the Government now established is unquestionably constitutional in its formation and that the Cabinet is of a high class representative character, and since the situation demands that the Government receive our official support immediately, I beg to request that I be authorized at once to state that the Embassy has established official relations with it.

(signed) Benjamin Sumner Welles

--◊◊◊--O--◊◊◊--

BENJAMIN SUMNER WELLES, US AMBASSADOR IN CUBA, WRITES TO
CORDELL HULL, US SECRETARY OF STATE

Havana, August 13, 1933   [Received 6:50 p.m.]

With the reported authorization of President Céspedes, Cuban gunboat ***Juan Bueno Zayas*** left Havana for Key West this afternoon to take to the United States the following members of Machado's family who were embarked at Havana or will be embarked on the high seas off the Coast of Varadero, Province of Matanzas:

Sra. Elvira Machado, wife of ex-President; José Emilio Obregón, son-in-law with wife and children; Rafael Jorge Sanchez, son-in-law with wife and children; Baldomero Grau, son-in-law with wife; and two or three servants said to be of Spanish nationality. No opportunity to obtain visas.

Vessel cleared without American consular documents in emergency after notification to and by advice of the Embassy. It is requested that facilities be provided for disembarkation at Key West and that ample police protection be provided on journey through Florida, particularly at Key West and Miami.

(signed) Benjamin Sumner Welles

--◇◇◇--0--◇◇◇--

BENJAMIN SUMNER WELLES, US AMBASSADOR IN CUBA, WRITES TO **CORDELL HULL,** US SECRETARY OF STATE

Havana, August 14, 1933   [Received 4:40 p.m.]

The United States Ships *Taylor* and the *Claxton* arrived at 1:30 this morning. I have just conferred with Commander Howard and have explained to him that there was in my judgment no reason now to anticipate any necessity for landing even one man. In the later afternoon the General Staff of the Army obtained better control of the situation. People were kept off the streets and patrols were established. In Marianao, a suburb, several casualties occurred, and the enlisted men turned on the officers. Looting and burning of houses was extensive. The situation now however is well in hand throughout the city.

President Céspedes has asked me to bring the commanding officers to visit him tomorrow morning. I feel very confident that the visit of these ships was essential for its moral effect alone. If the strike is broken today as I anticipate conditions may become normal rapidly and, in that event, the two ships might well leave after 48 hours.

(signed) Benjamin Sumner Welles

--◇◇◇--0--◇◇◇--

A cartoon published in **Bohemia** on June 5, 1938. It took a whimsical look at *La Pentarquía*, portraying each of the *pentarchs* as one of the *"Dionne Quintuplets,"* who were recently born, on May 28, 1934. **Carbó** is the first quintuplet on the left, holding the rattle. **Grau** is seated at the right, next to the toy horse.

BENJAMIN SUMNER WELLES, US AMBASSADOR IN CUBA, WRITES TO
CORDELL HULL, US SECRETARY OF STATE

Havana, August 14, 1933   [Received 2:00 p.m.]

At 3 a.m. this morning President Céspedes announced the formation of his Cabinet as follows:

1. Gobernación, Col. Federico Laredo Bru, Unión Nacionalista;
2. Justicia, Dr. Carlos Saladrigas, ABC;
3. Hacienda, Dr. Joaquín Martínez Sáenz, ABC;
4. Obras Públicas, Dr. Eduardo J. Chibas, Liberal;
5. Agricultura, Dr. Rafael Santos Jiménez, Marianista;
6. Instrucción Pública, Dr. Guillermo Belt, Unión Nacionalista;
7. Sanidad y Beneficencia, Dr. Antonio Presno, University of Havana;
8. Comunicaciones, Dr. Nicasio Silverio, OCRR;
9. Guerra y Marina, Demetrio Castillo Pokorny, non-partisan;
10. Presidencia, Dr. Raúl de Cárdenas y Echárte, Conservative.

In addition to the Cabinet appointments the President appointed Dr. Estanislao Cartana, Liberal, Mayor of the Central District of Havana, the most important political post in the province; and Miguel Angel Cisneros, another prominent Liberal as Chairman of the Municipal Council.

Yesterday was a day of as much political stress as it was of stress' in the maintenance of public order. The Cabinet as finally constituted represents a thorough new deal for Cuba. There is not a man appointed to the Cabinet who is not of high personal integrity and of individual ability. The younger generation and the ideas for which the organized groups of the former opposition have been struggling are very much in the fore. Because of the financial difficulties in which the new government finds itself in view of the fact that the members of the Machado Government systematically cleaned out the public treasury during the last days of their regime it is not easy to forecast how soon an effective administration can be set to work, At this juncture I can only state that I have the utmost confidence in the ability, integrity and patriotism of the President and of the members of his Cabinet. A great deal of criticism will undoubtedly ensue because of the two leading secret organizations which have in the past engaged in terroristic activities are represented in the Cabinet in very important posts. In this matter my point of view has been that it was impossible for any constitutional government to exist in Cuba if strong terroristic secret societies remained in existence and that the only possible solution was for these organizations to be brought into the light and to seek to achieve the ends for which they are working through political and constitutional methods. The ABC has a definite program

Finally, **Machado's days are over** on August 12, 1933. After an anti-Machado conspiracy in the army is forced into the open, a group of officers take possession of some military barracks and **proclaim a rebellion** against the government. Machado visits the Columbia Military Barracks to assess the situation, and a group of officers that includes **Julio Sanguily**, the son of the patriot who was rescued by Ignacio Agramonte in 1868, and **Erasmo Delgado**, Jefe Militar de La Havana, inform him that to save Cuba from intervention he should resign. Machado resigns the presidency, and flies to *Nassau* in the Bahamas. **Carlos M. Céspedes**, the son of Cuba's legendary leader, takes over as provisional president.
The event was reported in the press all around the world.

and a definite purpose. This program is radical in character but includes two salient features—social reconstruction and honesty in administration with punishment by law of those guilty of malfeasance in office. If these two ideals can be carried into effect now or later nothing could be more salutary for the Republic of Cuba.

I am considerably concerned by the increasing demand by the newspapers and by the members of the opposition for the immediate abolition of the existing Congress on the ground that the elections under which the members were sent to the Congress were unconstitutional. If this point is carried general elections would have to be held for the vacancies in the Senate and in the House in the immediate future and I do not think the country is in a state to stand a national political campaign. I am endeavoring to urge the acceptance of the same compromise which was accepted prior to the overthrow of the Machado Government in the mediation proceedings, namely, the retention of the existing Congress until the elections of 1934.

A good many omnibuses and taxis are circulating in the streets; many of the stores have opened; and I am informed the street cars will again be in operation by noon today and that the railroads will commence operating before nightfall. Conditions in the city this morning appear to be rapidly becoming normal and for the time being the danger of an anarchistic condition at least in the Province of Havana appears to have been averted. I have not yet had reports from the interior.

(signed) Benjamin Sumner Welles

--◊◊◊--0--◊◊◊--

BENJAMIN SUMNER WELLES, US AMBASSADOR IN CUBA, WRITES TO **CORDELL HULL,** US SECRETARY OF STATE

Havana, August 15, 1933

The Secretary of War came to my house at 8 o'clock this morning to tell me that in his opinion the situation was most disquieting; that public opinion was rolling up tremendously against the continuation in office of any national, provincial, or municipal executive or legislative authorities who had held office under the old regime; and that this feeling was shared by the great majority of the younger officers of the Army. During the past 2 days the resignations of certain provincial governors and of the mayors of some of the more important cities have been forced from them or else they have been violently removed from office. He told me that in his opinion if the Government insisted upon replacing the former officials in office by force the Army in many districts would refuse to carry out orders. He also told me that agitation was spreading alarmingly against the Government for having permitted the departure from the country of so many of the officials of the old regime who were connected in the public mind with the atrocities performed by the Machado administration. He urged me to see the President at once and impress him with the gravity of the situation.

I went immediately to see President Céspedes and I told him that I thought he must take immediate energetic action. I suggested that he issue two declarations immediately, after consulting with his Cabinet to the following effect:

1. That his Government was determined that all of those employees of the prior government who had been guilty of crime or of malfeasance in office should be brought to trial and punishment and that it was his intention that strict justice be done but that his Government would insist upon it that such punishment be administered through legal channels and through the verdict of the courts and could not for one moment permit mobs to take the punishment of guilty officials of the Machado Government into their own hands.

2. That the prime requisite in benefit of the Cuban people was the immediate restoration of peace and of normality and of the return to work by the Cubans; that for the time being he demanded a definite truce with regard to the removal from office of unpopular officials of the former government and that as soon as normal conditions had been restored his government would proceed energetically to carry out the will of the people through legal and orderly procedure; that for the time being such officials as had been appointed during the past 2 days to replace those who had either been ousted or who had resigned would be temporarily confirmed by the Department of the Interior but that such temporary confirmation would only continue until an orderly manner of obtaining the determination of the Cuban people in this regard had been achieved.

President Céspedes was in the utmost accord with the suggestion which I made and called his Cabinet together at once to take the necessary action, which all of the Cabinet members with whom I have spoken believe will do very much to control conditions. I feel that the prime necessity is to bring about at the first possible moment a restoration of discipline in the Army. Once this has been obtained the Government can count on its orders being carried out. At the present time this is unfortunately not the case. A great obstacle to the speedy control of the Army came about last night in the very serious illness of General Sanguily who had been appointed Chief of Staff by President Céspedes and who had been handling the situation admirably. He has had to undergo an operation and will be incapacitated, if he survives, for several weeks.

Reports from the interior in general today are more satisfactory but if immediate measures such as those indicated above are not taken by the Government to tranquilize opinion it is very difficult to foresee what may result.

The Secretary of War has urged me to leave the *Taylor* in the harbor here and has also requested me confidentially to advise the Department that in view of the danger which exists in the present situation reinforcements should be at hand both at Key West and at Guantanamo.

I am hopeful and now I believe that the situation will be controlled by the Government, but I do not expect to be able to reach a definite conclusion on this point until several more days have passed.

The exiles who are now returning from the United States are unfortunately doing a great deal to increase agitation. They are taking the attitude that a triumphant revolution has placed the Government in power and that they are consequently entitled to dictate the policies of the Government. Furthermore, the student group which is the most pernicious element in Cuban public life is constantly issuing inflammatory proclamations and making speeches of the same character over the radio. The representation of the ABC in the government fortunately will make it possible for the ABC to place itself squarely against the student activities and through the extraordinary organization which it possesses probably to dominate them but at the present moment both the Government, the Army, and the organized political parties or groups of public opinion are all equally afraid of making themselves unpopular and consequently the strong action which is needed to dominate and control the utterly lawless student groups is lacking.

(signed) Benjamin Sumner Welles

--◇◇◇--0--◇◇◇--

BENJAMIN SUMNER WELLES, US AMBASSADOR IN CUBA, WRITES TO **CORDELL HULL,** US SECRETARY OF STATE

Havana, August 19, 1933

Personal for the Under Secretary. I will appreciate it if you will lay the following considerations before the President at the earliest opportunity.

After considerable reflection I feel that in the best interests of our own Government I should be recalled and Caffery appointed to replace me, such change to take place not later than the first of September. My reasons for this belief are as follows:

> 1. *The Cuban people have a Government which commands their confidence. This Government is composed of capable and high-minded men who are seeking the best interests of the Republic. It seems unlikely that any grave political*

disturbances will take place soon unless unexpected events materialize.

2. This Government has for its program preparation through the passage of a new electoral code based upon McBain's recommendations and through the formation of new parties and reorganization of the old ones, for the holding of free and fair elections next year, which will make it possible for a permanent constitutional government to be installed and in the meantime in frank cooperation with the United States to take all possible steps to hasten the return of economic prosperity to the Republic.

3. As soon as the President and the Secretary of the Treasury have the opportunity to give me an accurate picture of the financial situation of the Government I desire to announce immediately that the final negotiations for a new commercial treaty are being undertaken and at the same time announce the discussion of measures tending to relieve the desperate financial straits of the Government of President Céspedes, I think that I should be instructed to undertake the initiation of measures referred to and likewise be instructed to continue the commercial treaty negotiations so that it will be at once apparent that the nature of my mission was as much to improve the economic conditions of Cuba as to assist in bringing about a restoration of political peace. My successor can of course push such negotiations to a Conclusion.

4. My personal situation is becoming increasingly difficult. Owing to my intimate personal friendship with President Céspedes and the very close relationship which I have formed during these past months with all of the members of this Cabinet I am now daily being requested for decisions on all matters affecting the Government of Cuba. These decisions range from questions of domestic matters affecting the discipline of the Army to questions involving appointments in all branches of the Government. This situation is bad for Cuba and bad for the United States. Now no one criticizes my relationship with the Government because of the United States is today more popular in Cuba than it has been since the early years of the independence of the Republic. On the other hand there will very soon commence to be a large party of disgruntled office seekers who, added to the sincere opponents of American influence in Cuba and to the old-time political leaders who are now out of the picture temporarily— and I hope permanently—, will constitute a very considerable mass of public opinion and who will inevitably utilize the relations which I have with the Government as a means of political attack.

Carlos M. Céspedes y Quesada (1871-1939), the son of Cuba's legendary *"Padre de la Patria"*, became the provisional president after he fall of Machado. He went to school New York City until 1885, and then his mother took him to Germany. He earned degrees in international law and diplomacy from the *Institut Stanislas* in Paris, in 1895, he returned to Cuba and from 1895 to 1898 he served as a lieutenant colonel in the War of Independence, and as governor of Santiago de Cuba. He was active in the overthrow of Machado. In August 1933, Céspedes was offered the position of President. He took office on August 12, 1933, his 62nd birthday. His Cabinet included as Minister of Interior, **Col. Federico Laredo Bru** (from *Unión Nacionalista*), Minister of Justice, **Dr. Carlos Saladrigas Zayas** (from *ABC*), Minister of Hacienda, **Dr. Joaquín Martínez Sáenz** (from ABC), Minister of Public Works, **Dr. Eduardo J. Chibás** (from *Liberal Party*), Minister of Agriculture, **Dr. Rafael Santos Jiménez**, (a Marianista), Minister of Education, **Dr. Guillermo Belt** (from *Union Nacionalista*) Minister of Health, **Dr. Antonio Presno**, (from Havana University), Minister of Communications, **Dr. Nicasio Silverio**, (from the OCRR), Minister of War, **Demetrio Castillo Pokorny**, Presidential Minister, **Dr. Raúl de Cardenas y Echarte**, (a *Conservative*). He died on March 28, 1939, of a heart attack.

A remarkable figure in the struggle to depose Gerardo Machado was **Julio Sanguily Echarte**, son of the Major General of the 1868 Independence Army **Julio Sanguily Garritte** (1845-1906), central character of the famous **"Rescue of Sanguily"**, on October 8, 1870, when he was rescued by Major General **Ignacio Agramonte** in a bold cavalry charge. **Sanguily Echarte** was Head of the *National Army of Cuba* in 1933, and head of the *Army Aviation Corps*. He is considered one of the most important leaders of the movement that overthrew Machado. He was promoted after August 12, 1933, to *Major General* by President *Céspedes*. On September 3, he suffered a perforated ulcer in the stomach, was immediately hospitalized and underwent emergency surgery by Dr. Núñez Portuondo. He moved to the **National Hotel**, where his son, also Julio Sanguily, was a lead physician, to recover. On September 4 he was deposed by Batista. Weeks after he left the Hotel fully recovered, he was run over by an automobile and died on December 15, 1933.

> *In my judgment the policy which this Embassy should from now on pursue is a policy which should have no connection whatever except in the event of urgent necessity with the political picture and which should limit itself to cooperating in the elaboration of constructive measures in benefit of the economic prosperity of Cuba and in benefit of American exports to the Cuban market.*
>
> *5. If all goes well, I should judge that the proper moment to make a change in the Embassy here would be September 1st. If as I hope the President still wishes me to return to the Department and desires me to cooperate in preparing for the Montevideo Conference I would like to suggest that if my recommendations are approved the announcement be now made that I am returning to the Assistant Secretary of State for that purpose and that Caffery has been designated as my successor here in order to complete with the greatest rapidity possible the negotiation of those economic and financial measures upon which both Governments may determine as of mutual benefit to our two countries.*

I feel that the recommendations I have made above are in the interest of my Government. It is unwise not only from the point of view of our relations with Cuba but with the whole of Latin America as well for the American Embassy here to possess the measure of control over the Government which it now does possess owing to the peculiar developments of the past 2 months. Caffery unquestionably will obtain all the needed influence immediately after his arrival but it will be an influence exerted behind the scenes and not apparent to the public.

If by any mischance the political situation again becomes troublesome it would presumably be best for me to remain until it is straightened out because of the contacts which I now have, but should conditions continue to improve I am confident that the recommendations I have made above should be adopted.

(signed) Benjamin Sumner Welles

--◊◊◊--0--◊◊◊--

WILLIAM PHILLIPS, US UNDER SECRETARY OF STATE, WRITES TO **BENJAMIN SUMNER WELLES**, US AMBASSADOR IN CUBA

Washington, August 21, 1933

Personal from the Under Secretary. Your Telex from August 19, noon. I at once laid your telegram before the President who has given it careful consideration. He is pleased that in your opinion political conditions have improved sufficiently to permit your returning to the Department in time to cooperate in preparing for the Montevideo Conference. At the same time, and while appreciating that the present relation between the Embassy and the Cuban Government may lead to some criticism, he believes it would be preferable for you to remain in Cuba until September 15th; he hopes that in the meantime you can make substantial progress with the commercial treaty negotiations.

The President approves the suggestions set out in numbered paragraph 3, as well as in the second sentence of numbered paragraph 5, and the final paragraph of your telegram.

Announcement of your return to Department will be shortly.

(signed) William Phillips

--◊◊◊--0--◊◊◊--

BENJAMIN SUMNER WELLES, US AMBASSADOR IN CUBA, WRITES TO
CORDELL HULL, US SECRETARY OF STATE

Havana, August 22, 1933

With the arrival this morning of Colonels Mendieta and Méndez Peñate all of the old-time political leaders of the opposition have returned to Cuba with the exception of Miguel Mariano Gómez who is due to arrive by the end of the month.

A determined effort is being made now by certain of these leaders, notably Menocal, in conjunction with the extreme radicals to transform the present Government of Cuba into a purely revolutionary *de facto* government. It is their announced intention to abolish the Congress and the existing judiciary and to remove all local provincial and municipal officials throughout the Republic in order to replace them with their own henchmen. During the past 3 days I have repeatedly emphasized in all of my conversations with these leaders and with the leaders of the groups and parties represented in the present Government that only through the maintenance of a constitutional form of government in Cuba until the next national elections would it be possible for the Government to make effective the urgent measures required to improve economic conditions here as well as the financial situation of the Government itself and in addition thereto to take steps to ensure the satisfactory result of the next elections through the enactment of a new electoral code and through the passage of constitutional reforms to be submitted to a constituent assembly. Furthermore, I have made it clear that a *de facto* government governing solely by decree would not in my judgment be able to retain the support and the confidence of the people for any protracted period owing to the unstable conditions which obtain in Cuba and that insistence upon a revolutionary *de facto* form of government would in all likelihood result in general chaos.

In an interview which I had yesterday with General Menocal I stressed my own belief, as above-indicated, and further made clear that we had continued official relations with the present Government of Cuba in view of our belief that whatever the cause of the change in the Government the result had been merely a change in the persons entrusted with the executive power of the Government through methods provided in the existing constitution. I told him that I felt it essential, as I knew my Government did, that in this moment of crisis all important leaders, of whatever faction they might represent, get together in support of the present Government and assist it in making effective, at the earliest possible moment, the program of reform, both political and economic, which it had already elaborated in principle....

A portion of the press is coming rather timorously to the support of the necessity of maintaining a constitutional form of government in Cuba. None of the real leaders of public opinion have, however, as yet had courage enough to come out openly against the popular agitation for revolutionary government and a resultant clean sweep of all of the former officeholders no matter whether they were legitimately entitled to the offices they were holding or not. Until I can persuade some of these leaders to come out positively against any such policy, I am afraid to urge the Government to take the stand because of the fact that the opportunity might then be used by certain self-seekers to attack the Government on that ground to their own advantage. I shall confer today and tomorrow with all the outstanding leaders, including those recently arrived, and I shall hope to be able to persuade them of the necessity for prompt action along the lines suggested in benefit of Cuba.

(signed) Benjamin Sumner Welles

--◊◊◊--0--◊◊◊--

BENJAMIN SUMNER WELLES, US AMBASSADOR IN CUBA, WRITES TO **CORDELL HULL,** US SECRETARY OF STATE

Havana, August 23, 1933

The President of the Republic this morning informed me that the appointment of Caffery as my successor here would be most acceptable to the Cuban Government.

(signed) Benjamin Sumner Welles

--◊◊◊--0--◊◊◊--

BENJAMIN SUMNER WELLES, US AMBASSADOR IN CUBA, WRITES TO **CORDELL HULL,** US SECRETARY OF STATE

Havana, August 24, 1933

I am rapidly coming to the conclusion that my original hope that the present Government of Cuba could govern as a constitutional government for the remainder of the term for which General Machado had himself elected must be abandoned. If the solid and unwavering support of the Army could be counted on, and if the groups and parties represented in the present Government were unanimous in their support of the administration, it might be possible for the existing Government to maintain itself, pass the necessary legislation of all kinds required, and hold the general national elections in November 1934 as originally anticipated. As a matter of fact, however, a general process of disintegration is going on. The Army is by no means in a satisfactory condition and the relapse in the health of General Sanguily, Chief of Staff and the one ranking officer in the Cuban Army who can command the support of his subordinates, has delayed the taking of the measures necessary to enforce discipline within the Army which he alone could have undertaken satisfactorily. The presence of General Menocal in Cuba is as always, an exceedingly disturbing factor. His insatiable ambition and his unwillingness to recognize that he no longer can count on the support of any, but a small group is causing him to attempt to undermine the authority of the Government and I am reliably informed that he is trying to promote dissidence among the Army officers.

The inability of the Government as yet to enforce the maintenance of public order has permitted an almost anarchic condition throughout the country as the result of which groups of so-called students and radicals of every shade are breaking into houses, promoting lynchings, forcing resignations from Senators and Congressmen and other public officials and only this morning forced the resignation of the sub-Secretary of Communications recently appointed by President Céspedes. The labor situation is of course disquieting and while the most serious strikes in the cities have been settled, conditions on the large sugar plantations are very grave and it was only through the acceptance of all the demands presented by the strikers that collected on the Punta Alegre sugar estate this morning that destruction of the property and possible loss of life of the American manager and of his family was averted. If conditions such as this continue a general state of chaos here is inevitable.

The only alternative to such a result that I can now see is for the program of the present Government to be modified in order that general elections may be held approximately 3 months from now so that Cuba may once more have a constitutional government in the real sense of the word, that is, supported by an evident and overwhelming majority of the Cuban people. In order to accomplish this the Supreme Court will have to declare that the existing constitution under which General Machado was reelected is unconstitutional in that the constitution of 1928 came into being through illegal and unconstitutional methods as the result of which the country would once more be governed by the original constitution of 1901. I have every reason to believe that the Supreme Court will so hold. Once such a decision is rendered the existing Congress, to which public hostility is so intense that I doubt if it could meet even with military protection, would be *ipso facto* abolished. The President would then by decree convoke national elections to be held 3 months from such date and at the same time issue a decree declaring that the electoral law under which such elections would be held would be the Crowder code of 1919 as amended by the recommendations formulated by Professor McBain, in his recent report. The parties, under the terms of this law, would then be afforded the opportunity of organizing and presenting their lists of candidates and the entire Government, executive and legislative, would be replaced as the result of such elections. After the installation of such government a constitutional convention would be called to adopt the constitutional reforms agreed upon during the mediation proceedings which reforms represent unquestionably the desire of a great majority of all elements of public opinion.

Yesterday I consulted with Colonels Mendieta and Méndez Peñate, Dr. Torriente, General Menocal, leaders of the ABC and other opposition organizations and with President Céspedes. There is not one of them who believes that the Congress as now constituted can again function. These leaders are now meeting with their own groups and I think will reach the conclusion that the program above indicated is the one solution which offers a reasonably safe outcome for Cuba under present conditions. The President will call them into session with him tomorrow and will try and reach a unanimous agreement as to the program which his Government should carry out and the way it is to be put into effect.

Conditions in the country of course are not ripe for general elections. I have likewise every reason to believe that during the electoral period, if the above program is carried out, disturbances will take place in many parts of the Republic. I feel, however, that a change in the policy which I had originally hoped to carry out is inevitable. I do not believe that the present Government can maintain itself in power for an indefinite period and I think that nothing would be more likely to prevent a further attempt at revolution than the prospect of elections soon. A solution of this character has the added advantage that it offers the hope of a constitutional and stable government in the near future rather than in the remote future and furthermore that negotiations for the commercial treaty can continue with the authorities now in power and that the individuals taking part in the next constitutional government will undoubtedly be willing to ratify beforehand any measures of financial relief that we may decide to suggest to the existing Government of Cuba.

(signed) Benjamin Sumner Welles

Former President **Mario García Menocal** played an important role in the solution of Machado's undesirable presidency. He had been a *Cornell University* graduate, a *Major General* in the War of 1895, a renowned *businessman* and CEO, the third *president* of Cuba, serving two terms, and the man *most trusted by Roosevelt* in the Cuba of the 1930s, as he had declared war on Germany a day after the US did in 1917. In 1940 he was a member of the *Constitutional Convention*, a few weeks before he died in Havana.

Above, photos **at war**, as **CEO** of *Central Chaparra*, as a presidential **candidate** and as a **mediator** in the solution of the Machado problem.

BENJAMIN SUMNER WELLES, US AMBASSADOR IN CUBA, WRITES TO
CORDELL HULL, US SECRETARY OF STATE

Havana, August 25, 1933

In view of the urgency of the situation President Céspedes yesterday evening decided to carry out the policy indicated in my telegram under reference. He was advised to adopt this course by all the members of his Cabinet and by all the political leaders that have now returned to Cuba. During a Cabinet meeting which the President held last night the following decree was drafted which was handed to me at 4 o'clock this morning. The decree reads as follows:

To the people of Cuba.

Whereas the Congress of the Republic in the exercise of the powers established in article 115 of the constitution resolved by the law of June 21st, 1927 to amend certain provisions of the constitution;

Whereas in the call of the election for delegates of the constitutional convention the laws by virtue of which the reorganization of political parties had been prohibited remained in force as well as that prohibiting the organization of new parties and other laws were enacted prohibiting the presentation of independent candidatures all of which legal provisions had no object other than to carry into effect the amendment to the constitution with absolute disregard of the popular will inasmuch as the electors opposed to said amendment were not able to elect delegates to aforesaid constitutional convention in manifest infringement of article 38 of the constitution which recognizes the right of suffrage to all Cubans over 21 years of age;

Whereas, the constitutional convention elected to that effect did not limit its acts to the approval or disapproval of the amendment voted by Congress in accordance with the provisions of article 115 of the constitution above-cited but overstepping its authority proceeded to change certain provisions of the law which contained the amendment;

Whereas, one of the provisions which was the one of modification was that by virtue of which the presidential term of office which should have expired on May 20, 1929, was extended for two years to May 20, 1931, and which, furthermore, prohibited the reelection of the President of the Republic then in office, the change consisting in permitting said chief executive to be reelected for the next presidential term;

Whereas, on May 11, 1928, the amendment of the constitution was promulgated by the President of the Republic, the same containing as has been said important changes in *the text of the law which had been voted and passed by Congress;*

__Whereas__, in the emergency electoral law of July 20, 1928, a series of provisions were included tending to assure the reelection of the person who at that time held the Presidency of the Republic and at the same time to prevent the presentation of other candidates for the same office which objects were achieved with absolute disregard of the popular will;

__Whereas__, the Supreme Court of Justice __en banc__ in several decisions handed down in writs of unconstitutionality has recognized that the constitutional convention in altering the text of some of the provisions of the amendment law infringed the provision contained in article 115 of the constitution so often cited;

__Whereas__, all the illegalities and overriding of authority which have been mentioned constituted a __Coup d'État__ against the popular sovereignty and gave rise to an intense revolutionary agitation which obliged the Government constantly to maintain in suspense the individual guarantees and to appeal to all class of violence in order to appease the protests of the people;

__Whereas__, the good offices of the Ambassador of the United States of America to procure a solution to such an intense political crisis having been offered and accepted and the President of the Republic having refused to give performance to the essential obligations acquired by the parties within the negotiations which were being carried on, the revolutionary state became more acute to such an extent that he was forced to resolve the abandonment of the power and withdraw from the national territory in use of a leave of absence at the same time leaving a full resignation of his office;

__Whereas__, by virtue of said leave of absence I have provisionally assumed the Presidency of the Republic;

__Whereas__, many Senators and Representatives have presented the resignation of their offices and others have left the country without requesting a leave of absence;

__Whereas__, in view of everything that has been set forth above and with the object of reestablishing constitutional legality and restoring tranquility to the country, interpreting the popular will which is clearly manifested at this time throughout the country, conscious of the national conventionalities and of the transcendency of the measures I am adopting, with my thoughts placed on the founders of the nation and on the welfare of the Republic, and having heard the opinion of my Cabinet, I proceed to issue the following decree:

1. The text of the constitution of 1901 is reestablished in its full force and effect and consequently the constitutional amendment promulgated on May 11th, 1928, remains null and without any value or effect.
2. Therefore, the mandate attributed to citizen Gerardo Machado y Morales as President of the Republic is hereby terminated.
3. The present Congress is declared dissolved and therefore the mandates of the Senators and Representatives as well as the rights of their substitutes to take their places are terminated.
4. The offices of Justices of the Supreme Court filled after May 20th, 1929, are hereby declared vacant.
5. The mandates of all the other officials of popular election are hereby declared at an end, nevertheless, those holding such offices at the present time shall remain in the discharge thereof until the Government shall order what it deems proper in each case.
6. On February 24th, 1934, general elections shall be held for the filling of all offices which have their origin in popular suffrage, the new Presidential term of office to be inaugurated on May 20th of that year.
7. An advisory commission shall be created charged with the proposing of the modifications considered indispensable to carry into effect the measures contained in this decree, and the recommendations of the said commission once approved in whole or in part shall be promulgated by the Executive.
8. The Government shall respect and give fulfillment to all international obligations contracted in the name of the Republic even though they may be dated after May 20th, 1929.
9. All the Secretaries of the Cabinet are entrusted with the fulfillment of this decree insofar as it may be pertinent to each of them.

Given at the Presidential Palace in Havana on August 24, 1933. (Signed) Carlos Manuel de Céspedes, President. (Signed) Carlos Saladrigas, Secretary of Justice and Acting Secretary of State."

For the reasons set forth in my telegram above referred to, I consider that the action taken by the Government is in the best interests of the Republic of Cuba. Furthermore, I believe that under the circumstances now existing it is calculated to promote stability and to quiet opposition.

Owing to the fact that three members of the Supreme Court were appointed during Machado's second term and that their appointments are consequently held to be illegal; that the President of the Supreme Court has resigned; and that one of the remaining members is seriously ill a quorum of the Supreme Court cannot meet for the time being. The Government has decided consequently to take upon itself the responsibility of declaring unconstitutional Machado's second term of office and not refer the constitutionality of that regime to the Supreme Court.

The eighth clause of the said decree which specifically announces the intention of the Government to comply with all of the international obligations entered into by the Cuban Government from May 20, 1929, until the present date should relieve anxiety on the part of American banks which have made loans or extended credits to the Cuban Government during that period.

The President will issue within the next few days a further decree containing the electoral code under which the national elections are to be held 6 months from now. It is the intention of the Government to adopt Professor McBain's suggested reforms in their entirety.

(signed) Benjamin Sumner Welles

--◊◊◊--0--◊◊◊--

JOHN P. HURLEY, US AMBASSADOR IN NASSAU, WRITES TO
CORDELL HULL, US SECRETARY OF STATE

Nassau, August 27, 1933

Machado and party left by the steamship *Lady Rodney* last night, destination Montreal via Bermuda.

(signed) John P. Hurley

--◊◊◊--0--◊◊◊--

BENJAMIN SUMNER WELLES, US AMBASSADOR IN CUBA, WRITES TO
CORDELL HULL, US SECRETARY OF STATE

Havana, August 30, 1933   [Received 2:15 p.m.]

I was visited yesterday by a delegation of 30 of the most prominent American businessmen in Cuba. They expressed themselves as exceedingly disturbed by the social and labor unrest which is current in Cuba and certain of them appear to be firmly of the opinion that Communist agitators "under the pay of Russia" are seizing this opportunity through the formation of unions and the promotion of syndicalism to plan the overthrow of the Cuban Government and the installation of a Communist regime.

It is true that during the past 2 weeks labor leaders, some of them foreigners, have been furthering unrest and have been responsible for the epidemic of strikes which have swept the Republic. I do not believe, however, that Communist theories as such have yet any support among the laboring classes. The present situation, disturbing as it is and increasingly serious as it may become, is primarily due to the fact that the laboring classes have suffered under an absolute dictatorship for the last 3 years; that their leaders have been arrested and frequently assassinated; and that any organization of labor has been made absolutely impossible. Even more important is the fact that for the same period the average laborer on the plantations has been paid less than the minimum amount required to feed himself and his family and the conditions of distress and actual destitution which exist cannot be exaggerated. The field consequently is particularly ripe for agitation by labor leaders and for the formation of labor unions under the control of such leaders. The demands which have been presented on the sugar plantations by the delegates of the newly formed unions have called for a living wage and an 8-hour day as well as recognition of the unions. In most instances these demands have been granted by the companies although many of the companies frankly state that they may be unable because of their own financial situation to carry out their promises.

In such cases where the demands have not been agreed to unruly mobs, frequently considerable, in size, have been formed and while violence has until now been averted loss of life and destruction of property may take place at any time. The condition is so general that the military forces of the Government can only cope with the situation where the detachments are sufficiently large to inspire respect and as I have already informed the Department the discipline within the Army, while improving, is not yet sufficiently good to give the Government assurance that its orders will be complied with in every instance.

The only sure solution for a situation which otherwise may get beyond control is for the sugar companies to be able to commence work within the near future and offer their laborers sufficient to enable them to live and support their families. This, of course, is contingent upon the determination in the immediate future of the amount of sugar which Cuba can produce during the next crop year. This in turn depends on the agreement which is to be reached in Washington as to the Cuban quota. If some fair adjustment is arrived at soon, I believe the labor situation on the plantations will solve itself within a comparatively few weeks.

The situation in the cities while still precarious is more satisfactory. The American employers of labor are fearful of the formation of labor unions which the Machado Government made impossible. In certain exceptional cases where American companies have not during the past years cut down wages and have treated their employees fairly the demands now presented by the latter to their employers are preposterous and if insisted upon the companies will have to close their doors. In many other cases, however, the demands formulated are in my judgment reasonable and can be complied with. There is a very strong desire on the part of the   >

Photos, top to bottom: **Menocal in exile** in Miami in 1931. After August 12, 1933, he stayed in Cuba and tried to do his best to placate the violent behaviour of the citizenry. *In the center and below*, some of the frustrations during the dictatorship of Machado were vented by **vandalism and aggression** on August 12, 1933, particularly the burning and sacking of **Heraldo de Cuba**, a newspaper owned by **Orestes Ferrara**, whose plane was attacked as he was leaving for exile in Miami.

Government to regulate the formation of unions by law soon so that the Government itself may act as arbitrator in disputes between foreign interests and their employees. This I think should be encouraged and many of the American interests represented here favor it.

While I recognize that a small number of foreign agitators are availing themselves of this opportunity to stir up strikes and labor unrest in general to their own profit and that if this policy is not checked by the Government serious consequences may ensue, I cannot see any indications of the *"red menace"* which certain Americans doing business here are fearful of. Immediate improvement of economic conditions in Cuba is a sure cure for the situation which now exists and I feel it obligatory for me to state to the Department that if the Government of the United States does not soon render friendly assistance in the determination of a fair sugar quota for Cuba and the formulation of other financing and economic recommendations such as those which I have proposed in previous telegrams to the Department a general chaotic condition throughout the country will probably arise which it will be much more difficult to put down than it would be to prevent.

(signed) Benjamin Sumner Welles

--◊◊◊--0--◊◊◊--

BENJAMIN SUMNER WELLES, US AMBASSADOR IN CUBA, WRITES TO
CORDELL HULL, US SECRETARY OF STATE

Havana, August 30, 1933   [Received 2:30 p.m.]

The President has appointed this morning Dr. Horatio Ferrer, Secretary of War and Marine in the place of Captain Castillo Pokorny, who has been appointed Secretary of Agriculture and Commerce to fill the vacancy created by the appointment yesterday of Dr. Rafael Santos Jiménez as Mayor of the city of Havana. Owing to the continued illness of General Sanguily, Chief of Staff, General Armando Montes, retired, has been brought back into active service to serve temporarily as Chief of Staff until General Sanguily is able to resume his duties.

The changes made hold the promise of an immediate improvement in the discipline of the Cuban Army, Dr. Ferrer was until recent years Surgeon General of the Army and has the confidence and support of the great majority of the armed forces.

(signed) Benjamin Sumner Welles

--◊◊◊--0--◊◊◊--

SEPTEMBER OF 1933

 Events in Cuba

September 1 A hurricane hits the areas of Cárdenas and Sagua la Grande.

September 3 At a meeting held at Columbia Military Hospital, a group of Sergeants urges the troops to file lawsuits and claims.

September 4 A meeting of officers and Army classes is held to present their demands. The Secretary of Defense disapproves of the meeting, although *Captain Torres Menier*, who organized it has the support of *Coronel Julio Sanguily*, who is sick. *Pablo Rodríguez* and *José E. Pedraza* leave for Matanzas in search of military support, while Batista oversees Columbia in Havana. In the course of the day, the military movement of the Sergeants becomes a *Coup d'État*. At night they are joined and supported by opposition civil organizations such as the radical ABC, the University Student Directory, Pro Law and Justice, and several university professors. The *Cuban Revolutionary Group* is created, and a Proclamation is launched to the People of Cuba in which they affirm they take political power as a provisional government. Among those involved are *Carlos Prío Socarrás, Rafael García Bárcena, Justo Carrillo, Juan A. Rubio Padilla, José Miguel Irisarri, Carlos Hevia, Emilio Laurent, Ramiro Valdés Daussá, Gustavo Cuervo Rubio, Guillermo Portela, Ramón Grau San Martín, Sergio Carbó* and *Fulgencio Batista*, head of the Armed Forces of the Republic.

September 5 The *Cuban Revolutionary Group* sends a delegation to President Céspedes, who signs his resignation. The movement becomes a bloodless *Coup d'État*. They adopt as an ideological platform the July program of the *Revolutionary Directory*. The Group gives full powers to an Executive Committee of five people, thereafter, known as La Pentarquía, consisting of *Guillermo Portela, Porfirio Franca, Sergio Carbó, José Miguel Irisarri* and *Ramón Gran San Martín*. Welles, upset by the Coup, asks Roosevelt for warships and the landing of troops in Cuba.

September 6 Cordell Hull, US Secretary of State, sends warships to Cuba, but does not land troops.

September 7 Mexico supports La Pentarquía. Roosevelt opposes restocking Céspedes by force but displaces 29 ships to the area.

September 8 Sergeant Batista is promoted to Colonel of the Army by Sergio Carbó. The rest of the Executive Commission, La Pentarquía, protests the appointment, considered unnecessary and dangerous because of the precedent it sets. *Pablo Rodríguez* and *J. Eleuterio Pedraza* are promoted to Captains.

September 9 Most former officers of the army, who refuse to join the new army commanded by Sergeants, are concentrated with long and short weapons in the newly opened *National Hotel*, where *Ambassador Benjamin Sumner Welles* is living. There they also take *Colonel Julio Sanguily Echarte*, head of the Army, who is convalescing of surgery. After a stormy meeting, *Porfirio Franca* and *José Miguel Irisarri* resign their pots in the Executive Committee. The remaining members dissolve the Commission and try to appoint a president. It becomes the end of La Pentarquía. The Student Directory, on its own, agrees to appoint the radical *Ramón Gran San Martín*, known Professor of Physiology, as president of the Republic of Cuba.

September 10 Grau repeals the 1901 Constitution and takes possession of the presidency declaring the *Enmienda Platt* null and begins to govern by decree. The US government doesn't recognize those decisions, but the governments of Spain, Uruguay, Peru and Mexico do recognize them.

September 11 Batista asks the former officers to return to the Army, but they refuse to be under the direction of their former subordinates. The US Secretary of State, *Cordell Hull,* informs all US diplomats in Europe, Japan and Germany that he will not intervene in Cuba, but wants a government *"capable of maintaining law and order."* The ABC, Menocal and Mendieta and the former officers openly oppose the new government.

September 12 Grau forms a new cabinet with *Antonio Guiteras Holmes* as Minister of the Interior, *Marquez Sterling* as Secretary of State (former US Ambassador), *Manuel Despaigne* (in Treasury), *Carlos E. Finlay* (in Health) and others. The employees of the National Hotel and the American Ambassador leave the hotel.

September 14 A call for a Constituent Convention. In Consolación del Sur, Pinar del Río, the former officials also revolt. Batista's soldiers begin to besiege the National Hotel. Officers contact the ABC of Martínez Sáenz for support. *Workers' Soviets* (councils) arise in several sugar plants.

September 16 An important meeting with President Grau, Martínez Sáenz of ABC, Miguel Mariano Gómez y Menocal and the Radical Revolutionary Cell Organization (OCRR) takes place. Ambassador Welles meets with the Revolutionary Directory to discuss the country's financial crisis.

September 17 A Grau-Welles secret interview also takes place, where President Grau says he cannot control Colonel Batista. Grau wants, apparently, to resign and seek a unity government, but Guiteras opposes. A new Army officiality is being created.

September 18 The opposition to the political alliance Grau-Batista-Guiteras asks Grau to resign, since his government comes from a military coup.

September 19 Antonio Guiteras, Secretary of the Interior, decrees the eight-hour working day. The Revolutionary Student Directory opposes Grau's resignation to the presidency.

September 20 All parties that supported Machado are declared dissolved, the Liberal, the Conservative and the Popular parties.

September 21 A Welles-Batista secret meeting takes place trying to replace Grau. Batista tries to meet Welles.

September 22 Batista meets with *Carlos Mendieta* and *Miguel Mariano Gómez*, and it results on a favorable impression of him.

September 26 Mella's ashes arrive in Havana from Mexico.

September 27 The government states that four important military, economic and political decrees will be announced soon.

September 29 Six dead and a score of wounded when the communists try to bury, without authorization, the ashes of Mella in the *Plaza de la Fraternidad*. Soldiers destroy the premises of the Anti-Imperialist League, the Confederation of Workers (CNOC) and the monument itself. The Army dissolves the Worker's Soviets (Councils) of the *Mabay, Jaronú and Senate* sugar mills, which had been created with little proletarian support. Guiteras holds the CNOC responsible for what happened, and states that they could induce and facilitate an American intervention by Welles, since he has ships already in the ports of Cuba.

September 30 Guiteras signs a decree to set popular rates for gas, electricity and telephones, and also issues provisions that delay the evictions of homes of insolvent people and forgives 50% of municipal taxes to the owners.

--◊◊◊--0--◊◊◊--

BENJAMIN SUMNER WELLES, US AMBASSADOR IN CUBA, WRITES TO **CORDELL HULL,** US SECRETARY OF STATE

Havana, September 5, 1933   [Received 3:45 a.m.]

To be handed to the Secretary immediately upon receipt. At 10 o'clock tonight as the result of a concerted movement which apparently exists throughout the Republic the soldiers in the garrisons of Havana have deposed all officers and have declared themselves in control of the Army. The action taken has been fomented by the extreme radical elements. The subversive movement has been announced by radio from the various barracks and in all probability violent disorder will break out before morning. From latest reports from Santiago an identical situation exists there. The President who has been visiting the provinces affected by the cyclone is absent from the capital.

The Cabinet Ministers who were holding a Cabinet meeting to determine what action should be taken have abandoned the Palace fearing an attack. There is consequently no semblance of authority remaining. The Secretary of War has just telephoned me to state that there is no hope of solution in his judgment.

The extreme gravity of the situation is apparent. There will by morning likely be a complete collapse of government throughout the island. For the moment I recommend the immediate necessity of sending at least two warships to Havana and one to Santiago de Cuba at the earliest moment. The commanding officers of the vessels sent to Havana should receive the same orders as those issued previously and the commanding officer of the ship sent to Santiago de Cuba should be instructed to report to the Consul with whom I will be in touch. I anticipate a renewal of the general strike as soon as the public becomes aware of the Army situation. Since telephone communication with Washington is interrupt >

ed, I beg to request advice by rush cable of whatever action is taken in response to this telegram.
(signed) Benjamin Sumner Welles
--◊◊◊--0--◊◊◊--

MEMORANDUM OF TELEPHONE CONVERSATION BETWEEN
CORDELL HULL, US SECRETARY OF STATE, AND
BENJAMIN SUMNER WELLES, US AMBASSADOR IN CUBA
SEPTEMBER 5, 1933, 8:10 A.M.

The Ambassador began by stating that during the last two hours there had been a change of a kind in the situation. He stated that a revolutionary government had been set up, composed of the most extreme radicals in Cuba; that all military officers had been removed and a sergeant named Batista had been installed as Chief of Staff; that the city at the present was quiet, but that as to how long it would remain so was very doubtful.

The Ambassador requested that two armed vessels be sent to Havana at once and one to Santiago. In answer to questions he further stated that there was no chance to maintain the old government; that no government was possible without the support of the army. He stated that disorders due to radical activities were prevalent, wherever his limited advices came from, over the island: but that information, however, was sporadic on account of the destruction of communications by the storm.

The Ambassador stated that President de Céspedes and other officials would be in Havana at 11:00 o'clock and that he would keep me advised as to any developments resulting. He stated that it was very important that a battle cruiser be sent to Havana at once; that the small destroyers we were sending would be of some help in the meantime, but not of enough use. I inquired whether these destroyers should not stand off just outside the Havana harbor, lest irresponsible individuals might fire on such vessel if close in the harbor. Welles thought it should go on in. I inquired as to the extent of the revolution among the soldiers, and he replied that the chief portion of them were involved and that the army was thus under ultra-radical control, while radical citizens in different parts of the island were precipitating more or less disorder.

I requested the Ambassador to keep in mind the question as to whether it would be advisable for our government to seek the cooperation of the ABC governments of South America and Mexico, in the event conditions became so serious that intervention might be seriously threatened. He promptly stated that he would keep this phase in mind and be ready to discuss it if conditions made it necessary.
(signed) Cordell Hull

BENJAMIN SUMNER WELLES, US AMBASSADOR IN CUBA, WRITES TO **CORDELL HULL,** US SECRETARY OF STATE

Havana, September 5, 1933   [Received 3:25 p.m.]

All the officers in the Havana Government have been forced to leave their posts by the non-commissioned officers and enlisted men. Some of the officers have been permitted to leave freely; some are detained in the barracks; and a few have been sent to the Army prison. Sergeant Batista has either named himself or been selected by the enlisted men at Camp Columbia as Chief of Staff of the Cuban Army. Major Boffil, Chief of police of Havana has been jailed; Lieutenant Laurent who was imprisoned by Machado for complicity in a plot against his Government 2 years ago has been named Chief of Police in his place.

The troops in Havana have announced that the mutiny in which they are engaged is receiving the support of the troops throughout the Republic but on account of the difficulty of communication since the cyclone I am unable to confirm this. The American Consul at Santiago reports troops there remain loyal to constituted Government.

At 5 o'clock this morning a so-called revolutionary government was proclaimed and has made the following announcement:

The revolutionary group of Cuba composed of enlisted men of the Army and of the Navy and of civilians belonging to various sectors headed by the university student group declares:

First. That it has constituted itself in order to carry out in whole the revolutionary program for which the great majority of the Cuban people is contending and will continue to contend within ample lines of modern democracy and based upon the pure principles of national sovereignty.

Second. This program in brief is as follows:

1. Economic reconstruction of the nation and political organization based on a constitutional convention to be held immediately.
2. Immediate elimination and full punishment of all those responsible for the previous situation both in civilian life as well as in the Army without which the reestablishment of real order and authentic justice is impossible, protecting at the same time the life and property of nationals and foreigners.
3. Strict recognition of the debts and obligations contracted for by the Republic.
4. Immediate constitution of adequate courts to insist upon the responsibilities above mentioned.
5. Reorganization within as brief a period as possible of all
>

Photos, on top: **Machado** surrounded by friends hours before the *Coup d'État* of August 12, 1933. On the left of him in the picture, with a mustache, **Carlos Manuel de Céspedes**, on his right, with sunglasses, **General Herrera**, the man he left in charge after resigning. *In the center*, the **Cabinet** formed by **Céspedes**; *below*, a group of politicians in 1933, seated are left to right, **Grau San Martín, Carlos Mendieta, Mario García Menocal** and **Miguel Mariano Gómez**.

>   *services and national activities obtaining a rapid return to normality.*
> 7. *Finally, to take all the measures not foreseen in this document in order to commence the march towards the creation of new Cuba founded upon an immovable foundation of justice and of the most modern conception of democracy.*

Third. Believing that the actual government is not responsive to the urgent demands of the triumphant revolution notwithstanding the good faith and patriotism of its members, the revolutionary group of Cuba takes charge of the reins of power as a provisional revolutionary government which will resign the sacred trust conferred upon it by the people as well as the Constitutional Assembly which is to be convoked to the constitutional government which will guide our destinies until the first general elections.

This provisional government will issue decrees and regulations which will have the force of law before the people of Cuba and with the unquestioned support of the people of Cuba, which we greet in the name of liberty and justice. This new government will march forward fully guaranteeing the stability of the Republic and will operate in accordance with existing treaties confident that Cuba will be respected as a new sovereign nation which arises full of vigor to take part in international life.

This proclamation is signed by Sergeant Batista who adds the title of *"Sergeant and Revolutionary Chief of all the Armed Forces of the Republic"* and is likewise signed by a group of the most extreme radicals of the student organization and three university professors whose theories are frankly communistic. Five of the signatories of this proclamation have constituted themselves an executive committee to govern the Republic and have announced their intention of taking possession of the Palace during this morning.

President Céspedes will arrive in Havana about 11 o'clock. The members of his Cabinet are now in session at the house of one of the members and a group of them will come to the Embassy to see me in an hour's time. I feel it inadvisable for me to make any specific recommendations until I have had an opportunity of talking with President Céspedes and his Cabinet.

The situation in the city this morning appears to be quiet. I repeat that it is urgently necessary in my judgment, however, that two destroyers arrive here at the earliest moment possible and that a battleship likewise be sent. As stated in my previous telegram a warship should be sent to Santiago without delay. It is very likely on account of the serious labor agitation which had existed already that additional vessels should be sent to other ports to guarantee the safety of American lives. I shall so recommend if I later believe it necessary.

I wish to make it emphatically plain that I shall do my utmost to prevent in every possible way the necessity of any armed interven-

tion by the United States. Since such a step, however, may have later to be taken by our Government I strongly urge the desirability now of explaining the Cuban situation fully to the representatives of all the Latin American Republics. It appears hardly likely that a so called revolutionary government composed of enlisted men of the Army and radical students who have occupied themselves almost exclusively during the last 10 days with the assassination of members of the Machado Government can form a government *"adequate for the protection of life, property and individual liberty"*. All of the important leaders of the existing political parties in the Republic notably the Unión Nacionalista and the ABC are definitely hostile to this movement and it is highly problematical how many hours or days will elapse before violence and open dissensions take place throughout the Republic.
(signed) Benjamin Sumner Welles

--◊◊◊--0--◊◊◊--

BENJAMIN SUMNER WELLES, US AMBASSADOR IN CUBA, WRITES TO
CORDELL HULL, US SECRETARY OF STATE
Havana, September 5, 1933   [Received 12:45 p.m.]

Sergeant Batista accompanied by Sergeant Santana called to see me at the Embassy.... Neither of them seems to have any clear conception of what the movement of the soldiers and non-commissioned officers is responsive to. The purport of their visit was to ascertain what my attitude was towards the so-called revolutionary group and whether the installation of a government headed by this group would be favorably regarded by the Government of the United States. I replied that I had no comment to make.

I inquired what steps they had taken to preserve the maintenance of public order in Havana and while in their reply they proffered most ample assurances it was made quite plain that no measures whatever had been taken in that sense beyond the stationing of soldiers outside of the foreign embassies and legations and the foreign banks. I concluded by stating that I would be glad to see them at any time they wished to call here.
(signed) Benjamin Sumner Welles

--◊◊◊--0--◊◊◊--

BENJAMIN SUMNER WELLES, US AMBASSADOR IN CUBA, WRITES TO
CORDELL HULL, US SECRETARY OF STATE
Havana, September 5, 1933   [Received 1:45 p.m.]

The Secretary of War Dr. Ferrer has just left me. He advises me that he has just held an interview with the members of the executive committee of the revolutionary group and has advised them that the entire Cabinet of President Céspedes would proffer their resignations if the revolutionary group would support President Céspedes and enter his Cabinet. The reply was given that President Céspedes had already been deposed and that the revolutionary group was in control of the Republic.

Dr. Ferrer informs me that at the Cabinet meeting which President Céspedes will have immediately after his arrival in Havana at 11:30 his Cabinet will advise him to make no effort to maintain himself in power since all of the armed forces of the Republic are in mutiny and he can count on only moral support which is not effective in this moment.

I have called for 12:30 a meeting of the following leaders: Colonel Mendieta, Colonel Méndez Peñate, General Menocal, Dr. Miguel Mariano Gómez, Dr. Martínez Sáenz, and Dr. Saladrigas. I shall advise the Department immediately by telegraph of the result of my interview with them.

(signed) Benjamin Sumner Welles

--◊◊◊--0--◊◊◊--

BENJAMIN SUMNER WELLES, US AMBASSADOR IN CUBA, WRITES TO **CORDELL HULL,** US SECRETARY OF STATE

Havana, September 5, 1933   [Received 5:05 p.m.]

At 1 p.m. the Céspedes Cabinet resigned, and President Céspedes left the Palace to go to his own house. Very little disorder took place. Immediately thereafter the Committee of five members of the revolutionary group took possession of the Palace as the executive power of the Cuban Republic. The members of the Committee are the following: Sergio Carbó; José Miguel Irizarri, a radical of the extreme type who is a law partner of General Menocal's son-in-law; Professors Guillermo Portela and Grau San Martín of the University of Havana, both of whom are extreme radicals; Porfirio Franca, a supposedly conservative business man of good reputation who is being used as window dressing. Immediately before the transfer of power at the Palace I had the conference with the political leaders referred to in my telegram No. 194, September 5, noon. I explained to them my own view of the situation and suggested that through consultation among themselves they determine whether they can devise any plan to prevent the utter break-down of government which in my judgment is inevitable under the present regime. They agreed to do so although with some reluctance on the part of General Menocal and arranged to return to the Embassy at 5 o'clock to advise me of their decisions.

(signed) Benjamin Sumner Welles

--◊◊◊--0--◊◊◊--

Gradually, events are increasing the presence and role of **Sergeant Fulgencio Batista** in the events after the fall of Machado. *Photo on top*: US Ambassador **Sumner Wells** meets **Batista**. *Photo at center*: Batista and Grau begin to develop a mutually rewarding friendship. *Photo below:* all the former high-rank military took refuge at the **Hotel Nacional** and the low-rank soldiers confront them with the choice of surrender or death. An unsuspecting Hotel resident, US Ambassador Sumner Wells, had to leave in panic.

Memorandum of Telephone Conversations Between
Cordell Hull, US Secretary of State and
Benjamin Sumner Welles Ambassador in Cuba
September 5, 1933, 5:30 p.m., and between

Jefferson Thomas Caffery, US Under Secretary of State and **Benjamin Sumner Welles** Ambassador in Cuba
September 5, 1933, 6:15 p.m.,

Conversation started at 5:15 o'clock between Mr. Sumner and the Ambassador:

SECRETARY: How are things coming along by this time?

AMBASSADOR: I think that the situation is gradually getting worse. I have had a conference with the political leaders of the Republic, and they are of the opinion that it would be wise to land a certain number of troops from the American ship. It would be my idea that what we would do in that case would be to have a certain number come to the Embassy as a guard and a certain number to the National Hotel. It would not imply any patrolling of streets or anything of that kind. The difficulty is that we have only 50 men on the *McFarland*, which is now in port, to be brought ashore. That number is not enough to make it wise to bring them ashore. Is the *Richmond* arriving tomorrow?

SECRETARY: I do not think it can get there before tomorrow morning. That is, the *Richmond* from the Canal Zone. There is no other battleship on the way just yet. We can take this matter up and have a conference about it. How would we define our policy that would contemplate what you suggest?

AMBASSADOR: Our policy would simply be on the ground of protection of the American Embassy and the protection of American nationals.

SECRETARY: Have you any other suggestions?

AMBASSADOR: The political leaders say that a government will be restored with the support of all the army officers, but this can only be accomplished with the aid of an American guard and thepresent small number of our men offshore is insufficient.

USS light Cruiser Richmond (CL-9) 1920-1946

***Conversation resumed at 6:15 o'clock between
Mr. Caffery and the Ambassador:***

AMBASSADOR: I think that it is indispensable that men be brought from the ship to the Embassy and to the hotel. A crowd is gathering in front of the Embassy now and there is no protection whatever except a few policemen we have in the Embassy building. I am not at all certain what will happen before very long if we do not have any men here.

MR. CAFFERY: You have no guard there?

AMBASSADOR: No guard anywhere. There is absolutely no semblance of order of any kind. I could not hear whether the Secretary said the *Richmond* is arriving tomorrow.

MR. CAFFERY: No, the *Richmond* is not due to arrive until Thursday—I think in the early afternoon.

AMBASSADOR: What time does the *Bainbridge* get here? Tomorrow, in the early afternoon?

MR. CAFFERY: Not early-I think, late afternoon. Now the *Mississippi* is on the way. She is 32,000 tons.

AMBASSADOR: The situation is increasingly serious here. What time will the *Mississippi* get here?

MR. CAFFERY: She cannot make it under three days. She is at Hampton Roads.

AMBASSADOR: I have just had another meeting with the political leaders and they seem to be all of the opinion that the only possible way is for a temporary landing of possibly a thousand men until a new government can be restored with the cooperation of all them—with all of the officers who are loyal to constitutional government and who have not gone over to the other side.

MR. CAFFERY: It is better to cable the whole thing. We miss words.

AMBASSADOR: All right. This evening I think we will have some men come from the *McFarland* to the Embassy and the hotel.

MR. CAFFERY: Have you seen anything more of the soldiers? Or the radical element who were allied with them?

AMBASSADOR: There is absolutely no evidence of any intention to maintain order. The soldiers are going anywhere that they want and pay no attention whatever to anyone's objections.

MR. CAFFERY: But you have not seen them any more yourself.

AMBASSADOR: No, not since the revolutionary group took over control of the Palace.

MR. CAFFERY: Only two of them came to see you this morning.

AMBASSADOR: Those two are supposed to be the head people, but I have heard nothing from them since. I will cable fully.

MR. CAFFERY: The Secretary, who is here now, asks if you know whether they have any intention of trying to see you again.

AMBASSADOR: I am unable to hear what you say.

(Note:—The last paragraph was repeated several times, but the Ambassador was unable to understand what was said.)

--◊◊◊--0--◊◊◊--

Memorandum of Telephone Conversations Between

Cordell Hull, US Secretary of State and
Benjamin Sumner Welles Ambassador in Cuba
September 5, 1933, 7:00 p.m.,

SECRETARY: I was just talking with the President and he agrees of course that if you or any of your folks in the Embassy are in physical danger, you should call on the commander to send all possible aid to you ashore.

AMBASSADOR: All right.

SECRETARY: But if you are not in physical danger, we are inclined to the opinion here that such a small number sent ashore might provoke trouble rather than quiet trouble.

AMBASSADOR: I understand that perfectly. I am quite in accord. I have not sent for them and am not going to unless I consider it necessary.

SECRETARY: By the time the battleship, the *Mississippi*, gets down there, and it is on its way, we can work out some of these other matters. But if we just have fifty men there for the moral effect and not necessarily to protect the Embassy from physical violence, we agree with you that it would probably be inadvisable and that we should work out a broader policy on that question.

AMBASSADOR: I quite agree, and I do not want to do it unless I cannot possibly help it. And only in an emergency to keep the embassy from being entered.

SECRETARY: Are the *de facto* people doing anything to restore order?

AMBASSADOR: I have one in the embassy now talking to me about it.

SECRETARY: I would make very sweeping demands upon them to protect the embassy and all foreigners.

AMBASSADOR: I am doing that, but as you understand it is impossible for them to attempt to control things.

SECRETARY: We will keep in touch with you in every way possible.

AMBASSADOR: Thank you so much. I will not take any steps of that kind unless I believe it indispensable.

SECRETARY: Unless there is physical danger to you folks in the Embassy.

--◊◊◊--0--◊◊◊--

BENJAMIN SUMNER WELLES, US AMBASSADOR IN CUBA, WRITES TO
CORDELL HULL, US SECRETARY OF STATE

Havana, September 5, 1933   [Received 11:20 p.m.]

At 5 o'clock my meeting with the political leaders, referred to in my telegram 195, took place at the Embassy. It was attended by all those present in the morning except for General Menocal who sent word that he had no concrete solution to propose yet. The opinion expressed by all was that the only possibility of avoiding American intervention was for the installation of a government composed of the chiefs of all the political groups. Before Colonel Mendieta's arrival the other leaders stated that Colonel Mendieta was by far the most acceptable man as head of the new government. Investigation had proved that the officers of the Army had refused to enter into any conversations with the present revolutionary group in control but would support any representative government such as that proposed.

It was the unanimous opinion that the enlisted men in great part would be loyal to their officers if they could be free from the control of the non-commissioned officers. It was the unanimous opinion likewise that the only way in which a government of the character proposed could be maintained in power, until a new Army could be organized under the Cuban Army officers, was for the maintenance of order in Havana and Santiago de Cuba and perhaps one or two other points in the island by American Marines. They were emphatic in their declaration that the present revolutionary group could not remain in control for more than a few days and would be then in turn forced to give way to an out and out Communist organization.

The tentative project as outlined to me is not yet entirely satisfactory, as many important details have not been determined upon. I shall be advised later tonight what the final decision may be.

Conversations have likewise been held this evening between the leaders of the Unión Nacionalista Party, Dr. Gómez and the two more Conservative members of the revolutionary group in control of the government, namely, Messrs. Grau San Martín and Franca, to ascertain whether the latter would agree to enter the government of concentration proposed. The tentative proposal appears to have been rejected.

Dr. Grau San Martín has just called to see me, and I have impressed upon him the fact that my Government would require of any government in Cuba the protection of life and property of American citizens. He is utterly impractical and appears to be obsessed with the idea that the soldiers are so devoted to the ideals of the "revolution", as he terms the mutiny, that they will take it upon themselves without any orders to maintain order and to guarantee life and property. He did say, however, that an attempt would be made to persuade the lower-ranking officers of the Army

Photos, on top: **Ramón Grau, Sergio Carbó** and **Fulgencio Batista** in the days prior to the **Pentarquía** (Pentarchy), before Batista's **September 4** *Coup d'État*. *At the center*, the **Pentarquía**: **Porfirio Franca, José Miguel Irizarry, Guillermo Portela, Ramón Grau San Martín** and **Sergio Carbó**. It ruled from September 4, 1933 to September 10, 1933. **Batista** had been offered to be part of the Pentarchy but declined to belong. Batista is sitting at the right end of the group, next to Sergio Carbó.

Below, when the Pentarquía is dissolved, Grau assumes the Presidency. Unfortunately for him, it was the first time the US refused to recognize a Cuban government, and his government fell. Batista was then fully in charge of the country.

to support the group in control of the government and in that event, they would be reinstated in their former positions.

(signed) Benjamin Sumner Welles

--◇◇◇--0--◇◇◇--

Memorandum of Telephone Conversations Between
Cordell Hull, US Secretary of State and
Benjamin Sumner Welles Ambassador in Cuba
September 6, 1933, 19:00 a.m.

SECRETARY: How is everything looking?

AMBASSADOR: I had four hours of sleep last night and I feel somewhat better.

SECRETARY: How are conditions?

AMBASSADOR: There was some trouble in the city last night, but not as bad as might have been expected. I think the presence of the destroyer did a great deal to prevent more disturbance. The situation in the interior seems to be becoming very serious and while Santiago during the early night was quiet, there is no word as to what happened after midnight.

SECRETARY: Have you any new suggestions over the telephone or not?

AMBASSADOR: I think I had rather keep those in the cables, Mr. Secretary. I have gone into full detail in the cable I am sending you now.

SECRETARY: We have been discussing this last evening and this morning as best we could. It seems to us that the whole thing down there revolves around the army, and the question comes up with us as to whether the landing of men before we are absolutely compelled to do so if we should land a thousand men there—it would in all probability mean intervention, and while we will not hesitate to go in if compelled to, we do not want to unless compelled. Because if we must go in there again, we will never be able to come out and we will have on our hands the trouble of thirty years ago. We feel that if conditions would justify your continuing your present and past policy of absolute neutrality towards each group and especially towards the group in power, Keeping their confidence and goodwill as you have with each group in the past, that that would give the Cubans themselves all the more opportunity to do something, to take steps to preserve some degree of law and order. Then when the crisis has passed there would be an opportunity to reorganize the present army to whatever extent they might feel would be helpful, as that cannot be done on short order if undertaken and if considered desirable. Now if in the meantime some of our American friends should get unduly alarmed, we might consider dropping submarine destroyers in at such ports as Guantanamo, Santiago and Cienfuegos for the time being. Everything is revolving around the army now and if they were to receive some cooperation from the different leaders, whether they are immediately a part of the army or not but very helpful. At a distance several of us are wondering how long any group of leaders representing each faction even would stay in power if they were put in, in view of the experience of Céspedes and those people, and that means the army, as now constituted, for the time being is in supreme control.

AMBASSADOR: I am in full accord with what you say.

SECRETARY: I am just getting these facts before you for what they may be worth, because we have implicit confidence in your judgment and in your ability to keep yourself ingratiated with all groups while we are giving Cuba and the dominant forces in it an opportunity to work out of the snarl or to take such steps as would make intervention by us unnecessary. I do not know whether I have said anything at all which would fit in there according to your judgment, but I wanted to get these things before you.

AMBASSADOR: I agree absolutely with everything you have said. One or two members of the present group in power I know, and one was here with me for an hour and a half last night. I will be in touch with them constantly, but for the time even to consider recognizing any government of this character, in my opinion.

SECRETARY: Until it has shown its ability to preserve law and order.

AMBASSADOR: What they want is an expression of opinion from me and I have refused to give any opinion whatever except to insist on the maintenance of orders.

SECRETARY: It is natural that from their viewpoint they would be urging us, just like our Chamber of Commerce friend last night, to rush in and intervene. But of course, you and I are keeping our eyes on the other side of the thing as well and we can only hope that those people will be patient and give such cooperation as the dominant forces are willing to receive. Have you anything further to suggest or to say over the telephone?

AMBASSADOR: No. I had rather have the suggestion come to you in cable form.

SECRETARY: We will keep in touch with you by cable and over the telephone.

AMBASSADOR: I will keep you informed all the time during the day.

BENJAMIN SUMNER WELLES, US AMBASSADOR IN CUBA, WRITES TO
CORDELL HULL, US SECRETARY OF STATE

Havana, September 6, 1933

I had a further meeting at 11 o'clock last night with the political leaders mentioned in my telegram 199, September 5, 9 p.m. I told them that upon careful consideration the basis of the proposal outlined to me by them, as reported in my telegram referred to, appeared to me undesirable inasmuch as it required the Government of the United States to assume responsibility for the maintenance of order in Cuba through the presence on Cuban territory of American armed forces whose number would not be determined in advance and the length of whose stay in Cuba might be for a protracted period. I further said that in my judgment action of this kind by the United States would constitute intervention even though limited in scope and intention and would be considered as intervention by the Cuban people and by the other nations of the world. I concluded by stating that I felt that the Cuban people themselves should make every possible effort to solve their own problems through their own agencies and that if we landed forces here to help install a new government, we would be justly accused of overthrowing the present regime.

As the result of my conversation the political leaders referred to have a further conference with Messrs. Grau San Martín and Franca. They then returned to see me at 1 o'clock this morning. They told me that they had advised these members of the revolutionary group in control of the government that in view of the fact that the group now in control had announced for government, program of government [sic] almost identically the same points as those agreed upon by the Céspedes government they and their followers would agree to lend support to the present government provided that the "revolutionary group was able to maintain order. They stated that in their opinion this was indispensable. Dr. Gómez and Colonel Mendieta further informed me that they had been assured that the revolutionary group desire to reappoint all of the junior officers of the Army up to and including the rank of Major in the course of the next 24 hours except in those instances where charges of crime had been preferred against them.

At approximately the same time the leaders of the ABC informed me that they had issued a statement announcing their intention to support the program of the revolutionary group but otherwise maintaining an attitude of *"watchful waiting".* In this manner the leading political forces of the country have made clear their intention not to attempt for the present to overthrow the present regime and to support the program for a constitutional assembly and for national elections.

I feel confident that the policy we have adopted during the past 2 days is the correct one. The presence in the harbor of Havana yesterday afternoon of an American destroyer and the announcement which the local newspapers made much of that three other American warships were on their way to Cuban waters has had a very sobering effect and has been highly useful in preventing untrammeled disorder. I have, made it perfectly clear to the members of the present regime that my Government will insist upon the maintenance of public order and the protection of foreign life and property. At the same time, I have stated emphatically that the United States had no intention of intervening provided life and property were fully protected. There is not one political leader with whom I have talked who did not of his own initiative suggest the dispatch of American warships and for the Department's confidential information the leaders of even so radical a group as the ABC urgently requested me yesterday afternoon to insist that the Department authorize the landing of American Marines both in Havana and in Santiago. The local press without exception is commenting favorably on the attitude assumed by the United States Government.

For the moment therefore the situation in Havana appears to be slightly more favorable than it did yesterday in so far as for the time being the early desire of the powerful political groups overthrow immediately the present regime has been avoided. As an indication of this intention yesterday afternoon at 2 o'clock a group of 1,500 members of the ABC, fully armed, assembled in the headquarters of the organization with the intention of leaving immediately for Camp Columbia in order to take possession of the barracks there by force. They were only prevented from doing so by the personal influence over them of Dr. Martínez Sáenz. If this action had been taken there would have been in all probability house-to-house fighting throughout a greater portion of the city last night.

The situation is such that in my opinion it is impossible at this time to attempt to lay down any specific policy other than the determination by us to avoid any act of intervention if life and property can be guaranteed. I feel that it would be decidedly prejudicial even to consider official recognition by the United States of this regime, certainly for some time to come. The government of Cuba today is an undisciplined group of individuals of divergent tendencies representing the most irresponsible elements in the city of Havana with practically no support whatsoever outside the capital. The attitude adopted by the major political organizations may keep things quiet for a time. For the moment I feel the only policy we can adopt is to solve each problem as it is presented in the light of immediate circumstances.

(signed) Benjamin Sumner Welles

--◊◊◊--0--◊◊◊--

Photos, top to bottom: a view of **Havana in 1933**; **Dr. Ramón Grau San Martín's** home (he called it "*la choza,*") at Quinta Avenida and 14th street in Miramar; **the ABC headquarters** at Neptuno Street near Belascoaín, in Havana.

Memorandum by Edwin C. Wilson,
Chief of the US Division of Latin American Affairs
September 6, 1933

At my request the following came individually to see me today:

The Minister of Guatemala, Dr. Recinos,
The Minister of the Dominican Republic, Mr. Despradel,
The Minister of Paraguay, Dr. Bordenave,
The Minister of Honduras, Dr. Paz,
The Minister of Haiti, M. Bellegarde,
The Chargé d'Affaires of Costa Rica, Mr. González,
The Chargé d'Affaires of Nicaragua, Dr. Debayle.
The Secretary of the Peruvian Embassy, Mr. Mendoza, the Ambassador being absent,
The Secretary of the Venezuelan Legation, Mr. Rivero, the Minister being absent,
The Secretary of the Panamanian Legation, Mr. Chevalier, the Minister being absent.

I explained to each of the foregoing gentlemen the situation in Cuba. In brief, I spoke of the condition which arose in Cuba a few weeks ago which had made it necessary for us to send some destroyers there. I said that at that time we had taken particular care to make our position clear, to the effect that there was no thought of intervention or interference with Cuban political affairs, but that the ships were sent to Cuba for the purpose of protecting American lives. The situation had cleared up at that time and the ships were withdrawn. Unfortunately, a new situation had now developed in Cuba, which appeared very serious, and we again found it necessary to send ships there for the purpose of protecting Americans if this should be necessary. I said that we attached great importance to the opinion of the Governments and people of the Americas and for this reason was explaining the situation and again desired to make it clear that we were not contemplating intervention or interference in Cuban affairs, but that our most sincere hope was that the Cubans would themselves work out a Cuban solution of their difficulties.

I received a very sympathetic response from all the above-mentioned gentlemen. In particular, the Ministers of Guatemala, Paraguay and Honduras expressed their full appreciation of the attitude of this Government towards Cuba, said that of course the United States had a right to intervene, and that they thought our effort to avoid intervention and to let the Cubans work out their own problems was making a fine impression in Latin America. All these diplomatic representatives stated that they would inform their Governments at once of the conversation. They all appeared to appreciate being informed.

(signed) Edwin C. Wilson

--◊◊◊--O--◊◊◊--

EDWARD LAWTON, US CHARGÉ OF AFFAIRS IN GUATEMALA, WRITES TO
CORDELL HULL, US SECRETARY OF STATE

Guatemala, September 6, 1933

Minister of Foreign Affairs requested me this afternoon to inform you that President Ubico feels the Cuban situation is exceedingly grave principally because of Communistic tendencies. Consequently, he is of the opinion that American intervention is essential to preserve order and insure establishment of constitutional government.
(signed) Edward Lawton

--◊◊◊--0--◊◊◊--

JOSEPHUS DANIELS, US AMBASSADOR TO MEXICO, WRITES TO
CORDELL HULL, US SECRETARY OF STATE

Mexico, September 6, 1933

Have just conferred with Dr. José Manuel Puig Casauranc, Secretary of State of Mexico at his request. Government here is seriously disturbed over fear of intervention in Cuba. Puig says he knows the four men composing junta are educated men with good background and no taint of Communism. He believes that they will organize good government. Mexican Government believes new order should be given sympathy and help. Puig believes and I concur that intervention would impair Pan American friendly relations and might in advance destroy the hopes in connection with the Montevideo Conference. If situation in Cuba demands outside action, I strongly urge that Mexico and ABCP countries of South America be asked to cooperate in restoring peaceful conditions and giving Cubans help in setting up a stable government.
(signed) Josephus Daniels

--◊◊◊--0--◊◊◊--

JOSÉ M. PUIG CASAURANC, MEXICO SECRETARY OF STATE, WRITES TO
CORDELL HULL, US SECRETARY OF STATE

Mexico, September 7, 1933

As information supplementary to the verbal communication that our Chargé d'Affaires, Mr. Padilla-Nervo must have made this afternoon to Assistant Secretary Mr. Caffery, I take the liberty of advising Your Excellency that we have accurate data concerning personality at least four persons who are serving as members of the Executive Commission of the new government of Cuba, data indicating that they are not Communists, but persons of undoubted preparation, intellectual capacity and social responsibility.

Mr. Guillermo Portela, who is Commissioner of Foreign Relations in the new government, is professor of criminal law, a scientist of standing, with ample financial resources, of high social position, and who, as soon as the university problem arose, distinguished himself as an opponent of President Machado.

Dr. Ramón Grau San Martín, Commissioner of Public Instruction and Health, was Dean of the Medical Faculty, with non-Communistic ideas, (was) also distinguished in the university opposition to President Machado, and until recently an exile in your country.

Porfirio Franca, Commissioner of Finance, may be considered as one of the best prepared men in Cuba for that position, with the highest connections in the best banks, a man of means, of no communistic views or antecedents.

Mr. Carbó, Commissioner of Gobernación, Commerce and War, was some years ago Consul of his country; he has been and is manager of the periodical, *La Semana*. There could be no basis for the supposition of his communist affiliations due solely to the fact of (his) having visited in Moscow and then written a book on Russia that is strictly literary. He was leader of the revolutionary movement against President Machado in 1931.

In the interest of the solidarity of the American continent and with the lofty purpose of bringing about *rapprochement* in every way we deem it our duty to submit these facts which we know to the consideration of the Department of State particularly in view of the cordial attitude of that Department in transmitting to the Government of Mexico, through Mr. Caffery, explanations of the situation in Cuba and proposals of your Government to continue its observation, assuring us that the sending of ships does not mean intervention in Cuba.

(signed) J.M. Puig Casaurano

--◊◊◊--0--◊◊◊--

CORDELL HULL, US SECRETARY OF STATE , WRITES TO

JOSÉ M. PUIG CASAURANC, MEXICO SECRETARY OF STATE

Washington, September 7, 1933

I greatly appreciate Your Excellency's courteous telegram and your kindness in furnishing me the information therein contained. As President Roosevelt and Mr. Caffery said yesterday to Mr. Padilla-Nervo in informing him of the situation in Cuba, we have sent ships to that country solely as a precautionary measure and there is not the slightest intention of intervening or interfering in Cuba's domestic affairs.

It is our fervent hope, which I am sure Your Excellency shares, that the Cubans themselves will work out in a peaceful and orderly manner a Cuban solution of their own difficulties. Certainly no one in the world will be more relieved and thankful than I if this takes place.

(signed) Cordell Hull

--◊◊◊--0--◊◊◊--

BENJAMIN SUMNER WELLES, US AMBASSADOR IN CUBA, WRITES TO **CORDELL HULL,** US SECRETARY OF STATE

Havana, September 7, 1933   [Received 4:10 p.m.]

Late last night Dr. Horacio Ferrer, Secretary of War in the Céspedes Cabinet, called to see me. He told me that he had spent the preceding 24 hours in continuous conferences with political leaders of all the groups which had supported the Céspedes Government and that the plan which he would outline to me met with the approval and support of all of them. He told me that he had been in touch with the sergeants in control of the Fortress Cabana; that they realized that they had been deceived in participating in the mutiny and that they were prepared to make any reparation for their action. They had prepared a written communication in this sense addressed to President Céspedes. Dr. Ferrer stated that he had arranged with them that they should request of the revolutionary group, which is now attempting to persuade the officers to resume their positions, the reappointment of Major Cardenas the former Commander of Cabana and all the former subordinate officers in whom Dr. Ferrer states he has implicit confidence; that as soon as these preliminary measures had been taken Dr. Ferrer accompanied by a group of some 80 loyal officers would proceed tomorrow, Friday, night to the Cabaña Fortress with President Céspedes and several other members of his Cabinet and that early Saturday morning he would proclaim the support of La Cabaña fortress to the legitimate Government of President Céspedes. He informed me that the Fortress was impregnable and that there was both food and water and enough ammunition for them to hold out if necessary, for a period of at least 2 months. Dr. Ferrer assured me that all the soldiers and non-commissioned officers in La Cabana would be loyal to him but that should there be any few disloyal individuals they would be immediately ejected. He stated that he had already been in touch with the officers of the military forces of Matanzas and Pillar del Río as well as in other portions of the Republic and that as soon as the proclamation from Cabana has been issued the loyal troops and officers throughout the country would make a simultaneous proclamation. He was confident that within a very brief period the present regime would be overthrown.

He inquired whether, should this action be taken, and should the Céspedes Government make such request the Government of the

United States would be willing to land troops from the battleships now due to arrive at Cojimar, immediately to the east of Cabana Fortress, in order to assist the Céspedes Government in maintaining order. He stated of his own initiative that he fully understood my position and that of my Government and that he wished merely to inform me of the plans which he had made without expecting or desiring any assurances of any character from me, and that he would follow through the plan he had in mind no matter what action the United States Government might take.

I told him I deeply appreciated his advising me of his intentions; that of course, as he stated, it was impossible for me to participate even tacitly in the elaboration of his plans; and that I could make no commitments to him at this time with regard to the landing of American troops.

Dr. Ferrer stated that the Céspedes Government was still the constitutional and recognized Government of Cuba; that President Céspedes had left the Palace through **force majeure** and had accepted the declaration of the revolutionary group that he had been "deposed" since he had no armed forces to keep him in power but that he had not resigned either orally or in writing.

If the plan formulated by Dr. Ferrer were carried out successfully, I desire to lay the following considerations before the President and yourself. The Céspedes Government came into power through constitutional procedure and was immediately recognized by all the nation's having diplomatic relations with Cuba including the Latin American Republics as the legitimate Government of Cuba. The President and his Cabinet have not voluntarily resigned but have had to give in in the face of a mutiny in the Army. If the legitimate and recognized Government of Cuba can make an effective demonstration of its intention to reestablish itself, it would most decidedly appear to me to be in the best interest of the United States Government to afford them immediate support. Any solution of this character is more advantageous to our interests and to our policy than full intervention and the possible necessity of an American Military Government. What I purpose would be a strictly limited intervention of the following nature:

The Céspedes Government should be permitted to function freely in the same manner as it did until the time of its overthrow, having full control of every branch of the Government. It is obvious, of course, that with a great portion of the Army in mutiny it could not maintain itself in power in any satisfactory manner unless the United States Government were willing, should it so request, to lend its assistance in the maintenance of public order until the Cuban Government had been afforded the time sufficient, through utilizing the services of the loyal officers of the Cuban Army, to form a new Army for which it would possess a nucleus in the troops which are still loyal and detachments of the rural guard, most of whom have not come out in support of the present regime.

Photos, on top: The **Cabinet** formed by Dr. Grau in September 13, 1933, integrated by distinguished men. *Seated in the picture, left to right:* **Col. Julio Aguado, Col. Manuel Despaigne, Dr. Grau, Dr. Carlos Findlay, Gustavo Moreno. Standing up, Dr. Manuel Costales Latatúd, Dr. Rios Balmaseda, Antonio Guiteras** and **Ramiro Casablanca**. *At the center*: the support of the armed forces, showing **Batista** with the Minister of the Interior **Antonio Guiteras**; *On the bottom:* the founding members of the ***Partido Revolucionario Cubano (PRC)***, with Grau (sitting in the center) as president, later in 1934.

Such policy on our part would presumably entail the landing of a considerable force at Havana and lesser forces in certain of the more important ports of the Republic.

If through the lending of a police force to the legitimate Government of Cuba for a comparative brief period we can assist the Céspedes Government to function, in all probability the Constitutional Assembly and the national elections which the Cuban people unanimously desire, could be held within less than a year's time with the result that a new constitutional Government in Cuba would come into power and by that time there will be functioning a Cuban Army capable of maintaining that Government in power and guaranteeing life and property and public order.

The disadvantages of this policy as I see them lie solely in the fact that we will incur the violent animosity of the extreme radical and communist groups in Cuba who will be vociferous in stating that we have supported the Céspedes Government because that Government was prepared to give protection to American interests in Cuba and that our policy is solely due to mercenary motives. It is worth emphasizing, however, that we always have had and always will have the animosity of this group and that the adoption of the measures above indicated will merely offer them an excellent opportunity for attack. Consequently, since I sincerely believe that the necessity of full intervention on our part is to be avoided at all hazards, the limited and restricted form of intervention above outlined would be infinitely preferable. When the recognized and legitimate government of a neighboring republic with which republic we have special contractual obligations, is confronted by mutiny in the army and can only maintain order and carry through its program of holding elections for a permanent constitutional government through the assistance of an armed force lent by the United States as a policing power, it would seem to me to be in our best interests to lend such assistance, and it would further seem to me that since the full facts of the situation here have been fully explained to the representatives of the Latin American countries, the landing of such assistance would most decidedly be construed as well within the limits of the policy of the *"good neighbor"* which we have done our utmost to demonstrate in our relations with the Cuban people during the past 5 months.

If Dr. Ferrer's plan is carried through immediate action by us will undoubtedly be required if such action is to be of any effective assistance. I consequently request instructions from the President and yourself at the earliest possible moment in order that I may be fully prepared to carry out such instructions whom [*when?*] the appropriate moment arrives.

(signed) Benjamin Sumner Welles

--◊◊◊--0--◊◊◊--

Memorandum from **Benjamin Sumner Welles,** to
Cordell Hull, US Secretary of State

September 7, 1933

In the conversation carried on to-day at one o'clock p.m., with the Assistant Secretary of State, Mr. Caffery, the Ambassador of Cuba, authorized by the Executive Commission of Government, set forth the following points:

First. The new Government of Cuba does not correspond to trends of a Communistic character; neither are the members composing it Communists. The suspicion that has arisen to that effect is due to the junta form of government which was adopted with the intention of protecting it from intimate political complications which do not affect the nature of the provisional regime.

Second. The elements composing the Executive Commission are not Communists nor were they the originators or leaders of the movement which placed them in the exercise of public power. The leaders of the movement, demonstrating exceptional disinterestedness, did not appropriate for themselves the fruits of the victory, and taking as their aim the greatest advantages of the country, entrusted the function of government to the persons whom they considered fitted for the mandate.

Third. Now order is being preserved throughout the Republic. The disorders that have taken place since the 4th instant have been of less importance than those which occurred under the preceding administration. And the events that transpired in some sugar centers, are not the consequence of the political and economic character of the present regime, but a continuation of the disturbances, of that kind, which were happening under the authority of the Government which terminated on the 5th.

Fourth. For the purpose of restoring the discipline and authority of the Army, the Executive Commission has decided to reestablish, and is reestablishing the commanders and officers of all arms to their corresponding grades and commands. In addition to the respect that the whole country is showing the Executive Commission, the reintegration of the Army, which is being accomplished with all possible speed, permits of the assurance that the life, property and liberty of the citizens are receiving full protection in the Republic.

Fifth. The idea that the Executive Commission is the result of the *coup* of a faction which can give it only a precarious and ephemeral existence is derived from vague reports, that are often exaggerated, with respect to the true situation now prevailing in Cuba; but it loses all appearance of reality by the fact of its having been put in contact with all sectors of those who were in opposition to the dictatorship, in order to form a strong cabinet of National Concentration in which there are truly represented all the militant groups that fought for the purpose of restoring in the Republic, right, civil liberties, the laws and the honor of the people as an homage to civilization. The Executive Commission, dedicated today to the accomplishment of this powerful coordination of legitimate desires and aspirations, for the welfare and prosperity of Cuba, trusts that before the dawn of tomorrow the said Cabinet, the task of which is to clothe the Government with the sublime confidence and the full representation of the Cuban people, will have been constituted.

(signed) Benjamin Sumner Welles

--◇◇◇--O--◇◇◇--

BENJAMIN SUMNER WELLES, US AMBASSADOR IN CUBA, WRITES TO **CORDELL HULL,** US SECRETARY OF STATE

Havana, September 7, 1933   [Received 4:20 p.m.]

The so-called Student Council last night determined to arrest Dr. Torriente and Colonel Mendieta, and likewise Drs. Martínez Sáenz, and Saladrigas. All of them left their homes and have gone into hiding, although in the case of the first two I do not believe that there is any intention of doing them any bodily harm.

Alfred Botet, who was a representative of the ABC in the revolutionary junta in New York City, called to see me this morning to inform me that the ABC are persuading some of the younger officers, who are identified with them, to return to their troops at Camp Columbia; tomorrow afternoon, Friday, in order to assist in the plan referred to in my telegram 206, September 7, noon.

The feeling in the city is increasingly tense and while the revolutionary group in control continues to issue reassuring statements as to the maintenance of order it seems to be the consensus that grave disorder may develop soon.

(signed) Benjamin Sumner Welles

--◇◇◇--O--◇◇◇--

BENJAMIN SUMNER WELLES, US AMBASSADOR IN CUBA, WRITES TO **CORDELL HULL,** US SECRETARY OF STATE

Havana, September 7, 1933   [Received 7:57 p.m.]

It is my impression that the situation here is breaking fast. Dr. Belt, Secretary of Public Instruction in the Céspedes Cabinet, has just called to inform me that Sergeant Batista has requested an interview with President Céspedes in order to inform him that the Army wishes to place itself at his disposal. Dr. Belt advises me that he is to act as intermediary since he has refused to permit the President to receive Batista. He further informs me that Carbó, one of the five members of the revolutionary group, has fled and that the others are only waiting in order to seek some solution which will guarantee their safety.

The sergeants and the ringleaders of the mutiny are in a state of panic and I have recommended to President Céspedes that he not turn down a request made by them to place themselves at his orders in view of the fact that if they are denied any hope they may get entirely beyond control tonight.

A large Communist demonstration to protest against everything and in particular against the United States and to urge the creation of a Soviet Government was scheduled to take place at 4 o'clock in the main park. Soldiers with machine guns have gone to the park and I am reliably informed that the meeting scheduled will not take place.

I am beginning to have the hope that the situation may turn out so that we may be able to avoid any act of intervention other than that of the landing of a moderate force, at the request of President Céspedes, to assist his Government, if it is reconstituted, in maintaining order.

(signed) Benjamin Sumner Welles

--◊◊◊--O--◊◊◊--

JOSEPHUS DANIELS, US AMBASSADOR TO MEXICO, WRITES TO
CORDELL HULL, US SECRETARY OF STATE

Mexico, September 7, 1933   [Received 9:00 p.m.]

Minister for Foreign Affairs told me this morning that he was telegraphing Mexican representatives in important South American countries to endeavor to secure cooperation of respective countries in bringing influence to bear on present Cuban Government to maintain order and to protect foreign interests in Cuba. Foreign Office has just telephoned that telegrams have been sent to Argentina, Brazil and Chile and that Mexican Chargé d'Affaires had been fully informed of Mexican position.

(signed) Josephus Daniels

--◊◊◊--O--◊◊◊--

Memorandum from **CORDELL HULL,** US SECRETARY OF STATE

September 7, 1933

The French Ambassador called and made inquiry about conditions in Cuba and stated he had just been informed that a French

The New York Times.

LATE CITY EDITION

FARLEY THREATENS MAIL FRAUD ACTION IN NRA VIOLATIONS

MACHADO FLIES TO A SECRET REFUGE; DE CESPEDES MADE PRESIDENT OF CUBA; 18 KILLED AS MOBS AVENGE MURDERS

DE VALERA SAYS AIM IS TO BAR CIVIL WAR

MACHADO NOW ON 'LEAVE'

CUBANS HERE HAIL CHOICE OF CESPEDES

ROOSEVELT SPEEDS CUBAN TRADE PACT

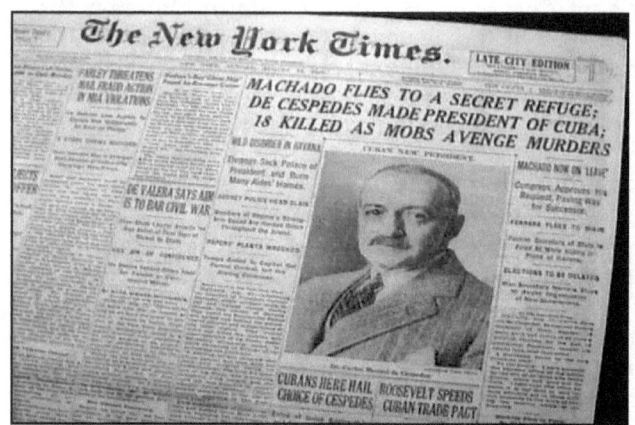

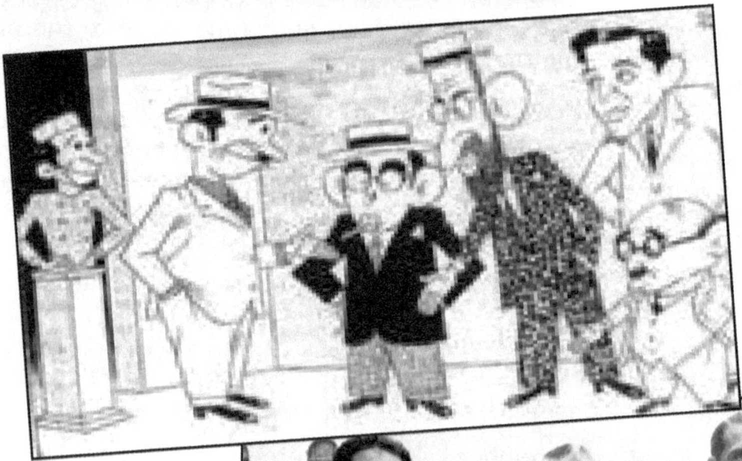

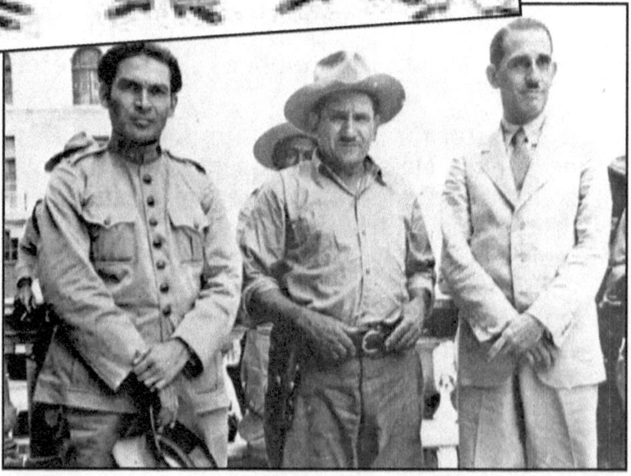

The **New York Times** reported on the events in Cuba, two days after the fall of Machado; a cartoon with a group of politicians who *"want to enter the theater to see the movie;"* finally, **Grau** and **Batista** with **Juan Blas Hernández** (*el Sandino de Cuba*), a prominent figure in the struggle against Machado, allegedly murdered by Batista's army after he surrendered at *Atarés Castle* on November 9, 1933 national had been killed by disorderly forces at Santiago. I expressed deep regret at this news and described fully to him the many precautionary steps the United States Government had taken, from the very hour that information reached Washington of the present revolution, to allay the lawless movements and to encourage the law-abiding forces of Cuba to create at the earliest possible moment a stable government that could maintain law and order. The Ambassador seemed pleased at the idea that our government had not overlooked a single precautionary step that might be helpful. I stated to him that I had talked to Ambassador Welles over the telephone an hour ago and he informed me at the time that conditions were grave in Santiago, although they had been quiet early in the morning. I added that he had not given me any information of the killing of the Frenchman or of any other person.

I assured the Ambassador that our government would continue to take every possible precautionary step in the interest of law and order in Cuba and that we would place at his disposal any and all information we might receive from there.

(signed) Cordell Hull

--◇◇◇--0--◇◇◇--

CORDELL HULL, US SECRETARY OF STATE, WRITES TO
BENJAMIN SUMNER WELLES, US AMBASSADOR IN CUBA

Washington, September 7, 1933

We fully appreciate the various viewpoints set forth in your telegram. However, after mature consideration, the President has decided to send you the following message:

"We feel very strongly that any promise, implied or otherwise, relating to what the United States will do under any circumstances is impossible; that it would be regarded as a breach of neutrality, as favoring one faction out of many, as attempting to set up a government which would be regarded by the whole world, and especially throughout Latin America, as a creation and creature of the American Government."

The President's conversations with the ABC representatives have received widespread approval in the United States and throughout Latin America and any action contrary to the policy outlined therein would have disastrous effects.

The above does not mean, of course, that you should do anything to block or in the least affect any movement by any faction; in other words, strict neutrality is of the essence.

All of us appreciate the heavy load you are carrying and hope you may bear up well in order to get the best possible results in these trying circumstances.

(signed) Cordell Hull

BENJAMIN SUMNER WELLES, US AMBASSADOR IN CUBA, WRITES TO
CORDELL HULL, US SECRETARY OF STATE

Havana, September 7, 1933   [Received 8:42 p.m.]

A meeting is called for 10 o'clock tonight at the Palace which will be attended by the leaders of all political groups. I am reliably informed that the revolutionary group in control will then turn over the Government and I am further advised that President Céspedes will be restored as head of the Government.

(signed) Benjamin Sumner Welles

--◇◇◇--0--◇◇◇--

BENJAMIN SUMNER WELLES, US AMBASSADOR IN CUBA, WRITES TO
CORDELL HULL, US SECRETARY OF STATE

Havana, September 8, 1933   [Received 3:53 a.m.]

The meeting at the Palace appears to have degenerated into a fruitless prolonged argument. I have just been visited by two of the delegates of the Unión Nacionalista present who stated that Mendieta and Menocal have left in disgust and that no compromise agreement can possibly be reached. During the discussion thereof, every political sector urged the group in power to turn over the government to a legitimate government of concentration on the ground that the present government represented only the students and the extreme radicals. Finally, a subcommittee was formed but it seems improbable that any useful result can be expected from its deliberations.

(signed) Benjamin Sumner Welles

--◇◇◇--0--◇◇◇--

BENJAMIN SUMNER WELLES, US AMBASSADOR IN CUBA, WRITES TO
CORDELL HULL, US SECRETARY OF STATE

Havana, September 8, 1933   [Received 12:40 p.m.]

For the President. I have this morning conferred with Admiral Freeman. I concur thoroughly in the policy of not having more than two destroyers in Havana harbor at one time. I do, however, consider it essential that the *Richmond* should remain in the harbor until conditions are changed materially for the better. There are two immediate possibilities of danger in the city to be considered: The first is an absolutely disorganized and demoralized army of some 2,000 men who now realize their mistake and while the majority of them are anxious to find any peaceful way out of the situation they have created for themselves, another group who are in close touch with Communist leaders in Havana may resort to desperate measures if they become sufficiently drunk. The other potential danger which I consider far less important is that possibility that crowds directed by the most radical agitators may commence a demonstration against Americans in the course of which American lives and more probably American property will be jeopardized. I shall not under any conditions request the landing of a single man unless I feel that American lives are in actual immediate danger. Under these circumstances I feel it is a wise precaution to have the *Richmond* anchored in the harbor where men can be landed at short order rather than outside the harbor, which would involve considerably more time in landing men in the event of urgent need. In so far as the effect upon the populace here is concerned, there is not the slightest difference in the impression made upon them whether the *Richmond* is outside the harbor or within the harbor. I have every reason to believe that no situation where American lives are in actual danger will develop but on the other hand, appreciating the possibilities inherent in the conditions which now exist in Havana, from the many contacts which I have and from information which comes to me from all sources, I feel precautionary measures are fully warranted.

(signed) Benjamin Sumner Welles

--◇◇◇--0--◇◇◇--

H. F. ARTHUR SCHOENFELD, US AMBASSADOR IN THE DOMINICAN REPUBLIC, WRITES TO CORDELL HULL, US SECRETARY OF STATE

Santo Domingo, September 8, 1933   [Received 1:15 p.m.]

The Minister of Foreign Affairs called on me this morning by direction of the President of the Republic, to inform me that in view of the confidence of the Dominican Government in the *"purity and justice"* of the policy of the President of the United States with regard to the Cuban situation, the President of the Republic desires to assure the President of the United States of his readiness to cooperate in any way desired. The Minister of Foreign Affairs mentioned that President Trujillo had given instructions that American military aircraft could utilize freely the territory of the Dominican Republic. The Minister informed me that the aircraft of the Dominican Republic would be placed at the disposal of the American Government if so desired.

The Minister added that the Dominican Government had received from the junta in Havana a number of communications requesting recognition but that the Dominican Government had not answered these messages and would be guided in the matter of recognition by the policy of the United States.

(signed) H.F. Arthur Schoenfeld

--◇◇◇--0--◇◇◇--

BENJAMIN SUMNER WELLES, US AMBASSADOR IN CUBA, WRITES TO
CORDELL HULL, US SECRETARY OF STATE

Havana, September 8, 1933 [Received 7:35 p.m.]

For the President and the Secretary. With reference to telegram 206, September 7, noon, and to the President's message contained in your 90, September 7, 8 p.m., I desire to submit the following summary of the present situation.

The Céspedes Government that was overthrown by the Army mutiny was supported by and participated in by members of the following political parties and independent groups: the Unión Nacionalista, which is the greatest political force in Cuba today and which likewise has the growing support of the old Liberal and Conservative Parties whose members have turned almost unanimously to Mendieta, the leader of the party; the Gómez Liberals, whose strength is concentrated in Havana and Santa Clara; the original ABC, which is a very powerful party organized throughout the Republic and directed by younger men of integrity and idealism; the OCRR, a revolutionary group, particularly strong in Matanzas and Camaguey; the followers of Menocal; the UR and the UNR Revolutionary Societies, which have considerable following in Oriente and Camaguey; the university professors except for six or seven radicals; all commercial and business groups; and all of the Cuban Army officers; in other words, the enormous majority of the Cuban people.

The Army mutiny was originally engineered by a few Communist leaders in Havana under the guidance of Martínez Villena, who got the soldiers to believe that their pay was to be cut, and their numbers reduced. At the last moment the student group intervened with the connivance of Carbó and persuaded the non-commissioned officers and the soldiers to depose their officers and join in creating a government installed by the students and committed secretly to the semi-Communist program published by the extreme radical students 2 weeks ago. This new regime is supported by the students, by a few university professors, group called ABC radicals which is chiefly composed of boys from 16 to 20 years of age, by heterogeneous mass of extreme radicals of every shade, and by the enlisted men of the Army in Havana and a few other cities.

At the meeting of the political leaders held last night, which broke up at 4 a.m., and is due to resume at noon today, the leaders of the parties supporting Céspedes held firm except for Gómez who tried to carry water on both shoulders. They urged a return to legality with Céspedes as President and a Cabinet of concentration. No basis for agreement was even indicated. The ABC leaders state the aviation officers are to seize the aviation camp this afternoon. They expect to seize Sergeant Batista and the other ringleaders at Camp Columbia but if they fail the camp will be bombed by the

Photos, top to bottom: **Mendieta** and **Batista** get to be good friends after Batista received a medal and a raise in rank in 1933; a not so happy photo of **Machado** when he reached *Nassau* with his family and friends. They soon moved to a friendlier *Miami Beach*; on the balcony at the Presidential Palace, a photo of **Prío, Grau, Batista** and **Sergio Carbó**, three of them future elected Presidents of Cuba.

aviators: the Ferrer plan is to be consummated tonight if no change in the situation occurs and the loyal troops at Matanzas will then march on Havana. It may be that an overturn in government will ensue.

In my considered judgment the present revolutionary government has neither popular support nor any means at its disposal with which it can maintain order. It continues to declare that order exists throughout the Republic notwithstanding cumulative evidence from every province that complete anarchy exists and that where quiet prevails it is the quiet of panic. If this government continues much longer and no counter revolt is successfully staged by the conservative groups, it will be replaced by a soldier-workman which will last until a concerted revolt of the majority takes place.

With regard to the President's message above referred to, I concur that we should make no promise implied or explicit as to whether we would land troops to maintain order if a counterrevolution to replace the Céspedes Government were successful. I fully agree that we should take no action which would permit the creation of the belief that any Cuban government was installed by us. My previous cables will make plain that I have strictly followed this policy. I wish, however, to make it very clear that Céspedes himself, who had not resigned and is recognized by us as the constitutional President of Cuba, represents no faction but was selected by all political groups after Machado's overthrow as a man who had the confidence of all and who, since he was known to belong to no political party, could as President guarantee fair elections. Consequently if he were reinstated with the support of all the groups above mentioned and we assisted his Government either financially, economically or through affording police service until the Cuban Government could clean up the condition created by the Army mutiny, we would not be *"favoring one faction out of many"*, but lending friendly assistance at its request to a Cuban Government presided over by an impartial President and supported by every element of importance in the Republic.

Finally, nothing, in my judgment, would create more disastrous effects in Latin America than a prolonged military intervention in Cuba. If, at the request of the Cuban Government, we temporarily afford them the moral assistance a small number of Marines would create in maintaining order after such Government had established itself and until a new Army could be organized, such assistance should be construed as just as much of a friendly act as the facilitating of a loan. In the one case we would lend the Cubans police and in the other money, neither of which they possess,

I fully agree that no such action should be taken by us unless it appeared indispensable. But I feel it would be a far wiser policy to do this, if necessary, rather than permit [conditions?] in Cuba to slide until complete anarchy prevails and we are forced into a military intervention.

There is, of course, no necessity for decision on this point now. It is, however, a contingency that may arise and it is for that purpose that I requested instructions.

I would appreciate having the President's wishes communicated to me in the light of the additional considerations above indicated.

(signed) Benjamin Sumner Welles

--◊◊◊--0--◊◊◊--

BENJAMIN SUMNER WELLES, US AMBASSADOR IN CUBA, WRITES TO
CORDELL HULL, US SECRETARY OF STATE

Havana, September 8, 1933   [Received 5:40 p.m.]

The Hotel Nacional in Havana, where many of the American colony are living at the present moment and to which I myself have moved since the lease on my house expired, has been decided upon today by the Cuban Army officers as headquarters. Approximately 500 officers fully armed are in the hotel. Some of them have received information that their houses have been sacked by the soldiers this morning and many of them are in fear of their lives. They refuse to leave the hotel since they state that it is the only place open to them in Havana which can be readily defended. At the present moment there appears to be no likelihood that the soldiers will attack the officers so long as they remain in the hotel but the possibility, of course, exists and in that event the protection of the lives of Americans resident in the hotel would be a very serious problem.

(signed) Benjamin Sumner Welles

--◊◊◊--0--◊◊◊--

MEMORANDUM BY **JEFFERSON THOMAS CAFFERY,**
US UNDER SECRETARY OF STATE

Washington, September 8, 1933

Dr. Marquez Sterling, in charge of the Cuban Embassy, came in to see me this afternoon under instructions from Dr. Guillermo Portela, who is a member of the Cuban governing group, and who is in charge of foreign affairs, to ask me if it were true that the United States Government intended to disembark marines at Havana this afternoon. He said that that report had been circulated throughout the city and that as a result a very disturbed feeling prevailed there. I told him that the report was false. He asked me if we had any intention of disembarking marines. I replied, "only for the protection of lives in actual physical danger". He asked me if this might be made public at Havana. I said yes that publicity might be given to the fact that *"we have no intention of landing marines except in* the single case where they are needed for the protection of lives actually in danger".

Dr. Marquez Sterling went on to say that the Committee composed of the five members of the governing group and leaders of the opposition parties were still in session; that it meant to stay in session until it had agreed upon a President acceptable to all and a concentration cabinet representing all the groups.

As Dr. Marquez Sterling had asked me if he might speak frankly to me on the question of landing marines, I said, "I would like now to ask you frankly a question". I said, "we hear that Communist elements are having an unfortunate influence and are causing disturbances in many parts of Cuba; what do you say to that?" He said that he could assure me that there were no Communist elements in the Revolutionary Government; that on the other hand, it was quite possible that the Communists were causing disturbances in various parts of the Island but he believed that with the formation of a concentration government it would be easy to put down the Communists. I said, "what is this I hear about anti-United States propaganda in various cities?" He said, "those are only irresponsible elements; not more than ten serious people on the Island are unfriendly to your country".

He asked me if I thought that the formation of a concentration government would be a good step. I said, "I will repeat what we have often said before, that we would welcome the formation of any Cuban Government able to maintain order and give adequate protection to the lives of inhabitants of Cuba. We have no desire to impose any individuals or select the members of your Government."

--◊◊◊--0--◊◊◊--

CARLOS SAAVEDRA LAMAS, ARGENTINE MINISTER OF FOREIGN AFFAIRS, WRITES TO CORDELL HULL, US SECRETARY OF STATE

Buenos Aires, September 8, 1933

The Argentine Embassy in Washington has communicated to its Government that it has been informed by His Excellency, the President of the United States, of the lofty principles with which he is considering the political disturbances in the Republic of Cuba, and of his ardent desire not to be obliged to intervene, notwithstanding the Platt Amendment.

The Argentine Government is grateful for the information which has so kindly been communicated to it and is pleased to learn that the action which the Chief Executive proposes to follow will correspond to those high ideals. It does not doubt that he will be able to maintain them, whatever may be the course of events which take place in the sister Republic, and which the Argentine people are observing with such heaviness of heart. The statements made will do honor to American traditions and by their example history will know that no state arrives at the maturity of democracy and the fullness of destiny without experiencing, as a necessary accompaniment, the travail of difficult conflicts.

The capacity to maintain order and to assure the reign of law emerges by itself as a fruit of this experience within the exercise of sovereignty, which must be characterized by absolute internal autonomy and complete external independence. Such principles are developed by a formative process in all youthful nations and, especially in recent times, by the demonstration that the reestablishment of normality requires a natural flow in the spontaneous development of national tendencies.

Argentina has invariably supported such doctrines throughout the course of its history. It believes that the only method which will assure on this continent the stability of political institutions is the maintenance of those standards as the mainstay of justice and international peace. It is confident that the Cuban people will overcome the difficulties through which they are passing and will be able to find a way to pursue their destiny, free to follow out the dictates of patriotism and the love of fatherland.

(signed) Carlos Saavedra Lamas

--◊◊◊--0--◊◊◊--

MEMORANDUM OF A TELEPHONE CONVERSATION BETWEEN
FRANKLYN D. ROOSEVELT, US PRESIDENT,
CORDELL HULL, US SECRETARY OF STATE
BENJAMIN SUMNER WELLES, US AMBASSADOR IN CUBA

Washington, September 8, 1933

At about 11:00 o'clock this evening, Mr. Welles telephoned the Secretary to advise him that about half the officers in the National Hotel had left, leaving about 250 (?) still there and that all of the soldiers surrounding the hotel had left.

Mr. Welles went on to say that due to the conditions prevailing in Havana at the moment he wished to have authority to issue a statement to the effect that the American Government had not and would not give consideration to the recognition of the revolutionary group at present in power at Havana. After an exchange of views between the Secretary and Ambassador Welles, the President was cut in on the conversation and gave Mr. Welles authority to issue a statement to the effect that no question of recognition or non-recognition of the group now in power in Cuba had been considered by the American Government up to the present time.

(signed) Hugh S. Cumming

--◊◊◊--0--◊◊◊--

BENJAMIN SUMNER WELLES, US AMBASSADOR IN CUBA, WRITES TO
CORDELL HULL, US SECRETARY OF STATE

Havana, September 9, 1933   [Received 1:45 p.m.]

Late last night I was informed that in disgust at the appointment of Batista as Colonel and permanent Chief of Staff of the Army, Porfirio Franca, the most conservative member of the revolutionary group at the Palace, had resigned and had gone into hiding fearing an attack upon him by Batista. José Irizarri, another member of the group, likewise resigned. Both have agreed to withhold publication of their resignations until Monday morning in order not to provoke a public crisis.

Franca stated to my informant that the attitude of Batista had now become intolerable since he was dictating to the so-called government instead of carrying out the orders given him by the government. Franca fears Batista will now undertake a new **Coup d'État** to do away with the revolutionary group and install himself in the Palace.

From the leaders other than Nacionalista, the ABC and the Menocalista Party, I am advised that when the discussions between the revolutionary group and the political leaders are resumed at the Palace this morning the representatives of the three groups mentioned will deliver an ultimatum insisting upon the immediate formation of a government created in the customary form and participated in by all of the important factions in the country. With the schism which now exists within the revolutionary group itself it appears likely that a compromise will be reached but in view of the attitude of Batista it would not seem as if such solution would afford any very favorable prospect of stability.

(signed) Benjamin Sumner Welles

--◊◊◊--O--◊◊◊--

BENJAMIN SUMNER WELLES, US AMBASSADOR IN CUBA, WRITES TO
CORDELL HULL, US SECRETARY OF STATE

Havana, September 9, 1933   [Received 3:20 p.m.]

Shortly after speaking to the President and yourself last night I was called urgently to the National Hotel which was again surrounded by soldiers and in the front of which a considerable number of soldiers was stationed with machine guns. I found in the hotel a small commission of sergeants with orders from Batista to search the hotel and to seize all arms found in it. The officers who feared, I have no doubt with justification, that most or all of them would be seized in the course of the search had again taken to the upper floors where they were prepared to defend themselves. The situation was complicated by the fact that there were many civilians fully armed who had joined the officers and a certain number of Americans also armed prepared to prevent any search of the apartments which they occupied. I explained to Sergeant Diaz, who was spokesman for the commission, that if the soldiers attempted to enter the hotel they would undoubtedly be attacked by the officers and that in the course of the grave disturbances which would probably result the lives of the Americans resident in the hotel would be unquestionably endangered. I explained to him the very serious possibilities of the situation should he proceed in his attempt. He advised me that he would telephone his superiors and explain to them the representations I had made and I also requested a group of Cubans present in the hotel who are on friendly terms with some of the members of the revolutionary group in the Palace to proceed there at once and explain the point of view I had expressed. Within half an hour telephone orders came from the Palace that all troops would be once more withdrawn, and orders were promptly carried out. An almost identical situation developed at half past two in the morning but in the latter case no soldiers entered the hotel. Finally, at 4 o'clock this morning the line of pickets and sentries which had been stationed on all streets leading to the hotel were withdrawn and since then the situation has remained quiet.

The fact that the officers have been unable or unwilling to leave the hotel until now has prevented the carrying out of any of the plans they may have had in mind. No attempt was made to seize the airfield or to take part in any counter revolt.

The same feeling of high tension exists in Havana this morning that existed yesterday. Except for the disturbances around the hotel the city last night was relatively quiet although good deal of shooting occurred in one or two suburbs.

(signed) Benjamin Sumner Welles

--◇◇◇--0--◇◇◇--

MEMORANDUM OF A TELEPHONE CONVERSATION BETWEEN
CORDELL HULL, US SECRETARY OF STATE AND
JOSEPHUS DANIELS, US AMBASSADOR TO MEXICO.

Washington, September 9, 1933

SECRETARY: Good morning, Mr. Secretary.
AMBASSADOR: How are you Mr. Secretary?
SECRETARY: It is good to hear your voice. What is going on?
AMBASSADOR: They told me you called me last night.
SECRETARY: I called and then cancelled the call. I did not understand fully now about the kind of recognition that Mexico was accustomed to extending to all countries situated like Cuba, but

I learned what the Estrada doctrine is. I got on to it and then cancelled this call. I was out of touch with my real advisers like Wilson and Caffery for the moment.

AMBASSADOR: That doctrine is that if their diplomatic representative remains, that is continuing the recognition.

SECRETARY: Exactly. What does the Mexican Foreign Office think about the attitude of the ABC countries?

AMBASSADOR: They like it very much.

SECRETARY: Have they got replies yet from all three of them?

AMBASSADOR: I do not know. I will find out and let you know.

SECRETARY: It will be interesting to have anything you get. There is no urgency. It can come by cable instead of telephoning.

AMBASSADOR: I will find out right away and cable it.

SECRETARY: The Argentine sent something to us last night. I wanted to know what she sent to Mexico to know her attitude accurately. We are doing everything We can. You can tell our Mexican friends to encourage the Cubans to build up a government there that will preserve law and order and will be stable and say that we are greatly appreciative about what the Mexican Government is doing on its own initiative.

AMBASSADOR: Yes, I will gladly do that. They are very tense down here. They feel that if we intervene it will destroy the Montevideo conference.

SECRETARY: We are going to resort to everything possible to prevent intervention. The last thing on earth we want to do is intervene. That is why we want the Mexicans so much as good friends, on their own initiative, to get it to the Cubans that they must get together and form a stable government. We have very persistent reports that there are communistic influences in there that are trying to keep anything from being done to restore order and that may be the chief trouble we have down there.

AMBASSADOR: I talked with the Minister of Sweden yesterday. He knows two of those men now at the head and says they are high-class.

SECRETARY: Tell him it may not matter who is in charge any more than it did when the Céspedes government was in. The whole thing revolves around the army and you might have a commission made up of the finest men in the universe there and the army might go back on them within a split second. That is the key to our trouble and that is what we must keep our eye on, as well as the personnel of the commission.

AMBASSADOR: I see. Goodbye.

--◊◊◊--0--◊◊◊--

A photo that travelled around the world: On January 18, 1934, **Colonel Carlos Mendieta**, a distinguished veteran of the *War of Independence* (1895-1898) became Cuba's provisional president. In the turbulent and confused political period that followed the fall of Gerardo Machado (August 12, 1933), Mendieta was succeeding **Carlos Hevia**, who was President of Cuba from 5 p.m. on Monday, January 15, 1934, to 1:20 a.m. on Thursday, January 18, 1934. He had succeeded Grau San Martín, who lasted a little longer.

On the center and bottom: an image of the Platt Amendment Repeal Accord, signed on May 29, 1934, granted in part after the efforts of **Drs. Grau San Martín** and **José Manuel Cortina**, as part of Roosevelt's **Good Neighbor Policy**. Also, a cartoon celebrating the occasion.

JOSEPHUS DANIELS, US AMBASSADOR TO MEXICO, WRITES TO
CORDELL HULL, US SECRETARY OF STATE

Mexico, September 9, 1933   [Received 7:45 p.m.]

With reference to our telephone conversation of this morning I delivered your message regarding his action looking toward producing peace in Cuba to Dr. Puig, who highly appreciated it. He said that he has not heard directly from any countries except Chile. He said that both Chile and Argentina are in harmony, but Chile thinks opportunity should be given to all countries to unite in concerted action, otherwise some who were not given this opportunity might feel slighted. According to a telegram from Mexican Chargé d'Affaires in Washington, sent after conferring with Latin American colleagues there, Argentina, without discussing the validity of the Piatt Amendment, would not approve of United States intervention even in case of civil war. Dr. Puig will let me know as soon as he hears further, and I will telegraph. He is doing everything possible to aid in securing order in Cuba. He says the feeling against intervention by the United States is deep-seated and unanimous.

He showed me a telegram from Mexican Chargé d'Affaires in Washington to the effect that some of the Latin American diplomats in Washington hesitate to sign a round robin to Cuba because such action might indicate they were trying to intervene in Cuban affairs.

(signed) Josephus Daniels

--◇◇◇--0--◇◇◇--

BENJAMIN SUMNER WELLES, US AMBASSADOR IN CUBA, WRITES TO
CORDELL HULL, US SECRETARY OF STATE

Havana, September 9, 1933   [Received 8:30 p.m.]

A commission of sergeants visited President Céspedes this morning in his house to inform him that Colonel, former Sergeant, Batista, was willing to support his restoration to the Presidency provided President Céspedes would confirm him in his position as Colonel and Chief of Staff of the Army and guarantee his safety and that of his associates in this mutiny. President Céspedes stated that he was unwilling to make any commitments whatever as to what would be done provided, he was reinstated in power. I have just been informed that the meeting of the political leaders at the Palace with the members of the revolutionary group has resulted in the determination to restore the presidential form of government. No decision has yet been reached as to the Presidency.

(signed) Benjamin Sumner Welles

--◇◇◇--0--◇◇◇--

JOSEPHUS DANIELS, US AMBASSADOR TO MEXICO, WRITES TO
CORDELL HULL, US SECRETARY OF STATE

Mexico, September 9, 1933   [Received September 15]

DEAR MR. SECRETARY: It was good to hear your voice over the telephone to-day. Sometimes I get lonesome for the voice of a friend in our country. It cheered me greatly when you said, *"I would rather walk from here to the South Pole than to have to intervene".*

In our conversation this morning you said, *"All reports are very persistent that there are more or less communistic [influences] in there behind a certain group that is trying to keep anything from being done, and that may be the chief trouble we have down there".* My information here is that the report of communistic influence in Cuba is very much exaggerated. In our own country and elsewhere people attribute to Communists all the agencies that work evil. I think it is so in Cuba, and if I were you, I would accept with many grains of allowance the attempt to saddle on the comparatively few Communists all that goes awry. Some years [ago] Lord Lochiel, a Cameron of Scotland, was visiting in North Carolina. *"The trouble in Scotland"* he said, *"is due to Communists and Bolsheviks".* I expressed surprise that there were any in Scotland, and said *"Lord, will you please define a Bolshevist".* He made several attempts, and each time said *"No, that will not do—that is not correct"* and then in his inability to give a definition satisfactory to himself, said, *"Oh, well, a Bolshevist is anybody you don't like".* I am inclined to think that it is not Communists who are making, the most trouble in Cuba, but they are made to bear sins of other groups.

Practically all the civil officials who had part in helping Machado in his reign of ruin have fled the country or been killed. Up to a few days ago most of the army officers, military men, who had more to do with the reign of terror in Cuba than the civilians were still holding high rank in the army. The Cubans who drove out the civilians whose rule was evil, feel that their cause will not be safe as long as their army is officered by men who were largely responsible for the downfall of the President who was then Commander-in-chief and carried out the bloody policy. Can you blame the men who risked all for a change to wish to be rid of reactionary military leaders as they ousted civilian leaders? You put your hand on the sore spot when you said in your telephone talk *"The whole thing revolves around the army".* Does it not—or may it not revolve—around army officers, who were in sympathy with Machado, but who still hold positions which them dangerous. Of course, we are alarmed get out of control of their officers, but may there not be times, as in Russia, when the high-up officers are so utterly out of sympathy with the good objects of a revolution that their continuance endangers reforms?

I do not know enough about Cuba to assert that such is the case there, but I do know that Machado and his associates, civil and military, were very close to high financiers in Cuba and the United States, and had no sympathy for reforms that would give bread to the hungry Cubans whose needs were not cared for by those in power. Army officers under a Machado are often the agents of repression and have no heartbeat for the oppressed and distressed. May not the rich and powerful in Cuba, and their allies in the United States, and imperialistic army officers, be behind the attempt to hide behind exaggerating the lawlessness of Communists? I do not know, but I submit the question for your consideration.

(signed) Josephus Daniels

--◊◊◊--O--◊◊◊--

Memorandum by Jefferson Thomas Caffery,
US Under Secretary of State

Washington, September 9, 1933

The Mexican Chargé d'Affaires came to see me this evening, 7:00 p.m., and told me that his Government had had a reply from the Chilean Government to Dr. Puig's telegram. The Chilean Government communicated its approval of the proposed action, adding the suggestion, however, that all Latin American countries be invited to subscribe. The Argentine and Brazilian Governments had not yet replied to Dr. Puig's telegram.

Note: Dr. Puig's telegrams to the Ministers of Foreign Affairs of the Argentine, Brazil and Chile, of course referred to the suggestion that the Governments of the ABC powers' and the Mexican Government instruct their representatives at Havana to urge the *de facto* Cuban authorities to endeavor to form a Government able to maintain order and protect lives and property.

(signed) Jefferson Thomas Caffery

--◊◊◊--O--◊◊◊--

Benjamin Sumner Welles, US Ambassador in Cuba, writes to Cordell Hull, US Secretary of State

Havana, September 10, 1933   [Received 7:09 p.m.]

At 2:30 this morning the three remaining members of the revolutionary group in the Palace designated Dr. Grau San Martín as Provisional President of the Republic and immediately afterwards selected Dr. Antonio Guiteras Secretary of Gobernación; José Barquín Secretary of the Treasury; Dr. Carlos Finlay Secretary of Sanitation; Eduardo Chibás Secretary of Public Works. They were either unable to agree upon, or unable to find, candidates for the other Cabinet positions. They announced, however, that additional Cabinet appointments would be made this morning and that Grau

San Martín would take the oath of Provisional President at noon today. None of the above have any party affiliation.

The creation of this presidential form of government was due to the strong antipathy which was noted in Havana to the commission form of government, with which the revolutionary group commenced, and to the belief that recognition by the United States would immediately be accorded if the type of government was changed. It should certainly be considered as a tendency towards a return to formality, the men who figure in the new Cabinet, except for ... are men whom I believe to be personally honest. I have no doubt that they are all sincere in the belief that the program of government which the student body has drawn up for them will meet the requirements of the Republic. The Army, I am advised by competent authorities, is showing signs of resentment at the promotion of Batista and the other ringleaders of the mutiny and that many of the other sergeants are demand- ing similar promotions. Even the appearance of discipline among the troops of Havana has vanished, there are continuous reports of local revolutionary movements in the interior particularly in Oriente Province and in Santa Clara, but it is impossible for me as yet to confirm the accuracy of any of them.

I am more than ever confident that in view of the very difficult situation which has now been presented the only path for the United States to take is that which the President indicated to me on the telephone the other night, namely one of watchful expectancy. None of the political or independent groups have yet shown an inclination to support this government. None of them, however except for the ABC has come out openly and strongly against it. It is yet consequently a group which is solely representative of the student body and of extreme radical elements. The next 2 or 3 days will determine whether any strong revolutionary movement against it will be made. There appears to be no indication now that any successful counter revolt can be carried through in Havana if after a reasonable period the government attracts popular support, appears to be able to maintain public order even nominally, appoints respond provincial and municipal authorities, and is able to function as a government in the sense that it complies with its obligations and collects and disburses public revenues; I should strongly recommend consulting with the Latin American Republics with a view to reaching a determination upon recognition; protracted period without recognition by the United State and our failure to recognize for an indefinite period if the requisites above-indicated are complied with would merely bring about in Cuba a more thoroughly chaotic and anarchic condition than that which already obtains.

Now, however, I cannot see much reason for anticipating so favorable an outcome. The leaders of the large political parties will not, I think, consent to the duration of a government of this character which is necessarily in the last analysis under the

Eduardo Chibás (1907-1951), during his University studies, was at the front lines of the struggles against Machado. He condemned *"great foreign monopolies"* along with their *"indigenous servants"* and concluded that the revolt against Machado sought not merely to depose him but also to *"change...the economic structure of Cuba."* Years later, he was the founder of the *Orthodox Party*, a political movement that had detached itself from the ruling *Authentic Party* in 1947, following the acts of corruption by the government of Ramón Grau San Martín. His charges of corruption were indisputable. **Francisco Ichaso**, one of the founders of the **ABC**, described Grau's last years in office as *"one of the most corrupt periods in the history of the Republic."*

The denunciations of Eduardo Chibás would continue during the government of Carlos Prío, since he would also be plagued by acts of corruption, privileges, embezzlement and repression.

Just as Grau's **Authentic Party** became in the early 1950s a great disappointment of the Cuban people, Eduardo Chibás and his political movement emerged as the great hope for a nation tired of living in poverty and exploitation. The people saw in Chibás a fighting leader, honest and who would play a historical role in Cuba.

The bases of the **Orthodox Party** were *anti-imperialism*, the *fight against corruption* and the *total rejection of repression*. He was completely against Fulgencio Batista and was also a *passionate opponent of Communism*. The main motto of the Orthodox Party was: *"Verguenza contra dinero"* (Shame against money), its symbol was a **broom**, symbolizing the full sweep of the corruption tolerated by the Authentic Party.

In 1948, Eduardo Chibás lost to Carlos Prío Socarrás as candidate for President of Cuba. He became a *whistleblower*, disclosing dubious transactions in government; his popularity was constantly rising. A May 1951 poll in **Bohemia**, Cuba's most popular magazine, indicated that Chibás, with multi-class support, was the leading candidate for president in all six of Cuba's provinces in 1952.

From a personal and psychological standpoint, Chibás was undoubtedly an eccentric, with intemperate remarks that helped popularize his radio program and the recklessness with which he made public accusations. His sense of drama, his inclination toward rashness, and his sincere desire to inspire people, came together in a final dramatic act: shooting himself in the stomach while broadcasting. No one knows whether he intended to take his own life or whether he merely sought, in a bizarre fashion, to shift attention away from a recent and not uncommon dispute with a politician. He died 10 days later.

control of the enlisted men in the Army. It is most probable that open revolt will not take long in showing itself in the interior provinces.

The local press is now undergoing as severe a censorship as it did in the time of the Machado Government. This censorship is exercised by groups of students who have even gone so far as to inform the Associated Press correspondent here that they will not permit him to send to the United States any material other than favorable regarding present conditions in Cuba; he has, of course, paid no attention to this demand.

The Embassy is being attacked because of its failure to accord immediate recognition to the revolutionary group and the possibility of intervention is being violently assailed. The proprietors of all the chief newspapers of Havana have yet, however, had enough courage to prevent the publication of any regular editorials criticizing either the attitude of the United States or of the Embassy.

The refusal of the Latin American powers to accord immediate recognition has incensed the students who are sending violent cables on the usual subject of American imperialism to the universities and radical associations throughout Latin America.

(signed) Benjamin Sumner Welles

--◊◊◊--0--◊◊◊--

BENJAMIN SUMNER WELLES, US AMBASSADOR IN CUBA, WRITES TO **CORDELL HULL,** US SECRETARY OF STATE

Havana, September 10, 1933   [Received September 11 1:34 a.m.]

This afternoon Dr. Ferrer called at the Embassy to advise me that the Army officers wished to petition me to agree to have a sufficient force of American Marines landed to disarm the soldiers and the innumerable civilians who are armed and that should I agree they would at once proclaim that President Céspedes was the sole legitimated President of Cuba and undertake the recruiting and training of a new Army. I replied that I would not even receive such a petition; and that it was absurd to imagine that the Government of the United States would undertake it at the request of 200 deposed Army officers. In reply to a further inquiry whether my Government would refrain from recognizing the new regime I replied that I most decidedly refused to make any such commitment. I stated that in the matter of recognition we had yet given no consideration to the question.

My replies to these inquiries, I was later advised by a civilian present, were accurately transmitted by Dr. Ferrer to the assembled officers. Notwithstanding this fact the Directorio Estudiantil this afternoon cabled to Latin American universities the charge that I was inciting the Army officers who have taken refuge at the National Hotel to disturb public order in order to find a pretext for landing Marines.

If inquiry is made by the press, I think the following facts should be stated:

I have never spoken to any of the Army officers either individually or in assembly nor have I ever received any message from them other than the one above-mentioned. I moved to the National Hotel because the lease on my own house had expired and I expected to sail on September 14th. I had been living there 2 days before any Army officers had taken refuge there. I have not changed my residence both because my doing so would have been at once misinterpreted and also because since the hotel is owned by an American company and many Americans have been residing there, I believed my continued stay was helpful in view of the complications existing.

(signed) Benjamin Sumner Welles

--◇◇◇--0--◇◇◇--

BENJAMIN SUMNER WELLES, US AMBASSADOR IN CUBA, WRITES TO **CORDELL HULL,** US SECRETARY OF STATE

Havana, September 11, 1933   [RECEIVED 3:33 P.M.]

The ABC, in many ways the best organized and most energetic political organization in Cuba, published this morning a very long proclamation making entirely plain its hostility towards the present regime in Havana. The following are the salient features:

"Less than 30 persons gathered together in the military camp appointed by their own responsibility and without previous consultation five individuals to exercise the Executive Power of the Republic. These five individuals in turn, after several interviews which had as object the attempting to obtain the support of the political parties of the nation for this committee, designated one of their own initiative and without the agreement of anyone else, a President who is one of the members of the committee and likewise a Cabinet.

"The military mutiny which took place can never be justified by history since there can be proved beyond doubt that the Government of Dr. Céspedes was essentially a Government of public opinion. A crisis of juvenile impatience has led to an unjustifiable act of violence against that Government with disastrous results for our political future. The attempt has been made to show that the Government of President Céspedes was not a spontaneous product but the result of mediation of the American Ambassador. The argument is good for demagogues to use because there is nothing that can incite the anger of a Latin American people more thoroughly than to wave the flag of North American imposition. But the falsity of this argument is notorious. The outstanding

leaders of the opposition parties suggested the name of Dr. Céspedes which was accepted unanimously because of his qualities of integrity and patriotism and his impartiality in political strife.

"This recent mutiny results in the placing of one class against another and took place contrary to the desires of the entire country. It was the result not of national desire but of the impatience of a tiny minority and far from preventing intervention it inevitably creates the danger of intervention.

"While the ABC. is positively opposed to any form of foreign intervention it is determined to oppose with equal energy those who have provoked the possibility of the intervention through their stupidity and inability."

In a formal statement issued this morning General Menocal in behalf of his political party states "We decline all present and future responsibility which may be derived from the formation of the Government."

In an interview which I had last night with Colonel Mendieta he advised me that in the course of the day he and his fellow leaders of the Unión Nacionalista would issue a public statement condemning the present regime and opposing its continuation in power.

The discipline of the Army is daily slipping and rivalry and dissension between the various sergeants is on the increase. Many the deposed officers remain at the National Hotel although a 24-hours' truce, expiring this evening at 6 o'clock, has been agreed upon. It is my hope that before the expiration of that period some arrangement will be made which will permit the officers to leave the hotel with guarantees.

(signed) Benjamin Sumner Welles

--◊◊◊--0--◊◊◊--

MEMORANDUM BY **JEFFERSON THOMAS CAFFERY**,
US UNDER SECRETARY OF STATE

Washington, September 11,1933

The Brazilian Ambassador called on me this afternoon to say that he had received a telegram from his Government stating that the President's action in calling in the Brazilian diplomatic representative here and explaining our point of view in regard to the Cuban situation had been highly appreciated at Rio.

The Ambassador then asked me if we approved of what the Mexican Ministry of Foreign Affairs was attempting to do in regard to the suggestion to be made by the ABCM powers at Havana that it was important for the Cubans to form a stable government capable of maintaining order in the country. I told the Ambassador that we approved of the attitude of the Mexican Government in the instance.

The Ambassador added that his Government desired him to say that in no case would Brazil take part in any action which might present possibilities of degenerating into a movement directed against the United States on the question of intervention. I said to Mr. Lima e Silva that we did not apprehend that the Mexicans had anything of that sort in mind; we believed they were sincerely desirous of giving good advice to the Cubans. Mr. Lima e Silva said that it was his understanding that as the Mexican proposal now stood the idea was that the diplomatic representatives of the four interested powers here in Washington should agree on a declaration to be made at Havana. However, he apprehended that the Argentine representative here would be unable to take part in a move of this kind, it being clear from the Argentine note published a few days ago that the Argentine Minister for Foreign Affairs was opposed to the Mexican suggestions.

I thanked the Brazilian Ambassador for his information.

(signed) Jefferson Thomas Caffery

--◊◊◊--0--◊◊◊--

MEMORANDUM BY **JEFFERSON THOMAS CAFFERY**,
US UNDER SECRETARY OF STATE

Washington, September 11, 1933

The Chilean Chargé d'Affaires *ad interim* came to see me this afternoon to say that he had instructions from his Government to pass on to the President and the Secretary of State his Government's thanks and high appreciation for the President's action in informing the Chilean representative here of our point of view in regard to the Cuban situation. Mr. Cohen added (as we already know) that his Government approved of the Mexican suggestion. However, it had made the added suggestion that not only the ABC powers be asked to participate in the informal representations at Havana, but that every Latin American country be included. Mr. Cohen gave me to understand that he doubted whether this were practicable, there being too many divergent points of view among the nineteen Latin American Governments represented here,—it does not seem possible that they could all agree on a definite course of action at Havana.

Mr. Cohen then said, *"well, in any event, I think that considerable good has been accomplished; the Cubans know how we, that is at least the Mexicans and ourselves, feel about the matter and, doubtless, this will have a salutary effect on their activities".*

(signed) Jefferson Thomas Caffery

--◊◊◊--0--◊◊◊--

CORDELL HULL, US SECRETARY OF STATE, WRITES TO
H. F. ARTHUR SCHOENFELD, US AMBASSADOR
IN THE DOMINICAN REPUBLIC.

Washington, September 11, 1933   [Received 6:00 p.m.]

You will please inform the Minister of Foreign Relations orally that this Government greatly appreciates the friendly gesture of the President and the Dominican Government and add that as we have already explained to the Dominican Minister in Washington, as well as to the other representatives of the American Republics, we are not contemplating intervention or interference in Cuban affairs, and that it is our most sincere hope that the Cubans will themselves work out a Cuban solution of their difficulties.
(signed) Cordell Hull

--◊◊◊--0--◊◊◊--

MEMORANDUM BY **CORDELL HULL,** US SECRETARY OF STATE
To several Diplomatic and Consular Missions
Washington, September 11,1933

For your information and appropriate use in case of conversations on the Cuban situation: This Government in view of disturbed conditions in Cuba has sent ships to that country solely as a precautionary measure and there is not the slightest intention of intervening or interfering in Cuba's domestic affairs. It is our earnest hope that the Cubans themselves will work out a solution of their own difficulties and that they will be able to form a government capable of maintaining order. We have not, and shall not, attempt to influence the Cubans in any way as to choose of individuals in the government.

The Department has explained its position as set out above to the diplomatic representatives in Washington of the Latin American countries and the President has himself repeated this to the representatives of Argentina, Brazil, Chile and Mexico.
(signed) Cordell Hull

--◊◊◊--0--◊◊◊--

BENJAMIN SUMNER WELLES, US AMBASSADOR IN CUBA, WRITES TO
CORDELL HULL, US SECRETARY OF STATE

Havana, September 11, 1933   [RECEIVED 8:30 P.M.]

In addition to the statements of hostility and determined opposition to the present regime announced this morning by the ABC and the party headed by General Menocal and the similar statement which is to be published this afternoon by the Unión Nacionalista, the fourth largest political organization, the OCRR, likewise will issue this afternoon a similar statement. As the result of these public declarations of opposition the political situation is crystallizing noticeably. The attitude thus taken makes it evident to the public that the organized political strength of the Republic which itself represents most of the Cuban people is opposed to a continuation of the present regime. Under these conditions I desire once more to emphasize that in my judgment it would be highly prejudicial to our interests to intimate in any manner that recognition of the existing regime was being considered by us. Every effort is being made and has already been made, through fictitious reports inserted in the local press, to create the impression that the Government of the United States is on the verge of recognizing the group headed by Grau San Martín as the provisional government of Cuba. Headlines appeared in the morning newspapers that President Roosevelt intended to afford immediate financial assistance to Grau San Martín and that recognition by the United States would be obtained within a few hours or days. In view of the campaign of misrepresentation and distortion of the truth which is being conducted by the group now in power and which is causing both consternation and resentment on the part of the powerful parties opposed to the existing regime, I feel it would be to be issued by you making unmistakably plain the attitude of the Government of the United States in view of the conditions which now exist in Cuba.

In accordance with my telephone conversation with you 2 days ago I venture to suggest a statement along the following lines:

"The chief concern of the Government of the United States is, as it has been, that the Cuban people solve their own political problems in accordance with the desires of most of the Cubans. The Government of the United States believes that only through a provisional government which responds to the will of the majority of the Cuban people can stability be obtained and assurance be given that national elections can be held under the jurisdiction of such government with such full and ample guarantees of impartiality, the fairness as to make possible the successful inauguration of a new permanent and constitutional government of Cuba. It would seem unnecessary to repeat that the Government of the United States has no interest in behalf of or prejudice against any political group or independent organization which is today active in the political life of Cuba. In view of its deep and abiding interest in the welfare of the Cuban people and the security of the Republic of Cuba it cannot and will not accord recognition of any government in Cuba other than a legitimate and constitutional government unless conclusive evidence is presented that such government effectively represents the will of a majority of the people of the Republic, that it is capable of maintaining order and of guaranteeing the protection of 'life, property and individual liberty' and finally that such government is competent to carry out the functions and obli-

While in Cuba, in late 1933, soldiers, students and politicians are battling for control of events, the world continues to spin. In every western country, the film **King Kong** by Edgard Wallace, featuring Fay Wray, tells the story of a giant gorilla, shackled in chains, taken to New York City and presented to a Broadway theatre audience as **"Kong, the Eighth Wonder of the World".** Cartoonists in the US, meantime, are depicting the numerous hassles that Uncle Sam has to endure to bring peace and quiet to Cubans.

gations which are incumbent upon any stable government."

The impression is very general today that the Grau San Martín regime is evanescent. Of the four Cabinet members appointed yesterday Chibás and Finlay have refused to serve, and I am likewise advised that Barquín will not take office. A complete Cabinet was to have been announced this morning and such announcement has now been postponed until 10 o'clock tonight. There seems to be very little probability that any Cubans of standing or reputation will accept office. I wish to emphasize again that conclusive evidence has now been presented to my satisfaction that the existing regime represents only the student, a few radical agitators and a small number of insignificant radical groups which have no political importance or following whatever.

The longer the present regime continues in power the more dangerous the situation becomes. For over a week no government department has been able to function and all semblance of order and discipline in the Army is vanishing rapidly.

(signed) Benjamin Sumner Welles

--◊◊◊--0--◊◊◊--

CORDELL HULL, US SECRETARY OF STATE, WRITES TO
BENJAMIN SUMNER WELLES, US AMBASSADOR IN CUBA

Washington, September 11, 1933   [RECEIVED 12:00 P.M.]

The President authorizes me to make the following statement which is now being released for Tuesday morning papers:

"The chief concern of the Government of the United States is, as it has been, that Cuba solve her own political problems in accordance with the desires of the Cuban people themselves. It would seem unnecessary to repeat that the Government of the United States has no interest in behalf of or prejudice against any political group or independent organization which is today active in the political life of Cuba. In view of its deep and abiding interest in the welfare of the Cuban people, and the security of the Republic of Cuba, our Government is prepared to welcome any Government representing the will of the people of the Republic and capable of maintaining law and order throughout the island. Such a Government would be competent to carry out the functions and obligations incumbent upon any stable Government. This has been the exact attitude of the United States Government from the beginning. This statement has been communicated to Ambassador Welles and meets his full approval."

(signed) Cordell Hull

--◊◊◊--0--◊◊◊--

BENJAMIN SUMNER WELLES, US AMBASSADOR IN CUBA, WRITES TO
CORDELL HULL, US SECRETARY OF STATE

Washington, September 12, 1933   [RECEIVED 5:18 P.M.]

The Unión Nacionalista last night issued a statement signed by the four leaders of the party—Colonels Mendieta, Hevía, Méndez Peñate and Dr. Torriente—in which the party declared that its advice that in these moments of danger to the Republic only a strong government of concentration could govern the country until a permanent constitutional government had been installed as the result of national elections had been disregarded by the group now in power and that the party consequently notified Cuba that it "refuses to accept any responsibility for the circumstances which now exist".

With the attitude of open opposition to the Grau San Martín regime adopted by the four most powerful party organizations in Cuba, namely, the Unión Nacionalista, the ABC, the Menocal party and the OCRR it is very apparent that a majority of the Cuban people will not at present support the government now in power. Cuban commercial circles are unanimously opposed to the regime. During the past 8 days no revenues have been collected, no taxes are being paid, and if the insistent demands of the soldiers for the payment of back pay are complied with no available cash will remain in the Treasury.

Grau San Martín this morning announced the following Cabinet:
Marquez Sterling, Secretary of State;
Antonio Guiteras, Secretary of Gobernación;
Carlos Finlay, Secretary of Sanitation;
Manuel Costales Latatú, Secretary of Public Instruction;
Gustavo Moreno, Secretary of Communications;
Colonel Julio Aguado, Secretary of War;
Dr. Ramiro Capablanca, Secretary of the Presidency;
Dr. Joaquín del Rio Balmaseda, Secretary of Justice.

Dr. Capablanca, Dr. Costales Latatú and Dr. Finlay are all university professors, identified with the student movement. Colonel Aguado was imprisoned by the Machado Government for having been involved in a revolutionary plot. Jointly enjoy a favorable reputation. Judge del Rio Balmaseda is a judge of a Court of First Instance of Santiago. Gustavo Moreno, appointed Secretary of Communications, related to the Unión Revolucionaria, the smallest of the revolutionary groups participating in the mediation negotiations.

Announcement was made while Colonel Manuel Despaigne had been appointed Secretary of the Treasury. Colonel Despaigne was Secretary of the Treasury under President Zayas and was appointed administrator of the national lottery by President Céspedes. He is a man of absolute integrity and of the highest character, but he is now very old and he accepted the position offered him by President

Céspedes with the understanding that he would only retain it a short period since he advised me his health would not permit him to undertake any arduous work.

There is no politically organized strength represented in the Cabinet. With the exception of Marquez Sterling and Despaigne, none of the individuals mentioned have held any public office before and they are all with the same exceptions closely identified with and responsive to the student group.

The present outlook therefore in brief is as follows:

All of the important political parties have announced themselves as opposed to this Government; the financial situation of the Government is disastrous; the new members of the Cabinet with two exceptions have no governmental experience and will be entirely under the domination of the student group; the Army officers with few exceptions have positively refused to support the Government or to return to the troops and the discipline within the ranks of the troops is degenerating; such public order as now prevails in the Republic is being maintained by civilian committees acting in some instances in the conjunction with the soldiers. Under these conditions the Government of the United States can do nothing more than await developments. None of the political leaders will agree even to tacit support of the present regime and while I have consistently urged the force of public opinion be the only weapon they employ should they desire to attack the Government I have every reason to believe that it is only a question of a short time before General Menocal will attempt to lead a revolution. The sole action I have been able to take in order to prevent this is through the leaders of the other parties who have refused him their cooperation in such a movement at the present time and have counseled him consistently that he awaits developments without resorting to violence.

(signed) Benjamin Sumner Welles

--◊◊◊--0--◊◊◊--

BENJAMIN SUMNER WELLES, US AMBASSADOR IN CUBA, WRITES TO
CORDELL HULL, US SECRETARY OF STATE

Havana, September 12, 1933   [RECEIVED 9:35 P.M.]

The sole motive, I presume, for the editorial published this morning in the *New York Herald Tribune* and reprinted here in the Cuban morning newspapers is for the purpose of making a political attack on the administration. The result, however, of course, of at tacks of this character in newspapers of influence in the United States is to weaken very materially the influence which I possess here and to impair the probability of a successful outcome of our policy. To the best of my knowledge no American correspondents have cabled any such reports as those alleged to have been sent in the editorial referred to. In any event the attitude which I have consistently adopted with reference to the Cuban Army officers who have taken refuge in the National Hotel has been fully reported to the Department. They had as much right to engage rooms there as any tourist would and the question of extraterritoriality was never raised by me nor could it have been except in so far as my own apartments were concerned. Moreover, far from delivering *ultimata* to the revolutionists now in control of the government, my contacts with them have been limited to the one conversation I had with Grau San Martín which I reported at once by cable to the Department. It must be perfectly apparent that it would have been a far more agreeable course for me to have left the hotel as soon as the Army officers came there. If I had done so, however, I would at once have been charged with personal fear, which is of considerable psychological importance in these countries and I would moreover have been unable to have prevented the very real danger to the lives of the American residents who had congregated in the hotel, in the event that fighting between the officers and the soldiers had taken place within the hotel which upon two occasions at least appeared to be imminent.

In so far as the dispatch of United States vessels to Cuban waters for the purpose of safeguarding American lives is concerned there are very few if any Americans resident in Cuba today who do not believe that they might be in jeopardy so long as this abnormal condition continues should the American warships be recalled.

I believe that we have followed the only wise course and the one course that gives promise of any hope in an excessively difficult and complicated situation. We have taken the necessary precautionary steps to insure so far as may be possible the lives of our citizens. We have, on the other hand, not landed a man on Cuban soil nor have we threatened nor attempted to dictate the solution which the Cuban people themselves should bring about. The statement which you issued last night regarding our policy concerning recognition makes our position perfectly plain to the Latin American world and is heartily approved by all those representatives of the Latin American Republics with whom I have been able to get in touch. It is unanimously approved by all the important Cuban political groups. Under these very trying circumstances it is impossible naturally to contradict every malicious and utterly unfounded falsehood that may be spread regarding my own official activities. They have emanated from the extreme radical group, which is connected with the present regime here, just as similar reports were spread regarding the Embassy during the last few days of the Machado administration. I feel very strongly, however, that personal considerations are of no importance whatever where a matter of public policy is concerned. If the President and you believe for any reason that it would be advantageous to the administration to have [me] carry out my original plans and leave for the United States within the next few days I must of course do so. I suggested to you on the telephone that it might be preferable for me to remain here

On September 1933, the world press continued to report extensively on Cuban affairs and events. *Top two photos:* **News Week** magazine, September 14, 1933, offered full coverage of the ascent to power of Grau San Martín;

lower image: the devastating hurricane of 1933. In the lower photo, the results in the town of **Isabela de Sagua**. The hurricane hit on September 1, category 4, had winds of 120 mph (190 km/h), and all along Cuba left about 100,000 people homeless and killed over 70, mostly on the central part of the island.

until the prospects seem clearer because of my belief that I had had, and still retain, the confidence of the leaders of all of the political groups, with the exception of the so-called student organization, and that for that reason it might be easier for the Embassy in an emergency to prevent sporadic and isolated outbreaks which would not tend to clear the atmosphere but merely complicate matters still further. I shall welcome a frank expression of the President's desires and your own in this regard.

Owing to the fact that all of the servants in the National Hotel left the hotel last night, and that the electric light and water supply will be cut off in the course of the day, I and the Americans still remaining there were forced to leave the hotel this morning. No adjustment as to the situation of the Army officers in the hotel has been reached. Since I left the hotel the American manager telephoned the Embassy at 1 o'clock this afternoon to state that his life had been threatened and the destruction of the hotel property would be undertaken by the student group unless he promptly cut off the water, light, and telephone services. Under the conditions which now obtain there is no authority to afford protection other than nominal. I have, therefore, notified him and the American manager of the American Electric Light Company that if they receive orders from some governmental authority in the sense indicated it would be wiser on their part to comply with the demand made. Since the hotel manager has appealed to the Embassy for protection, I consider that this was the only possible policy for me to pursue.

(signed) Benjamin Sumner Welles

--◊◊◊--0--◊◊◊--

Memorandum by Jefferson Thomas Caffery, US Under Secretary of State

Washington, September 13,1933

The Mexican Chargé d'Affaires ad interim came to see me today at noon and said that he had had a telegram from the Minister of Foreign Affairs at Mexico City instructing him to inform the Department that, as it seemed that a stable government capable of maintaining order had been formed in Cuba, it did not seem necessary to go any further with efforts to induce other Latin American countries to make suggestions at Havana that a stable government capable of maintaining order be formed. The Chargé indicated that, following his conversations with the other Latin American representatives here in Washington, it was his opinion that this view was shared by the great majority of his colleagues. He indicated also that his Government, and most all of his colleagues, believed that we should remove our naval vessels from Cuban waters because they (he and his colleagues) feel that the opposition political leaders in Cuba will not cease their efforts to overthrow the *de facto* government as long as our naval vessels remain there.

Sr. Padilla told me also that the real difficulty which the Mexican Government found in its efforts to secure general Latin American action at Havana arose from the fact of the Argentine Government's failure to cooperate, many of his colleagues here fearing to take a definite position until they knew what the Argentine Government would do. As the Argentine Government had done nothing, his Government had found it impossible to proceed. His chief, Dr. Puig, had instructed him to tell me that, therefore, the Mexican Foreign Office would take no further steps in the premises.

I again expressed the Department's appreciation for the Mexican Government's friendly interest in this whole matter, and our appreciation of his (Sr. Padilla's) friendly efforts here in Washington.

I then said our position remains the same as it was in the beginning, that is, we have no interest in individuals and will express no opinion as to who should form a Cuban Government—we desire only to see a stable government capable of maintaining law and order formed. *"Speaking very frankly,"* I said,

> *"I must invite your attention to the fact that all of the principal political leaders have come out in opposition to Dr. Grau San Martín. In the face of that, can you say that his government will be able to extend its authority over the Island and, especially, will he be able to secure the support of the army? Will the de facto authorities be able to secure the support of the mass of the Cuban people over the heads of the political leaders? It seems to me that the point at issue is important. Either the government of Dr. Grau San Martín will be able to exist notwithstanding the political opposition or the politicians will turn the government out."*

Sr. Padilla admitted that these questions were pertinent and indicated that he was not yet convinced himself that Grau San Martín will be able to count on the army's loyalty, nor was he convinced that Grau San Martín would be able to gain the support of the mass of the people of the Island in the face of the opposition of the political leaders. He remarked, however, that Dr. Márquez Sterling (the Cuban Ambassador here) had said to him this morning that he believed that none of the political leaders in opposition could now count on a large following in the Island; that the only well-organized political party in Cuba was the Liberal Party, adherents of Machado, who are now dispersed. Perhaps the *de facto* authorities would be able to secure support from the erstwhile Liberal mass.

I said also (in effect),

> *"no one is more anxious than we are to take our ships out of Cuban waters, but we frankly do not yet feel that we can do so in view of the circumstances we have just discussed. Would not it be far worse for us to take them out and*

have to send them back than to keep them there a while longer?" "Yes", said the Chargé, "that would be disastrous". I said, "please explain that to Dr. Puig". The Chargé said, "I will do so gladly".

Sr. Padilla then went on to talk at some length. He said that his Government, and other Latin American governments, understood our position thoroughly but that, owing to the efforts of the Cuban students, the students in other Latin American countries were becoming excited and they were charging their governments with sympathizing with American intervention. He said,

"we know the charges are not true, but the matter might easily become a domestic political one for us." He added, *"it is almost miraculous how President Roosevelt has been able to change Latin American feeling towards the United States in a few months. We do not want to see that good feeling fade away now, especially since we are all interested in seeing something done at Montevideo next December."* I assured the Chargé that we understood their (Latin American governments) difficulties, as well as our own. We appreciated the Mexican Government's frankly putting their ideas before us; we would always be glad to receive from Dr. Puig any ideas or suggestions he cares to make. I then repeated our position—*"we have no interest in individuals or any desire to suggest names; we desire only to see a stable government formed in Cuba capable of maintaining law and order in the Island. We have no desire to keep our vessels in Cuban waters one minute longer than is absolutely necessary".*

Sr. Padilla then said, *"well, if you cannot withdraw your vessels can you do something else to alleviate the situation."* I said, *"what do you mean?"* He said, *"could not you make some sort of public declaration to the press here that you hope that Dr. Grau San Martín's government will be able to establish itself solidly in the Island and be able to maintain law and order throughout the Republic."* I said, *"that would be a partisan declaration, whereas we desire to remain neutral; that declaration would be construed to mean that we have decided to support the **de facto** authorities and we would be attacked for it by all of the Cuban political leaders. We cannot commit ourselves that far yet."*

(signed) Jefferson Thomas Caffery

--◊◊◊--o--◊◊◊--

BENJAMIN SUMNER WELLES, US AMBASSADOR IN CUBA, WRITES TO **CORDELL HULL,** US SECRETARY OF STATE

Havana, September 13, 1933   [RECEIVED 5:30 P.M.]

The general political situation has not changed materially since yesterday. Dr. Grau San Martín has sent an urgent request to Colonel Mendieta for an interview which has been accorded and will be held at 6 p.m. today. I shall cable the Department tonight the result of the conversation. There are increasing and apparently well-founded rumors of dissension and the part of the soldiers. The student body is with frantic haste attempting to organize a student militia with its headquarters in the university. My informants, who belonged to the student group although opposed to the present regime, advise that this effort is due to the realization by the students that the feeling among the soldiers is becoming increasingly dangerous both in so far as the present government is concerned and likewise in so far as communist propaganda is involved.

I was visited this morning by General Asbert, a former Governor of the Province of Havana and a former very prominent member of the Liberal Party who created a personal following during the last 2 years of the Machado administration. He gave me to understand although without saying so openly that he desired to join those groups of the opposition to the present regime who desired to commence an immediate revolution for the purpose of restoring the Céspedes Government. I counseled patience and a waiting policy. I am informed that the students are now dissatisfied with the constitution of the Grau San Martín Cabinet and that they are insistently demanding that all Cabinet members other than those identified with the student body be dismissed from office.

The officers remain at the National Hotel. They were joined last night by a small group of additional officers from the interior and apparently succeeded in getting into the hotel an additional quantity of arms and ammunition. While the ordinary water supply is cut off, they have enough stored in tanks to last them for 10 days as well as food supplies for a much longer period. General Sanguily has taken command. All immediate hope of agreement with the present regime appears to have failed and the officers now appear to desire an encounter if the soldiers are willing to provide it.

(signed) Benjamin Sumner Welles

--◊◊◊--0--◊◊◊--

CORDELL HULL, US SECRETARY OF STATE, WRITES TO
BENJAMIN SUMNER WELLES, US AMBASSADOR IN CUBA

Washington, September 13, 1933   [RECEIVED 11:00 P.M.]

The President and I are in accord that you should remain at Havana for the present as indicated by you.

(signed) Cordell Hull

--◊◊◊--0--◊◊◊--

The **US Federal Reserve** once had not one, but two offices in Cuba,(the first from Atlanta, the second from Boston. There were there in response to the Cuban government request, "for the redemption of all old and deteriorated currency circulating on the Island, because it was regarded as dangerous to public health." They also, of course, helped both countries to engage in business across the gulf.

On the top photo, cash brought to Cuba by Eugene Black (in a circle) and the offices of the Atlanta Federal Reserve in Havana.

Photo in the center left: **Luis Eleuterio Tiant** (1906-1976) was a Cuban pitcher whose career extended from 1926 through 1948 in the **US Negro Leagues**; he played for the *Havana Red Sox, Cuban Stars West* and *New York Cubans*, between 1928 and 1947. In 1933, the sport press in the US reported he had the **seventh best screwball of all time.**

Photo on the center right: a cartoon showing the Communist propaganda dispersed across the world.

BENJAMIN SUMNER WELLES, US AMBASSADOR IN CUBA, WRITES TO
CORDELL HULL, US SECRETARY OF STATE

Havana, September 14, 1933   [RECEIVED 12:10 P.M.]

Admiral Freeman advises me this morning that the French dispatch boat *Dentorereaux*, now at Charleston, South Carolina, is under orders to proceed to Havana Friday September 15th. The French Minister 2 days ago advised me that he had requested that the projected visit to Havana be indefinitely postponed. The visit here of a foreign war ship would undoubtedly complicate matters considerably and it is my earnest hope as it is that of Admiral Freeman that no such visit be made at this time.

I suggest that the French Embassy in Washington be advised of the circumstances with the hope that the orders which have apparently been given notwithstanding the request of the French Minister here be modified.

(signed) Benjamin Sumner Welles

--◊◊◊--0--◊◊◊--

MEMORANDUM BY **CORDELL HULL,**
US SECRETARY OF STATE

Washington, September 14, 1933

The French Ambassador called on my invitation and I proceeded to show him the copy of telegram, attached hereto, from Ambassador Welles at Havana. I then explained in much detail the extremely delicate and hair-trigger conditions existing in Cuba at this time and said that nothing would be much easier than to arouse the populace and bring about unfortunate confusion that might result in consequences that could not be foreseen. I pointed out just how our government is resorting to every possible method to preserve the goodwill of the Cuban people in their present confused and inflamed state of mind, and to encourage them in every possible way to establish a stable government at once that can maintain law and order. I then stated that this did not present a question of Cuban nationals or their property being in danger of serious injury and that if such question should later arise, we could then discuss all its phases. I told the Ambassador that this was merely a request that the French Government consider the danger of starting serious complications by having this vessel enter the harbor at Havana at this time. He agreed that he would at once communicate all the facts as to how our government is undertaking to encourage peace, law and order in Cuba and the speedy setting up of a stable government; that he would emphasize the efforts of our government to safeguard human lives throughout the island; and also emphasize the question of whether the French Government could not consistently direct this vessel to remain out of Cuban ports at present. The

Ambassador remarked that he thought it was merely on a general cruise from northeast Atlantic ports to the Antilles.

(signed) Cordell Hull

--◊◊◊--0--◊◊◊--

CORDELL HULL, US SECRETARY OF STATE, WRITES TO
BENJAMIN SUMNER WELLES, US AMBASSADOR IN CUBA

Washington, September 14, 1933

I talked this afternoon with the French Ambassador regarding this matter and have also telegraphed the Embassy at Paris to take it up immediately with the Foreign Office.

(signed) Cordell Hull

--◊◊◊--0--◊◊◊--

CORDELL HULL, US SECRETARY OF STATE, WRITES TO
BENJAMIN SUMNER WELLES, US AMBASSADOR IN CUBA

Washington, September 14, 1933

In accordance with the recommendations made in your telegram No. 191 of September 5, the President authorized the dispatch of certain naval vessels to Santiago and Havana purely as a precautionary measure in case American citizens should find themselves in immediate physical danger. When the revolutionary movement extended throughout the Island/with resulting disturbances, additional ships were ordered to various other ports. The Secretary of the Navy also ordered other ships to proceed to Key West and stand by for orders.

In view of the publicity not only in this country but throughout Latin America which attended the dispatch of these vessels, the President, after consultation with the Secretary of State, considered that it might be helpful if the governments of all of the Latin American countries were fully informed of our action and reasons therefor. Accordingly, during the afternoon of September 5 and the morning of September 6 Assistant Secretary Caffery and the Chief of the Latin American Division saw all of the Latin American diplomatic representatives, those of Salvador and Cuba being excepted for obvious reasons. Mention was made to them of the conditions which arose in Cuba a few weeks ago, because of which the President had then felt constrained to send vessels to Cuba. Atthat time the President had made it perfectly clear that the dispatch of the ships to Cuba did not mean intervention or interference of any kind with Cuban political affairs, but that their presence was for the sole purpose of protecting American lives should they be physically in danger. When the situation had cleared up the ships were withdrawn. They were informed that unfortunately disturbances had again broken out in Cuba which appeared very serious and the President had again reluctantly found it necessary to send naval vessels for the purpose of protecting Americans should the occasion arise. The various diplomatic representatives were informed that this Government attached great importance to the opinion of the Governments and people of the Americas and, for this reason, desired to explain the situation and to reiterate that the United States was not contemplating intervention or interference in Cuban affairs, but sincerely hoped that the Cubans themselves would work out a Cuban solution of their difficulties.

On the afternoon of September 6 the President personally informed the Ambassador of Argentina and the Chargés d'Affaires of Brazil, Chile and Mexico in the sense above indicated. The President stated that intermeddling in the internal political affairs of Cuba was the last thing that he desired and that the United States would land troops only to afford protection to American lives in immediate physical danger. He reiterated his reluctance in having felt obliged to send ships to Cuba, and that having done so, he desired to explain the situation and to make it clear that he was not contemplating intervention; in fact, that it was his most sincere hope that the Cuban people would set up a stable government capable of maintaining law and order.

The following day the Mexican Government, on its own initiative, telegraphed to the Foreign Offices of Argentina, Brazil and Chile suggesting that, in an effort to render unnecessary intervention in Cuba by the United States under the Piatt Amendment, they join with Mexico in an appeal to the Cuban Government and people for a prompt restoration of law and order. The Chilean Government, in communicating its approval of the proposed action, added the suggestion that all the Latin American countries be invited to subscribe to the joint appeal.

On Wednesday afternoon, September 13, the Mexican Chargé d'Affaires informed Assistant Secretary Caffery that he had received a telegram from the Minister of Foreign Affairs of Mexico City instructing him to inform the Department that as it seemed that a stable government capable of maintaining order had been formed in Cuba, it did not seem necessary to go any further with efforts to induce other Latin American countries to make suggestions at Havana that a stable government capable of maintaining order be formed. He also indicated that his Government, and most of all his colleagues in Washington, believe that the United States should withdraw its naval vessels from Cuban waters; they feel that the opposition political leaders in Cuba will not cease their efforts to overthrow the *de facto* government as long as American naval vessels remain there. Furthermore, he told Mr. Caffery that the real difficulty which the Mexican Government encountered in its efforts to secure general Latin American action at Havana arose from the fact of the Argentine Government's failure to cooperate. As the Argentine Government did nothing, his Government had found it impossible to proceed. (See attached memorandum of conversation between the Mexican Chargé d'Affaires and Assistant Secretary Caffery.)

There are enclosed herewith copies of various memoranda and telegrams bearing on this matter.

Very truly yours,
For the Secretary of State:
(signed) Jefferson Caffery

--◇◇◇--O--◇◇◇--

BENJAMIN SUMNER WELLES, US AMBASSADOR IN CUBA, WRITES TO **CORDELL HULL,** US SECRETARY OF STATE

Havana, September 14, 1933   [RECEIVED 10:05 P.M.]

Dr. Carlos Saladrigas, Acting Secretary of State in the Céspedes Government and one of the most influential and prominent members of the ABC, called to see me this afternoon. He told me that in view of the present emergency Dr. Martínez Sáenz had been made dictator of the party and that the ABC was cooperating with the Menocalistas and the other parties opposed to the present government for the purpose of forcing a compromise and the creation of a national government of concentration. He told me that if the student group refused to compromise and preferred to attempt to drive the Republic to disaster his party and those associated would have no other alternative than immediate military action. He further told me that a rapid and effective organization of themselves and commercial groups was being made for the purpose of protecting themselves against the possibilities which they foresaw in the continuation of the present regime. Organization of commercial and financial interests is likewise progressing rapidly in other parts of the Republic. He stated that they would make every effort to force a national compromise upon the present regime in the true interest of the Republic but he expressed himself as being extremely pessimistic and feared that since the students neither have any grasp of the dangers which confront the Republic nor the slightest conception of the unselfish friendship which the United States has displayed for Cuba during the Roosevelt administration they would be unwilling to agree to anything other than their own complete retention of control of the Government.

(signed) Benjamin Sumner Welles

--◇◇◇--O--◇◇◇--

BENJAMIN SUMNER WELLES, US AMBASSADOR IN CUBA, WRITES TO
CORDELL HULL, US SECRETARY OF STATE

Havana, September 14, 1933   [RECEIVED SEPTEMBER 15 1:43 A.M.]

The Grau San Martín Government this evening issued a long proclamation which appears to be a combination of a program of procedure and a temporary constitution. The two most important paragraphs are the following:

> "Since the Provisional Government would incur grave responsibility if it abandoned the security of power to seditious ambitions it may temporarily subordinate individual rights to a system of governmental correction and control of whose use account will be given to the Constituent Assembly."

> "With full realization of its historic responsibility the Provisional Government declares its profound respect for the sanctity of those international treaties spontaneously entered into in the name of the Republic of Cuba and its firm and decided intention of complying with them to satisfy the revolutionary purposes which gave lire to its organization."

In my judgment the use of the word *"spontaneously"* in this context clearly implies the intention of denouncing the permanent treaty with the United States.

Full text will be sent by air mail.

(signed) Benjamin Sumner Welles

--◊◊◊--0--◊◊◊--

HUGH S. GIBSON, US AMBASSADOR IN BRAZIL, WRITES TO
CORDELL HULL, US SECRETARY OF STATE

Rio de Janeiro, September 14, 1933   [RECEIVED SEPTEMBER 23]

SIR: I have the honor to furnish the Department herewith, as serving to indicate the attitude of Brazil with respect to the political situation in Cuba and the relations thereto of the United States, Mexico, and Chile, a copy of a memorandum of a conversation I had with the Brazilian Minister for Foreign Affairs on September 11.

(SIGNED) HUGH S. GIBSON

--◊◊◊--0--◊◊◊--

JESSE ISIDOR STRAUS, US AMBASSADOR IN FRANCE, WRITES TO
CORDELL HULL, US SECRETARY OF STATE

Paris, September 15, 1933   [RECEIVED 7:55 A.M.]

I saw the Director of Political Affairs at the Foreign Office this morning who told me that the orders had been given more than a week ago for the dispatch boat to alter its schedule and not to proceed to Havana. The French have no desire to send any ship there at the present time as it would raise questions of recognition and protocol in which they do not wish to become involved.

(signed) J.I. Strauss

--◇◇◇--0--◇◇◇--

BENJAMIN SUMNER WELLES, US AMBASSADOR IN CUBA, WRITES TO **CORDELL HULL,** US SECRETARY OF STATE

Havana, September 15, 1933   [RECEIVED 9:15 P.M.]

A further move is under way for conversations between the leaders of the Unión Nacionalista, the ABC, Menocalistas, OCRR and representatives of the Grau San Martín regime with a view to attempting to achieve a peaceful compromise for the installation of a concentration Cabinet. A meeting is to be held tonight at 6 o'clock to discuss the bases for such agreement. The morale of the student group seems to be breaking down. The widespread labor disorders throughout the Republic, the attempt at revolt in the Province of Pinar del Río last night, the fact that even in Havana strikers are breaking into shops and that disorder is on the increase and finally the fact that the Army is almost hourly becoming more unmanageable has brought them to the realization that they need help and that they need it quickly. Two delegates of the Unión Revolucionaria, a relatively small group which is the only one of the groups represented in the mediation proceedings that accepted office from the present government have just called at the Embassy to inform me that they foresaw a breakdown of all government quickly unless a solution is found. This feeling is shared, of course, by every other group of political importance. I spent all of yesterday, as well as all of today, urging upon the political parties opposed to the present regime the necessity of making every possible effort to reach a peaceful compromise and I think my efforts have been successful in so far as the leaders have now consented to a further meeting with Grau San Martín and representatives of the student body.

As the result of an indication on the part of students acting under the orders of the Directorio Estudiantil, I requested Adolf Berle late last night to have a conversation with some of the principal members of the Directorio. In a long conversation he pointed out that the criticism of the policy of the United States, which they had been so loudly proclaiming during the past week, was quite unjustified and that the charges they had concocted regarding the policy of the Embassy were utterly baseless. I was told by one of the students present that Berle's conversation with them had an exceedingly salutary effect. This morning a representative of the Directorio came to see me to ask if I would be willing to meet with the Directorio tonight. I said that I would be very happy to do so and that I had repeatedly indicated to the students, all of the leaders of whom were either in exile or in prison during the course of the mediation negotiations, through certain professors of the university identified with the student movement that I would welcome an opportunity to talk matters over with them but that in view of their lack of response I had not felt warranted in pressing the matter any further. I expect to hold my meeting with them tonight at the House of Sr. Chibás, who was Secretary of Public Works in the Céspedes Cabinet and is the father of one of the most extreme radical members of the student group, the author of the cable sent to Latin America accusing me of complicity in the officers' plot.

(signed) Benjamin Sumner Welles

--◊◊◊--O--◊◊◊--

BENJAMIN SUMNER WELLES, US AMBASSADOR IN CUBA, WRITES TO
CORDELL HULL, US SECRETARY OF STATE

Havana, September 16, 1933   [RECEIVED 2:36 A.M.]

I had an interview tonight with the full membership of the Directorio Estudiantil. I indicated the reasons for the recent features of our policy towards Cuba and expressed very emphatically our earnest desire to be of friendly assistance should the Cuban people desire it. I stated my belief that in these very grave moments all elements of Cuban public opinion should put all feelings of rivalry and ambition to one side and cooperate for the benefit of the Republic. The interview was extremely cordial and most of the lady members were not unreasonable.

The meeting between the political leaders and Grau San Martín came to an impasse. It has, however, resumed its sessions and the negotiations are still in progress.

(signed) Benjamin Sumner Welles

--◊◊◊--O--◊◊◊--

MEMORANDUM OF A TELEPHONE CALL BETWEEN
CORDELL HULL, US SECRETARY OF STATE, AND
BENJAMIN SUMNER WELLES, US AMBASSADOR IN CUBA

Washington, September 16, 1933

SECRETARY: ... If they should reach a stage where they would get together in a broad way, would we want to take up then as rapidly as we could the question of dealing with them further? >

Photos of **Dr. Ramón Grau San Martín,** the man who raised expectations of progress and honesty in the uncertain days after the fall of Gerardo Machado.
Photos, top to bottom, left top right:
Grau in 1931; **José Grau San Martín**, his nephew, Civil Engineer, known in his time as "**Pepe Plazoleta**;" A group with his other nephews, Paulina, Polita, Ramón and Francisco; Grau San Martin with his successor and follower, future President **Carlos Prío Socarrás**. Prío, among the University students, and Batista, as leader of the Cuban Army, were the top two figures during the start of the 1933 Revolution in Cuba.

AMBASSADOR: Yes. I think under those conditions, it is the only possible solution.

SECRETARY: That would cause the more unintelligent people everywhere, who do not know our real attitude, to see that we were doing our best to go along with the Cubans.

AMBASSADOR: Exactly. Under those conditions I think we could safely waive the maintenance of order question, because no government here will be able to maintain absolute order for some time to come. If we did not, now it would give US the enmity of groups that have been friendly to us, I believe.

SECRETARY: If we should go ahead, it would give us better team work there in the future no matter what happened—and all south of it too.

--◊◊◊--O--◊◊◊--

BENJAMIN SUMNER WELLES, US AMBASSADOR IN CUBA, WRITES TO
CORDELL HULL, US SECRETARY OF STATE

Havana, September 16, 1933 [Received 5:25 p.m.]

At the meeting between the political leaders and Grau San Martín which commenced last night at 6 o'clock and with a recess terminated at 3 o'clock this morning, Colonel Mendieta acted as principal spokesman and had at all times the unfaltering support of Dr. Martínez Sáenz of the ABC; General Menocal on behalf of his own party; and the delegates of the OCRR. Dr. Miguel Mariano Gómez pursued his usual policy of taking neither one side nor the other but made it very evident, however, that he realized that the present government could not continue in power. Colonel Mendieta stated to Grau San Martín that the sole hope remaining to save Cuba was the cooperation in the national government of all the important political groups and factions in the Republic. He stated that the present government represented nothing except the students; that it had the opposition of all the principal parties as well as financial and commercial interests; and that its continuation was meeting with increasing hostility in all the provinces of the Republic. He concluded by saying that Dr. Grau San Martín must present his resignation as President and that then by common agreement a government of national concentration could be set up. He made it clear that none of the opposed parties intended to designate any specific person for the Presidency or for any other office but were willing to enter discussions with an open mind.

Grau San Martín assumed his usual attitude of insistence that his government was supported by an enormous majority of the people but stated that he would consider the proposals offered and meet with the political leaders tomorrow, Sunday, to deliver his reply.

In my conversation with the members of the student group last night I gained the very distinct impression that the three or four real leaders of the Directorate were weakening materially in the uncompromising attitude they had heretofore taken. They are gravely worried by the fact that the soldiers are no longer inclined to obey any orders issued and that the labor agitation seems to have passed beyond the control which they had deluded themselves they possessed. After having left the meeting, perhaps the most prominent of the students stated to me that he felt a solution was necessary and could be arrived at. The Department will understand that Grau San Martín is entirely under their orders and whatever decision they reach he will be forced to abide by. The student directorate contains 30 members of whom about 4 are girls and the rest men ranging from 20 to 30 years of age. The general impression I gained was one of complete immaturity, of a failure to grasp even in a rudimentary sense the grave dangers which the Republic confronts and a feeling of almost impermeable self-satisfaction. I am having Berle explain to three or four of them today who have some slight grasp of economics just what the Cuban financial and economic picture really is; that the American companies—public utilities, importers and sugar mills—cannot and will not do business under present conditions; that the situation of the Cuban Treasury is such that it will be empty within a period of between 2 weeks and a month; that the food supplies in Havana and the other ports are barely sufficient to last for 10 more days; that the Communist wave is spreading with the utmost rapidity and facility throughout the country. Once they [realize?] these obvious and simple facts, I am inclined to think that the already shattered morale of the student leaders will be further weakened, and a more patriotic and conciliatory attitude will be adopted.

As an indication of the fact, which is presumably not grasped by the American public, that the actual control of the government of Cuba is today vested solely in the hands of this group of immature students the following incident which occurred yesterday is illuminating.

The *American Electric Company* refused to shut off the light and power connections of the National Hotel without a written order from the government, which was not forthcoming. A group of the leading students thereupon proceeded to the office of the Secretary of War and demanded an escort of soldiers in order that they might go to the office and the power plant of the company and either take control themselves or wreck the buildings. Upon the refusal by Colonel Aguado to agree to their request they broke up the furniture in his office and told him to leave his office and not return. The Secretary immediately resigned. Incidents of this character, which are taking place in Havana, are, of course, occurring in every part of the Republic.

In conversation with me last night they were both courteous and deferent and the students responsible for the sending of cables both to the United States and to Latin America accusing me of various crimes and misdemeanors apologized profusely for the action they had taken which they said was due *"to the excitement of the moment"*.

They feel that recognition by us is not something which we are entitled to determine for ourselves but that it is on the contrary their right to be accorded recognition and that by our failure to recognize we are defrauding them of something to which they are legitimately entitled. On this feature, of course, I merely reiterated the statement issued by the Secretary 2 days ago and emphasized the fact that in my judgment the present government had not demonstrated that it counted upon the support of the Cuban people nor that it was maintaining public order.

The surprisingly friendly attitude shown towards me was in part due, in my belief, to their realization that recognition by the United States Government is essential to any government in Cuba and further to a desire to express a feeling of regret for the unwarranted and unjustifiable criticism directed against this Embassy.

(signed) Benjamin Sumner Welles

--◊◊◊--0--◊◊◊--

BENJAMIN SUMNER WELLES, US AMBASSADOR IN CUBA, WRITES TO **CORDELL HULL,** US SECRETARY OF STATE

Havana, September 17, 1933 [Received 3:42 a.m.]

Colonel Mendieta and Dr. Martínez Sáenz have just asked me in behalf of all the groups opposed to the present regime which now include every party except that of the students that they will inform Grau San Martín in their interview Sunday afternoon as follows:

They will accept as Provisional President any impartial Cuban of national reputation provided he is not under the domination of the Student Council; they will agree to recommend men of similar qualifications for Cabinet positions so that the Cabinet will have no political tinge; if a government can be formed in this manner they will support it consistently and actively until a new constitutional government can be inaugurated; they will under no conditions support Grau San Martín nor any government selected by and solely responsive to the Student Council.

I have arranged for an unofficial and private interview with Grau San Martín in the house of a friend early tomorrow morning. At my request Berle has seen him and outstanding members of the Student Council this evening to make entirely plain the fact that the Republic is on the brink of economic, financial and social disaster and that immediate action is imperative if the situation is to be saved.

The members of the original revolutionary junta of five have now come out against Grau San Martín and are insisting upon the necessity of the constitution of a national government to meet the existing grave emergency.

(signed) Benjamin Sumner Welles

--◊◊◊--0--◊◊◊--

BENJAMIN SUMNER WELLES, US AMBASSADOR IN CUBA, WRITES TO
CORDELL HULL, US SECRETARY OF STATE

Havana, September 17, 1933 [Received 6:40 p.m.]

I have just finished a secret conversation of 2 hours' length with Grau San Martín at a friend's house.

I told him that I had requested Berle to see him last night in order that he might realize how desperately serious the situation had become and how rapidly dangers of every kind were increasing both in number and in extent. I said that in my judgment confidence in his Government was daily diminishing and the attitude now assumed by financial, commercial and agricultural elements in refusing to pay taxes, in closing down or in canceling orders wherever possible to do so, and in protesting publicly their opposition to a continuation of the present regime must certainly convince him, as it had me, that the Government was not supported by exceedingly important elements in the country. I said that in my opinion lack of confidence was not directed in any sense against him personally nor most of the men with whom he had surrounded himself but in the basic fact that his Government had been installed as the result of a mutiny in the Army which in itself shattered all confidence in authority and in the second place that it was responsive solely to one numerically small group in the country, namely, the student group. I called his attention to the fact that I was constantly receiving accurate information from all over the Republic and that no matter how often his Government might announce that order was being maintained, I knew, and I had no doubt that he knew, that disorders were increasing every moment and that neither the lives nor the property of Cuban citizens at the present time were safe and I was by no means certain that the lives and properties of American citizens or other foreigners were safe except in those ports where American warships were stationed. He admitted this fact quite frankly. I then referred to the official declaration regarding recognition issued by my Government in Washington 4 days ago. I told him that in my judgment none of the requisites which he [sic] had mentioned in that declaration existed in his government; that the government did not have the support of the Cuban people other than that of a relatively small group; that public order was most decidedly not being maintained; that the government certainly was not stable and that no government could be considered as carrying out the functions of government when, as I had no doubt he knew, a great number of the provincial and municipal internal revenue offices were now filled by soldiers who were pocketing such few receipts as might come in and when furthermore it was plainly apparent that at the same time that the government did not collect revenues it likewise did not have sufficient funds in reserve to meet the ordinary daily charges upon it for more than an extremely brief period.

At this point he argued with me regarding popular support leaving the other features of my statement uncontroverted. He said that everyone in the country would support the government if the United States would accord recognition. I reminded him that our recognition could not in the first place be employed by him as a means of obtaining popular support but was a matter which rested entirely within our own sovereign discretion and that we did not, in justice to the Cuban people, intend to exert that power as a means of attempting to keep a minority group in control of the Cuban government.

I told him that my conversations with the leaders of the really important political groups opposed to his regime had convinced me that they were unanimously in accordance with the main features of the program which he had announced as the ideal of his government and of the student group and that on that point consequently there was no question at issue. I told him, however, that they all felt that the present government had been selected by the students and that the members of his Cabinet were subservient to every whim of the students; and that they felt that no government of this kind could either last or even attempt to carry out the program which it had set for itself. I asked him in the true interest of the Republic in this moment of gravest emergency what possible objection the student group or he himself could have to a government of concentration composed of men who were not active politicians and who were individuals of high standing and reputation who might be indicated by the various opposition groups because of the fact that they had confidence in them which confidence they did not have in most of the members of the present Cabinet.

In his reply Grau San Martín adopted an extremely conciliatory attitude. He said that he believed such a solution was necessary and that he himself favored it. He said he recognized that practical considerations must be taken into account and that at a meeting with the political leaders this afternoon he would maintain that attitude since he did not consider that individuals were of any importance in comparison with the necessity of saving the country. The attitude so expressed to me is, of course, exactly the reverse of what he has previously repeatedly said to the political leaders in past conferences. It was very apparent throughout the conversation that Grau San Martín was extremely apprehensive. When I touched upon the subject of the Army and the conditions in the Army and the imminent danger which I foresaw from the fact that the sergeants and soldiers now felt, quite correctly, that the real control of the country is in their hands and that they can exercise such con- >

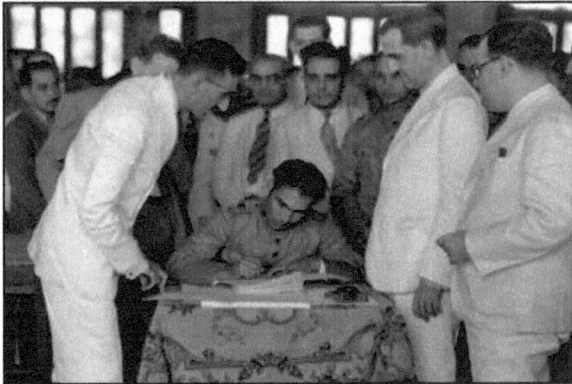

Three important photos of **Dr. Ramón Grau San Martín** during the early days of the 1933 Revolution. *Photos, top to bottom:*
The meeting where the **Partido Revolucionario Cubano (Auténtico)** was organized by Grau San Martín, February 8, 1934.
Signing ceremony on Oct 12, 1933, a formal ceremony with the presence of 1933 revolucionaries, when Batista was appointed **Chief of the Army** by Grau.
Grau watching a parade in his honor as the survivor of the *Pentarquía*.

trol whenever they see fit, it was apparent that that question was the cause of his apprehension. He told me that Batista wanted to be President but that he thought that Batista would try to gain popular support for the coming elections among the laboring classes and would not now attempt a further *coup d'état* in order to install himself in the Palace. He admitted that Batista "had to be handled" and that no orders could be given to him with any expectation of their being carried out. He said there was no alternative whatever to leaving Batista in his present post as Chief of Staff and that if any attempt were made to remove him the Army would at once become unmanageable. I reminded him that in my previous conversations with him he had expressed the opinion that the sergeants and soldiers who had joined in the mutiny were so pure in mind and were so devoted to the ideals of the students that they had no ulterior ambitions. He told me that he was willing to admit that he had been gravely mistaken on this point.

The Department will easily gather from this summary of my conversation how utterly impractical and visionary Grau San Martín is and how little hope of success there can be from a government controlled by him and by the students. The effects of his present apprehension, however, will make a compromise this afternoon more likely. The meeting referred to will be held at 3 o'clock and upon receipt of information as to the result of such meeting I shall telegraph the Department.

(signed) Benjamin Sumner Welles

--◊◊◊--O--◊◊◊--

BENJAMIN SUMNER WELLES, US AMBASSADOR IN CUBA, WRITES TO **CORDELL HULL,** US SECRETARY OF STATE

Havana, September 17, 1933   [Received September 18 1:05 a.m.]

The meeting between Grau San Martín and the leaders of the political parties lasted 5 hours the former stated he was willing to present his resignation but would only resign provided the Army and the Student Council accepted his resignation as well as the political parties. An agreement in principle was reached on the program of government as well as on the constitution of a national concentration Cabinet. The leaders of the opposition groups are now in session to determine whether they will insist upon Grau San Martín's resignation or whether they will support him, provided a new Cabinet is created in which they have confidence. They will meet again with Grau San Martín tomorrow morning at 9 o'clock to reach a final decision.

I have repeatedly today urged upon all the need for unanimous cooperation and joint support of a national government. The general situation in the country becomes hourly more serious. Even if a national government is at once constituted and we determine to accord recognition the most immediate and effective assistance on our part may not be sufficient to avert the dangers I foresee from the social revolution which is taking place and from the entire breakdown of discipline which has occurred both in the Army and among civil authorities.

(signed) Benjamin Sumner Welles

--◊◊◊--0--◊◊◊--

BENJAMIN SUMNER WELLES, US AMBASSADOR IN CUBA, WRITES TO **CORDELL HULL,** US SECRETARY OF STATE

Havana, September 18, 1933   [Received 2:45 p.m.]

The session of leaders of the political groups opposed to the government sat until early this morning. It was attended by the leaders of the Unión Nacionalista, ABC, OCRR, Menocalistas, as well as by Miguel Mariano Gómez in representation of his own party. The determination was reached that the parties represented would act jointly and present a united front on all matters at issue. Gómez has decided to join the opposition groups without further hesitation and in confirmation of this decision read a letter addressed by him to Grau San Martín in which he maintained that the government neither had popular support nor was able to maintain order and, furthermore, attacked him bitterly for the hostility demonstrated by the governmental group towards the United States and the policy followed by the Roosevelt administration and this Embassy.

It was decided that under no conditions would they support Grau San Martín as President in view of the fact that he is generally considered in great part responsible for the crisis in which the country has been plunged. There was no difference of opinion as to the program to be followed by the Provisional Government and the acceptance in the same manner of a non-political Cabinet. They further decided that they would hand their written reply to Grau San Martín this afternoon at 2 o'clock but would refuse to have further conferences with him.

It is highly unlikely that Grau San Martín and the students will give in. However, from the reports I have received this morning, the student leaders are more reasonable than Grau San Martín himself.

The political leaders are decided that no government can govern the Republic so long as the students dominate the political life of the country and are not in the university where they belong. They furthermore believe that Batista and the Army will not continue to lend support now that it is evident that public opinion throughout the Republic has crystallized strongly against the government and that under these conditions recognition from the United States will not be forthcoming. They feel that he will either seek an understanding with the political parties to oust the Grau San Martín regime or, failing that, seek to install himself in control of the government. In the latter contingency they seem to believe that the student groups will be eliminated by the Army and that in this manner this disturbing element will be removed from the scene. Those of them who have personal contacts with Batista appear to be very confident that a direct understanding with him is possible and will avoid the danger of a military dictatorship.

One healthy sign at least seems to have appeared and that is that the leaders of the political parties have reached the conclusion that the Government of the United States is not going to impose a solution and that the responsibility of finding a solution now rests upon their own shoulders. I am more than ever confident that the wisest policy for us to pursue is to keep our hands off except insofar as the protection of American lives is involved. If the solution is long postponed it will be difficult to lift Cuba from the economic and financial prostration towards which it is rapidly headed. It is also within the bounds of possibility that the social revolution winch is under way cannot be checked. American properties and interests are being gravely prejudiced and the material damage to such properties will in all probability be very great. All these contingencies seem to me preferable to intervention. By intervention we not only would seriously jeopardize our continental interests but we also would once more give the Cuban people and particularly the Cuban leaders to understand that they do not have to assume the responsibility for their own lack of patriotism or lack of vision, and that the United States Government stands always ready to repair the damage which they themselves cause their own country. It is my sincere belief that Cuba can never become a self-governing republic so long as this feeling persists.

(signed) Benjamin Sumner Welles

--◊◊◊--O--◊◊◊--

BENJAMIN SUMNER WELLES, US AMBASSADOR IN CUBA, WRITES TO **CORDELL HULL,** US SECRETARY OF STATE

Havana, September 18, 1933

I am informed by one of the persons present when the reply to the leaders of the political groups was read to Grau San Martín and to the members of the Student Council that after considerable discussion Grau San Martín announced his intention of presenting his resignation to the Army and to the students and not to the groups opposed to his regime but that he intended in any event to resign his office. As he started to rise from his chair to end the conference, Escalona, one of the leaders of the students who was standing behind him forced him back into his chair by physical force and told him that he was going to remain as President as long as the students desired him to whether he himself wished to or not. Varona, another of the student leaders, was so incensed by Grau San Martín's statement that he showed his displeasure by breaking several pieces of furniture in the room where they were sitting. These incidents are merely indicative of the way the government is conducted.

At dawn this morning Colonel Juan Blas Hernández, the revolutionary leader whom Machado was never able to suppress, commenced a revolution near the town of Moron in Camaguey Province. He is accompanied by about 300 men none of whom are well armed. Batista sent immediately a special car of soldiers and students to that region to attempt to intercept Bias Hernandez. A further revolutionary movement is imminent in the city of Santa Clara.

Grau San Martín and the Student Council are now in conference drafting their reply to the ultimatum presented by the political leaders last night. I learn on good authority that approximately half of the student leaders are in favor of accepting the compromise suggested but that it would seem probable that the more radical among the students will prevent this saner opinion from making itself effective.

(signed) Benjamin Sumner Welles

--◇◇◇--0--◇◇◇--

BENJAMIN SUMNER WELLES, US AMBASSADOR IN CUBA, WRITES TO
CORDELL HULL, US SECRETARY OF STATE

Havana, September 20, 1933

Dr. Santos Jiménez, chief political adviser of Miguel Gómez, advises me that certain of the leaders of the Student Council are in conference with Gómez for the purpose of having him serve as intermediary between the government and the leaders of the opposition groups to attempt to work out a solution for a national government based upon the ultimatum presented to Grau San Martín by the opposition leaders. In view of the very strong stand which Gómez has now taken against the government and of his support of the attitude taken by the other political leaders this move is significant. All evidence seems to point to a general weakening on the part of the students except for two or three of the most radical members.

It has been very noticeable during the past 3 days that the members of the government and of the students themselves have ceased entirely their attacks upon the United States and upon this Embassy. A demonstration consisting of about 3,000 persons, many of them ordinary street loiterers and the rest university and high school students and members of a few heterogeneous groups such as the Lithographers Union and the women revolutionists, marched to the palaces yesterday afternoon as a sign of their support of the government. Grau San Martín and several of the students made speeches to the crowd but in none of their speeches was there shown any hostility to the United States. The same change is noticeable in the radio propaganda speeches emanating from governmental sources.

In the interior evidence of armed and concerted opposition to the government is increasing. All evidence I have been able to obtain despite the strict governmental censorship tends to confirm the fact that the revolutionary government started by Bias Hernandez is gaining force and that the number of men now supporting him has increased to over 500. Two other local leaders in Santa Clara Province affiliated with the Unión Nacionalista have come out in revolt with approximately 50 supporters each.

The American Consul at Antilla informs me by telephone that he is advised Major Balan has risen in revolt in Oriente Province with approximately 800 men and apparently sufficient arms; that he took possession of the town of Gibara yesterday and is marching on Holguin today.

To the great relief of the more moderate residents of Havana the economic corporations comprising all the financial and business interests of Havana which have organized during the last few days in determined opposition to the government have agreed to postpone their threatened lockout. It is my belief that had the lockout been declared immediate sacking would have taken place and a general strike would have been declared which unquestionably would have played into the hands of the Communist leaders.

My general impression of the situation this morning is that the prospects of a national provisional government are decidedly more favorable. The revolutionary outbreaks, while bad in themselves should the movement be long continued, have the effect of weakening the attitude assumed by the students and of breaking down resistance on the part of the disorganized Army, many of whose units were forced into the mutiny against their better judgment.

(signed) Benjamin Sumner Welles

--◊◊◊--O--◊◊◊--

BENJAMIN SUMNER WELLES, US AMBASSADOR IN CUBA, WRITES TO **CORDELL HULL,** US SECRETARY OF STATE

Havana, September 21, 1933

I have just concluded an interview with Batista. He expressed this morning the desire through an intermediary to have a conversation with me. His attitude throughout the conversation was extremely reasonable and he repeatedly emphasized the fact that neither the stubbornness of the Student Council nor that of Grau San Martín should be permitted to stand in the way of a solution of the immediate political problem. It was obvious, from my talk with him, that the students and presumably Grau San Martín himself have misled Batista as to the attitude of the United States Government since September 4th. I made clear to him our policy, convinced him that we have no prejudice and no partiality and emphasized the fact that we would welcome any government in Cuba no matter by what individuals it was composed which fulfilled the requirements made clear in the official declaration of the Secretary of State last week.

He expressed the belief that solution was imperative but that some solution must be found which would not result in open hostility on the part of the students and at the same time does not result in open hostility on the part of the important groups and factions opposed to the present regime. He expressed rigorous opposition to all communist propaganda and activities.

Antonio Mendoza, Dr. Granados of the Rotary Club of Havana, and Batista's aide, Captain Ferrer, were present at the interview. At its conclusion it was proposed by Granados that Batista exert his influence with the students and with the present regime so that as a counter-proposal to the ultimatum delivered by the groups opposed to the present government a list of names of five nonpolitical Cubans should be presented from which the opposition groups will select one name to replace Grau San Martín as Provisional President, such individual then to appoint a neutral Cabinet composed of individuals acceptable to all concerned. This suggestion met with Batista's entire concurrence and he stated that he would at once support it with the students and members of the present government. I made it thoroughly clear that I had not come to the interview to make suggestions as to the nature of the formula and that my Government had no desire to offer its views as to how a solution should be found but that on account of our deep concern, because of the gravity of the situation we were keenly anxious that all groups and parties in Cuba should come to a political understanding so that a government might exist which would have the support of all.

The influence of Batista currently is, of course, very powerful. He appears to have increased his control over the troops in Havana although he complains bitterly of the attempts which are being made by the opposition to impair the loyalty of the soldiers to him. I am by no means confident that he can force the students to accept his point of view in which I think he is sincere. A willingness to compromise on such a basis as that now proposed will, I think, be demonstrated by all the opposition groups except that of General Menocal. The conversations which will ensue, as the result of the initiative which will now be undertaken by Batista, will commence tonight and presumably continue throughout tomorrow. It is my considered judgment that the probability of a favorable outcome would be greatly enhanced if the President himself were willing to address a message to the Cuban people. In my opinion the extreme gravity of the situation warrants this step. It will be recalled that the message delivered to the people of Cuba by the President

Building the **National Capitol** in Cuba was a major project that demanded time, funding and engineering and architectural expertise. The process was started in 1917, during the Menocal government, when plans were drawn by **Félix Cabarrocas**, who conceived a monumental staircase and a majestic portico topped with a grandiose classical dome. The work was paralyzed in 1921, due to the economic crisis. The project continued tears later, when the government of Machado signed the firm **Govantes and Cabarrocas**, in 1925, emphasizing the importance of the staircase and attaching large pilasters to the side porches; The dome became even more classic. In the same year 1925 **Raúl Otero** and the French architects **Heitzler** and **Leveau**, from the **Forestier** firm, made changes, such as further accentuating the vertical stair-porch-dome axis and giving more transparency to the lateral bodies. In 1927 **José María Bens Arrarte** made other changes, which made the building more classic and grandiose, with elements of art deco.

Final construction, overseen by the US firm of **Purdy and Henderson** began on April 1926, during the **Machado** administration. The size of the building is 681 by 300 ft. Its design although it is often compared to that of the United States Capitol, it is not a replica of it. It is similar to that in Washington DC, but a meter higher, a meter wider, and a meter longer, as well as much richer in detail. To finish its construction more than 5000 workers, 3 years, 3 months and 20 days were needed. Inside, it houses the world's third largest bronze statue. the inspiration for the cupola came from the **Panthéon** in Paris. The cupola, which is stone clad around a steel frame, is set planimetrically forward on the building to allow for the apse that contains a statue of La Republica, a work by **Angelo Zanelli**. It weighs 49 tons with a height of 49 ft., covered with 22 carat gold leaf. At almost 302 ft. high, the dome was the highest point in the city of Havana until 1956 when the FOCSA Building was built reaching a height of 121 meters (397 ft). The *Capitolio* had the third highest dome in the world at the time of its construction. The 56 steps leading to the main entrance, La Escalinata, are flanked by two 21 ft statues, also by Zanelli; to the left is **Work** (El *Trabajo*), to the right is **Virtue** (La *Virtud*).

on the 1st of July last met with an exceptionally favorable response. I believe that a message now would be welcomed by all except the professional agitators and those who are opposing friendship with the United States for ulterior motives and that it might well have a decisive effect. I wish, therefore, to present to your consideration and to that of the President the desirability of his issuing a statement based upon the following facts, and I would like to emphasize that if such a message is to be sent it should be made public within the next 48 hours. My suggestions are as follows:

1. There exists in Cuba today a situation where it is apparent that not only is public order not being maintained but that there is likewise a rapidly increasing disregard for the protection of individual and property rights guaranteed by the constitutions which have been adopted by the Cuban people and reasserted in the permanent treaty between the United States and Cuba.

2. The economic condition of the Republic is fast verging upon complete prostration.

In the state of uncertainty and confusion which now obtains, confidence on the part of financial and commercial interests operating in Cuba has been seriously impaired; the import and export trade has been partially paralyzed; the agricultural production of the nation upon which in great part the prosperity of the Republic rests has been very largely checked; unemployment as the logical result of such conditions has mounted rapidly until such estimates as can be prepared show that approximately one-third of Cuba's wage earners are unemployed.

3. The financial condition of the Cuban government is rightly a cause for the gravest disquiet. During the past 2 weeks a deficit in the collection of normal revenues has steadily mounted and it is obvious that the ordinary obligations of the government cannot long be met.

4. It is very plain that in order to counteract such conditions which are a matter of just and friendly concern to every republic of the continent and in particular to the Government of the United States because of the traditional ties between our two countries, stability in government must be assured. In the disturbed state of the political, economic, and social phases of Cuban life which now persists, such stability can only be secured if the Cuban people support and have confidence in their government.

The Government of the United States has officially declared it would welcome the creation of any government in Cuba which was responsive to the will of the Cuban people, which was capable of maintaining public order, and which consequently could carry out the functions of any stable government. Those conditions do not now exist.

We favor no group nor party in Cuba in preference to any other. We sympathize deeply with those ideals of social reform and honesty in government which so many of the important factors in Cuba's public opinion of today are proclaiming. We hope they will be carried into effect. But the Government of the United States believes that what is imperative in this moment of grave crisis is not alone the determination of a far reaching program but the immediate cooperation of all groups in Cuba in the formation and maintenance and support of a government responsive to the will of the people lest all government in Cuba be destroyed. No party advantage, no political strife is the issue currently. On the program of the provisional government all groups are in accord. The issue is, on the contrary, the urgent need for the support by the people of a provisional and temporary government which can prepare the way through the carrying out of this program for the installation of a constitutional government elected by the majority of the Cuban people.

It would afford the American Government and people the deepest satisfaction if all representative groups in Cuba through their responsible leaders were, without delay, in the interest of the Republic of Cuba, to lend their support to a provisional government in which they all have confidence. We would not only welcome such a government, but we would likewise tender it all possible assistance in these difficult moments should such assistance be desired of us.

(signed) Benjamin Sumner Welles

--◇◇◇--0--◇◇◇--

BENJAMIN SUMNER WELLES, US AMBASSADOR IN CUBA, WRITES TO **CORDELL HULL,** US SECRETARY OF STATE

Havana, September 22, 1933   [Received 5:45 p.m.]

At the same time that Batista was engaged in conversations yesterday evening with a view to forcing a compromise agreement, Dr. Miguel Mariano Gómez, together with one or two of the most influential professors of the university, had a long conference with the Student Council for the same purpose. As the result of the latter negotiation the leaders of the student group agreed to propose the following compromise to the leaders of the opposition parties:

1. The retention of Grau San Martín as President.
2. Appointment of a *Junta Consultiva* composed of 20 members, one-half of which to be selected by the opposition groups, and the remaining half by the government supporters to function as a legislative council.

3. The *Junta Consultiva* to determine all appointments to the Cabinet, including sub-secretaries as well as directors of bureaus in the Executive departments, all such appointments as are recommended to be made automatically by the President; no removals to be made automatically except with the consent of two-thirds of the members of the *Junta Consultiva*.

Mendieta is inclined, in behalf of the Unión Nacionalista, to agree to this compromise; it is likewise acceptable to the leaders of the OCRR. The other groups of the opposition are opposed to any decision which involves the retention of Grau San Martín.

With reference to my conversation, by telephone this morning with the Secretary, I wish to call attention to the fact that revolutionary outbreaks are increasing in number and extent. I am advised this morning that a revolutionary movement of considerable importance has commenced in the southeast portion of the Province of Matanzas. Notwithstanding the government's reports to the contrary the revolutionary movement commenced by Bias Hernandez has not been checked but is on the contrary increasing in extent. The revolutionary movement in Oriente Province continues. If a compromise is rapidly reached, which all the opposition groups will publicly support, these revolutionary movements will cease. If, on the other hand, no agreement is now reached or it is long postponed the revolutionary movements will gather momentum, extreme bitterness of feeling will be engendered as the result of casualties and it may be exceedingly difficult to prevent a continuance for an indefinite period of general guerrilla warfare. It is for that reason that, in my belief, it is wise policy for us to do everything, we can further a speedy agreement by all influential groups in Cuba. I realize that professional agitators might seize any statement issued by the President as a pretext for renewed anti-American propaganda. On the other hand, an enormous majority of the Cuban people would not only not resent but would welcome an appeal in the name of the American people to all Cubans to support a provisional government satisfactory to all on the program of which all elements are already in entire accord. I fear that the Department may have the impression that a statement of this kind might be considered as favoring one faction as against another. That, of course, is not the case. What Cuba requires until national elections can be held for a constitutional government, is a provisional and temporary government which has the confidence of all so that the usual claim of partiality or intimidation during the electoral period cannot be raised. If the Cubans cannot reach an agreement as to the formation of a temporary government which possesses the confidence of all it will be readily understood that during the electoral period disturbances will be bound to occur. With a view to that future danger it is most decidedly to our own interest to foster in every possible way the creation now of a government in which all elements will participate and in which they all feel they can repose confidence before increased revolutionary activities make such agreement more difficult, if not altogether impossible.

(signed) Benjamin Sumner Welles

--◊◊◊--0--◊◊◊--

BENJAMIN SUMNER WELLES, US AMBASSADOR IN CUBA, WRITES TO
CORDELL HULL, US SECRETARY OF STATE

Havana, September 22, 1933   [Received September 23 2:00 a.m.]

At their interview this afternoon with the university professors who were proposing a solution based upon the retention of Grau San Martín as President and the selection of a national Cabinet both the Student Council and Grau San Martín reversed completely the conciliatory attitude assumed last night and stated they would agree to no compromise whatever. At the same time Batista was holding an interview with Mendieta and Gómez upon both of whom he made an extremely favorable impression. He stated that the solution proposed yesterday (reported in my telegram of September 21, 7 p.m.) should be acceptable to any Cuban who thought first of his country and that he would again see the Student Council tonight at 9 o'clock and deliver an ultimatum to them in the sense that they must accept it. After this interview he will meet with the leaders of all the opposition groups to report the result. All the opposition groups have now decided to support any government formed as the result of such solution.

In the meantime, the revolution gathers strength in Matanzas Province. It is reliably stated that the cities of Cardenas and Matanzas will join the revolt tonight with the support of the troops stationed there.

The students this afternoon refused to permit a truck loaded with pay for the officers in the National Hotel to enter although the soldiers on the truck bore a written order from Batista authorizing entrance, and although an officer by order of Batista directed the entrance of the truck. Since officers in the hotel only have food for one day more, they will presumably try to fight their way out tonight or tomorrow. There is general apprehension in Havana tonight; all leaders of the opposition group have however informed me that they have strictly forbidden any counter movement so long as there is any hope of a peaceful solution.

(signed) Benjamin Sumner Welles

--◊◊◊--0--◊◊◊--

Political caricatures in Cuba in the early 1930s. *Top to bottom, left to right:* Cuban **President Zayas** taking orders from US Ambassador **General Enoch Crowder**; **Einstein** visiting Havana; Cuban President **Mario Menocal**; US **President Herbert Hoover**; **the Stalin-Hitler** non-aggression Pact; **President Grau San Martín**.

BENJAMIN SUMNER WELLES, US AMBASSADOR IN CUBA, WRITES TO
CORDELL HULL, US SECRETARY OF STATE

Havana, September 23, 1933   [Received 7:35 p.m.]

The interview of Batista with the opposition leaders was postponed until 3 o'clock this afternoon. The students have learned of it and have insisted upon being present.

I have very little hope of any agreement being reached owing to the interposition of the Student Council. The latter at half past 2 o'clock this morning issued a statement rejecting all compromise insisting that patriotic Cubans should support the present government and making it very plain that the students themselves and no others are the government.

Owing to peremptory orders issued by the political leaders here last night a halt was called to the revolutionary movement in Matanzas Province. The revolutionists, however, have retained their arms and are awaiting developments.

(signed) Benjamin Sumner Welles

--◊◊◊--0--◊◊◊--

BENJAMIN SUMNER WELLES, US AMBASSADOR IN CUBA, WRITES TO
CORDELL HULL, US SECRETARY OF STATE

Havana, September 23, 1933   [September 24—12:55 a.m.]

The conference between the student representatives and the leaders of the political parties lasted 6 hours. There were present Batista, three members of the Student Council, Mendieta, Gómez, two representatives of Menocal, Martínez Sáenz for the ABC, two delegates of the OCRR and Dr. Coro for the university. Batista took a very strong attitude in line with his position in his conversation with me 2 days ago. After very violent dissension at the outset the discussion took a more constructive turn and it was unanimously decided that a substitute for Grau San Martín should be considered the basis of a compromise. The opposition leaders meet again tomorrow at 10 o'clock and in the afternoon they will once more discuss a solution with the government's representatives. There appears to be some feeling of optimism on the part of those present as to the possibility of an agreement.

(signed) Benjamin Sumner Welles

--◊◊◊--0--◊◊◊--

BENJAMIN SUMNER WELLES, US AMBASSADOR IN CUBA, WRITES TO
CORDELL HULL, US SECRETARY OF STATE

Havana, September 25, 1933   [Received 3:45 a.m.]

I feel that the time has come when I must emphasize my conviction that the statement by yourself suggested in my cable No. 289 is the one remaining chance we have of persuading the Cubans to agree upon' a solution of their problem which will offer promise of being satisfactory [to] all groups and which can in any way be regarded as satisfactory to our Government. The entire day of today has been spent by all leaders in joint conference and now an agreement is as remote as it has been at any time this week. The conference will meet again tomorrow night, but all leaders have lost hope that any agreement can be reached of their own initiative. There now remain two alternatives if you decide to refrain from making our position clear by urging a common accord. The first will be a desultory revolutionary movement which will probably take a considerable time before it proves successful and which will impoverish still further the interior provinces and inevitably entail damage to American and foreign properties; the second is the displacement of the present regime by a more radical group in connivance with a portion or the whole of the Army and which will be headed by some profession agitator... or some one of the Army sergeants. In the latter event likely, the government would assume completely dictatorial powers and abandon the program for the re-establishment of constitutional government as the result of national elections.

While the delay in reaching a solution continues the economic conditions grow steadily worse, the field grows more propitious for Communist propaganda and the breakdown of all semblance of unity or discipline in the Army is fast reaching to point where hope must soon be abandoned of using even a part of the Army again as a national military force.

You know how sincerely I believe in the policy of nonintervention in Cuba. I likewise am convinced that the Cubans can never govern themselves until they are forced to realize that they must assume their own responsibilities. But you also appreciate the psychology of the peoples of the Caribbean Republics. We have been generous, and we have shown the utmost patience. The impression is fast growing that our attitude is due to fear of public opinion in Latin America and that we will countenance a complete disregard by the Cubans of any international or individual rights we may possess here. Respect for us is diminishing and the belief is rising, sedulously fostered by the radicals, that the United States can be flouted with complete impunity. That attitude in my judgment is due to the mistaken impression that our continued abstention from announcing a more definite stand than we have is caused by a policy of weakness rather than by the policy of generosity and non-interference which we have pursued.

I feel very strongly that a statement of the nature suggested in my telegram No. 289 would have a decisive effect. I do not think it is too late. But if some measure of that kind is not taken, I fear that the situation here will take a turn which can only be regarded as disastrous to the Cuban people themselves as well as to our national interests.

(signed) Benjamin Sumner Welles

--◊◊◊--0--◊◊◊--

BENJAMIN SUMNER WELLES, US AMBASSADOR IN CUBA, WRITES TO **CORDELL HULL,** US SECRETARY OF STATE

Havana, September 25, 1933   [Received 11:47 p.m.]

Colonel Juan Blas Hernandez who had attempted to lead a revolution in Santa Clara Province during the past 10 days arrived in Havana this morning to make an ostensible peace with the Grau San Martín government. The motive for his apparent surrender is the fact that he was ordered to do so by Colonel Mendieta whose supporter he is on the ground that no satisfactory plans have as yet been formulated for a nation-wide revolution since there is still the possibility of a peaceful solution and because Bias Hernandez has neither sufficient arms nor ammunition for a successful revolt.

(signed) Benjamin Sumner Welles

--◊◊◊--0--◊◊◊--

BENJAMIN SUMNER WELLES, US AMBASSADOR IN CUBA, WRITES TO **CORDELL HULL,** US SECRETARY OF STATE

Havana, September 25, 1933 [Received September 26 12:22 a.m.]

The negotiations between the leaders of the national political parties and the representatives of the Grau San Martín regime have broken down. At a meeting this morning of all political leaders it was decided that they would act jointly in all negotiations and that they would under no conditions accept Grau San Martín as President on the ground that the public had no confidence in him, that he had already proved thoroughly unfitted for his task and because he was merely the puppet of the Student Council. They agreed to accept any other formula of solution that the Government and Batista might propose, including the suggestion by the Student Council of the designation of Grau San Martín's substitute in the Presidency, provided that a national concentration Cabinet was formed. I was advised that during the debate the students admitted quite cynically that the attacks which they had directed against the United States and against the Embassy had been made solely for the purpose of creating popularity for the government and with full realization that there was neither truth nor motive for the charges alleged.

The opposition leaders have determined to hold no further conversations with the students or with Grau San Martín and have designated Antonio Mendoza and Dr. Granados of the Rotary Club as intermediaries should the government delegates desire to treat further with them.

(signed) Benjamin Sumner Welles

--◊◊◊--0--◊◊◊--

BENJAMIN SUMNER WELLES, US AMBASSADOR IN CUBA, WRITES TO
CORDELL HULL, US SECRETARY OF STATE

Havana, September 26, 1933

I spoke to the President yesterday evening on the question of the suggested message, but he said that thus far he has not felt justified in sending another message.

(signed) Benjamin Sumner Welles

--◊◊◊--0--◊◊◊--

BENJAMIN SUMNER WELLES, US AMBASSADOR IN CUBA, WRITES TO
CORDELL HULL, US SECRETARY OF STATE

Havana, September 27, 1933   [Received 3:05 p.m.]

Professor Cuervo Rubio, who was at first identified with the Student Council and the present regime and who determined to oppose it about a week ago, last night on the radio delivered a bitter attack against it. He stated that the administration not only lacked the support of all the political parties but was also opposed by most of the public opinion. He criticized the regime for the adoption of measures in imitation of those employed by General Machado. He concluded by condemning the government for encouraging propaganda against the Roosevelt administration and its diplomatic representatives here and stated that "The American Government is demonstrating its greatest respect for our independence and its vehement desire not to intervene". He urged as the only possible solution a concentration Cabinet supported by all factions.

Dr. Cuervo Rubio was joined in his attacks on the present regime by prominent individuals who have formerly been identified with the administration including representatives of the Unión Revolucionaria and of the Feminist Alliance both of which groups formerly supported Grau San Martín.

Sergio Carbó this morning asked if I would consent to meet him this afternoon in order to discuss the situation. I have announced that I would be willing to do so. I am informed that realizing that the Grau San Martín government cannot long continue he is associating himself with Batista in order to prepare to expedite its fall.

(signed) Benjamin Sumner Welles

--◇◇◇--0--◇◇◇--

CORDELL HULL, US SECRETARY OF STATE, WRITES TO
BENJAMIN SUMNER WELLES, US AMBASSADOR IN CUBA

Havana, September 28, 1933

From Caffery. Dr. Carlos Finlay came to see me informally this morning. I told him that we are not interested in what individuals make up the Cuban government, but we are very much interested in seeing a government formed capable of maintaining law and order throughout the Island. I told him that I see no reason why a concentration government able to carry out the normal functions of government cannot be formed.

Dr. Finlay, and Marquez Sterling who was also present, stated that they would take immediate steps to work to that end.

(signed) Cordell Hull

--◇◇◇--0--◇◇◇--

OCTOBER OF 1933

 Events in Cuba

October 1 *Emilio Laurent* resigns his post at police headquarters.

October 2 At 6 AM, soldiers and civilians, without prior notice, start the attack on the *National Hotel*, where former officers have taken refuge. Artillery is used in the attack, but soon they run out of munitions, and they must surrender. Between 12 and 16 officers are killed while held in detention. The fight is settled with almost one hundred dead between soldiers and officers. Survivors are taken prisoners to the La Cabaña fortress, the Columbia Camp and the Castle of El Príncipe.

October 4 Grau is the subject of an attack. Batista and Welles meet again. The American ambassador supports Batista. Welles asks Batista for a solid and democratic government that the US could recognize.

October 6 The University of Havana is granted autonomy.

October 7 New interview Batista-Welles, where the first states that he has the support of businessmen and financiers, along with former opposition politicians. **October 10** Campaign to issue a decree regulating that at least 80% of Cuban nationals most be in the payroll of every company.

October 13 The militarization of the High Schools (Institutes) and forcing students to wear military uniform are repealed.

October 20 Pedraza sent by Batista to Oriente to control the military situation.

October 24 The radical ABC is divided into two branches, one of which continues to support the government.

October 26 A powerful bomb detonates at Mendieta's house. He escapes unharmed.

October 29 A group of members of the opposition asks Mendieta to preside over a provisional government. He declines even after the support of the idea by both Welles and Batista.

Washington Telex

BENJAMIN SUMNER WELLES, US AMBASSADOR IN CUBA, WRITES TO **CORDELL HULL,** US SECRETARY OF STATE

Havana, October 1, 1933   [Received 7:20 p.m.]

Martínez Sáenz informed me this morning that the Uruguayan Consul here had advised him earlier that he and the Chargé d'Affaires of Chile and the Chargé d'Affaires of Mexico were offering to mediate between the government and the opposition to help find a solution of the present problem. He told me he had replied that he felt that no effort of this kind would be successful unless I agreed to join and requested my opinion. He also said he was confident Grau San Martín would not accept the offer.

I replied that I would of course welcome any effort by the diplomatic representatives of American Republics to help the Cubans reach a solution of their difficulties and that I could only express my sincere hope for their success; that I appreciated his reference to myself but that I felt it would be advisable not to raise the question of my participation.

(signed) Benjamin Sumner Welles

--◇◇◇--0--◇◇◇--

The World and Cuba in late 1933. Newspapers report on Hitler and his policy of **Anti-Semitism**. Reporters are amazed at the stamina of **Nikola Tesla**, the electrical engineering wizard, In Cuba, hundreds of **worker's demonstrations** for higher wages and fewer workhours... mainly an 8-hour workday.

BENJAMIN SUMNER WELLES, US AMBASSADOR IN CUBA, WRITES TO
CORDELL HULL, US SECRETARY OF STATE

Havana, October 1, 1933   [Received October 2, 2:27 a.m.]

I had at his request a further interview with Sergio Carbó this afternoon.

Owing to the increased strength which the Army has obtained since the events of Friday the government itself has felt itself correspondingly weaker. There is in the first place a healthy reaction among the soldiers themselves against those elements in the government and especially those members of the Student Council whom they consider identified with the Communist organization, and in the second place, there is an increasing divergence between those individuals in the government who support the attitude of the soldiers and believe in the necessity of maintaining public order and those who wish frankly to join with the extremist labor and Communist groups. The Army is more united in Havana than at any time during the past month and Batista's position is correspondingly stronger. Owing to his close connection with Batista and his present influence over him Carbó has more power today than the Student Council and consequently than Grau San Martín whose sole support is in the students.

Carbó stated that he had reached the conclusion that a change in the present government was desirable provided such change was predicated from this fusion into a national party of those existing factions which favored the realization of a program of social reform—by this he meant, he explained, a fusion of the ABC, the less radical portion of the Student Council, the progressive elements in the Unión Nacionalista and Gómez parties, and the OCRR, such fusion to support the new provisional government. In reply to my inquiry he stated that any such project must, of course, imply not only the support but the active participation of the Army. He made it clear that the Army leaders were no longer willing to stand the attempt on the part of the students to dominate by emphasizing that the soldiers were already disarming students as well as other civilians and intended to disband the so-called "caskets army" composed of about 2,000 students armed with rifles and machine guns.

I told him that I was heartily in favor of any government in Cuba that could rally popular opinion of real importance and that could prove it was capable of maintaining order and that could inspire confidence in its intent to carry out the general program already agreed upon. I told him further that in my conversations with the leaders of the groups which he had mentioned I had obtained the clear impression that they would agree to the project he had in mind provided they were offered a fair deal; that if he offered them authority as well as requesting their support they would in all probability accede to the suggestion. I told him that I would not agree in any sense further to mediate but that if he and they desired to consult me behind the scenes I was willing to be of all possible service for the purpose of unifying Cuban public opinion in the support of a provisional government in which all classes could have confidence.

He discussed with me at great length the administration's policies in the United States. He asked if the United States would oppose a policy of social and economic reform in Cuba. I stated that in my judgment my Government would not only not oppose but would in every proper manner actively support such a program provided it were carried out with the consent of a majority of the Cuban people through the medium of a constituted government. He promised me he would oppose any move by the present government to declare a moratorium on the foreign debt in the hope that change in the existing situation would result in the creation of a government that would be recognized and which could handle that question in a constructive and friendly manner with the bankers. He told me that in compliance with his promise to me in our last interview a decree would be issued tomorrow ordering the Army to dislodge from any sugar central all individuals other than the employees whom the managers desired to retain and calling for the expulsion from the Republic of all foreign agitators and Communists.

He will begin tomorrow conversations with the leaders of the political parties above mentioned.

(signed) Benjamin Sumner Welles

--◊◊◊--0--◊◊◊--

BENJAMIN SUMNER WELLES, US AMBASSADOR IN CUBA, WRITES TO **CORDELL HULL,** US SECRETARY OF STATE

Havana, October 2, 1933   [Received 2:30 p.m.]

According to reliable information two trucks heavily loaded with arms and ammunition broke through the sentries stationed around the National Hotel just before dawning this morning. This incident gave rise to shooting between the officers and the soldiers which resulted in the death of one soldier and the wounding of several others. Shortly after 6 o'clock the soldiers who had in the meantime collected a large force which they had thrown around the hotel opened fire upon the hotel with light artillery. The engagement lasted for the better part of 2 hours as the result of which at least 15 soldiers were killed, and a much greater number seriously wounded. At half past 8 Dr. Grau San Martín sent his aide to inform me that the soldiers intended to bring heavy artillery into play in order to force the officers to surrender or else to kill them. He desired to ascertain if there were any Americans still in the hotel. After ascertaining from the manager of the hotel that all   >

American citizens had left I advised him accordingly. Shortly before this time I received a letter from General Sanguily, the commanding officer of the officers, in which he stated that the attack had been made upon the hotel by the soldiers and that the officers were determined to resist it and to bring about the reinstallation of the *"legitimate Government of Cuba presided over by Dr. Carlos Manuel Céspedes"*.

At 7:15 an American citizen employed by Swift and Company named Lotspicht who was watching the fighting from the balcony of his apartment in the Lopez Serrano Apartment House a short distance from the National Hotel was seriously wounded and died an hour later in the hospital to which he had been taken. There is every reason to believe that the shot which resulted in his death was a stray bullet. Now the firing on the hotel continues and one wing of the hotel had been very badly damaged. An increasing number of troops are being brought into the city from the garrisons around Havana and are being stationed about the hotel.

The Cuban Red Cross has attempted to obtain a protracted armistice without success. As the result of my suggestion a period of approximately 30 minutes was permitted for the civilians living in the houses immediately adjacent to the National Hotel to remove to positions of safety. Since many of the telephone wires have been cut it has been impossible for me to speak personally to other members of the Diplomatic Corps. I have, however, communicated with the Spanish Ambassador, the Dean of the Corps, through his secretary and have suggested that certain of the diplomatic representatives of the Latin American Republics might to advantage attempt to mediate between the soldiers and the officers in the hotel in order to prevent not only casualties among the officers and soldiers but likewise danger to the lives of foreigners living in the Vedado district from stray bullets and shells.

So far there has been no counter revolution attempted in this city which, except for the district around the National Hotel, appears to be quiet. Consular reports from all points in the interior show no signs of serious disturbances.

(signed) Benjamin Sumner Welles

Lieutenant Arsenio Ortiz, aka the Jackal of the East, for his "personal justice actions," bypassing established judicial procedures, was a thug personally protected by Gerardo Machado. He began working for the president when he arrived in Havana from Holguin, where he was already famous for his excesses. Machado appointed him Army Supervisor in Santiago de Cuba, in order to prevent possible uprisings against him. His appointment was subsequent to the murder, in a well-planned attack, of the previous supervisor Captain Calvo.

Ortiz established his residence in 1930 in a house on the outskirts of Santiago de Cuba, bordering on the Santa Bárbara neighborhood, located on a small elevation near the shooting range and the San Juan river, in the town of Santa Elena. Because of the proximity of a training camp to his home, Ortiz spent two or three hours a day training and they say he possessed an enviable aim, even throwing coins into the air which he hit in the same center. From his home he could see much of Santiago de Cuba, which he considered his fief. Early in the morning he went down in his mule by an old trillo called Madre Vieja, who led him directly to the Moncada Barracks. At the side of his house was a cave, which many said kept the remains of criminals and young opponents of the Machado government. Nearby was also the famous Loma Colorada, one of their favorite places to execute their victims.

For many months Ortiz extorted merchants and prostitutes from the region. It is said that, drinking in a bar, he sent to kidnap a dependent nicknamed the Galleguito; They put him in a police car in front of several friends and sent him to hang. Then he went to a farm with the group and drank until dawn.

On another occasion, on the beach of Caletón, west of Santiago, when one night one of his enemies was asleep in a hammock, he surprised him with a successful blow to the head, with a wooden pylon, and when he fell they riddled with bullets.

Arsenio Ortiz married young and had three children, two females and one male, the latter bore his same name. He lived for many years near Los Caballitos, in Madre Vieja, Oriente. Machado sent him to Germany to refresh the political spirits against him. From Germany, Ortiz went to the Dominican Republic in the shelter of Trujillo, for which he worked together with the famous Dominican gigolo Porfirio Rubirosa, who taught the art of how to get rid of some unpleasant characters for Trujillo. Ortiz died in 1949, still on the payroll of Generalissimo Trujillo.

MEMORANDUM OF A TELEPHONE CONVERSATION BETWEEN
CORDELL HULL, US SECRETARY OF STATE, AND
BENJAMIN SUMNER WELLES, US AMBASSADOR IN CUBA.
Washington, October 2, 1933

SECRETARY: Hello, Mr. Ambassador, how is the situation now?

AMBASSADOR: Mr. Secretary, I wanted to call you up a little earlier because I finally succeeded in getting hold of the Spanish Ambassador, and a meeting of the Diplomatic Corps has been called for four o'clock. We are going then as a body to propose, for humanitarian reasons, that a solution be found for a peaceful settlement between the officers and the soldiers.

SECRETARY: How many of the Diplomatic Corps?

AMBASSADOR: Every member of the Corps.

SECRETARY: Have they all agreed?

AMBASSADOR: Yes. They are all entirely in accord. It will simply be a formal way of doing what we have already agreed upon. In the meantime, conditions have been proposed to the officers which I think should be acceptable to them. The conditions are that if they will agree to come out unarmed, five at a time their lives will be guaranteed, and they will be given all possible respect but will be held as prisoners until some definite decision is reached—as to what is to happen to them. Under the circumstances, that is the best that can be done.

SECRETARY: Were these conditions proposed by the civil government or by the army?

AMBASSADOR: They were received just from the army.

SECRETARY: At the present time that is all that counts.

AMBASSADOR: Yes. I think that what the Diplomatic Corps will have to do, and I want to speak to you specifically about this, is to support any agreement the officers may come to with the soldiers along those lines. Because if we do not take some action of that kind, there is so much agitation and so much ill feeling that it might be doubtful if those conditions would be carried out. I think we are perfectly justified, do you not, in taking that action?

SECRETARY: At first impression, that would seem to be the most feasible thing that would be open to you.

AMBASSADOR: Of course, we won't assume any individual responsibility on behalf of our governments, but as the Diplomatic Corps we can lend our moral support.

SECRETARY: The Diplomatic Corps would be acting as a unit?

AMBASSADOR: As a unit, yes.

SECRETARY: At first blush, it would seem to me to be the feasible thing to do. I do not think there is anything else we can do.

Caffery and Phillips are listening in and their first impression is the same.

AMBASSADOR: It means that if we do that, we may possibly prevent a massacre, and for purely humanitarian reasons I think we are justified in doing so. But I will send you a cable, Mr. Secretary, just as soon as the meeting of the Corps is over, and I know what happens.

SECRETARY: What has happened to the Americans in those apartments in the vicinity of the hotel?

AMBASSADOR: A truce was maintained, and we got them all out. Automobile omnibuses were sent up there and the Americans were all banded up and are out of there.

SECRETARY: That is a mighty fine piece of work. Phillips and Caffery both said so before I had time to say it.

AMBASSADOR: I am hopeful that now at any rate we can prevent a needless slaughter, and I will work along those lines.

SECRETARY: That proposed action by the entire Diplomatic Corps might lead to some help all along the line.

AMBASSADOR: I am not sure about that, but this preliminary step I think will be very useful anyhow.

SECRETARY: It is very interesting to hear from you, and we are very well pleased with the way you are handling those matters.

AMBASSADOR: Thank you very much. I appreciate it. I will send you a cable as soon as I have the facts to report.

--◊◊◊--O--◊◊◊--

BENJAMIN SUMNER WELLES, US AMBASSADOR IN CUBA, WRITES TO **CORDELL HULL,** US SECRETARY OF STATE

Havana, October 2, 1933   [Received 10:40 p.m.]

The meeting of the Diplomatic Corps, referred to in my telephone conversation with the Secretary, took place at 4 o'clock. There were present, besides the Spanish Ambassador, the Dean of the Corps, and me, the Ministers of Chile and Paraguay and the Chargés d'Affaires of Argentina, Brazil, Mexico, Colombia and Venezuela, together with the French Minister. The other members of the Corps either could not be reached by telephone or else like the Ministers of Great Britain and Germany were afraid to leave their Legations on account of the shooting that was going on in their vicinity.

At the meeting of the Corps it was unanimously agreed to authorize the Spanish Ambassador as Dean to obtain an immediate interview with Dr. Grau San Martín in behalf of the entire Corps and request for the sake of humanity an immediate truce between the officers and the soldiers, to continue until some peaceful agreement might be reached between the two contending forces.

It is as yet impossible to locate the whereabouts of Dr. Grau San Martín but if he can be found the Spanish Ambassador will make the representations indicated.

At noon today Batista offered the following terms to the officers: That they were to leave the hotel disarmed in groups of five at intervals of 10 minutes; that they would be taken into custody but that their lives would be guaranteed, and their persons would be treated with complete respect. At 3:30, the time limit set by Batista for the acceptance of these conditions, the officers were yet unwilling to accede and firing consequently commenced.

At a quarter before 5, after heavy firing, the officers surrendered to the soldiers. The soldiers immediately entered the hotel and lined the officers up by twos outside of the hotel grounds. A very large crowd had collected and radical agitators in the crowd endeavored to incite the mob to seize the officers and kill them. In order to prevent the mob from getting closer the soldiers first fired in the air and later the mob and dispersed it. I understand that the officers are now being taken to Cabana Prison.

Captain Velasco of the General Staff has sent word that the city tonight will be patrolled by soldiers and that complete order will be preserved. During the day very considerable numbers of the lawless element have collected particularly in the Vedado and it will be difficult in my judgment to prevent a considerable amount of sacking and robbery.

(signed) Benjamin Sumner Welles

--◇◇◇--0--◇◇◇--

BENJAMIN SUMNER WELLES, US AMBASSADOR IN CUBA, WRITES TO **CORDELL HULL,** US SECRETARY OF STATE

Havana, October 2, 1933   [Received 9:00 p.m.]

There has been during the past 2 hours a great deal of shooting throughout the city. At one time the shooting around the Embassy was considerable as well as at the Palace a block away. So far as I can ascertain it is due to cars filled with opposition groups who drive at all speed about the city firing on soldiers or known adherents of the government and in part to encounters between soldiers and lawless elements.

The circumstance that gives me most concern is the fact that the soldiers are looting the wine cellars of the National Hotel and the probability is that many of them will be dangerously drunk before midnight. I have just sent a message to Batista urging him to place a guard in which he has confidence at the hotel to prevent the soldiers from having access to the wine stored there. The mobs have so far been kept out of the hotel grounds. The report has reached me that while the bulk of the officers were safely transported to the prison a few were murdered by soldiers and a number were shot by the mob while a few who refused to surrender are still in refuge on the top floor of the hotel prepared to fight to the last.

(signed) Benjamin Sumner Welles

--◊◊◊--0--◊◊◊--

BENJAMIN SUMNER WELLES, US AMBASSADOR IN CUBA, WRITES TO **CORDELL HULL,** US SECRETARY OF STATE

Havana, October 2, 1933   [Received 10:58 p.m.]

Batista has just sent me word that he has placed a guard around the National Hotel to prevent any further looting by soldiers and especially distribution of contents of wine cellars. He assures me that the lives of all the officers now in custody will be personally guaranteed by himself and that I may feel confident that order will be maintained in the city tonight.

From all information I can obtain, in view of the difficulty of communications, all sections of the city have been relatively quiet during the past 2 hours.

(signed) Benjamin Sumner Welles

--◊◊◊--0--◊◊◊--

BENJAMIN SUMNER WELLES, US AMBASSADOR IN CUBA, WRITES TO **CORDELL HULL,** US SECRETARY OF STATE

Havana, October 3, 1933

It appears to be now established that the following are the casualties in Havana yesterday: of the officers, 14 killed and 17 wounded; of soldiers and civilians associated with them, 80 killed and approximately 200 wounded. It seems to be equally clearly established that none of the officers was killed up to the time of their surrender. Approximately six were killed either by soldiers or by the crowd around the National Hotel as the result of violent shooting which broke out from an unexplained cause after most of the surrendered officers were already lined up in front of the hotel. Of the remaining officers who were killed, three were killed by soldiers in the truck in which they were being taken to the ferry in which they had to cross the harbor in order to enter Cabana Prison and the remainder at the ferry landing either by the crowd or by the soldiers who were guarding them.

There have been continued rumors last night and this morning that the Student Council and a portion of the soldiers wish summarily to execute the officers who are now in prison. So far as I can ascertain Batista, his own personal supporters, and some of the members of the Government are vigorously opposing this move. I expect to see Batista this afternoon and I shall endeavor to learn what positive guarantees for the safety of the officers he has been able to provide. I feel of course and am sure the Department will concur in my belief, that should there be any real danger of the execution of the officers I will be justified on the grounds of humanity alone, in making the most vigorous representations to the existing authorities against such a measure which would be a blot on the civilization of the continent, for there is absolutely no justification whatever for mass assassination of this character, particularly when there are no charges pending against the great majority of the officers.

(signed) Benjamin Sumner Welles

--◊◊◊--0--◊◊◊--

BENJAMIN SUMNER WELLES, US AMBASSADOR IN CUBA, WRITES TO **CORDELL HULL,** US SECRETARY OF STATE

Havana, October 3, 1933

The Minister of Paraguay who leaves tomorrow for Mexico City to which post he is also accredited advised me this afternoon that it was the unanimous opinion of all of the Latin American members of the Diplomatic Corps here, with whom he had been in constant consultation during the past few days, that the policy pursued by the Government of the United States in Cuba was absolutely right and proper. He stated that in his own judgment we had made every possible effort to permit the Cuban people to solve their own problems without interference and that they must assume the sole responsibility for the difficulties with which they are now confronted. He likewise told me that he understood the offer of some of the Latin American representatives here to act as friendly intermediaries had been rejected by Grau San Martín.

signed) Benjamin Sumner Welles

--◊◊◊--0--◊◊◊--

BENJAMIN SUMNER WELLES, US AMBASSADOR IN CUBA, WRITES TO **CORDELL HULL,** US SECRETARY OF STATE

Havana, October 4, 1933

Batista came to the Embassy this morning to see me and I had a conversation with him alone for about one hour and a half.

He gave me in detail the history of the battle between the officers and the soldiers at the National Hotel. He insists that the causes of the fighting were primarily the continued and successful efforts of the officers to pass arms and ammunition through the lines of sentries around the hotel and, secondly, to the report that had come to him that the officers had planned a concerted

The role of Batista on September 4, 1933.

After August 12, Cuba was in a state of chaos; it was evident that President Céspedes could not control the situation. There were conspiratorial meetings of soldiers and officers, attended by **Sergeant Fulgencio Batista** as a stenographer. At the meetings on the Infantry Battalion 2, he interacted and conspired with students, news people and revolutionary leaders, particularly with **Carlos Prío** and **Sergio Carbó**. Belonging to the *Branch 7 of the ABC*, he was advised that the *ABC* supported the government, hence he had to be calm and wait for orders from above. Batista, however, decided to move in another direction.

On August 18, Batista was at *Columbus Cemetery* for the funeral of **Miguel Ángel Hernández**, an army man. At the burial place no one had been appointed to speak on behalf of the *Army General Staff*. Sergeant Batista *impromptu* decided to take the floor, and with fiery and eloquent words, he spoke of the injustices of the moment, of necessary reforms and of several other hot topics.

Batista was now in full swing. He made contacts with members of *"Pro Ley y Justicia"* the student group of **Carlos Prío**. A week later, on September 3, he met with **Sergio Carbó**, the director of the magazine *La Semana*, and traveled to Matanzas to talk to sergeants of Regiment 4 of the *Guardia Rural*. He got a commitment of support and returned to Havana, following talks with soldiers in Pinar del Rio. Carbó and Prío now became two of his strongest supporters.

On September 4, the General Staff granted a permit to hold a meeting at *Columbia's Enlisted Club*, presumably to discuss and resolve certain grievances. Batista attended that meeting and, once finished, he headed to the *Master Barracks*, a short walk from the *Enlisted Club*. Soldiers began to concentrate there, and someone shouted, **"Long live Batista!"** After addressing the group, he left and began to tour different military units located in other parts of the city, finally returning to Columbia. He learned that *Infantry Battalion One*, cantonized in the old *Artillery Depot*, did not support the movement, and without losing a second, he went to the depot and gained their loyalty. Afterwards he went to Sergio Carbó's, house; together, they sent orders to his followers: «*Each Sergeant Major shall take charge of his unit. If for any eventuality he does not accept that responsibility, any soldier will take over.*»

Batista and Carbó, at the Regiment Headquarters, integrated a *"Revolutionary Board,"* and five eminent citizens were appointed to assume the functions of government (**La Pentarquía**). They issued *"The Proclamation of September 4"*, with 19 signatures, Carlos Prío the first, Batista the last one. A delegation was sent to Palacio to inform Dr. Carlos Manuel de Céspedes that he was dismissed. At that point Céspedes agreed to leave the Presidential Palace. The *Coup dÉtat* of September 4 was swift, bloodless and successful.

revolutionary movement for the afternoon of October 2nd in connivance with other revolutionary groups within the city of Havana. He referred to the conditions which he had offered the officers at noon and to which they made no reply as well as to the fact that the renewal of the fighting at 3 o'clock that afternoon was due to the officers at a moment when he himself was prepared to agree to an extension of the truce until the following morning at least. Finally, he assured me that the deaths of officers and soldiers after the surrender of the former was due to firing by the officers and that in the excitement which ensued it was utterly impossible for him to control the soldiers.

(signed) Benjamin Sumner Welles

--◊◊◊--0--◊◊◊--

Benjamin Sumner Welles, US Ambassador in Cuba, writes to **Cordell Hull,** US Secretary of State

Havana, October 5, 1933

I have just discussed your telegram of October 4, with the President, who desires me to say that it appears to him that public opinion as reflected in the press here seems to regard the capture of the officers as indicating a consolidation of the position of the present government. He also believes that Cuba now is going through a period of storm and stress, and that given all the circumstances, there must be some latitude, on the part of ourselves and of other states, in the application of the customary principles of international practice (e.g. as regards recognition) in view of these conditions.

The Cuban representative here left today at the Department an informal memorandum setting out that Grau San Martín had authorized him to state that he expects to make changes in his cabinet, giving participation therein to outstanding personalities who would inspire public confidence, *"without taking into account whether they are affiliated with any political group or any strictly revolutionary body".*

(signed) Benjamin Sumner Welles

--◊◊◊--0--◊◊◊--

Benjamin Sumner Welles, US Ambassador in Cuba, writes to **Cordell Hull,** US Secretary of State

Havana, October 5, 1933   [Received October 6—4:06 a.m.]

Your telegram of October 5, 7 p.m. I coincide, of course, in the belief expressed by the President that in view of all the circumstances now existing in Cuba there must be some latitude in the application by us of the customary principles governing recognition of a Cuban government. I wish, however, to make it very plain that the capture of the officers does not indicate consolidation of the position of the government but solely a decidedly increased prestige for the Army as distinguished from the government. I appreciate fully the difficulty of realizing that such a distinction can exist in view of the apparent identification of the Army with the Grau San Martín government. It might be remarked, however, that the Army mutiny did not take place in order to place Grau San Martín in power. It occurred for the sole purpose of displacing the officers and when Batista and the other ringleaders found at the last moment that the students and a few others would join with them they then agreed to support a so-called revolutionary government in which Grau San Martín participated. The divergence between the Army and the civilian elements in the government is fast becoming daily more marked. As Batista becomes more influential the power of the students and Grau San Martín diminishes.

There will be held tomorrow night a general assembly of the university students at which I am informed a large majority of the students will pass a resolution repudiating the actions of the Student Council and urging the constitution of a government in which all factions can have confidence. Once this action is taken the Grau San Martín regime will in strict reality only represent some 30 members of the Student Council, a few professors, and the office-holders whom they have appointed.

If our Government recognized the existing Cuban government before it has undergone radical modification such action would imply our lending official support to a regime which is opposed by all business and financial interests in Cuba; by all the powerful political groups and in general, so far as I can estimate the situation after 5 months' intensive study, not only by all the elements that hold out any promise of being able to govern Cuba but by a very great majority of the people as well. Such action on our part would undoubtedly help to keep the present government in power for a while but popular reaction against it, while delayed, would continue and would increase, until after a series of exhausting efforts which the Republic cannot effect, the government would either be overthrown or else, which is more probable, the country would be plunged into utter anarchy.

Under existing conditions no government can survive whether we recognize it or not unless the major political groups support it and unless the commercial and business classes have confidence in it.

If we extend recognition now, we do not promote permanent stability for the reasons above expressed and we incur the antipathy of those classes in Cuba which in reality constitute the dominant portion of public opinion and which, once these abnormal conditions have passed, will govern the country.

If we refrain from acting now a solution is probable. The students confidentially are stating to their friends that they can no longer hold out. Batista is today already pressing for a compromise. The [memorandum?] left today at the Department announcing a proposed change in the Cabinet is indicative of the change in the uncompromising attitude on that point formerly maintained by the students. I consequently most earnestly recommend that in the true sense of the term we give the Cuban people a further opportunity to settle their own problems without hindering that end through premature action on our part. If a change in the Executive branch of the government in whole or in part can now be brought about which will result in popular support and restore confidence, I would most decidedly recommend immediate recognition without waiting until those customary objectives such as the complete maintenance of public order are attained. But I wish to emphasize my strong belief that if we recognize a government now which does not possess at least a considerable measure of popular support we postpone a return by Cuba to normal and stable conditions and we incur once more the same measure of animosity on the part of the mass of the Cuban people as that which we possessed during the last 4 years of the Machado Government.

(signed) Benjamin Sumner Welles

--◊◊◊--0--◊◊◊--

Memorandum by Jefferson Thomas Caffery, US Under Secretary of State

Washington, October 6, 1933   [Extract]

The Brazilian Ambassador, Mr. R. de Lima e Silva, came to see me this morning to ask me if there had been any change in our attitude toward recognition of the Grau San Martín Government. I told Mr. Lima e Silva that there had not yet been any change in our attitude. He asked me to let him know if we decided to recognize, because his Government desired to act in accord with us in the matter.

(signed) Jefferson Thomas Caffery

--◊◊◊--0--◊◊◊--

Mr. William C. Burdett, US Chargé d'Affairs in Panamá, writes to Cordell Hull, US Secretary of State

Panama City, October 6, 1933   [Received 1:10 p.m.]

With reference to press reports Panamá's recognition of present government Cuba, acting President Diaz informs me that report is substantially correct, and that Panama has chosen to follow the principle of a continuous recognition by instructing its diplomatic representative in Havana to establish conversations with the government there.

Acting President thought President Arias might call on Grau San Martín at Havana.

(signed) William C. Burdett

--◇◇◇--0--◇◇◇--

BENJAMIN SUMNER WELLES, US AMBASSADOR IN CUBA, WRITES TO
CORDELL HULL, US SECRETARY OF STATE

Havana, October 6, 1933   [Received 5:30 p.m.]

I am advised this morning that at a full meeting of the Student Directorate yesterday the majority of the students determined that they would be inevitably forced to get rid of Batista. They were moved to this decision by the strong popular reaction in his favor due to his determined stand against Communist agitation and to the increasing prestige which this popular reaction had given him as well as by their desire to shift all responsibility for the death of the officers on last Monday to the Army. The bitterness of feeling engendered by the National Hotel incident is becoming increasingly strong and many of the students in the Directorate fear the public antagonism to them which this is creating.

In the meeting a possibility of an armed attack on Batista was seriously discussed as was likewise the attempt to obtain the support of the ABC and other revolutionary organizations in the endeavor to overthrow Batista.

Three of the members of the Directorate on several occasions during the past 24 hours have stated to my informants that the Army and Batista were now in control and that it was their patriotic duty to find at once means of doing away with the latter in order to avoid the creation of a military dictatorship.

(signed) Benjamin Sumner Welles

--◇◇◇--0--◇◇◇--

BENJAMIN SUMNER WELLES, US AMBASSADOR IN CUBA, WRITES TO
CORDELL HULL, US SECRETARY OF STATE

Havana, October 6, 1933   [Received October 8:00 p.m.]

At a meeting of the Diplomatic Corps held this afternoon to discuss the measures taken by the Dean in behalf of the Corps to insure the safety of the captive officers, the Chilean Minister and the Argentine and Brazilian Chargés d'Affaires stated to me that their Governments would not consider recognition of the present Cuban government until it had been so reorganized as to obtain the support of at least a considerable portion of public opinion. They further stated that unless such support was obtained, they saw no hope for the maintenance of even a semblance of public order.

The British Minister expressed very considerable alarm at the conditions of disorder existing in Havana.

Up to the present time, although the government daily announces impending recognition by the United States and by Latin American Republics, only Mexico and Uruguay are maintaining official relations with the government. I can find no evidence of the belief on the part of any other diplomatic representative here that there is any justification for recognition at this time.

(signed) Benjamin Sumner Welles

--◊◊◊--0--◊◊◊--

BENJAMIN SUMNER WELLES, US AMBASSADOR IN CUBA, WRITES TO **CORDELL HULL,** US SECRETARY OF STATE

Havana, October 6, 1933   [Received October 8:00 p.m.]

It seems evident that the fear which the increasing power of Batista has caused the Student Council is creating a very salutatory desire for an immediate understanding with the opposition political groups and parties. Last night Batista held a meeting with the principal leaders of the Army and determined that the students should be immediately informed that they must withdraw from all contact with the government and refrain from any interference with the installation of a concentration government. This afternoon the Student Council passed a resolution appointing a committee of three professors of the university to act as mediators between the opposition sectors and the government in order to reach a solution as to a new government. The leaders of the opposition, from what they have stated to me today, will meet these advances halfway.

I had this afternoon an interview with Sergio Carbó. He stated his ignorance of any intention on the part of Gran San Martín to appoint a concentration Cabinet and expressed the opinion that such a step would be worse than futile unless it had the previous approval of the opposition. He is firmly convinced that the government as now constituted must fall, and since he is the strongest member of the present regime, his insistence upon the need for a compromise acceptable to all factions is significant.

Grau is speaking to the press of appointing new Secretaries of the Interior and of Agriculture but since both candidates he mentions are individuals who have supported him from the outset of his government and are completely unacceptable to any opposition faction, such changes could hardly be considered as bringing about a *"concentration Cabinet".*

I believe a change for the better in the attitude of all parties towards a fair compromise is rapidly impending.

(signed) Benjamin Sumner Welles

--◊◊◊--0--◊◊◊--

Two views of Havana in late 1933. The **Capitolio Nacional** and the **America Building** on Galiano Street. *Below*, a reportage about the **1933 Atlantic hurricane season**, the second-most active season on record, with 20 storms breaking the record set by **1887**. About 40% of Cuban crops were destroyed, many houses wrecked, hundreds homeless, there were 23 deaths and $30 million in damages.

BENJAMIN SUMNER WELLES, US AMBASSADOR IN CUBA, WRITES TO
CORDELL HULL, US SECRETARY OF STATE

Havana, October 8, 1933

At a conference, a local diplomat admitted to me that he now fully realizes that the present regime is a complete failure and that a concentration government in which, the political groups and the commercial interests of the country would have confidence was an absolute necessity. He also stated that he appreciated the fact that recognition by the United States was essential before any improvement in conditions here could be expected.

He has already arranged for interviews with Mendieta and Gómez tomorrow and Monday and assured me that he would not cease his pressure until a new government supported by public opinion was installed through peaceful methods.

He was deeply impressed by the fact that delegates of all the important business and financial groups in Cuba had visited him this afternoon before I saw him to insist upon the creation of a government in which the public could have confidence.

The students today selected as their representatives in the negotiations for the solution of the political problems the following university professors: Drs. Dolzvieta and Carrera Jústiz. All of these are disposed to work for a complete change in the present administration.

Batista told me that he had already advised the Student Directorate that the Army would not permit any interference by the students in government here and that they must return to the university which reopens next week and remain there.

He also assured me of his intention to proceed immediately with a firm hand in all of the American sugar plantations where labor troubles still existed, by arresting and removing all Communist leaders and by using the troops to restore order wherever it was necessary.

(signed) Benjamin Sumner Welles

--◊◊◊--0--◊◊◊--

BENJAMIN SUMNER WELLES, US AMBASSADOR IN CUBA, WRITES TO
CORDELL HULL, US SECRETARY OF STATE

Havana, October 9, 1933   [Received 3:53 a.m.]

Today I had a long conference with Mendieta. He is now authorized to speak in the name of all the important opposition groups in his interview tomorrow morning with Batista. There is a very strong current of belief that the latter will urge the appointment of a concentration government headed by Mendieta himself.

The Student Council had a violent altercation with Batista last night. The open break which resulted has been temporarily repaired at the urgent insistence of a delegation of the students who called upon Batista this morning.

There is a growing feeling of optimism among those who are close to the city authorities and the government that a representative government will replace the present regime in the very near future.

(signed) Benjamin Sumner Welles

--◇◇◇--0--◇◇◇--

BENJAMIN SUMNER WELLES, US AMBASSADOR IN CUBA, WRITES TO
CORDELL HULL, US SECRETARY OF STATE

Havana, October 9, 1933   [Received 4:07 a.m.]

For Caffery. Negotiations today have been materially handicapped by the return of Finlay who has alleged to Grau San Martín that you stated to him that the inclusion in the Cabinet of three individuals of the opposition parties would bring immediate recognition of the United States. Grau is consequently thinking of appointing individuals who have in the past been connected with the opposition groups but who have been identified with the student movement since the overthrow of Céspedes and who have no support whatever from the parties to which they used to belong.

I have, of course, denied any such commitment by the Department. It would be helpful, however, at once if you would cable me that your discussion with Finlay was predicated on the support of parties or groups for a concentration government and in no sense upon the appointment to office of individuals who were not representative of the parties to which they formerly belonged.

(signed) Benjamin Sumner Welles

--◇◇◇--0--◇◇◇--

CORDELL HULL, US SECRETARY OF STATE, WRITES TO
BENJAMIN SUMNER WELLES, US AMBASSADOR IN CUBA

Washington, October 9, 1933

From Caffery. Your telegram of October 9, 2 a.m. I have not seen Finlay since September 28th, when I made statement set out in my telegram No. 112. I did not say that *"the inclusion in the Cabinet of three individuals of the opposition parties would bring immediate recognition"* by the United States.

(signed) Cordell Hull

--◇◇◇--0--◇◇◇--

Benjamin Sumner Welles, US Ambassador in Cuba, writes to
Cordell Hull, US Secretary of State

Havana, October 10, 1933   [Received 5:12 a.m.]

The negotiations for a concentration government are momentarily seriously complicated by the reports Finlay has given of his alleged conversation in the Department of State and by the hope on the part of the students that the propaganda in which they are now engaged in the United States will meet with favorable response.

All of the powerful party leaders, namely, those of the Unión Nacional, ABC, OCRR, Gómez and Menocal have agreed unanimously to support Mendieta as their spokesman and to urge him to accept the Provisional Presidency. It is their belief that should he be willing to make this sacrifice, since it is recognized by all elements that in national elections he would be elected to the constitutional Presidency by a sweeping majority, he would have the confidence of all elements in the political and business world and that his great popularity in the interior would be of immediate avail in checking unrest in the agricultural districts. He furthermore possesses the entire confidence of Batista and is not personally opposed by the students. Negotiations in this sense proceeded yesterday very rapidly and apparently successfully until the Finlay reports began to be given credence by the Student Directorate in its session last night. As a result, the conference adjourned this morning without any further action.

In his desire to appoint three individuals of previous connections with the parties of the existing opposition Grau San Martín has encountered an obstacle in the unwillingness of Batista to agree to the changes indicated. The latter has sent me word tonight that he has felt it necessary to postpone his conference with Mendieta for a 48 hour period since some of the students have been busy circulating reports today that if a new government was formed it would at once request the United States to land Marines to disarm the Cuban Army. In the excited condition of the soldiers this rumor, together with reports resulting from Finlay's conversations with the students as to the imminence of recognition by the United States, has necessarily had a prejudicial effect and Batista quite rightly fears that conferences between himself and Mendieta would be misconstrued by a portion of the soldiers.

As a result of the failure of the Directorate to act the three professors they had selected to act as their delegates have refused to serve.

In estimating the manner in which public opinion is lined up at the moment, the following is an accurate summary: All of the political parties, all of the commercial and financial groups, a majority of the university professors, a probable majority of the university students outside of the Directorate are insistent upon the need for the creation of a concentration government. Batista with the presumed support of the Army is pressing for a change satisfactory to all in the existing government. Grau San Martín is determined to retain the Presidency and the Student Directorate is divided.

The feeling as to the likelihood of a favorable solution is generally optimistic. I am doubtful, however, after the complications which occurred today, that any change will be decided upon in the immediate future.

(signed) Benjamin Sumner Welles

--◊◊◊--0--◊◊◊--

BENJAMIN SUMNER WELLES, US AMBASSADOR IN CUBA, WRITES TO
CORDELL HULL, US SECRETARY OF STATE

Havana, October 10, 1933   [Received 7:35 p.m.]

The propaganda circulated among the soldiers yesterday by the students to the effect that the Cuban Army would be disarmed if a concentration government was formed caused Batista not only to postpone his interview with Mendieta until tomorrow but likewise to issue a statement declaring no change in Government was impending and that there was no divergence between the Army and the present regime. Furthermore, a general assembly of the delegates of the university students which met last night, in view of the reports from Dr. Finlay that recognition by the United States was impending within 48 hours, determined to postpone any action urging the creation of a concentration government and adjourned until tomorrow night when the proposed resolution will again be presented for adoption.

Batista last night refused to agree to the changes in the Cabinet which Grau San Martín desired to make. Batista's objection was based on the very logical ground that changes were futile unless they implied the support of the political parties and unless they would strengthen the Government in public opinion. He was further induced to take this stand because of his personal lack of confidence in the appointee selected as Secretary of Gobernación who is technically his superior.

The proposal has now been revived of the creation of a supergovernmental advisory committee composed in equal parts of the opposition and of the present government, such committee to have practical control of the Executive power. Discussions are in progress this afternoon between delegates of the opposition and of the Student Directorate with a view to ascertaining whether the present government will offer to accept this proposal.

There is a constantly growing universal realization of the need for an immediate change in the present intolerable situation in government. The obstacles to the realization of this end are the reluctance of the students to accept the blame for the situation into

The Cuba lived everyday by common men and women in 1933.

which the country has been plunged and the hesitancy on the part of Batista to press the formation of a new government until he is sure that his troops will support such a move. There is of course likewise the inevitable rivalry between the leaders of different factions and the lack of courage on the part of the overwhelming majority of the university professors and a decided majority of the university students in expressing their convictions by condemning the activities of the Student Directorate.

The American Consul at Santiago in a telegram this morning reporting upon conditions in that city states that there exists "universal dissatisfaction and expectancy and no harmony of opinion." That diagnosis is equally applicable to the present situation in Havana and, from every account I have received, to that in all other parts of the Republic.

(signed) Benjamin Sumner Welles

--◊◊◊--0--◊◊◊--

CORDELL HULL, US SECRETARY OF STATE, WRITES TO
BENJAMIN SUMNER WELLES, US AMBASSADOR IN CUBA

Washington, October 10, 1933

At the press conference this morning the Under Secretary reiterated the third, fourth and fifth sentences of the statement communicated to you by telegram 96, September 11.

(signed) Cordell Hull

--◊◊◊--0--◊◊◊--

BENJAMIN SUMNER WELLES, US AMBASSADOR IN CUBA, WRITES TO
CORDELL HULL, US SECRETARY OF STATE

Havana, October 11, 1933   [Received 2:40 p.m.]

For Caffery. The statement made yesterday by the Department has created an extremely beneficial effect here. While the leading newspapers of Havana are not being published the reporters and other employees of these papers are getting out temporary editions and these have carried the news in very effective form. The statement so made has counteracted the daily propaganda coming from the political parties and from the Student Directorate that Grau San Martín regime is on the verge of being recognized by the United States.

Dr. Guillermo Portela, who has been acting as intermediary between the students and the leaders of the political parties and to whom I denied" the truth of the Finlay reports, yesterday telephoned Marquez Sterling and was told by the latter that in his last conversation with you, you had given him to understand that the inclusion by Grau San Martín of "three national figures" in the Cabinet would be regarded by us as a concentration government which would receive recognition by the United States.

I reiterated to Portela that any such statement on the part of Márquez Sterling was not based on fact and after your telegram No. 117, October 10, 7 p.m., was received I emphasized to Portela, for the benefit of the students, that the policy of the United States Government remained exactly the same. I suggest you call Márquez Sterling to the Department and reiterate for his benefit the statements yesterday made at the press conference as to our policy on recognition and request him to inform his Government accordingly. He has unquestionably made Grau San Martín believe that any change in the Cabinet would be regarded by us as resulting in an acceptable concentration government.

I shall appreciate it if you will cable me summaries of such conversations as you may have with Marquez Sterling so that I may be prepared accordingly.

(signed) Benjamin Sumner Welles

--◊◊◊--O--◊◊◊--

CORDELL HULL, US SECRETARY OF STATE, WRITES TO
BENJAMIN SUMNER WELLES, US AMBASSADOR IN CUBA

Washington, October 11, 1933

From Caffery. I am glad you liked the statement we gave out yesterday morning at the press conference.

This morning Márquez Sterling came in to see me and I told him that I was annoyed by what Finlay had said at Havana about his conversation with me and I said (what I had repeatedly said before to him) that our position on recognition was that set out in the press conference yesterday morning. Márquez Sterling has upon several occasions said something about plans of Grau San Martín for changes in his government. A few days ago, he said something about the possible inclusion of *"three national figures"* in the Cabinet but I, of course, gave him no assurances thereon. I shall show this telegram to Márquez Sterling.

(signed) Cordell Hull

--◊◊◊--O--◊◊◊--

BENJAMIN SUMNER WELLES, US AMBASSADOR IN CUBA, WRITES TO
CORDELL HULL, US SECRETARY OF STATE

Havana, October 11, 1933   [Received 9:00 p.m.]

The Spanish Ambassador has just informed me that the new Spanish Cabinet has instructed him to recognize the Grau San Martín government tomorrow *"the day of the Spanish race"*. The Ambassador is deeply chagrined at this instruction and has protested it although without hope that it will be modified. The entire Spanish colony is opposed to the present regime because of the decrees it has issued in prejudice of the Spanish regional and benevolent associations and because of the bad business conditions for which the powerful Spanish commercial groups hold the government responsible.

The Ambassador can only suppose that recognition is being extended by the new Spanish Cabinet for sentimental reasons in view of tomorrow's holiday and because the new Secretary of State is unfamiliar with the reports the Ambassador has sent on conditions here.

(signed) Benjamin Sumner Welles

--◊◊◊--0--◊◊◊--

HUGH SIMONS GIBSON, US AMBASSADOR IN BRAZIL, WRITES TO
CORDELL HULL, US SECRETARY OF STATE

Rio de Janeiro, October 13, 1933   [Received 3:30 p.m.]

Minister for Foreign Affairs would value any information as to our progress toward recognition of Cuban government. Says he is anxious to follow our lead in this matter of primary interest to us but is now at a disadvantage in standing off pressure for recognition through lack of up-to-date information. Suggest Department keep me advised of developments from time to time.

(signed) Hugh Simons Gibson

--◊◊◊--0--◊◊◊--

BENJAMIN SUMNER WELLES, US AMBASSADOR IN CUBA, WRITES TO
CORDELL HULL, US SECRETARY OF STATE

Havana, October 13, 1933   [Received 10:15 p.m.]

The Secretary of Gobernación announced officially this morning that an arrangement had been made with the Government of Mexico for the services of a military mission composed of Mexican officers to be used in the training of officers in the present Cuban Army.

I learned last night that this suggestion had been made to Batista by the Mexican Chargé d'Affaires 3 days previously. In view of the existing situation here and particularly in view of the fact that since the independence of the Republic of Cuba the training of Cuban officers has been undertaken solely in the United States or under the direction of American officers this step can only be construed as a deliberate effort by the present government to show its intention of minimizing any form of American influence in Cuba.

Carlos Saladrigas, the Secretary of State in the Céspedes Cabinet, upon whose conversations with the Mexican Chargé I have reported, advised me today that Spindola has within the past 10 days obtained further interviews with the directors of the ABC in order to urge them to unite with the elements supporting the present government as a means of lessening American influence in Cuba, in which effort, Spindola alleged he was acting by full instruction of his Government. This plea has been repeatedly and most emphatically turned down by that party. He has again offered the present government the sending from Mexico of delegates of the National Revolutionary Party to assist in the creation of the revolutionary party in Cuba which Carbó is sponsoring.
(signed) Benjamin Sumner Welles

--◊◊◊--O--◊◊◊--

BENJAMIN SUMNER WELLES, US AMBASSADOR IN CUBA, WRITES TO **CORDELL HULL,** US SECRETARY OF STATE

Havana, October 13, 1933   [Received October 14, 3:50 a.m.]

The Brazilian Chargé d'Affaires this evening advised me that in response to an inquiry from his Government as to the stability of the present Cuban government replied that *"it was built on sand"* since in his opinion its sole support was an *"undisciplined and mutinous Army and a band of students."*

I should appreciate having any opinions which may be expressed to you by the Argentine, Brazilian or Chilean Ambassadors in Washington regarding political conditions in Cuba. As I have reported, the representatives of those countries in Havana have frequently expressed the belief that the policy we have so far carried out in Cuba met with the complete support and approval of their own Governments.
(signed) Benjamin Sumner Welles

--◊◊◊--O--◊◊◊--

BENJAMIN SUMNER WELLES, US AMBASSADOR IN CUBA, WRITES TO **CORDELL HULL,** US SECRETARY OF STATE

Havana, October 14, 1933   [Received 4:35 a.m.]

I had a conference with Finlay tonight. He stated that the reports attributed to him had all emanated from Marquez Sterling and that the sudden change in attitude on the part of the Student Directorate was due solely to them.

He requested my opinion as to the desirability of further efforts for conciliation expressing the belief that an immediate common accord between all the political parties was urgently necessary in view of the danger presented by the attitude now adopted by the Army. He added that this belief was shared by the students. I assured him that I felt such a move was of the utmost interest to the Republic and that I had been repeatedly assured by the leaders of all parties of their readiness to agree to any reasonable compromise.

After long discussion he said that he would request full powers from the government for a delegation composed of himself, Dr. Irizarri and Dr. Portela to negotiate with the political leaders. He requested my assistance which I said I would gladly give provided my participation in the negotiations was maintained completely confidential since the utter lack of discretion displayed in previous conferences had been the primary cause of their failure.

(signed) Benjamin Sumner Welles

--◇◇◇--0--◇◇◇--

BENJAMIN SUMNER WELLES, US AMBASSADOR IN CUBA, WRITES TO
CORDELL HULL, US SECRETARY OF STATE

Havana, October 14, 1933   [Received 8:10 p.m.]

For Caffery. I have just received, through his wife, a message from Dr. Ferrer, Secretary of War in the Céspedes Cabinet, who is now confined as a prisoner in Cabana prison, that the authorities are circulating among all of the officers in prison a letter which has been drafted by Octavio Seigle, a paid propagandist for the Grau San Martín regime, and which the officers are requested to sign declaring that the assembling of the officers in the National Hotel and their conduct subsequent thereto was due to my instigation. Dr. Ferrer has sent me word that most of the officers have disregarded the communication, but it is to be presumed that some of them, in order to get in the good graces of the present authorities, will probably sign the letter. This is merely one of a long series of allegations regarding me published by the adherents of the present government and concocted in each instance without even a shred of fact upon which to base them. They have included charges that I was conspiring with various revolutionary leaders; that I had engaged in an attempt to foment a revolution in Pinar del Río Province and as recently as this morning that I was being bribed by the American Sugar Refining Company and by the National City Bank.

The present effort, however, is more plausible in that by obtaining the signatures of a few officers to such a declaration the charge will probably meet with a certain amount of belief both in Cuba and in the United States. I consequently suggest that you discuss the matter with the Secretary and if he concurs advise the press that the Department is aware of the effort which is being made to involve the Embassy in the action taken by the officers last month and that the Embassy's position in the matter has already been made clear by the Department.

The charge is as ludicrous as it is unfounded. It is only possible for me to reiterate that I never had any connection with any of the officers at any time and that with the exception of Colonel Sanguily whom I have not seen since August 13th, the day after that upon which the Céspedes Government came into power, I do not even know personally any of the officers who were in the National Hotel. The only other officer whom I knew, who was in the National Hotel, was Dr. Ferrer himself and my acquaintance with him was due to his service as Secretary of War. Once he took refuge in the National Hotel, I never communicated with him in any manner and the Department is fully informed in every detail of my conversations with him prior to that time.

I do not believe there is any way in which this extremely vicious attack can be prevented from gaining credence except through a statement by the Department in the sense indicated.

(signed) Benjamin Sumner Welles

--◇◇◇--0--◇◇◇--

Cordell Hull, US Secretary of State, writes to Benjamin Sumner Welles, US Ambassador in Cuba

Washington, October 15, 1933

From Caffery. The following statement has been released to the press this afternoon:

"The Department has been informed that an effort is being made to involve the Embassy at Havana in the action taken by the Cuban Army officers last month in taking refuge in the National Hotel, and in subsequent events.

With regard to this matter the Department can state unequivocally that far from instigating the assembling of the officers in the National Hotel, Ambassador Welles had no knowledge of their intention until the event took place. Moreover Mr. Welles was equally unaware of any of their subsequent plans, having never spoken to any of them either individually or collectively or having attempted to communicate with them since they took refuge in the National Hotel."

(signed) Cordell Hull

--◇◇◇--0--◇◇◇--

BENJAMIN SUMNER WELLES, US AMBASSADOR IN CUBA, WRITES TO
CORDELL HULL, US SECRETARY OF STATE

Havana, October 16, 1933   [Received October 17, 4:18 a.m.]

It seems an appropriate moment, in view of the apparent impasse that has been reached between the supporters of the Grau San Martín government and the elements opposed to it in the negotiation of an agreement which would provide for a government which might meet with general popular support, to lay before you the following considerations in view of my belief that we must now decide upon a definite course in accordance with a permanent policy towards Cuba which will further the ultimate interests of the United States both political and commercial not only in Cuba but on the continent as well.

The situation now existing and the events leading up to it are in brief summary as follows:

The Céspedes Government was supported by every one of the so-called revolutionary parties or associations opposed to Machado with the exception of the students. It was accepted by the bulk of the old Liberal, Conservative and Popular Parties, who realized the fall of Machado made a reorganization of those parties possible and felt that the rank and file of the parties would receive both political and individual guarantees. It was strongly supported by all commercial and financial interests as is demonstrated by the fact that an unprecedented revival of business took place commencing 10 days before the downfall of the government. While mob lynching of spies and criminals employed by Machado and the imprisonment of his chief henchmen occurred during that period the government was taking measures to restore authority and there was neither intimidation, assassination nor censorship of speech or press by the government itself.

The downfall of the Céspedes Government was due I believe to an Army mutiny. The mutiny was caused partly by the desire of the sergeants and soldiers to remove most of their officers; partly by their well-founded belief that some of the officers were plotting for the restoration of General Menocal to power; and principally because of the propaganda spread by Communist and radical agitators among the soldiers that their pay was to be cut from $22 to $13 a month. The mutiny was not directed against Céspedes or his Cabinet; it was not political in its origin and it was not, as appears to be believed in the United States, in any sense responsive to a social movement.

The students did not even know of the movement until 24 hours before it took place. Batista himself has confirmed my knowledge that they and the radical professors were not called in until the sergeants felt they dared not carry out their protest mutiny without civilian support. It was only at the last moment that these

Pictures, top to bottom:
Businessmen in 1933 make their rounds across Cuba in **hydroplanes**, like the one shown in Cienfuegos bay. Two newspapers carrying **news from Cuba** in 1933 almost anywhere in the US.

civilian elements joined by other extreme radicals succeeded in persuading the soldiers to turn the mutiny into a political revolution to place a new government in power.

During the past 6 weeks that the present government has been in control the following developments have taken place: The government is supported by a small number of professors and a portion, probably a minority, of the university students; by a scattered number of small offshoots from the large secret societies most of which offshoots are concentrated in Havana; by a few radicals of all shades belonging to the "lunatic fringe" of the older parties; and by the Army. It has sedulously cultivated the labor unions and has probably gained the sympathy of some of them but since there is not yet in Cuba effective national organization of labor outside of Communism such support as there may be by the unions is regional.

The government is opposed by all of the five organized revolutionary parties who were opposed to Machado; by the three old political parties whose strength in the provinces is still very strong; small merchants and business men; by the small farmer and *colono* class which constitutes the bulk of the population in the provinces; and finally by all the larger Cuban and foreign commercial and financial interests.

During these 6 weeks no constructive measure has been undertaken; many decrees have been issued and most of them have been disregarded; every branch of the public administration has been utterly disorganized; employees who have spent their life in the public service and who had no political color have been replaced by boys of 20 or 21 who have neither training nor qualifications. The Customs, Public Instruction, Post Office and Sanitary services are in a state of utter chaos; almost every judge in the Republic has been replaced by a so-called revolutionary.

The condition of the treasury is desperate; salaries can be paid for one more month; customs receipts are constantly shrinking and since taxpayers are refusing to pay taxes internal revenues are practically non-existent.

There is neither protection for life nor property. The houses of all political leaders opposed to the government are searched by squads of soldiers at any time; imprisonments occur without any semblance of legal authority; properties belonging to Cubans, foreigners and Americans have been seized by laborers, the owners' representatives have fled or have been driven off and the government has been unable or unwilling to restore the properties to their rightful owners; assassinations are recommencing and as in the days of Machado the President and his chief supporters only go about in armored cars surrounded by soldiers with machine guns. Those who dare to attack the government on the radio or in the press are in danger of seizure by soldiers or students if they do not go into hiding. The flight of political exiles to the United States has already commenced and two of the principal leaders of the revolutionary parties have now fled in justified fear of their lives.

As cynically admitted by one of the leading members of the Student Directorate the government has sought to gain popular support by raising the cry of anti-Americanism but in reality, the groups now supporting the government are the only elements in Cuba which are actually anti-American. It is only in the university and among the professional agitators that there exists any real anti-Americanism in Cuba so far.

In determining our course in view of these facts and bearing in mind the ultimate objectives which you have laid down it seems to me that we have the following alternatives:

(1) To recognize the present government without further delay.

The advantages of this step are as follows: We would presumably allay anti-American propaganda; we would avoid the present difficulties arising from having to deal with an unrecognized government; we might through influence prevent dangerous economic and financial measures being taken; recognition might offer us the opportunity of bettering the disastrous economic conditions in Cuba which affect every class and which are gravely prejudicial to our own export trade; finally recognition would help temporarily to strengthen and to maintain the present government.

The disadvantages are as follows: We would recognize a government supported by a scant minority and only capable of maintaining itself through the present adherence of a disorganized and undisciplined Army; we would incur exactly the same reproach which the Hoover administration incurred for not withdrawing recognition from Machado, namely, that through recognition and the moral and financial support which that implies we are forcing upon the Cuban people a dictatorship against the will of the great majority of the people; we would incur the lasting hostility of the organized political parties who will not go to national elections held under this regime as well as of the professional and commercial classes who foresee ruin under this government; we would apparently favor the small anti-American as against the large pro-American groups; we would not promote permanent stability for the reason that with the political parties refusing to go to elections and all the financial and commercial interests clamoring for a government in which they can have confidence, there is no possible doubt that one revolutionary attempt after another will be made until the government is overthrown and in the meantime there will be no sugar crop and no permanent economic improvement; finally for all of these reasons we would postpone the time when national elections can be held and a permanent constitutional gov-

ernment be elected with which we can undertake the ratification of new treaty relations, and which would itself be fitted to undertake those permanent social and economic reforms which alone can bring about real stability in Cuba.

(2) The second alternative is to withhold recognition until a provisional government is constituted which offers guarantees acceptable both to the political and non-political forces in the Republic.

The arguments above set forth are of course applicable to this alternative in reverse order. From the point of view of immediate expediency, the first alternative is preferable. From the point of view of permanent policy in Cuba the second alternative seems to me the one we must adopt. It is a policy based on justice to the Cuban people, one which will hasten rather than retard the creation of a constitutional government in Cuba and one which will expedite eventual stability. Our own commercial and export interests in Cuba cannot be revived under this government. Only confidence can accomplish that and there is no confidence either in the policies nor stability of this regime, whether it be recognized or not.

I have felt it essential to lay these facts before you for the determination by the President and yourself of the policy we should pursue. While my knowledge of sentiment in Latin America is largely based upon my conversations with the Latin American representatives here, it would seem as if we were supported generally in the continent in the attitude we have so far assumed.

(signed) Benjamin Sumner Welles

--◊◊◊--O--◊◊◊--

HUGH SIMONS GIBSON, US AMBASSADOR IN BRAZIL, WRITES TO
CORDELL HULL, US SECRETARY OF STATE

Rio de Janeiro, October 17, 1933   [Received 11:40 a.m.]

Minister for Foreign Affairs tells me Argentine Ambassador yesterday urged that the time had come for the South American states to agree as to recognition of government in Cuba. He was told reports just received from Brazilian Legation were distinctly discouraging and that Brazilian Government would await more favorable developments.

(signed) Hugh Simons Gibson

--◊◊◊--O--◊◊◊--

BENJAMIN SUMNER WELLES, US AMBASSADOR IN CUBA, WRITES TO
CORDELL HULL, US SECRETARY OF STATE

Havana, October 18, 1933   [Received 2:14 a.m.]

Negotiations between Mendieta and Batista will be resumed tomorrow. In a conference I had with the former this evening he expressed his willingness to make any personal sacrifice which might be necessary to bring about the formation of a national government.

Owing to the growing dissension between the students and Batista the latter intimated his desire today for immediate change in the present situation and expressed the belief that conditions in the Army now warranted his proceeding with conversations with Colonel Mendieta.

(signed) Benjamin Sumner Welles

--◇◇◇--0--◇◇◇--

BENJAMIN SUMNER WELLES, US AMBASSADOR IN CUBA, WRITES TO
CORDELL HULL, US SECRETARY OF STATE

Havana, October 18, 1933   [Received 3:05 p.m.]

Developments of the past 12 hours are disquieting. It appears that the issue between the students and Batista will be joined in the case of the Chief of Police of Havana. Batista some 2 weeks ago appointed to that office Captain Franco who is understood to be loyal to him and who has improved materially the discipline and authority of the police force. The students 2 days ago decided to remove Captain Franco and have appointed in his place a member of the secret society affiliated with the students known as *"Ley y Justicia"*. The name of the individual selected is Labourdette, some 27 years of age. The society to which he belongs committed most of the acts of terrorism and assassinations sponsored by the students during the last years of the Machado Government. He and his associates are the equivalent in Cuba of the American gangster.

The announcement of the desire of Dr. Grau to appoint Labourdette to this position created general consternation in Havana and open opposition both from Franco and Batista. Last night the Student Council met to determine its attitude and voted by a majority of one to insist upon Labourdette's appointment being made effective. Batista until the present moment has refused to permit such action. If he is overruled, he will necessarily lose prestige and influence as well as control of the Havana police force amounting to approximately 2,000 men.

Batista's position seems to have weakened materially during the past few days. He has been forced by the sergeants most closely associated with him to remove the three commissioned officers who joined him after the mutiny and upon whose advice he had largely depended. It is probable that the weakening of his position is the principal motive for his desire, as I informed the Department in my No. 370, October 18, 1 p.m., to resume negotiations with Mendieta immediately.

(signed) Benjamin Sumner Welles

--◊◊◊--0--◊◊◊--

BENJAMIN SUMNER WELLES, US AMBASSADOR IN CUBA, WRITES TO CORDELL HULL, US SECRETARY OF STATE

Havana, October 19, 1933   [Received October 20, 12:22 a.m.]

At last there appears to be definite evidence that Grau San Martín and the civilian elements associated with him are willing to take the initiative in seeking a compromise solution. This afternoon I talked with Fernando Ortiz who is now close to Grau San Martín and with leaders of the ABC. A form of solution of the following nature has been accepted by Grau and has been accepted in principle by the ABC. directors: The retention of Grau as President; complete change of Cabinet in such manner as to obtain the support of three and probably all of the political parties; the creation of an administrative commission which would have the deciding voice in all matters affecting electoral and financial decrees and which would be composed in equal parts of governmental and opposition appointees; and the proclamation of a provisional constitution which would define the duties and the duration of the provisional government.

Batista will support this formula. Mendieta and Gómez are, I believe, favorably inclined although they will attempt to insist on Grau's withdrawal. The OCRR will abide by Mendieta's decision.

This formula is in my judgment a reasonable compromise and should offer a basis for agreement. In a conference held today with authorized representatives of the commercial and financial interests I was informed that they would support it although they object to the retention of Grau.

The desire for a mapped-out accord is due to the open disagreement now existing between Batista and the students. The determined refusal of the former to agree to the removal of the Chief of Police of Havana and the inability of the students to force the issue have caused a marked diminution in their influence in the Palace.

They are already conspiring to overthrow Batista or to assassinate him. The fear on the part of Grau and many members of the Cabinet of the results of an open struggle between the students and the soldiers will hasten a solution.

Rionda

Gómez-Mena

Lobo

All throughout Machado's government in Cuba, he spent millions of dollars on public works and funding for industrial development, particularly through credits and tariffs support. When the sugar industry needed tariff relieve, Machado enacted the **Customs Tariff Law**; many historians consider it the most important economic legislation in the Cuba's first century. It granted duty-exception for many sectors of the industry. Added to the containment of "radical" forces of social unrest, Machado gained the support of the business classes that only it faded during his second term.

Cuba, before and after its independence, was a good soil to nurture great entrepreneurs, and of course some of the most successful were the so-called **Sugar Barons**. What follows is a short story of their roots and their efforts.

In 1870, **Manuel Rionda** left his native city of Gijón to try his fortunes in New York, where he worked for *Czarnikow-Macdougall Sugar Company* and first learned the sugar business. In 1891, he joined his brother **Francisco** in Cuba and with financial help from US tycoons **Henry O. Havemeyer** and **Walter E. Ogilvie**, they bought and restored the *Tuinicú Sugar Mill*. After his brother passed away in 1899, he built the *Francisco Sugar Mill* in Camagüey, naming it in memory of his brother. After the death of Caesar Czarnikow, Rionda reorganized the firm with a new name: **Czarnikow-Rionda Co**. It became one of the wealthiest corporations in the New World.

In 1878, **Andrés Gómez Mena** left Burgos for Havana to carve out his future. After many years of hard work, he bought the city block comprised by the streets Zulueta, Monserrate, Neptuno and San Rafael, across from Havana's Central Park, with the proceedings of a sale of several processing sugar mills to an American company in 1920. There he built the famous **Manzana de Gómez.** He died at age 68 during surgery after been attacked by a jealous husband named Fernando Neugart.

When **Rionda** died, his nephew grandson **Alfonso Fanjul** took over the business. When **Gómez-Mena** died, his granddaughter **Lilian** became the heiress of his fortune. In 1933 **Alfonso** and **Lilian** met and after 2 years they married, giving rise to the greatest empire of the sugar industry in Cuba, controlling 17 sugar mills and selling 18% of the sugar consumed in the US.

In 1898, **Julio Lobo Olavarría** was born in Caracas, Venezuela. He emigrated to Cuba in 1906 when his father worked at the *North America Trust Company*. Julio studied in the US and soon returned to Cuba to get involved in the family's sugar business. In 1932, he married **María Esperanza Montalvo**, the great-niece of la **Comtesse de Merlin**, *María de las Mercedes Santa Cruz Montalvo*, known in Paris as *La Belle Créole*. He turned his father's business into the world's largest sugar trading firm.

I have urged the immediate consideration of the compromise proposed throughout today on all elements. Unless the students are again successful in blocking its acceptance, I am inclined to be hopeful that the end of this impasse may be in sight.

(signed) Benjamin Sumner Welles

--◊◊◊--0--◊◊◊--

BENJAMIN SUMNER WELLES, US AMBASSADOR IN CUBA, WRITES TO **CORDELL HULL,** US SECRETARY OF STATE

Havana, October 20, 1933   [Received 8:45 p.m.]

Grau San Martín has just sent me, through drs. Portela and Granados, the written draft of the compromise solution referred to in my telegram of October 19, 10 p.m. It appears to me an entirely satisfactory solution provided two basic points are made clear. These points involve fair representation of all-important sectors on the Administrative Council or *"Council of State"*, as it is termed in the draft referred to.

I am advised that Grau San Martín himself and the Student Directorate have formally approved the draft and that, after receiving confidential advice from me as to whether I consider it a fair proposal, Grau San Martín himself will request the agreement of the individual leaders of the opposition parties.

In this project, copy of which will be sent by air mail, the powers of the President are limited, and principal executive and legislative authority is vested in the chief of the Cabinet and in the Council of State.

Portela likewise stated that Grau had informed him that should the new government be organized he himself would resign as President.

(signed) Benjamin Sumner Welles

--◊◊◊--0--◊◊◊--

BENJAMIN SUMNER WELLES, US AMBASSADOR IN CUBA, WRITES TO **CORDELL HULL,** US SECRETARY OF STATE

Havana, October 21, 1933   [Received October 23]

SIR: Referring to my telegram No. 382 of October 20, 4 p.m., I have the honor to transmit herewith a copy, in English translation, of the draft of a compromise solution which was handed to me yesterday by Dr. Felix Granados by instruction of Dr. Grau San Martín.

(signed) Benjamin Sumner Welles

--◊◊◊--0--◊◊◊--

BENJAMIN SUMNER WELLES, US AMBASSADOR IN CUBA, WRITES TO
CORDELL HULL, US SECRETARY OF STATE

Havana, October 21, 1933   [Received 8:43 p.m.]

In conversations yesterday afternoon and evening I ascertained that the leaders of the Unión Nacionalista and of the ABC are disposed to accept the form of compromise solution, full copy of which was transmitted with my dispatch No. 182, October 21.

A meeting will be held tonight at the Palace at which an authorized delegate of the business and financial interests of Cuba will express to the students and to Grau San Martín the support of these interests for this form of solution and insist upon its being made effective. The request was made of me by Dr. Portela at the instance of Dr. Grau San Martín to keep the matter strictly confidential in view of his fear that if the students knew that the proposed solution had been discussed with the Embassy, they would refuse to agree to it.

For the reasons above expressed I should prefer that this solution be not discussed with Marquez Sterling for the time being unless he brings it up of his own initiative.

(signed) Benjamin Sumner Welles

--◇◇◇--0--◇◇◇--

BENJAMIN SUMNER WELLES, US AMBASSADOR IN CUBA, WRITES TO
CORDELL HULL, US SECRETARY OF STATE

Havana, October 23, 1933   [Received 6:35 p.m.]

The Student Directorate yesterday passed a resolution with only three opposing votes declaring that Grau San Martín must determine within a period of 24 hours from the delivery this ultimatum whether he will undertake to govern the country as President or whether he will continue to be subservient to Batista. I am informed that the ultimatum will be delivered this afternoon.

The issue has been raised by the continued refusal of Batista to permit Grau San Martín to remove Guiteras, the Secretary of Gobernación, and by his refusal to permit the students to remove Captain Franco, present Chief of Police of Havana. As already reported, there are many further causes of disagreement between the students and Batista.

On Saturday the ABC Radical, the largest of the secret organizations supporting the government, formally announced its withdrawal of such support and made overtures to the ABC of which it originally formed a part for reincorporation in that party.

A significant indication of present conditions is the fact that the government on Saturday issued a regulation prohibiting all radio stations from permitting addresses to be broadcast in opposition to the government. In view of this regulation, at most of the theatres in Havana Saturday night and yesterday members of the ABC, surrounded by armed bodyguards, forced themselves upon the stages of the theatres and made addresses in which they attacked the government violently. In every instance the audiences received them with tremendous applause.

In view of the crisis with which he is now confronted within the government, Grau San Martín has made no progress in his negotiations with the opposition sectors.

(signed) Benjamin Sumner Welles

--◇◇◇--0--◇◇◇--

BENJAMIN SUMNER WELLES, US AMBASSADOR IN CUBA, WRITES TO **CORDELL HULL,** US SECRETARY OF STATE

Havana, October 23, 1933   [Received October 24, 1:54 a.m.]

Fernando Ortiz handed me this afternoon the drafts of a provisional constitution and of a program for the Provisional Government which he told me were approved this morning by Grau San Martín and by the Student Directorate. Both documents coincide in a general way with the draft agreement sent to me by Grau San Martín through Dr. Granados of which a copy was forwarded the Department. The parliamentary feature is, however, omitted. Ortiz told me that Grau would offer three Cabinet positions to the ABC and full equality to all the opposition sectors in the legislative council if they would agree to the compromise proposed. He is to confer tonight again with Grau to reach a complete agreement on details. He asked me to use my personal influence with the political leaders to urge a rapid agreement and I replied that in my conversations with them as with the business representatives I had ascertained that they were fully disposed to concur in any solution which promised political and individual guarantees and public confidence. I stated that I was in full accord with him that a speedy agreement was necessary inasmuch as it was now obvious to all that the position of the government was growing hourly weaker and that if the government did not take a rapid initiative the political leaders would prefer to await the anticipated collapse notwithstanding the dangers that involved.

Ortiz informed me he had been offered the Embassy in Washington or to be the Secretary of State; that he preferred the former but would not accept it unless a stable government were formed as a result of the present negotiations.

As a result of the ultimatum delivered him by the students Grau went out to Batista's headquarters at Camp Columbia this afternoon to attempt to come to an agreement. I am not yet advised of the outcome.

A general closing of all retail as well as wholesale business was determined by Havana business this afternoon to commence at midnight for 24 hours as a protest movement.

(signed) Benjamin Sumner Welles

--◇◇◇--0--◇◇◇--

BENJAMIN SUMNER WELLES, US AMBASSADOR IN CUBA, WRITES TO **CORDELL HULL,** US SECRETARY OF STATE

Havana, October 24, 1933   [Received 12:35 p.m.]

As a result of the resolution passed by the directors of the ABC Radical withdrawing their support from the government the group has broken up into two parts—one, a small fraction headed by Oscar de la Torre has remained with the government; the other, containing approximately 90% of the members, has organized as a political party and has come out in violent opposition. This latter group published this morning an inflammatory attack on Grau San Martín charging that his government was a worse dictatorship than that of Machado; claiming that he was plunging the country into anarchy; insisting that friendly relations with the United States were imperative for Cuba; and that a complete change of government was necessary immediately. This majority group had possession of most of the arms and ammunition distributed to the ABC. Radical by Batista in the early days after the mutiny. Although ordered by the government to turn back these arms to the Army some time ago they have retained possession of them and have now secretly conveyed them to the members of the ABC itself. Fearing reprisals of this action four of the leading members of the opposition wing fled last night by air to Miami.

The speeches in the theaters attacking the government continued last night notwithstanding the efforts of the military to prevent them.

(signed) Benjamin Sumner Welles

--◇◇◇--0--◇◇◇--

BENJAMIN SUMNER WELLES, US AMBASSADOR IN CUBA, WRITES TO **CORDELL HULL,** US SECRETARY OF STATE

Havana, October 24, 1933   [Received 12:35 p.m.]

I was informed this morning that Colonel Blas Hernández, who will be remembered as the only revolutionist whom Machado was unable to capture, was sent for yesterday by Batista for a private interview. Batista stated to him that the situation had now reached the point where it could no longer be tolerated and that he believed the only possible solution of the problem was the removal of the present government and the placing of Mendieta in the Presidency.

He requested Hernandez' support and upon receiving a favorable reply advised him that he would see him again tomorrow and that the step would have to be taken within the next few days. Batista has requested an interview with Colonel Mendieta to take place secretly tomorrow morning.

For the first time a majority of the Student Directorate have sent word to Saladrigas that they desire the support of the leaders of the ABC in effecting an immediate change of government, but the ABC leaders are unanimously opposed to any agreement with the students. They feel that the students are responsible for the disasters of the past 6 weeks and that no solution is possible unless it comprehends their complete elimination from political activities. The ABC directors are willing to support either the parliamentary form of government solution, as already communicated to the Department, or the placing of Mendieta in the Presidency. They will not agree to the plan proposed by Fernando Ortiz, and referred to in my telegram of October 23, 11 p.m.

Rubén de León, the foremost member of the Student Directorate, left this morning by airplane for Mexico. He gave as his ostensible reason for making this voyage, at a moment of the gravest tendencies for the government in which he has played so conspicuous a part, his desire to attend the centennial anniversary of the school of medicine of a university in Mexico.

(signed) Benjamin Sumner Welles

--◊◊◊--0--◊◊◊--

BENJAMIN SUMNER WELLES, US AMBASSADOR IN CUBA, WRITES TO **CORDELL HULL,** US SECRETARY OF STATE

Havana, October 26, 1933   [Received 2:30 p.m.]

At 2 o'clock this morning a large bomb exploded with great force at the entrance to the house of Colonel Mendieta, Chief of Unión Nacionalista. Considerable damage was done. Colonel Mendieta informs me that it was a time bomb and that the explosion took place only a few minutes after he had entered the house.

His conversation with Batista yesterday resulted in the latter agreeing to cooperate completely with Colonel Mendieta in solving the existing situation. He requested Mendieta to advise him at the earliest possible moment of his decision as to the best plan to pursue in the interest of the country but expressed the hope that the assumption of the Presidency by Mendieta now would not be indispensable since he believed that it would be more in the interest of the country if Mendieta were elected for the next constitutional term. Mendieta appears to be entirely satisfied with the conference. A meeting will be held this afternoon at 2 o'clock between Mendieta and his fellow directors of the Unión Nacionalista, the directors of

Colonel **Juan Blas Hernández** (1879-1933), popularly known as *El Sandino de Cuba*, was a prominent figure in the 1933 revolt against Gerardo Machado. He rose in arms and led various successful campaigns against Machado's troops before being invited to Havana on the request of Ramón Grau and Fulgencio Batista. He was asked to enter Havana unarmed because both of them feared he would raise again in rise up in arms against the revolutionary government. Ideologically, Blas Hernández was known to support land reform through small holdings, hence he was considered a political enemy of Antonio Guiteras, who favored collective holdings. He eventually rose in revolt against Batista, with assistance from the ABC membership, and found refuge at Atarés Castle in Havana. (Batista used heavy artillery especially from the Cuban Naval Vessel *Patria* firing from the Harbor. The artillery caused massive losses at Atarés and forced the troops inside to surrender. He was asked to come forward at a line-up of officers and soldiers once the fortress surrendered. As he was called out by name and stepped forward from the line, he was unarmed and was shot by a member of Batista's army. People that favored the revolution of 1933 in Cuba, considered Blas Hernández a true and brilliant hero and a masterful strategist of guerilla warfare; a champion to be respected and admired, whose motivation for waging war against Machado was to combat tyranny, not to secure power for himself. With time, the perception of his role, personality and ideology has been opposite to what Hugh Thomas presented in his book *Cuba, or the Pursuit of Freedom* in 1971.

Blas Hernández was born in Remedios, Las Villas. In 1933 his area of operations was Sancti Spíritus, Remedios and Placetas. He was a self-titled colonel, although he always avoided fighting with the Rural Guard, which exceeded him in men and equipment. He became an ally of Carlos Mendieta when he took part in the Mediation process. Mendieta and other traditional politicians fed Hernández ego and used it for their purposes. On September 17, he rose against the government of Grau in a protest that lasted only a week. Batista used him to bring Mendieta to his side. After trusting Batista for several weeks, he rose again against him on November 8 in concert with the ABC. When faced with an overwhelmingly strong army, he took refuge in Atarés, which eventually cost him his life.

the ABC and Miguel Mariano Gómez, to determine upon the reply to be given to Batista. In the meantime, Batista's own position is rapidly weakening. I was confidentially informed yesterday that four out of the five commanders of barracks in Havana had agreed to take immediate action to oust Batista replacing him with Colonel Perdomo, in command of Camp Columbia during the Céspedes Government, and to force the immediate resignation of the Grau San Martín regime. One of the commanders involved is Major Rodriguez who now commands Camp Columbia where Batista's headquarters are located. Gómez, who is involved in the plan, has urged postponement until the opposition leaders can reach a complete and detailed accord.

Grau San Martín yesterday held two Cabinet meetings to consider plans suggested for a concentration government. The parliamentary plan which he sent me word a week ago he would support was rejected by the students although he had previously advised me that the students were in favor of it. They are now going through the form of studying another plan similar to that outlined by Fernando Ortiz although with full knowledge that none of the opposition members will agree to it.

Innumerable arrests were made by the police last night, among them some 25 arrests for political motives including 3 women and over 200 labor leaders. All those arrested were imprisoned. Some 33 soldiers and noncommissioned officers in various barracks were likewise arrested for conspiracy.

There is such hostility to the government in Havana today and such widespread resentment throughout the laboring classes as well as among the armed forces that disturbances in the city appear inevitable soon.

(signed) Benjamin Sumner Welles

--◇◇◇--O--◇◇◇--

BENJAMIN SUMNER WELLES, US AMBASSADOR IN CUBA, WRITES TO
CORDELL HULL, US SECRETARY OF STATE

Havana, October 27, 1933   [Received October 27, 12:14 a.m.]

The meeting of the delegates of the political parties this afternoon resulted in the unanimous agreement to support Mendieta for the Provisional Presidency with a non-political Cabinet; to draw up immediately a program of government limiting the duration of the government to a period of from one and a half to not more than two years specifying each step to be taken until national elections are held and guaranteeing the security of Batista and the Army in general. It was further agreed to present this agreement to Batista in accordance with the understanding reached between him and Mendieta yesterday.

(signed) Benjamin Sumner Welles

BENJAMIN SUMNER WELLES, US AMBASSADOR IN CUBA, WRITES TO
CORDELL HULL, US SECRETARY OF STATE

Havana, October 27, 1933   [Received October 27, 12:14 a.m.]

Batista has sent word tonight that he is in full accord that Mendieta as Provisional President with a Cabinet of outstanding men and a legislative assembly composed of representatives of all political factions, labor, commerce, finance and the university is the only solution that promises success. He has informed Mendieta that he will at once take the necessary steps to carry out this program. He has, however, indicated that he desires Carbó appointed Secretary of the Interior and War. Neither the opposition parties, the commercial groups, nor Mendieta himself, will agree to the proposal. Negotiations on this point will continue tonight and it appears probable that the insistence of Batista for this appointment will be abandoned.
(signed) Benjamin Sumner Welles

--◇◇◇--0--◇◇◇--

BENJAMIN SUMNER WELLES, US AMBASSADOR IN CUBA, WRITES TO
CORDELL HULL, US SECRETARY OF STATE

Havana, October 29, 1933   [Received 4:10 p.m.]

After 36 hours of continuous negotiations as the result of which a detailed program was drawn up by common accord between the Directors of the Nationalist and ABC parties with the agreement and support of Batista for a Provisional Government headed by Mendieta, the latter late last night went back on the assurances he had given the leaders of his own party and the leaders of the A. B. C. and refused to accept the Provisional Presidency. His refusal is due primarily to his fear that Batista cannot control the Army and that he himself, as he puts it, would merely be Batista's prisoner. He has likewise been influenced to refuse the Presidency by certain members of his own party who do not wish him to injure his chances for the constitutional term during which their own personal interests would be better served. The leaders of the ABC and many of the leaders of his own party are highly indignant at his refusal and the attitude he has now adopted makes it improbable that the ABC will consent to a fusion with Unión Nacionalista.

Under these conditions, in view of the extreme gravity of the situation here and the very definite possibility that the general strike which is scheduled for tomorrow will give rise to a communistic movement, the extent of which is as yet incalculable, I have urged the adoption of the plan proposed by Fernando Ortiz providing for the retention at least temporarily of Grau San Martín as President with a completely new Cabinet composed in accordance with the desire of the main opposition parties and with a council of state or legislative assembly having control over all Presidential decrees and having the capacity to reject Presidential appointments and composed like the Cabinet of individuals selected by common accord between all of the opposition parties, as the only remaining solution that shows any signs of becoming successful.

In conferences last night with leaders of the Nationalist and ABC parties I expressed to them this point of view and ascertained that they would be willing to consent to such a plan in preference to no plan at all and a probable complete breakdown of the government; they are meeting this morning and this afternoon with Ortiz, who is acting as intermediary between them, and Grau San Martín and I am inclined to believe that a final agreement on this basis can be arrived at before tomorrow. Grau San Martín stated to Ortiz last night that he would agree to any Cabinet and any legislative assembly, requesting only that the present incumbents in the Treasury and Labor Departments be retained.

The former, Despaigne, is acceptable to the opposition; the latter, Giraudy, is not.

(signed) Benjamin Sumner Welles

--◊◊◊--0--◊◊◊--

BENJAMIN SUMNER WELLES, US AMBASSADOR IN CUBA, WRITES TO **CORDELL HULL,** US SECRETARY OF STATE

Havana, October 29, 1933   [Received 7:55 p.m.]

I had a conference this morning with Miguel Mariano Gómez. He told me he would support the Ortiz plan of government and the program agreed upon recently by the opposition leaders provided it was impossible to procure a change in the Presidency. He is in touch today with the five recently promoted sergeants opposed to a continuance of Grau San Martín, four of them in command of the key barracks in Havana and the fifth in command of the troops in Santiago. If he believes that they can successfully bring about a complete change of government without disorders he will support them. If successful, the result would then be a government set up in accordance with the Ortiz plan and program but with a new President and a new Chief of Staff. If he does not obtain satisfactory assurances within 48 hours, he will support the Ortiz plan *in toto.*

Batista this morning sent word to me that Mendieta must be forced to agree to serve as Provisional President; that he was the sole candidate in whom all political leaders and the country as a whole had confidence and that if he were requested by all elements to serve Mendieta must consent.

I am continuously urging upon all the necessity for a peaceful solution and the fatal results which are bound to occur if, through conspiracies, the Army is split up into factions. The consensus of opinion, I am glad to say, is against revolution and against a new *Coup d'État* but the latter is a definite possibility if an agreement on the basis of Mendieta or upon the basis of the Ortiz plan is not reached and carried out immediately.

(signed) Benjamin Sumner Welles

--◊◊◊--0--◊◊◊--

BENJAMIN SUMNER WELLES, US AMBASSADOR IN CUBA, WRITES TO **CORDELL HULL,** US SECRETARY OF STATE

Havana, October 29, 1933   [Received October 30 7:53 a.m.]

Batista has sent me word tonight that a change in government is imperative. He will insist that Mendieta accept the Provisional Presidency and if he persists in his refusal, he will urge Gómez to accept the position. He states that he will only ask that the Secretaries of the Interior and of War be appointees in whom he has confidence. He advises that he tonight will urge the Student Directorate of their own initiative to suggest the change but that if they refuse, he will force them to abandon politics and return to the university.

With one exception all the small civilian organizations supporting Grau San Martín have now withdrawn their support publicly. The general public expects the fall of the government tonight or tomorrow although the change will not in my opinion take place before the middle of the week.

The general strike announced for tomorrow will not materialize as planned. Some of the unions will strike but the Army has forced several of them including laborers of the Shell Mex Company to return to work tomorrow and consequently the lockout of the Standard Oil and Sinclair companies will be revoked.

(signed) Benjamin Sumner Welles

--◊◊◊--0--◊◊◊--

BENJAMIN SUMNER WELLES, US AMBASSADOR IN CUBA, WRITES TO **CORDELL HULL,** US SECRETARY OF STATE

Havana, October 30, 1933   [Received 1:40 p.m.]

I had late last night a conference with Mendieta. We discussed the desperate situation of the country and the problems arising from student activities, the imprisonment of officers and present conditions within the Army. I told Mendieta with regard to the former that this afternoon the Student Directorate and the Grau San Martín government would be formally deauthorized by the university students and that in the Student Directorate itself all but five or

Driven by the prospects of emancipation and an opportunity to play a prominent role in nation building, **blacks in Cuba** enthusiastically joined the struggle for independence against Spain. Cuban elites of the early twentieth century, however, viewed black's cultural forms as the antithesis of the European culture, civilization and progress they sought to implement in their society. More than 600,000 Spaniards immigrated to Cuba between 1902 and 1931, and while *'whitening'* had lost all intellectual respectability in the 1930s, it did shift the demographics of Cuba. One of the most valuable contributions of **Gerardo Machado** to Cuba's culture was his invitation of a **black band to play at his birthday** in 1925. It symbolically moved black music from the social spaces of working-class neighborhoods into mainstream.

In the photos above, two cartoons from the 1910's and 1920's, during the campaigns of the *Partido Independiente de Color* founded by Evaristo Estenoz; on the bottom right, a cartoon dealing with **non-white immigration** in the 1930's.

six are hostile to the present regime and would favor a new government. I further stated that Batista's anticipated ultimatum to the students would hasten the resumption of normal university life and the withdrawal of all students from interference in the government. I expressed my realization of the extreme difficulties involved in the necessary reorganization of the Army but at the same time my conviction that Batista would be willing to cooperate wholeheartedly with Mendieta for this purpose and would strongly favor the return of a large percentage of the former officers to commands in the Army.

At the conclusion of our conversation Mendieta gave me positively to understand that if all of the political parties, representatives of commerce and industry and the Army through Batista requested him to accept the Provisional Presidency he would be willing to do so.

(signed) Benjamin Sumner Welles

--◊◊◊--0--◊◊◊--

BENJAMIN SUMNER WELLES, US AMBASSADOR IN CUBA, WRITES TO
CORDELL HULL, US SECRETARY OF STATE

Havana, October 30, 1933   [Received 2:15 p.m.]

Personal for the Under Secretary. Referring to our telephone conversation, every sign seems to indicate a change in government here which would make prompt success possible. I believe change will take place this week and if so, I could be relieved a week or so thereafter or as necessary [sic] as soon as necessary measures of economic assistance to new government had been initiated.

(signed) Benjamin Sumner Welles

--◊◊◊--0--◊◊◊--

BENJAMIN SUMNER WELLES, US AMBASSADOR IN CUBA, WRITES TO
CORDELL HULL, US SECRETARY OF STATE

Havana, October 30, 1933   [Received October 31, 12:18 a.m.]

The University Student Assembly this afternoon was attended by about 1,500 students. The meeting from beginning to end was in continuous disorder. Chibás, a member of the Directorate, was permitted to make a speech, not in that capacity, but solely as a student. He announced that the Directorate had delivered an ultimatum to Grau San Martín *"to change the identity of the government"* before November 4th and requested those supporting the Directorate to leave the hall with him. About 100 left with him. The remaining 1,400 students are still in session. All of these oppose the government and the Directorate.

(signed) Benjamin Sumner Welles

--◊◊◊--0--◊◊◊--

BENJAMIN SUMNER WELLES, US AMBASSADOR IN CUBA, WRITES TO
CORDELL HULL, US SECRETARY OF STATE

Havana, October 31, 1933   [Received November 1, 12:45 a.m.]

Batista requested urgently an interview with Mendieta this afternoon. The latter postponed the meeting until late tonight in order to be afforded the opportunity for a final agreement with the other political leaders.

Batista has stated tonight that he is willing to place the entire decision as to the solution in Mendieta's hands but that the solution must be reached immediately. The two possibilities are the Ortiz plan which would permit the retention of Grau San Martín with an entirely new Cabinet selected by the opposition and a legislative assembly vested with some executive functions and composed of individuals selected in accord with the opposition, or the Provisional Presidency of Mendieta with a completely new government.

The situation tonight appears to promise an immediate crisis and Batista is apprehensive; the chief of the national police and two of the commanders of the four remaining armed forces in Havana went to see Mendieta this evening to urge him to accept the Presidency, and it is obvious that unless a solution is rapidly found the Army will disintegrate. At this moment it appears likely that Mendieta will finally reach an agreement with Batista tonight.

(signed) Benjamin Sumner Welles

NOVEMBER OF 1933

 Events in Cuba

November 1 Mendieta declares he would accept the presidency if it is recognized by the radicals of the Board; no agreement reached.

November 3 The Grau cabinet prevents him from resigning from the presidency. Meeting at the house of *Sergio Carbó*, where Grau slams at Batista for meeting with Welles without authorization from the president. The DI.T proposes that Batista be shot for treason. Grau opposes that and lets him go. Grau ratifies Batista as head of the army.

November 4 The University Student Directory is dissolved. The majority adopts the decision of not exercising any further activity in the government.

November 8 The *50% Law* is passed, which requires companies to have at least 50% of Cuban employees. An armed uprising takes place among Columbia Military Aviation Corps. Most agitators are enlisted ABC members, led by *Carlos Saladrigas*. They join the San Ambrosio Barracks, the Dragon Barracks and the garrison of the Castle of Atarés. A large group take refuge in the Castle of Atarés, from where they resist the regular army. The Castle is bombed by land artillery and from the cruises Cuba and Patria, right in the bay in front of Atarés.

November 9 Atarés surrenders. His leader, officer *Ciro Leonard*, commits suicide. There are numerous executions, including that of *Colonel Blas Hernández*.

November 14 *Captain Gregorio Querejeta* is promoted to Commander for having stifled the uprising in Atarés.

November 17 An Army assault of the Federation of Torcedores is successful. The leader of the Torcedores revolt is the communist leader *César Vilar*.

November 19 Welles meets with Roosevelt in Warm Springs, Georgia, behind the back of the Secretary of State, Cordell Hull, who was traveling to Montevideo to attend the VII Inter-American Conference. The Warm Springs meeting confirms Welles' non-recognition policy. The philosopher, writer and hero *Enrique José Varona* (1849-1933) dies. His funeral is a popular manifestation of grief.

November 22 Grau sends a letter to Roosevelt asking him to end Welles' interference in Cuba.

November 23 A statement is issued from Warm Springs by President Roosevelt, declaring that he will not recognize any government that does not have the support and approval of the Cuban people.

November 27 The Uruguayan ambassador to Cuba proposes a conciliatory plan to get out of the crisis of recognition of the Cuban government.

--◊◊◊--0--◊◊◊--

 Washington Telex

BENJAMIN SUMNER WELLES, US AMBASSADOR IN CUBA, WRITES TO
CORDELL HULL, US SECRETARY OF STATE

Havana, November 1, 1933   [Received 12:05 p.m.]

Mendieta last night had his anticipated meeting with the other political party leaders and agreed upon a program and upon most of the names for a new provisional government. He was then visited by the five members of the Student Directorate who have been outstanding in the Grau San Martín government. The students urged him to support the Ortiz solution permitting the retention of Grau San Martín but giving him to understand that should he refuse to accept it they would not openly oppose a provisional government headed by himself. Mendieta's meeting with the students lasted so late that he did not have his anticipated meeting with Batista.

Batista at 2 o'clock this morning reached the following decisions: to call this morning a meeting of the four members of the revolutionary junta who had elevated Grau San Martín to the Presidency and obtain from them a demand for Grau's immediate resignation; thereupon to call at 1 p.m. a meeting of all of the opposition leaders and the individuals who had taken part in drafting the revolutionary proclamation which had been issued as a result of the mutiny of September 4th and which had caused the constitution of the present revolutionary government; to state to them that the Army considered that the present government had resulted in absolute disaster to the Republic and that in the interest of Cuba a new provisional government was imperative and that only a provisional government headed by Colonel Mendieta offered any sure prospect of success.

(signed) Benjamin Sumner Welles

--◊◊◊--0--◊◊◊--

BENJAMIN SUMNER WELLES, US AMBASSADOR IN CUBA, WRITES TO
CORDELL HULL, US SECRETARY OF STATE

Havana, November 1, 1933 [Received November 2, 12:52 a.m.]

Mendieta has delayed the carrying out of the plan determined upon by Batista and supported by the political leaders in the hope that he can persuade the Student Directorate to agree to it. They are so far completely recalcitrant and none of the opposition groups have any belief that the Student Directorate will accept any solution except one based upon the continuance of Grau San Martín in the Presidency. Mendieta has, however, now taken the position that he must make every effort to obtain the acquiescence of the seven or eight leading members of the Directorate before he will consent to form a government.

This new evidence of vacillation has created a crisis which I think will force Batista to request the political leaders to agree upon some other candidate.

(signed) Benjamin Sumner Welles

--◊◊◊--0--◊◊◊--

CAPTAIN ELOY ALFARO, MINISTER PLENIPOTENTIARY
FROM ECUADOR, WRITES TO
CORDELL HULL, US SECRETARY OF STATE
Washington, November 1, 1933
[Received November 2, 12:52 a.m.]

MR. SECRETARY: The Minister of Foreign Relations, in compliance with the request of the Legislative Power, instructs me to bring to the knowledge of Your Excellency's enlightened Government the following resolution passed on September 16, last:

"*The Congress of the Republic of Ecuador:*
Whereas: *According to the principles of international public law, States are sovereign and are the only ones called upon to judge and settle their own problems of domestic politics.*
Resolves: **1.** *To proclaim that it would view with sympathy the non-intervention of the United States of North America, as well as of any other State, in the domestic politics of the sister Republic of Cuba; and* **2.** *To communicate this Resolution to the Government of the said Republic, to that of the United States of America and to those of the countries of Spanish America.*"

(signed) Captain Eloy Alfaro

--◊◊◊--0--◊◊◊--

MEMORANDUM BY **EDWIN C, WILSON**, CHIEF OF THE
US DIVISION OF LATIN AMERICAN AFFAIRS
Washington, November 2, 1933

Captain Alfaro, Minister of Ecuador, came in and handed me the attached note, communicating at the request of the Legislature of

Ecuador a resolution adopted by that body on September 16 stating, among other things, that the Legislature *"would look with sympathy upon non-intervention by the United States as well as by any other state in the internal politics of Cuba."*

Captain Alfaro, in handing me the note, said that he wished to put on record the fact that this communication was not to be regarded as in any way a criticism of the policy of the United States towards Cuba. On the contrary, the Ecuadoran Government appreciated the policy of the United States in having refrained from any act of intervention towards Cuba and thought that this policy had had an excellent effect throughout Latin America.

I said that, as Captain Alfaro knew from previous conversations with me, our policy had been and was today to avoid at all costs any possibility of intervention in Cuban affairs, and that we earnestly hoped that the Cubans themselves would work out a solution of their problems.

(signed) Edwin C. Wilson

--◊◊◊--O--◊◊◊--

BENJAMIN SUMNER WELLES, US AMBASSADOR IN CUBA, WRITES TO **CORDELL HULL,** US SECRETARY OF STATE

Havana, November 2, 1933   [Received 1:00 p.m.]

I had an interview with Mendieta and Méndez Peñate last night. The former states he is unwilling to reach any conclusion as to accepting the Provisional Presidency without at least the tacit acquiescence of the more unruly members of the Student Directorate. He tells me that he has no doubt from what they have said to him that they would be equal to provoking an encounter with the soldiers should a new government be installed in the course of which several students might be killed and the government would then have to confront the concerted antagonism of all of the student body because of the death of these *"martyrs"*. In such event Mendieta says the students would conduct a campaign against the government not only through acts of terrorism but also by fomenting strikes and other labor disturbances. I suggested to him that it seemed highly unreasonable to attribute more importance to the selfish opposition of a score of immature students than the unanimous desire of the rest of Cuban public opinion for a government headed by him which could restore peace to Cuba and commence the task Torriente and Méndez Peñate are meeting with the Student Directorate this morning and again this afternoon but I have no reason to believe that the attitude of the students will be modified.

After repeatedly requesting interviews with Mendieta during the past 24 hours Batista finally persuaded Mendieta to see him early this morning just after my own interview with Mendieta terminated.

It was a **convulsive world in 1933**. *Photos, top to bottom*: a **Communist parade** in New York city; a grandiose *meeting of the Nazis* at Berlin's Brandenburg Gate; in Cuba, however, politicians, wealthy Americans of the business world and musicians hungry to be a part of the hot, wild rhythms of Cuba, **rushed to the Nightclubs**. They did not suspect that Havana was already a wounded capital about to collapse.

The crisis therefore continues in increasingly acute form. Every newspaper this morning urges Mendieta to accept the Presidency as the sole means of saving the country. One of them, *La Manana*, concludes a front-page editorial with the following appeal:

"Colonel Mendieta, if you have any scruples, overcome them in view of the dramatic evidence of this Cuban crisis. Let it never be said that because of timidity or self-interest, which must always [be?] sacrificed on the altar of one's country, this opportunity of saving the Republic has been lost".

The City of Havana was in a state of continuous disturbance all last night. Nine bombs exploded in various points, one of them wrecking the offices of *La Semana*, the paper published by Sergio Carbó. A bomb brought into the central police station late yesterday afternoon killed one policeman and seriously wounded four others. Shooting occurred in all parts of the city and shots were fired at the Palace by passing automobiles.

(signed) Benjamin Sumner Welles

--◊◊◊--0--◊◊◊--

BENJAMIN SUMNER WELLES, US AMBASSADOR IN CUBA, WRITES TO **CORDELL HULL,** US SECRETARY OF STATE

Havana, November 3, 1933   [Received 2:06 p.m.]

Batista was summoned to the Palace by Grau San Martín last night but refused to attend the interview.

At 10 o'clock he met with the four members of the revolutionary junta which selected Grau for the Presidency together with Prío Socarras of the Student Directorate; Carlos Hevia; Alejandro Vergara; the two students Barrientos and Barreras (accused of complicity in the murder of the President of the Senate 2 years ago); and Nogueira and Labourdette, both of them expelled from the revolutionary parties to which they had previously belonged. The four last named were not invited to attend the meeting but were brought by Prío Socarrás on the ground that they were pre-sent at Camp Columbia when the mutiny was declared on September 4th. The discussion lasted for some hours. Of the four members of the revolutionary junta Franca, Irizarri and Portela favored a complete change of government. The others favored the retention of Grau as a figurehead and a national government of concentration. Batista declared that the Army desired a government that was responsive to popular demand and that in no event did he believe the retention of Grau San Martín could satisfy public opinion.

In view of Mendieta's refusal to reach a definite decision Batista and the others who demand a complete change of government were at a disadvantage in that they were unable as yet to propose the name of a new Provisional President and a definite program for a new government. No formal action was taken. It was solely the consensus to promote with the utmost rapidity an understanding between all the revolutionary parties which would result in the creation of a government that all could support.

The negotiations between Mendieta and the other directors of the Unión Nacionalista and the Student Directorate broke down entirely yesterday afternoon as I had anticipated. Mendieta stated that under no conditions would his party agree to any formula based upon the retention of Grau in the Presidency and the students representing the irreconcilable minority of the Student Directorate declared that they would agree to no compromise except one based upon the retention of Grau. A referendum is to be taken during the course of tomorrow among the various classes of the university students to ascertain formally the attitude of the student body with reference to, (*a*), continued intervention of students in the government and, (*b*), the dissolution and deauthorization of the Student Directorate.

The trend of opinion among the political parties is now turning strongly towards Gómez.

I had a conference with Dr. Gómez last night. He told me that no personal interest and no political ambition would enter his consideration of accepting the Provisional Presidency. He said that no solution could possibly save Cuba in this crisis except a completely new government supported by an overwhelming majority of public opinion and in which business would have confidence. He stated that no one had done more than he to help the students during the past 3 years but that should he head a new government he would deal with the students in the event that they attacked the government or provoked public disorder in exactly the same manner as that in which he would deal with any other lawbreaker. He is convinced that the university must be immediately opened and that once this is done the student problem for the time being will be solved. He told me that in his belief it was a greater honor to undertake the Provisional Presidency today than to take over the government at any other time because of the gravity of the moment and because of the fact that the safety of the Republic was obviously at stake. He added that the sole reason for any hesitancy on his part would lie in lack of confidence in Batista and in the Army generally. Word having been brought to him that Batista desired to ascertain if he would accept the Presidency, he replied that he desired 24 hours in which to consider the Army situation before giving a definite reply. Gómez is now enthusiastically supported by all the political parties except for that of Menocal and is perhaps more highly regarded by business circles in Cuba than any other outstanding political leader. As Mayor of Havana he had an efficient and honest administration and while his popularity in the country is not comparable to that of Mendieta except in the provinces of Santa Clara and Oriente the prestige of his father would be of great advantage to him.

(signed) Benjamin Sumner Welles

--◊◊◊--0--◊◊◊--

BENJAMIN SUMNER WELLES, US AMBASSADOR IN CUBA, WRITES TO
CORDELL HULL, US SECRETARY OF STATE

Havana, November 4, 1933   [Received 2:10 p.m.]

Negotiations between the chiefs of the political parties were in progress all yesterday afternoon and evening. Batista's attitude continued firmly to be that a final effort should be made by every element to agree upon Mendieta as Provisional President and to insist upon his accepting the office but that failing such effort Gómez was the candidate with the greatest likelihood of forming a successful government. During the afternoon Grau San Martín was handed the written resignation of all his secretaries and reached the decision himself to resign. At the same time the Student Directorate agreed to withdraw completely from the government of Cuba.

At half past 7 o'clock the *País Libre*, a newspaper published by the reporters and workmen of the País, was issued with the headline declaring that American intervention had been decreed and bearing on the front page a false cable concocted at the instigation of certain students and alleged to have been sent from Washington by special correspondent stating that the United States Government has determined upon intervention and that Marines would be landed and the Cuban soldiers disarmed by force. A mutiny immediately developed in the Cuban Navy barracks and agitation of the most dangerous character broke out in Camp Columbia and in the other Army barracks. I immediately telephoned Batista to send his aide and I handed him a written statement that the rumor was false and without foundation of any character. Batista has [had?] my statement read over the radio, announced it himself at Camp Columbia and had copies sent to the other Army and Navy barracks. The agitation promptly died down, but the harm had already been done. The promoted sergeants in the Army and Navy were suspicious that any change of government favored by Batista might imply danger to themselves and their attitude was reflected in the meeting of the revolutionary representatives called together last night at Sergio Carbó's house to meet with Grau San Martín and the students and to agree upon a new government. After long discussion which lasted until 4 a.m. this morning Grau San Martín withdrew his resignation and the individuals present at the meeting who were the same individuals who attended a similar meeting the night before declared their continued support of Grau San Martín.

The governmental crisis therefore continues. All governmental activities are at a standstill and the situation this morning in brief is as follows:

Grau San Martín remains in the Presidency supported by a few individuals. The Student Directorate has declared its intention of withdrawing from the government and will in all probability disband either before or after a vote of censure has been passed upon it

today or tomorrow by the university student assembly. The Army is in a state of unrest as a result of the false cable published last night regarding intervention, although still controlled by Batista. The political parties and the remainder of the country are more than ever determined that Grau must go.
(signed) Benjamin Sumner Welles

--◊◊◊--0--◊◊◊--

BENJAMIN SUMNER WELLES, US AMBASSADOR IN CUBA, WRITES TO **CORDELL HULL,** US SECRETARY OF STATE

Havana, November 4, 1933   [Received 7:40 p.m.]

Dr. Antonio Guiteras, the Communist Secretary of *Gobernación*, made his resignation effective this morning. He gave it as his opinion that the failure of the government was since it did not turn sharply to the Left and announced his intention of working for a government composed of soldiers, sailors, small shopkeepers and workers. He made evident a definite break between himself and Batista, because Batista was resolutely opposed to Communism and the disorders promoted by labor agitators and threatened to get rid of Batista soon. So far as I can ascertain, the other Cabinet secretaries are uncertain whether their resignations accepted yesterday afternoon still remain effective in view of Grau's withdrawal of his own resignation.

A university student referendum is in progress this afternoon. The Student Assembly meets tomorrow morning and the result of the votes on the following two points will then be announced:

(a) whether the Student Directorate should cease all governmental activities.

(b) whether the students approve the activities of the self-appointed representatives of the students during the past 2 months.

Torriente this morning informed me that he and the other directors of the Unión Nacionalista Party were so incensed at the attitude adopted by Colonel Mendieta in refusing to assume the responsibilities of government when they were offered to him that they intend to withdraw their support from Mendieta and leave the party organization as soon as a solution of the present crisis has been reached.
(signed) Benjamin Sumner Welles

--◊◊◊--0--◊◊◊--

BENJAMIN SUMNER WELLES, US AMBASSADOR IN CUBA, WRITES TO **CORDELL HULL,** US SECRETARY OF STATE

Havana, November 5, 1933   [Received 2:30 p.m.]

The referendum of the university students taken in an orderly manner yesterday afternoon showed an overwhelming majority opposed to the continuation of student activities in the government and a similar majority against the present Student Directorate.

In order to attempt to prevent a vote of censure by the meeting of the student delegates the Student Directorate last night formally dissolved. Some of the members at once announced that they would remain in the Palace *"as individuals"* to *"advise"* Grau.

The dissolution of the Directorate and the vote of the university students officially deprives Grau San Martín and his government of the apparent support of the university which he had made it appear he possessed.

The relations between Batista and Grau are increasingly strained.

--◊◊◊--0--◊◊◊--

BENJAMIN SUMNER WELLES, US AMBASSADOR IN CUBA, WRITES TO **CORDELL HULL,** US SECRETARY OF STATE

Havana, November 6, 1933   [Received 3:55 p.m.]

The student paper *Alma Mater* yesterday morning carried a front page editorial demanding my immediate withdrawal from Cuba on the ground that I was *"an envoy of Wall Street";* that I was conspiring to establish a government in Cuba which would obey orders from Washington; and that I was engaged in preventing *"a Cuban delegation from reaching Montevideo to unmask the shameful conduct of the Yankees".* This tendency was repeated yesterday afternoon at a meeting in the university in which the members of the former Student Directorate joined forces with the Left or Communist wing of the student groups. A speech was made by Eddie Chibás, author of the cables sent to Latin America last September 9th accusing me of having taken the Cuban Army officers to the National Hotel, in which he urged a student parade in support of my leaving Cuba and claimed that I was *"working for the interests of my own Government".*

The public recognizes, judging by the press, that the student groups are now effectually divided and with the dissolution of the Student Directorate and as the result of the referendum demanding the withdrawal of students from governmental activities the influence of the students in so far as their support of the present government is concerned is practically null.

I was visited last night by the two foremost leaders of the groups in Oriente Province which had been organized against the Machado Government. They told me that these groups were now consolidated with the old political parties and that complete and comprehensive preparations had been made for an immediate revolution in Oriente against the Havana government. They stated that they were supported by all of the soldiers in the province with the exception of the 250 men recently sent to Santiago from Havana; that the old officers were ready to take charge of the troops at a moment's notice and that approximately 11,000 men were under orders. They told me that whether the government in Havana was overturned or not the revolution in Oriente would break out; that the situation there was absolutely intolerable and that it had only been with the utmost difficulty that the movement had been so far controlled and then only because of their belief that the Havana government was to be replaced last week by a government headed by Mendieta. I did my utmost to persuade them [to] hold back. I told them that in the condition in which Cuba now was that civil war would have almost fatal effects and, in any event, make infinitely more difficult the process of economic rehabilitation which was the prime necessity of the moment. They assured me that they would make one last effort with the Havana leaders for a pacific settlement, but they warned me that any unexpected spark in Oriente might start a conflagration which they themselves could not control.

Negotiations proceeded yesterday in Havana for the purpose of consolidating opinion of the political parties in favor of Gómez. He has now definitely determined to accept the Provisional Presidency without any more hesitation. In the course of the day it will be ascertained whether Batista feels that he has enough control of the troops in Havana to make a move successful. Batista's own violent animosity to Grau San Martín which is now growing due to his knowledge of a plot favored by Grau Saturday to seize Batista and replace him with another sergeant makes it inevitable that Batista will move against Grau provided he can be reasonably confident of the loyalty of the soldiers in the various Havana barracks.

The newspapers continue to clamor for Grau's withdrawal and the general feeling regarding Grau's position is reflected in a cartoon in *La Manana* this morning which supported Grau until last week in which those individuals who still support Grau are referred to as *"one or two corporals"*.

(signed) Benjamin Sumner Welles

Photos, top to bottom: Photos taken on the same day, Holy Thursday, April 13, 1933, in three places around the world: **Cortejo de la hermandad de los Gitanos**, una cara diferente de la Semana Santa de 1933 en **Sevilla**; **Times Square**, lots of traffic in New **York City**; in all probability for reasons other than religiosity; finally, a deserted Tverskaya Street, in **Pushkin Square, Moscow**.

BENJAMIN SUMNER WELLES, US AMBASSADOR IN CUBA, WRITES TO
CORDELL HULL, US SECRETARY OF STATE

Havana, November 6, 1933   [Received 2:50 p.m.]

Personal for the Under Secretary. Referring to our telephone conversation this morning, the possibilities of a momentary change in the situation are such that it is impossible to foresee with any assurance what line the developments may take. General conditions are more precarious than they have been at any moment during the last 2 months. The possibilities are as follows:

(**a**) Ah immediate *Coup d'État* against Grau by Batista which if successful will result in the formation of a center government headed by Gómez or a military dictatorship;

(**b**) Outbreak of revolution in Oriente and Camagüey Provinces;

(**c**) General strike tomorrow instigated by the Communist organization;

(**d**) Displacement of Batista through violence by elements in the Army upon whom Guiteras the present Secretary of Gobernación is working;

(**e**) Reorganization of the government under Grau bringing into the Cabinet new elements probably of Communist tendencies which could only result in repeated revolutionary attempts against it.

Under these circumstances I cannot help but feel, much as I would prefer accompanying the Secretary to Montevideo, that a change in the Embassy at this moment will be prejudicial to our own interests. The personal contacts and relationships that I have formed during the past 6 months are necessarily of value in a critical moment like this and it is because of this that I believe I should not leave Havana until after a solution of one kind or another has been found.

(signed) Benjamin Sumner Welles

--◇◇◇--0--◇◇◇--

BENJAMIN SUMNER WELLES, US AMBASSADOR IN CUBA, WRITES TO
CORDELL HULL, US SECRETARY OF STATE

Havana, November 7, 1933   [Received 2:20 p.m.]

The letters which Seigle was able to obtain are published this morning in the student paper *Alma Mater* on the front page. Four of the letters are signed. One of the officers states that he believes that the *"condition which existed in the National Hotel was due to the hopes of the attitude which the Ambassador of the United States might assume as mediator in the problem of the Army and Navy officers."*

Another one states that he believes that the attitude of the American Ambassador contributed to encourage a great number of officers *"without being able to specify upon what the opinions of those officers was based"*. Two other letters state in general terms that they believe the attitude of the officers was due to their encouragement by me. The fifth letter and the only one in which any definite charge is made alleges that I made Colonel Sanguily move to the hotel as well as all the other officers through the offer of protection and assistance. It is significant that this letter is unsigned and the newspaper states that the signature is omitted *"for reasons of high policy"*.

In any discussion of this matter with the press I shall limit myself to referring to the statement issued by the Department on this matter and to the previous statements which I have made here at the Embassy.

(signed) Benjamin Sumner Welles

--◊◊◊--0--◊◊◊--

BENJAMIN SUMNER WELLES, US AMBASSADOR IN CUBA, WRITES TO **CORDELL HULL,** US SECRETARY OF STATE

Havana, November 7, 1933   [Received 6:32 p.m.]

The President and Secretary of the Cuban Red Cross Dr. Angulo, and Sr. Victor Mendoza, who in that capacity have access daily to the Cuban officers who are imprisoned or in the hospitals, have just visited me to state that they have been requested by the officer body to inform me of the profound indignation caused the officers as a whole by the letters published in the *Alma Mater* this morning. The officers in the hospitals are already signing a letter to be published in the *Diario de la Marina* tomorrow denying absolutely the insinuations and charges made in the letters published this morning, and such of the officers as are imprisoned who are enabled to do so will likewise sign this denial.

Dr. Angulo told me that two of the officers who signed the letters published this morning told him today that they had done so under false pretenses. Dr. Angulo further stated that Octavio Seigle had visited the hospitals on October 12th and on October 14th ... in order to obtain further signatures to charges of this character and had been unable to do so.

Dr. Angulo was likewise requested to state to me that the officers as a whole were confident that a monetary inducement had been used in two of the five cases where signatures were obtained.

(signed) Benjamin Sumner Welles

--◊◊◊--0--◊◊◊--

BENJAMIN SUMNER WELLES, US AMBASSADOR IN CUBA, WRITES TO
CORDELL HULL, US SECRETARY OF STATE

Havana, November 9, 1933   [Received 11:45 a.m.]

At 3 o'clock this morning, by concerted arrangement, the oppositionists in Dragones and Ambrosio barracks evacuated, passed through the city with all of the arms and ammunition and other supplies from those barracks and joined the opposition garrison in the fortress of Atarés situated on a high hill dominating the lower part of the harbor. Not a shot was fired to prevent this movement. So far as can be ascertained the total force now defending Atarés amounts to approximately 3,000 men fully armed and with ample ammunition. The leaders of the rebellion appear to be Colonel Collazo, Major Leonard, Bias Hernandez, and Rafael Iturralde.

The major part of the province of Santa Clara outside of the capital city is reported to have joined the revolution and to be in arms under the command of Colonel Carrillo. Reports received early are that the entire province of Matanzas is in arms including the soldiers, all supporting the revolution. No dependable reports yet have been received from the rest of the interior.

I beg to request that reports of the above character be not given to the press by the Department. All reports given out by the Department are invariably cabled to Havana and republished in the press here and under present circumstances it is desirable that no reports coming from me be made public.

(signed) Benjamin Sumner Welles

--◇◇◇--O--◇◇◇--

BENJAMIN SUMNER WELLES, US AMBASSADOR IN CUBA, WRITES TO
CORDELL HULL, US SECRETARY OF STATE

Havana, November 9, 1933   [Received 11:35 a.m.]

Dr. Guiteras, Secretary of the Interior and War, has just stated to my contact with him that it is intended in the course of the day to hold summary courts martial and execute immediately all soldiers or police who joined the opposition movement and who have been captured. I fear that the opportunity will be taken on some pretext to execute at the same time some of the officers who have been imprisoned since the National Hotel incident. I am advising the Spanish Ambassador of these facts in order that he may, as Dean of the Diplomatic Corps, make such representations as may be possible in the matter on the grounds of humanity.

(signed) Benjamin Sumner Welles

--◇◇◇--O--◇◇◇--

BENJAMIN SUMNER WELLES, US AMBASSADOR IN CUBA, WRITES TO
CORDELL HULL, US SECRETARY OF STATE

Havana, November 9, 1933   [Received 11:55 a.m.]

Later and perhaps more accurate reports tend to show that a portion of the oppositionists evacuating Ambrosio and Dragones barracks last night passed through the outskirts of the city into the province of Havana. Only seven or eight hundred men joined the garrison at Atarés. The total garrison there is consequently slightly over a thousand and some 1,500 oppositionists proceeded into the country. The government officers admit that all the arms and ammunition were taken from the evacuated barracks.

The commanding officer of the destroyer at Banes reports that representatives of the ABC arrived there yesterday consisting of a revolutionary force with the apparent support of the local groups.

Cienfuegos and Santiago de Cuba are reported to be quiet.

(signed) Benjamin Sumner Welles

--◇◇◇--0--◇◇◇--

BENJAMIN SUMNER WELLES, US AMBASSADOR IN CUBA, WRITES TO
CORDELL HULL, US SECRETARY OF STATE

Havana, November 9, 1933   [Received 3:40 p.m.]

Certain elements of the ABC have been broadcasting on the radio during the morning that beginning at 3 p.m. this afternoon foreign property and particularly American and British property would be destroyed and that foreigners themselves would be attacked. I have not until now attributed much importance to this propaganda but I have just received the visit of the head of one of the so-called *"action"* sectors who visited the Embassy at the risk of his own life since orders have been given for his immediate capture, to inform me that the members of his own group were completely out of hand and notwithstanding his efforts to prevent it would probably attempt to carry out wholesale destruction of foreign property tonight with the purpose of forcing intervention. He said the lives of foreigners would be in danger. These men have been made desperate by the reports circulated that many of the ABC members had been summarily executed and by the realization that they can hope for no guarantees of any kind should they be defeated.

There is a great deal more shooting throughout the city this morning than even yesterday. Shooting in front and to the side of the Embassy was frequent. An anarchic situation which may have very serious possibilities seems imminent for tonight particularly if the electric light plant is closed and the city is without light. Several shells have already struck the plant and if any shell strikes the high-pressure boilers the plant will be wrecked, and many employees killed. The management may consequently be forced to close the plant.

(signed) Benjamin Sumner Welles

--◊◊◊--0--◊◊◊--

BENJAMIN SUMNER WELLES, US AMBASSADOR IN CUBA, WRITES TO
CORDELL HULL, US SECRETARY OF STATE

Havana, November 9, 1933   [Received 6:14 p.m.]

After bombardment lasting 2 hours a red cross was hoisted on Atarés Fortress. Batista's soldiers, however, continued to fire with artillery and from a gunboat upon it. A white flag has now been hoisted. Firing upon the fortress, however, continues.

A Government report intercepted by the *Richmond* states that Batabanó in the southern portion of the province of Havana is in the power of the revolutionists and reports received by the American press correspondents confirm reports earlier received from Cuban sources that the revolutionists are marching through the southern portion of Matanzas and Havana Provinces.

The anticipated revolutionary movement in Oriente Province appears to have commenced with an outbreak in Palma Soriano to the north of Santiago.

(signed) Benjamin Sumner Welles

--◊◊◊--0--◊◊◊--

BENJAMIN SUMNER WELLES, US AMBASSADOR IN CUBA, WRITES TO
CORDELL HULL, US SECRETARY OF STATE

Havana, November 9, 1933   [Received 9:05 p.m.]

The oppositionists who have surrendered at Atarés amount to some 400. I am advised that the remainder who had gone there during the night left the fortress before noon with their arms and proceeded towards the south of the province.

(signed) Benjamin Sumner Welles

--◊◊◊--0--◊◊◊--

BENJAMIN SUMNER WELLES, US AMBASSADOR IN CUBA, WRITES TO
CORDELL HULL, US SECRETARY OF STATE

Havana, November 10, 1933   [Received 8:05 p.m.]

Havana has remained quiet on the surface today. There has been shooting in a few sections. There is deep apprehension of the result of the courts martial being held this afternoon. Captain Creecy at my request has remained at Camp Columbia all day and is in contact with Batista and his aides. Assurances are still maintained that no civilians will be executed.

The commander of the destroyer at Nipe Bay has radioed unconfirmed reports that a concentration of revolutionists is taking place in that section of Oriente; that some 500 have gathered at Cristal, 10 miles from Preston; and that a small detachment of soldiers has gone to Tánamo to put down disturbance there.

There is unquestionably developing an extremely violent reaction in every element in Havana against the present government because of the incidents of yesterday and because of the slaughters of some prisoners after they had surrendered. There is an open demand for intervention by the United States. The foreign colonies are criticizing the failure of the United States to land troops. I have stated today, as I have consistently throughout the past 2 months, that my Government had officially declared that warships had been sent to Cuba to protect American and foreign lives and for no other purpose; and that it was likewise our declared intention to adopt no policy which would prevent or hinder the Cuban people from freely determining their own destinies.

I have noted in certain reports from the American press of today that the assertion is made that recognition of the Grau government would have prevented revolutionary outbreaks. I do not believe that any competent observer present here during the past 2 months would confirm that assertion. Recognition would probably have delayed revolt, but it would not have prevented it. And recognition would have been construed by the bulk of the Cubans as evidence of our willingness to ignore their right to determine their own destinies by lending the support both moral and material which our recognition represents to a government which had come into power after [*against?*] the desires of the great majority of the Cuban people.

(signed) Benjamin Sumner Welles

--◊◊◊--O--◊◊◊--

BENJAMIN SUMNER WELLES, US AMBASSADOR IN CUBA, WRITES TO **CORDELL HULL,** US SECRETARY OF STATE

Havana, November 13, 1933   [Received 3:20 p.m.]

In view of the increasingly complicated problem presented as the result of recent developments here, I feel it is very desirable that I have an opportunity of discussing the situation personally with the President and with the Department, and for that purpose I suggest that I be authorized to return to Washington within the next few days. There has been such a virulent propaganda of absurd and entirely baseless charges directed against me by the agitators close to Grau San Martín and the Student Directorate during the past

Photos, top to bottom: an ambulance of the **Cuban Red Cross in 1933**; a unique view of one of the gloomiest spots in all Havana, known as *"the death hole."* It was here that the **troops under Batista set their artillery** to surrender the army officers that had taken refuge in the **Atarés fortress** in Havana. The city of Havana is in the background. *On the right*, the page of *Bohemia Magazine* reporting the death of **Antonio Guiteras**; *on the left* a picture of *Guiteras* as Minister of Gobernación.

weeks that if the President authorizes my return for conference it would make the position of the Embassy stronger if the Department would announce on the day I leave here (and not until such time) that I am proceeding to Washington at my own request for the purpose of discussing the Cuban situation with the President and with the Department and that I will thereafter return to Havana, should the policy we have followed until now be changed it would be preferable for Caffery to substitute me as special representative as it might be preferable in any event. But the authority of the Embassy would be gravely impaired if any suggestion to that effect were made known now.
(signed) Benjamin Sumner Welles

--◊◊◊--0--◊◊◊--

WILLIAM PHILLIPS, US UNDER SECRETARY OF STATE, WRITES TO
BENJAMIN SUMNER WELLES, US AMBASSADOR IN CUBA

Washington, November 14, 1933   [Received 3:20 p.m.]

I have consulted the President, who agrees with you that it would be helpful to discuss recent developments. Inasmuch as the President will arrive in Warm Springs on Saturday afternoon, he suggests that you come to see him there on Sunday.
(signed) William Phillips

--◊◊◊--0--◊◊◊--

STATEMENT BY **WILLIAM PHILLIPS**, US UNDER SECRETARY OF STATE

Washington, November 15, 1933

In view of recent developments in Cuba, Ambassador Welles has requested permission to have an opportunity to discuss the situation with the President.

Inasmuch as the President is to be in Warm Springs for the weekend and as Warm Springs can be quickly reached from Havana, the President has indicated that he will receive Mr. Welles there on Sunday. After his conference, Mr. Welles will return to Havana.
(signed) William Phillips

--◊◊◊--0--◊◊◊--

BENJAMIN SUMNER WELLES, US AMBASSADOR IN CUBA, WRITES TO
CORDELL HULL, US SECRETARY OF STATE

Havana, November 15, 1933   [Received 8:09 p.m.]

There are already strong indications of an urgent desire on the part of the civilian element of the Grau government to come to terms with the opposition groups. Leaders of the organizations known as the ABC Radical and the Ley y Justicia, which withdrew their support from the government 2 weeks ago but supported it when the revolt took place, have visited during the past 24 hours important leaders of the opposition to endeavor to secure their agreement to new compromise negotiations. In a public statement which Sergio Carbó himself issued a definite indication of this desire is given in view of his statement *"It is obvious that the government cannot govern against the tide of public opinion."*

From accounts which reached me today the civilians in the government with the exception of Grau and Guiteras are exceedingly apprehensive for their own safety and even more apprehensive as the result of the dominating role which the Army is now taking.

The leaders of the Unión Nacionalista are willing to consider a compromise but none of the other opposition leaders will entertain that possibility at this moment. All of the leaders of the ABC have either fled to the United States or are in hiding as is the case of the leaders of the OCRR Dr. Gómez remains in his house under the strictest surveillance. The *Menocalistas* are as firmly opposed to compromise as the ABC leaders but with one exception—all the important figures in the Menocal group are in the United States or in the provinces.

(signed) Benjamin Sumner Welles

--◊◊◊--O--◊◊◊--

BENJAMIN SUMNER WELLES, US AMBASSADOR IN CUBA, WRITES TO **WILLIAM PHILLIPS**, US UNDER SECRETARY OF STATE

Havana, November 13, 1933   [Received 3:20 p.m.]

Batista has just sent his aide Captain Hernandez to visit me. The ostensible reason for the visit was for me to receive Batista's assurance that he deeply deplored the attacks which were being made in governmental circles against the United States and against this Embassy in particular and to advise me that neither he himself nor the members of his staff had any participation in those attacks nor had any belief in the allegations made. The statement was further made by Captain Hernandez that the false and malicious propaganda which was being spread was solely the work of the civilians close to Dr. Grau. It was plain, however, that Batista is very much exercised as to my own views concerning the present situation in the light of the announcement made this morning of my intended conference with the President at Warm Springs on Sunday.

I requested Captain Hernández to advise Colonel Batista that I appreciated his message and his assurances and that I could only repeat what I had previously said personally to Colonel Batista, namely, that at a moment like this in order to prevent further disturbances and to permit the Cuban people to have confidence in their government and to devote their energies until such time as elections could be held for a new constitutional government towards a reconstruction of their shattered national economy, it should be the purpose of every patriotic Cuban to find through compromise some satisfactory arrangement as the result of which a government in Cuba might be constituted which would be responsive to the natural will and capable of providing guarantees to all Cubans. Hernández assured me that this was Batista's own desire and that he more than anyone else realized the necessity of it. He further informed me that Batista was already working towards that end.

(signed) Benjamin Sumner Welles

--◇◇◇--0--◇◇◇--

WILLIAM PHILLIPS, US UNDER SECRETARY OF STATE,
AT SEA EN ROUTE TO THE SEVENTH INTERNATIONAL CONFERENCE
OF AMERICAN STATES AT MONTEVIDEO
At sea, November 20, 1933

Press thus far nearly unanimous in approval of recognition of Russia, stressing trade possibilities and improvement in Far Eastern relations.

Sumner Welles called on the President yesterday at Warm Springs and is now here in the Department. The President announced that Welles will return to Havana in a few days. Welles plans to remain in Havana not more than 2 weeks and upon his return here will assume his duties of Assistant Secretary. Coincident with his return, Jefferson Caffery will proceed to Cuba as Special Representative of the President.

(signed) William Phillips

--◇◇◇--0--◇◇◇--

STEPHEN TYREE EARLY, SECRETARY TO PRESIDENT ROOSEVELT, WRITES TO
WILLIAM PHILLIPS, US UNDER SECRETARY OF STATE

Warm Springs, Ga., November 22, 1933   [Received 10:57 a.m.]

I have received a letter addressed to the President signed by Ramón Grau San Martín, President of Cuba. This communication was transmitted by Alfred Betancourt, who says it is very confidential and its early delivery to the President most urgent. The letter says briefly that the Grau government has quelled revolt against it; that it purposes to continue the renovating task; that its goal is to enact Constitution that Cuba now lacks which will be submitted to a plebiscite of the nation at the earliest possible date thereby ensuring freedom of suffrage and fulfillment of international obligations;

that Grau wishes quickly to end his mission and return to the peace of his home; that moved by these longings he is led to request in his own name as well as that of his government that the President put an end *"to the perturbing action of Ambassador Sumner Welles";* that Welles has repeatedly disclosed his partiality by communicating and dealing with enemies of the Grau government; that Cuba will welcome any representative of the President's good-neighbor policy etcetera. Please advise whether it is proper for the President to receive this communication. Meanwhile I will hold it.
(signed) Stephen Tyree Early

--◊◊◊--0--◊◊◊--

WILLIAM PHILLIPS, US UNDER SECRETARY OF STATE, WRITES TO
STEPHEN TYREE EARLY, SECRETARY TO PRESIDENT ROOSEVELT

Washington, November 22, 1933   [Received 1:30 p.m.]

Reference your wire of today's date. I believe the President should not receive the communication as method suggested for transmitting it is not the proper one to be used in the circumstances. I also suggest very confidentially that caution be exercised in dealing with the intermediary mentioned.
(signed) William Phillips

--◊◊◊--0--◊◊◊--

WILLIAM PHILLIPS, US UNDER SECRETARY OF STATE, WRITES TO
FRANKLYN D. ROOSEVELT, PRESIDENT, AT WARM SPRINGS, GA.
Washington, November 23, 1933

We have reduced the statement as far as seems possible and submit the following for your comment.

"During the months which have passed since the fall of the Government of President Machado, we have followed the course of events in Cuba with a most friendly concern and with a consistent desire to be of help to the Cuban people.

Owing to the exceptionally close relationship which has existed between our two peoples since the founding of the Republic of Cuba and in particular because of the treaty relations which exist between our two countries, recognition by the United States of a government in Cuba affords in more than ordinary measure both material and moral support to that government.

For this reason we have not believed that it would be a policy of friendship and of justice to the Cuban people as a whole to accord recognition to any provisional government in Cuba unless such government clearly possessed the support and the approval of the people of that Republic. We feel that no official action of the United States should at any time operate as an obstacle to the free and untrammeled determination by the Cuban people of their own destinies.

We have been keenly desirous during all this period of showing by deed our intention of playing the part of a good neighbor to the Cuban people. We have wished to commence negotiations for a revision of the commercial convention between the two countries and for a modification of the permanent treaty between the United States and Cuba. On the economic side, we have been hopeful of entering upon a discussion of such measures as might be undertaken by common consent between the two Governments which would redound to the benefit of both the American and Cuban peoples. No progress along these lines can be made until there exists in Cuba a provisional government which through the popular support which it obtains and which through the general cooperation which it enjoys, shows evidence of genuine stability.

As has already been officially stated, the Government of the United States has neither partiality for nor prejudice against any faction or individual in Cuba. It will welcome any provisional government in Cuba in which the Cuban people demonstrate their confidence. We earnestly hope that in the near future through a spirit of compromise on all sides, the Cuban people themselves will reach some peaceful agreement which may result in general support of a government and thus avoid continued civil disturbance with its attendant tragic loss of life and grave prejudice to the economic interests of the Republic.

Ambassador Welles is returning to Havana within the next few days. As previously announced, upon the termination of his mission which will be in the near future he will return to Washington to resume his former duties as Assistant Secretary of State, and will be replaced by Mr. Jefferson Caffery, now serving as Assistant Secretary of State."

(signed) William Phillips

--◇◇◇--0--◇◇◇--

Memorandum by **Jefferson Thomas Caffery**, US Assistant Secretary of State

Washington, November 25, 1933

The Chilean Ambassador, Sr. Don Manuel Trucco, came to see me twice recently, on Thursday and Friday. He was very vague as to exactly what he wanted on Thursday, but on Friday he came out with it. His Government wants to know what our attitude would be

Since the end of 1929, the **Cuban Communist Party**, committed to an agrarian and anti-imperialist revolution, proposed the creation of a **single front** of all nationalist organizations in Cuba. Communists had maintained for several years the political line of *"la lucha de clases."* The creation of numerous independent guerrilla units in areas of Santiago, Holguin and Las Villas, however, none of which had been inspired by the Communists, alerted the Party about the need to redouble their education work among the masses. In mid-June 1931, its *Central Committee* met with **Rubén Martínez Villena**, a renown Cuban Communist recently arrived from the USSR. The *Committee* recognized that *"revolting and noisy actions"* would keep the Cuban government in check and resolved that, wherever possible, all their militants should infiltrate all active armed guerrilla, to raise their political level and popularize the Party's agrarian and anti-imperialist agenda. Immediately after the fall of the Machado government, the Party held its *V Plenary* on August 29 and 30. Numerous delegates came from all provinces, as well as foreign guests from the *Communist International* and the *Red Trade Union International*. During the plenary session, they instructed all members to set up **Soviets** in Cuba. A week later, the first Soviet was established under the direction of Francisco Calderio (aka **Blas Roca**).

At that time in Cuba, three co-existing movements had popular support: a reactionary **right** commanded by **Fulgencio Batista** and the army; a **center** led by President **Ramón Grau San Martín** with a reformist ideology; and the revolutionary **left** led by **Antonio Guiteras** (*Minister of Interior, War and Navy* in the Grau government).The Party leaders knew they could only infiltrate the last two, and the strategy was to bring Antonio Guiteras to their side, not an easy task.

Antonio Guiteras Holmes (1906-1935) was a leading politician in Cuba during the 1930s. A believer in revolutionary socialism, he participated in the government that came to power in Cuba after the overthrow of President Gerardo Machado.

Guiteras' political beliefs were nurtured in the volatile political climate of the 1920s. He first became widely known as a student leader and friend of **Julio Antonio Mella**, a young Communist revolutionary. Mella believed that people's liberation could only be achieved through violent confrontation with the established authorities. Guiteras did not. When Guiteras was named *Minister of the Interior* under President Grau San Martín government, he was able to introduce many reforms, including minimum wages, minimum labor regulations, academic freedom, and nationalization of important sectors of the economy. After *"Grau's government of only 100 days,"* Guiteras became even more radical, and this would cost him his life.

Due to his intense revolutionary activity against Batista, Guiteras tried to leave the country. A cowardly traitor denounced his plans, and on May 8th, 1935, Guiteras was assassinated, alongside Venezuelan Carlos Aponte, by Batista thugs in a place called **El Morillo** in Matanzas province, during a failed attempt to escape to Mexico.

if various Latin American countries decided to recognize the Grau San Martín Government before the Montevideo Conference convenes.

(signed) Jefferson Thomas Caffery

--◊◊◊--O--◊◊◊--

MEMORANDUM BY **WILLIAM PHILLIPS**,
US ACTING SECRETARY OF STATE
Washington, November 25, 1933

In reply to the Chilean Ambassador's inquiry, I would say that President Roosevelt on the 23rd of November issued a statement setting out the attitude of the Government of the United States to eventual recognition of the Government of Cuba. I would hand him a copy of this statement.

I would say that my Government very much hopes that the other interested governments will take no precipitate action at Montevideo in regard to recognition, which might possibly compromise the success of the Conference there. I would say also that I hope the other interested governments will bear in mind that any action they take might have important consequences on the possibility of the Cubans themselves reaching an agreement for a Government, which represents and is backed by the will of the Cuban people.

(signed) William Phillips

--◊◊◊--O--◊◊◊--

EDWARD L. REED, US CHARGÉ D'AFFAIRS IN CUBA, WRITES TO
WILLIAM PHILLIPS, US ACTING SECRETARY OF STATE

Havana, November 27, 1933

Killing of five ex-Army officers has aroused widespread indignation. All five had been accused of responsibility for execution of three Alvarez brothers in the summer of 1932. Batista has promised thorough investigation and punishment of guilty persons if found.

Conciliation negotiations have received a setback due to reported declaration of General Menocal that he would accept no solution involving continuance of Grau as Provisional President and divergent tendencies in ranks of ABC.

(signed) Edward L. Reed

--◊◊◊--O--◊◊◊-

CORDELL HULL, US SECRETARY OF STATE, WRITES TO
WILLIAM PHILLIPS, US ACTING SECRETARY OF STATE

"S.S. American Legion," November 27, 1933

For the Acting Secretary and Caffery. Please telegraph me at Montevideo the controlling facts and conditions to date against recognition of the Grau San Martín regime in Cuba.
(signed) Cordell Hull

--◊◊◊--0--◊◊◊--

EDWARD L. REED, US CHARGÉ D'AFFAIRS IN CUBA, WRITES TO
WILLIAM PHILLIPS, US ACTING SECRETARY OF STATE

Havana, November 28, 1933

The Uruguayan Minister, Dr. Fernández Medina, who has been acting for the last 10 days as self-appointed mediator with the consent of Dr. Grau, announced to the press last night that his negotiations had virtually terminated with the formulation of a plan of conciliation which he was confident would be accepted by all sectors excepting that of Menocal.

As his plan as described in the press contemplates the continuance in office of Dr. Grau until elections are held and no change in the command and organization of the Army, I feel that Dr. Fernandez' optimism as to its acceptance is unwarranted. This impression is confirmed by information that has reached me from opposition sources.
(signed) Edward L. Reed

--◊◊◊--0--◊◊◊--

WILLIAM PHILLIPS, US ACTING SECRETARY OF STATE, WRITES TO
CORDELL HULL, US SECRETARY OF STATE

Washington, November 28, 1933

We have maintained that the criteria of Cuban recognition are: (1) popular support, and (2) ability to maintain law and order and carry on the functions incumbent upon any stable government.

The Embassy at Havana insists that these criteria have not been met. With regard to No. 1, Mr. Welles emphatically expressed to me his judgment that Grau does not have the confidence of the mass of the Cuban people but is supported by a minority bent upon remaining in power despite all costs. With regard to No. 2, Mr. Welles believes that the Grau regime can maintain order only by the most extreme and dictatorial methods, (although it appears to have strengthened itself by the suppression of the November 8th revolt which has tended to discourage counter-revolutionary movements).

In view of this situation, and the President's Warm Springs statement of November 24, I am awaiting further report from Welles, who arrives at Havana tomorrow. I will keep you fully informed of developments.

(signed) William Phillips

--◊◊◊--0--◊◊◊--

CORDELL HULL, US SECRETARY OF STATE, WRITES TO
WILLIAM PHILLIPS, US ACTING SECRETARY OF STATE

Montevideo, November 29, 1933

An evening paper yesterday and a morning paper today, both of Montevideo, published what purported to be an interview with me in which I was quoted as being in favor of recognition of the present government in Cuba and as having expressed an opinion on other questions pending. I have given no interview whatever since I left the United States and have only given out statements already transmitted to you. Believe interview above referred to be an adaptation of an Associated Press article giving the opinion of a correspondent on attitude which might be taken by our Government on questions discussed.

In this adaptation local newspapers deliberately put Associated Press opinion into quotations as if I had uttered them. Will be careful to keep you informed of all authorized statements.

(signed) Cordell Hull

--◊◊◊--0--◊◊◊--

BENJAMIN SUMNER WELLES, US AMBASSADOR IN CUBA, WRITES TO
WILLIAM PHILLIPS, US UNDER SECRETARY OF STATE

Havana, November 29, 1933   [Received 1:55 p.m.]

Resumed charge.

(signed) Benjamin Sumner Welles

--◊◊◊--0--◊◊◊--

Franklyn Delano Roosevelt,
(1882-1945)
32nd President of the US,
a cartoon from 1933.

DECEMBER OF 1933

 Events in Cuba

December 2 Welles has an interview with the Uruguayan ambassador and approves the Uruguayan conciliation plan.

December 3 Cuba is represented by *Angel Giraudy, Herminio Portell Vilá, Alfredo Nogueira, Carlos Prío* and *Juan A. Rubio Padilla* at the VII Pan American Conference of Montevideo.

December 4 A popular demonstration takes place before the presidential palace in support of a law that ensures not 50%, but 80% of Cuban workers in the country's businesses.

December 5 *César Vilar*, Secretary General of the CNOC (both man and organization are of Communist tendency) declares against the 50% law.

December 6 A reduction of 45% on the price of electricity goes in effect. Merchants, mostly Spaniards, threaten to close their businesses due to the 50% law. Laws against usury and protection against occupational accidents are passed.

December 9 President Grau meets with the opposition.

December 10 Grau refuses to declare many previous agreements void and the meeting turns out to be a failure.

December 13 Cuba's finally bids good-bye to Benjamin Sumner Welles, the disliked personal representative of President Roosevelt.

December 15 The principle of "No Intervention" in inter-American affairs triumphs in Montevideo.

December 16 Speeches by Grau and Batista before a large demonstration in the Presidential Palace gardens.

December 17 A series of riots take place during preparation of demonstrations against the *50% Law*. A mob destroys the premises of the *Workers' Federation* and looted and burns the newspaper *El País* for being against that law. Seven were dead and many others gunshot wounded.

December 18 President Roosevelt replaced Welles by Jefferson Caffery.

December 21 A massive demonstration of some 100,000 people takes place against the Platt Amendment in front of the US embassy. Government troops occupy the US-owned *Chaparra* and *Delicias* sugar mills for refusing to organize the year's harvest. Management indicates that it is *"too burdensome"* to pay a 5 cent raise to agricultural workers.

December 25 More than 600 prisoners are amnestied for the events of the Atarés Castle.

December 29 The harvest is limited to 2.3 million tons and its beginning is set for January 15. A new and technologically powerful new radio station, CMQ, is inaugurated, under the direction of Miguel Gabriel and Angel Cambó. The year ends with the important publication of *Martí, the Apostle*, by *Jorge Mañach*.

 Washington Telex

BENJAMIN SUMNER WELLES, US AMBASSADOR IN CUBA, WRITES TO **WILLIAM PHILLIPS,** US UNDER SECRETARY OF STATE

Havana, December 2, 1933   [Received 1:10 p.m.]

The newly arrived Italian Minister called to see me yesterday. He advised me that he was instructed by his Government that it would make no move towards recognition of any Cuban government until such government had received the approval of the United States. He stated that he himself had informed his Government that in his judgment there was no possible basis for recognition of any government such as the present Cuban government. He told me confidentially that his Foreign Office had been in communication with the French and British Foreign Offices concerning the recognition question and that the three Governments were in entire accord to follow the lead of the United States in this matter. He added that the question of recognition by Great Britain had arisen solely due to the initiative of the British Minister here who, as I had surmised, believed that the hardships and injustices being occasioned Jamaican negroes now in Cuba by the existing authorities might be lessened if recognition from Great Britain were forthcoming. The French Minister and the German Minister have personally stated that their Governments would take no action until we had moved in the matter.

The Chilean Minister yesterday informed me that he had consistently advised his own Government against recognition of the present Cuban regime and that he had received no intimation whatever from his Minister for Foreign Affairs that recognition was even under consideration. He repeated to me that Cruchaga was entirely in accord with the policy pursued by the United States here in every way. The Brazilian Minister and the Argentine Chargé d'Affaires have given me most positively to understand that their Governments have shown no indications of changing the policy they have pursued up to the present time of withholding recognition until a representative Cuban government comes into power.

(signed) Benjamin Sumner Welles

--◊◊◊--0--◊◊◊--

BENJAMIN SUMNER WELLES, US AMBASSADOR IN CUBA, WRITES TO
WILLIAM PHILLIPS, US UNDER SECRETARY OF STATE

Havana, December 2, 1933   [Received 9:00 p.m.]

Since my return I have been engaged in conferences with the leaders of the various political groups. During my absence, after the publication of the President's statement, Dr. Grau authorized the Uruguayan Minister to represent him in discussing with the opposition leaders some compromise agreement for the formation of a new government. The Uruguayan Minister yesterday informed me fully of the details of the proposal which he had presented.

The suggestion involved the continuation of Grau in the Presidency until a date still to be determined early in the spring prior to the holding of elections for a constitutional convention upon which date he was to agree to resign and transfer the Provisional Presidency to a substitute selected in a joint session of the Cabinet and a Council of State to be composed of approximately 50 individuals representative of all political and non-political groups of importance in the Republic; the Cabinet to be completely reorganized, Grau to name four of his own partisans, the opposition leaders to name six members, and the remaining two members to be selected by common accord from among impartial and non-political individuals to fill the posts of Interior and War. The Cabinet, by majority vote, would be given complete veto power over all Presidential decrees and control over the selection of any substitutes to fill vacancies in the Cabinet. The Uruguayan Minister informed me that his proposal had been accepted by Grau and was acceptable to the Unión Nacionalista leaders; to Miguel Mariano Gómez and to the leaders of the ABC; that the latter could not commit their party to it until a referendum now in process determined whether the party would agree to the proposal or not. I told the Uruguayan Minister that in my own belief the proposal offered a perfectly satisfactory basis for settlement and that I most heartily approved it.

It is evident, however, that the Uruguayan Minister has been either intentionally or unintentionally deceived as to the acceptability of this proposal by the opposition members and as to the willingness of Grau himself to agree to it. The referendum of the ABC in Havana which is now practically completed appears to show that approximately 80 percent of that party are opposed to any conciliation with the government and from the information that the leaders of the [apparent omission] have as to the sentiment of their partisans in the interior feeling there is even stronger against any compromise. While Colonel Mendieta was originally disposed to accept the agreement and his fellow director in the Unión Nacionalista Party, Dr. Torriente, has been openly working for it, the rank and file of the party have given every indication of their entire unwillingness to follow the advice of their leaders in this regard. Mendieta has consequently changed his own course completely and last night sent me word that under no condition whatever would he accept any settlement on the basis of the retention of Grau in the Presidency and that were he to do so he would undoubtedly be deposed immediately from his leadership of the party. The OCRR leaders advise me that they have never agreed even to consider the possibility of such a settlement as this and that they would openly oppose it. Gómez will follow the lead of Mendieta and the leaders of the ABC It is unquestionable that a compromise agreement which will permit Grau to continue in the Presidency is strongly opposed by public sentiment. The feeling of hostility to the government seems to be even stronger than when I left Havana. For the time being there is an attitude of expectancy throughout the country based upon the impression that the Government of the United States will step in and settle the situation to the satisfaction of the Cubans in general. Revolutionary activities are suspended. They will undoubtedly break out again with renewed violence as soon as the public in general is convinced either that the United States will not impose a solution or that a satisfactory peaceful agreement is impossible.

Bomb explosions are frequent in all the large cities. Two nights ago, a bomb exploded in Dr. Torriente's house which only through chance failed to kill several persons. Considerable material damage and loss of life has been caused by others. I am reliably informed that a very large number of highly explosive bombs are now in readiness for use by the terrorist organizations of the opposition and that the assassination of the most hated figures of the present regime, notably Carbó and Grau, has already been planned.

Dissension among the leaders of the Army is sharply on the increase. I was reliably informed yesterday from an authoritative source that the Secretary of the Interior Guiteras, in connivance with the leaders of the Cuban Navy and of two of the Havana barracks, intends to create a new mutiny directed against Batista and Grau should any compromise agreement for a concentration government be entered into, their objective being the creation of an extreme Left dictatorship.

(signed) Benjamin Sumner Welles

In 1933, the **New York Giants** were professional baseball's *Word Series Champions*. The *ad on the top right* seem pretty audacious and outrageous by today's standards: **"21 of 23 Giants,"** in other words, almost the *entire Giants team,* were smokers of **Camel**, and were happy to endorse this cigarette above all others... no surprise, because in 1933 the company was publicizing the **smoking habits of medical doctors** and touting the **safety of cigarettes**. Out of some thirty brands available.... Most of them also preferred **Camels**. *The top left image*, Rival brand **Lucky Strike**, on the other hand, was concentrating on **flavor**... and it was a fact that **Lucky Strike** was the **preferred cigarette of football players**...The picture at the center shows **Franklin D. Roosevelt** prepared to throw a ceremonial first baseball at Griffith Stadium in Washington, D.C. at Game 3 of the 1933 World Series, on Oct 5 1933.

BENJAMIN SUMNER WELLES, US AMBASSADOR IN CUBA, WRITES TO
WILLIAM PHILLIPS, US UNDER SECRETARY OF STATE

Havana, December 5, 1933   [Received 4:22 p.m.]

I have had additional conferences Sunday and yesterday with leaders of the political parties and with representatives of Dr. Grau. All of the opposition leaders will themselves accept the form of solution proposed in my telex of December 2, 1 p.m., provided Grau will agree definitely to resign the Presidency not later than April 1st next and will agree that his substitute be elected at a joint session of the new Cabinet and the Council of State as provided in the compromise agreement proposed. The leaders state that the sentiment within their parties at the present time is almost unanimously opposed to any formula that would permit Grau to retain office, but they have given me assurances that they themselves will accept the solution and believe that they can persuade their followers to support their decision. Dr. Grau, however, has reversed the agreement he originally expressed to the plan proposed and is now holding out for his continuation in the Presidency until May 20th and the election of his substitute by the constitutional convention which convention if the members are elected while he is in the Presidency would in all likelihood be composed of individuals selected by himself and it is therefore obvious that when the time came to select his successor the convention would either reelect him or select someone indicated by him. If he maintains his present attitude therefore there is not the remotest hope that the opposition parties will agree to the compromise formula.

General Menocal yesterday issued a manifesto to the Cuban people from Miami rejecting in the name of the revolutionary junta all possibility of the acceptance of the formula proposed by the Uruguayan Minister and attacking principally any solution based on the retention in control of the existing Army.

Most of Menocal's principal followers, however, are opposed to his present insistence on revolution. I saw yesterday Dr. Desvernine who was Menocal's Secretary of State for 7 years and Dr. Albanés one of Menocal's outstanding supporters in the last Congress. Both have notified Menocal they will not support him in his present attitude until all possibility of a peaceful solution has passed.

There is a very strong feeling among the leaders of all parties that Grau's intention is to prolong the negotiations for conciliation until he has obtained the large quantities of arms and ammunition for the government which have been ordered from Europe and from the United States and that as soon as he considers himself sufficiently prepared to terminate negotiations and declare without any further equivocation his intention to continue the present government as a radical dictatorship.

I am not inclined to believe that he would be supported in any subverted program by Batista. The latter is again actively seeking a change in government. He is apprehensive because of his knowledge of the movement within the Army directed against himself and inspired by Dr. Guiteras, Secretary of the Interior. He likewise fears constant attempts at revolution which he realizes are inevitable and he is particularly afraid of the possibility of intervention by the United States. I have reason to believe from messages he has sent me during the past 2 days that he will again try to rally support within the portion of the Army sincerely loyal to him in favor of the overthrow of Grau and his replacement by some nationalist acceptable to all elements such as Mendieta or Miguel Mariano Gómez. Mendieta once more has modified his attitude and is now permitting it to be generally known that he will accept the Presidency should all parties again request him.
(signed) Benjamin Sumner Welles

--◇◇◇--0--◇◇◇--

WILLIAM PHILLIPS, US ACTING SECRETARY OF STATE, WRITES TO
CORDELL HULL, US SECRETARY OF STATE

Washington, November 5, 1933

The President said today to say to you that in the event other Latin American nations desire to recognize the present Cuban authorities, we should not attempt to block them; that meanwhile, we should stand by the policy set forth in his Warm Springs statement but should be prepared to consider developments in order to determine whether the situation at any future time fulfills the criteria of recognition maintained in that statement.
(signed) William Phillips

--◇◇◇--0--◇◇◇--

BENJAMIN SUMNER WELLES, US AMBASSADOR IN CUBA, WRITES TO
WILLIAM PHILLIPS, US UNDER SECRETARY OF STATE

Havana, December 7, 1933   [Received 8:40 p.m.]

For the President. At the urgent request of Dr. Grau I had a long interview with him at midnight last night in a private house. He attempted at some length and in detail to excuse the utterly unjustifiable and false charges which he and the members of his government had formulated against me on the ground that he has been misinformed. I stated that this was entirely a personal question; that the allegations made had been completely ignored by me; and that the conduct of my official duties would be in no way affected thereby. He spoke with great indignation of the *"international con-*

spiracy" which had been formed to prevent recognition of his government and stated that the *"boycott"* so created presented an insurmountable obstacle. I replied that I was not competent to speak for any government but my own and that in the case of the United States neither any conspiracy existed nor had I before heard any rumors of such a conspiracy; that the policy that we were pursuing as announced by the President of the United States was based upon our desire to take no official action which would result in injustice to the Cuban people; and that that policy would be continued in the most friendly spirit towards every element in Cuba without prejudice and without favoritism.

He then related *in extenso* what he considered the achievements of his government. He felt that only malicious intrigues could have prevented his government from obtaining the confidence of all. I remarked that every liberal minded person must favor what he claimed was his desire to benefit the conditions of the laboring classes in Cuba but that I could not help but feel that the lack of study and the confiscatory nature of many of the decrees which he had issued affecting legitimate and vested interests in Cuba must necessarily impair confidence. I called his attention specifically to the decree issued yesterday affecting the Cuban Electric Company and to various other decrees of recent date affecting the just rights of many foreign interests other than American in Cuba. After a long harangue on the purity of the ideals of his colleagues, their opposition to Communism and their desire to benefit the Republic he admitted that some of his decrees and notably the Cuban Electric Company decree might not have received sufficient preparation and in the case of the latter assured me that the government would abide by any decision of the Supreme Court modifying the more obnoxious features of that decree.

He then requested me to help him in finding a solution of the political problem. I reminded him that in September I had expressed to him my belief that any provisional government in Cuba could only govern successfully if it adopted a spirit of compromise and sought popular support in order to carry out its obligations. I said that it was increasingly apparent that every day that passed made a concentration government less possible; that the many deaths and imprisonments for which his government had been responsible had aroused popular hostility to a high pitch; that the attacks directed by his government against the legitimate political groups and organizations had inspired the belief that the government intended through force to prevent those organizations from having any fair chance in the coming elections and that the government had determined to control the form of the proposed new constitution without giving the Cuban people any opportunity freely to express their opinion with regard thereto; and that finally the instability of the government and the ill-considered and radical decrees issued had vitally impaired business confidence. I stated that it was well known that revolutionary plans were being formulated on a very large scale and that these plans would almost inevitably be carried out and that in that event, given the disturbed social condition of the country, any fair minded observer could foresee widespread destruction of property and bloodshed on an extensive scale.

I questioned him as to why, when a formula of solution had been proposed through the Uruguayan Minister a week ago which was in a form acceptable to the majority of the opposition parties, he himself had not accepted it after a prior expression of his willingness to agree to it. His reply to this query led me to believe that he had agreed to it at a moment when he feared for his own security and that later, upon being reassured, he had gone back upon his commitments.

I then requested him to advise me what he was prepared to do in order to seek a solution of the country's difficulties. He then stated clearly and definitely that if no conciliatory agreement was possible he was willing to resign at any moment; that if an agreement was possible based upon the form suggested by the Uruguayan Minister, namely, his retention in the Presidency for a relatively brief period, virtual control of the government to be vested in a concentration Cabinet and an advisory council composed of representatives of all groups, he would only demand the outward semblance of control as a means of justifying his continuation in office. I thereupon stated that I could assure him that I would do everything possible to urge a joint agreement along the lines proposed but that my participation in such negotiations must necessarily be entirely confidential and informal and that so far as I was concerned the control of these negotiations must be retained by the Uruguayan Minister.

There is a very strong move on foot among the more influential of the present Army officers with the full support of Batista to remove Grau and his government and replace it by a National Government under the Presidency of Mendieta. In order to combine the two tendencies I have suggested to Torriente that he prepare a modification of the Uruguayan Minister's formula so as to include agreement by all that upon the resignation of Grau he be replaced by Mendieta. If this can be accomplished, and Mendieta has assured me that he would accept the proposal, the growing dissidence in the Army will be stopped and revolutionary plans will be checked since Mendieta is the only Presidential candidate who has the complete confidence of the present leaders of the Army and upon whom all political factions have agreed.

I do not wish to appear unduly pessimistic, but I am not hopeful of the outcome of the present negotiations. Grau is now under the complete domination of the worst elements in his government and while at times, as last night, he [apparent omission] to grasp the extreme gravity of the situation, I have no confidence in the sincerity of his desire to seek a solution unless this is forced upon him through fear. Between the individuals in the government who are seeking to create a frankly communistic government in Cuba and those who are solely in the government for the profits they can obtain, both of which elements have the upper hand and are working together, Grau remains the figurehead he has been from the beginning. There is strong reason for thinking that his renewed attempt to seek a compromise responds to a plan on the part of his Secretary of the Interior to prolong these negotiations until a favorable moment arises for a new *Coup d'État* and the replacement of Grau and the present Cabinet by a dictatorial government composed solely of elements of the extreme Left.

(signed) Benjamin Sumner Welles

--◊◊◊--0--◊◊◊--

BENJAMIN SUMNER WELLES, US AMBASSADOR IN CUBA, WRITES TO
WILLIAM PHILLIPS, US UNDER SECRETARY OF STATE

Havana, December 8, 1933   [Received 1:15 p.m.]

Personal for the Under Secretary. In view of the possibility which seems more favorable today that a political crisis is in fact approaching, because of the serious issues involved in the questions affecting the interests of the *Cuban Electric Company* and the *Cuban Telephone Company* and because of the general belief that labor disturbances on a large scale are impending, I have decided that it is inadvisable for me to make any definite plans at this moment for my return. We can tell more precisely early next week what the developments may be. The political crisis will apparently be settled one way or the other before the 12th. If on that date, there seems no hope for immediate settlement and there is no urgent matter regarding the interests of these American companies in conjunction with which my continuance would be useful I shall arrange to leave about the middle of the week and cable you accordingly. If, on the other hand, the political crisis is prolonged it would be better for me to remain until a day or so before Caffery's arrival.

I think it is exceedingly important that nothing whatever be said to the press concerning my plans at this time. I shall commence my duties in the Department immediately upon my arrival without taking any leave.

(signed) Benjamin Sumner Welles

--◊◊◊--0--◊◊◊--

BENJAMIN SUMNER WELLES, US AMBASSADOR IN CUBA, WRITES TO
WILLIAM PHILLIPS , US UNDER SECRETARY OF STATE

Havana, December 9, 1933   [Received 3:05 p.m.]

The night before last Torriente had a confidential interview with Dr. Grau. He explained at great length to Grau the political and economic situation of the country and received from him the same expressions and assurances which Grau had given me the preceding night. Grau told Torriente in unequivocal language that he was willing to resign but still insisted that he wished to remain in office until a constitutional convention could be convoked. Torriente explained to him that in the disturbed situation in which the country now was, that was materially impossible since disturbances would not cease until a change of government had taken place and no fair elections under proper guarantees could possibly be held until the parties had a chance to organize and until the active intervention of the Army in every phase of Cuban existence as is now the case can be prevented. Grau appeared to be convinced by the arguments advanced.

The Uruguayan Minister came to see me yesterday afternoon to show me the revised formula he has now prepared to provide for an understanding between all factions. This formula includes in addition to the points already communicated to the Department a new article, the essential portion of which reads as follows:

"Upon the retirement of Dr. Grau San Martín from the Provisional Presidency on blank date Colonel Carlos Mendieta will assume the functions of the Provisional Presidency."

The remainder of the article in question provides for the manner in which a substitute for Mendieta should be selected in the event of his inability to serve. The Uruguayan Minister stated that he was going to urge upon Grau the abandonment by the latter of his desire to continue in office until a constitutional convention had assembled and likewise urge that the date of his resignation be set for the very near future. He told me that he was going to explain to Grau that in his own opinion no solution of this character would be possible unless it was carried out immediately and included the provisions above mentioned.

Batista sent word to me this morning that he and the officers of the Army were insistent that the agreement be entered into by Grau and that there was a general unanimity of opinion among the leading officers of the present Army in favor of the above formula. Dr. Presno, the newly appointed Director of the University of Havana who represents the opinion of all the professors and the great majority of the student body, asked for an opportunity to see me last night and advised me that not only was the student body extremely anxious for an agreement along the lines proposed but also that in a recent meeting of the members of the former Student Directorate almost all of the students had expressed their intention of going over to the opposition and openly opposing the present government. He stated that he would see Grau today and urge upon him ratification of the agreement as now formulated. Grau has requested me to have a further interview with him tonight and I have agreed to meet him at midnight as previously in a private house. In general, the prospects seem more hopeful. The press without exception has come out in open support of the suggested agreement

Some of the large companies in Cuba in the 1930s. *Photos, top to bottom:* **Francisco Sugar Company,** refining and marketing of sugar; **Curtis Aviation Company**, mail and passenger transports; **Cuban Telephone Company**, communications; **Cuban Electric Company**, electricity and streetcars; the **Cuba Company**, sugar and agriculture.

which is now a matter of common knowledge. Public opinion has rallied in favor of it and even the soldiers in the streets are speaking enthusiastically of the hoped-for change in government.
(signed) Benjamin Sumner Welles

--◊◊◊--0--◊◊◊--

WILLIAM PHILLIPS, US ACTING SECRETARY OF STATE, WRITES TO
BENJAMIN SUMNER WELLES, US AMBASSADOR IN CUBA

Washington, December 9, 1933

The President asked me to say that he believes it would be well for you to make your plans to leave on the evening of the 12th or the 13th. Caffery is now at his home in Louisiana and will presumably reach Havana a few days after your departure. We all feel that it would be best for him not to give the appearance of hastening to Havana immediately after you have left.
(signed) William Phillips

--◊◊◊--0--◊◊◊--

BENJAMIN SUMNER WELLES, US AMBASSADOR IN CUBA, WRITES TO
WILLIAM PHILLIPS, US UNDER SECRETARY OF STATE

Havana, December 10, 1933   [Received 2:15 p.m.]

In my conference with Dr. Grau last night he told me that he withdrew all the conditions he had previously imposed for the formation of a new government; that he was willing to come to an immediate agreement with the opposition leaders for the constitution of a concentration Cabinet and that he was prepared to retire as President immediately. He said that he would solely insist that the new government obligate itself to carry out the "revolutionary program". Since all factions are in accord on this program, I do not anticipate any difficulty on this point.

Grau has summoned the opposition leaders to meet him secretly tonight at 11 o'clock. They will support only Mendieta as his substitute. Should a complete agreement be reached during the night, as now seems possible, Batista will be called in and will be given full guarantees as to his retention of his present position.
(signed) Benjamin Sumner Welles

--◊◊◊--0--◊◊◊--

BENJAMIN SUMNER WELLES, US AMBASSADOR IN CUBA, WRITES TO
WILLIAM PHILLIPS, US UNDER SECRETARY OF STATE

Havana, December 11, 1933   [Received 2:05 p.m.]

The leaders of the Unión Nacionalista, ABC and Marianista Parties met with Grau last night. I am advised that after very ample discussion an agreement in principle was reached both on the program to be carried out by the provisional government and as to the way the provisional government should be formed. An entirely conciliatory spirit existed throughout. A subcommittee of the opposition has been appointed to meet with Grau this afternoon at 5 o'clock. At this meeting, details will be fixed including the exact date upon which Grau will retire from the Presidency. Tonight, a full meeting will again be held to determine upon the names of the individuals to be selected for the new concentration government as well as the members to compose the Council of State. Batista is in full accord with the agreement and has given assurance that he will support the new national government.

Should the conferences this afternoon and tonight be successful it is highly probable that the agreement will be completed in final form tomorrow and be made public shortly afterwards. While the public has knowledge of the fact that the negotiations are proceeding favorably the nature of the agreement has yet been kept confidential.

(signed) Benjamin Sumner Welles

--◊◊◊--0--◊◊◊--

BENJAMIN SUMNER WELLES, US AMBASSADOR IN CUBA, WRITES TO **WILLIAM PHILLIPS,** US UNDER SECRETARY OF STATE

Havana, December 11, 1933   [Received December 12, 1:18 a.m.]

Personal for the Acting Secretary. In view of the unexpected and complete collapse of negotiations this afternoon I shall leave Havana by airplane Wednesday, arriving Washington Friday morning. Leaving Matthews in charge. The sub-commission of the opposition parties appointed at last night's meeting in Grau's presence and with his full approval, and composed of Dr.Torriente, Méndez Peñate and Dorta Duque called at the Palace at 5 o'clock as arranged. It was immediately apparent that Grau's attitude had completely changed. He had been in constant conference with Carbó and Guiteras during the afternoon and it is the impression of the opposition leaders that the change is due to the threat of immediate revolt made by them should Grau agree to a national government. Grau refused listen to any appeal or arguments, decried the necessity of recognition by any foreign governments and declared that the only possible solutions were cooperation with his government by the political parties or else its overthrow through [*force?*].

The opposition leaders consequently in view of this complete reversal of attitude consider all present possibility of a peaceful solution terminated.

The Uruguayan Minister after the breakdown of negotiations this afternoon made a statement to the Associated Press in which he said that I had not followed his advice, should solely have sought the cooperation of the ABC Party, and had organized the meeting of the opposition leaders held last night without his knowledge. Torriente has sent for the Minister to request a published retraction. Should this not be forthcoming I shall tomorrow morning make a brief statement making clear the facts.

As have already informed the Department the Uruguayan Minister came to me to request my cooperation in his efforts at conciliation. I replied that while I could take no action whatever I fully sympathized with his endeavors and should my opinion be requested, would counsel a peaceful adjustment of all disputes through patriotic compromise. My conversations with the party leaders have of course been limited to this. The meeting between Grau and the political leaders last night was arranged for by Grau directly with the latter. In my conversations with Grau himself, when he requested my assistance, I made it thoroughly clear that I could take no part whatever other than that of a friendly observer and that the role of go-between was undertaken not by me but by the Uruguayan Minister.

(signed) Benjamin Sumner Welles

--◊◊◊--O--◊◊◊--

BENJAMIN SUMNER WELLES, US AMBASSADOR IN CUBA, WRITES TO
WILLIAM PHILLIPS, US UNDER SECRETARY OF STATE

Havana, December 12, 1933   [Received December 12, 1:30 p.m.]

The Uruguayan Minister late last night went to the office of the Associated Press to state that he had never made any such statements as those transmitted by the Associated Press and quoted in my telegram under reference. He requested that the story be killed. When he was told that this was impossible, he requested that a new statement be transmitted in place of the one which he had previously made in which all reference to me was omitted.

In view of the action taken I do not consider any statement by me necessary particularly since none of the statements originally made are carried by the local press for this morning.

(signed) Benjamin Sumner Welles

HARRISON FREEMAN MATTHEWS, US CHARGÉ IN CUBA, WRITES TO
WILLIAM PHILLIPS , US UNDER SECRETARY OF STATE

Havana, December 13, 1933   [Received 4:20 p.m.]

Ambassador Welles departed by airplane this afternoon
(signed) Harrison Freeman Matthews

--◊◊◊--0--◊◊◊--

HARRISON FREEMAN MATTHEWS, US CHARGÉ IN CUBA, WRITES TO
WILLIAM PHILLIPS, US UNDER SECRETARY OF STATE

Havana, December 14, 1933   [Received 2:20 p.m.]

At the request of several student leaders, after very careful consideration and in view of the breakdown of conciliation negotiations, I conferred last evening with Batista and three students, namely, Rubén de León, (see Embassy's telegram of October 24) Curtis and Maceo all formerly associated with the Directorate.

León who spoke for the students present emphasized the weakness of Céspedes and his Government, the increasing lack of control (mentioning Occident Sugar Mill troubles during its brief regime) and the growing rivalry thereunder of the *"old political groups"*. He expressed fanatically the determination of the students to continue fighting *"for the aims of the revolution, which means not only a change of leaders but a change of system"*. He said that the Grau government is *"nationalistic"* and aims to improve the lot of the Cuban people (in this connection he mentioned the 50 % labor law) without, however, overturning the *"capitalistic system"*. He attempted to compare these aims to the *"new deal"* in the United States. Both León and later Batista emphatically denied any sympathy for or tendency toward *"Communism"* and point to the communistic opposition to the present government to which element they laid the continuing nightly bomb explosions. They also emphatically denied that they or the present regime were either anti-American or anti-foreign.

Batista then told his story calmly and at length. He gave as reasons for engineering the September meeting, first, alleged intrigues going on among the Army officers particularly the partisans of Menocal looking toward a replacement of Céspedes; second, the desire of the younger officers to oust their elders in order to obtain immediate advancement and third, the danger of either complete disintegration or establishment of a military dictatorship similar to Machado's. Batista expressed his grave regret at the National Hotel incident and emphasized his efforts to give the officers every opportunity to come to an agreement. He disavowed any political ambitions other than to support a government which would preserve the *"ideals of the revolution."*

Both Batista and León naturally attempted to minimize the strength of the various opposition sectors asserting that the latter were composed chiefly of *"front page photograph"* leaders without substantial following but aided by the entire press. This opposition they claimed would rapidly subside once present regime were recognized by our Government. They asserted that the Grau government has been in power now nearly 4 months and has demonstrated its *"stability;"* that it is carrying on the normal functions of government, laying stress on the opening of normal schools and institutions and the prospective opening of the university in January. That Grau had any ambitions to continue in office after the establishment of a Constitutional Assembly they denied.

When they had finished, I limited myself to expressing interest in what they had told me and to reiterating our position with respect to the question of recognition. I emphasized that we had no interest in any particular person or group and that our sole desire as Ambassador Welles had frequently stated was that the Cubans themselves compose their difficulties. I added that Mr. Caffery would be arriving within a few days and that I felt sure that he would be glad to see and talk with them just as he would be equally anxious to meet leaders of the various opposition sectors in order to acquire a thorough knowledge of the Cuban situation.

Batista and the students, particularly León, seemed to be on very friendly terms. Our interview was most cordial throughout. I transmit the foregoing brief factual outline of what was said for what it may be worth. Ambassador Welles will upon his arrival doubtless fill in the necessary background and interpretation.

(signed) Harrison Freeman Matthews

--◊◊◊--0--◊◊◊--

HARRISON FREEMAN MATTHEWS, US CHARGÉ IN CUBA, WRITES TO
WILLIAM PHILLIPS, US UNDER SECRETARY OF STATE

Havana, December 18, 1933   [Received 10:00 a.m.]

Dr. Grau expressed a desire to meet me yesterday and I accordingly called at the Palace last night. The press having learned of the visit, I stated that I had merely told Dr. Grau that Mr. Caffery would arrive this morning.

(signed) Harrison Freeman Matthews

--◊◊◊--0--◊◊◊--

JEFFERSON THOMAS CAFFERY, PERSONAL REPRESENTATIVE OF THE
PRESIDENT, WRITES TO
WILLIAM PHILLIPS, US UNDER SECRETARY OF STATE

Havana, December 18, 1933   [Received 2:30 p.m.]

Arrived

(signed) Jefferson Thomas Caffery

--◊◊◊--0--◊◊◊--

CORDELL HULL, US SECRETARY OF STATE, WRITES TO
WILLIAM PHILLIPS, US UNDER SECRETARY OF STATE

Montevideo, December 21, 1933   [Received 10:15 a.m.]

Havas dispatch from Havana to morning paper here says that *Wyoming* with 1,800 men arrived and opinion is that it is to protect Spanish interests under existing treaty. The dispatch then adds that it is believed that the Americans are taking precautions in case it should be necessary to comply with the stipulations in the Treaty of Paris which obliges the United States to protect the lives and interests of Spanish residents in Cuba. It further adds that the government accuses the Spaniards of favoring American intervention. Please wire quickly exact facts. I do hope no vessel movements about Cuba will be found necessary before this Conference adjourns.

(signed) Cordell Hull

--◊◊◊--0--◊◊◊--

JEFFERSON THOMAS CAFFERY, PERSONAL REPRESENTATIVE OF THE
PRESIDENT, WRITES TO
WILLIAM PHILLIPS, US UNDER SECRETARY OF STATE

Havana, December 21, 1933   [Received 4:17 p.m.]

I saw Carlos Hevia (at his suggestion) privately last evening. We went over the whole situation in both its political and economic aspects. As regards the political I said (in effect):

"As the situation appears today (I repeated some of the well-known deficiencies of the regime) we cannot recognize your government; you say that you are only a provisional governor with no political affiliations and no political interests and that your only object is to hold honest elections and then get out; but I do not feel that you offer adequate assurances for guaranteeing free elections for the proposed constitutional assembly."

I said also that we had been disturbed at certain seemingly communistic tendencies in the present regime and at the apparent lack of preparation with which important decrees affecting some of our interests had been issued: some of these decrees such as that affecting the electric light rates appeared confiscatory and others such as the Workmen's Compensation Law appeared entirely unworkable. (Hevia readily agreed concerning the latter and indicated that he believed it could be modified into a workable law). We discussed the importance of solving the sugar question and the present strenuous campaign here apparently primarily backed by

Photos of 1933 Cuba, top to bottom: the building of the **Diario de la Marina** newspaper with a **Havana Electric Railway** company streetcar; Cartoon showing **Presidents of Cuba** involved in the Political life of 1933: **Gerardo Machado, José Miguel Gómez, Fulgencio Batista** and **Mario García Menocal**; photo in Diario de la Marina of April of 1933, showing the **dirigible USS Defender** flying low over Paseo Avenue, in Havana. It was piloted by 45 marines and crashed during a storm in the coast of New Jersey with only three survivors; the building of the **Centro Asturiano** in Prado and Virtudes Streets, Havana, in 1933.

speculators (here and in the United States who had sold short) in favor of an unrestricted crop. Hevía was patently much worried concerning this situation. He has asked to see me again this evening.

(signed) Jefferson Thomas Caffery

--◊◊◊--0--◊◊◊--

TELEGRAM FROM
WILLIAM PHILLIPS, US UNDER SECRETARY OF STATE
TO **CORDELL HULL**, US SECRETARY OF STATE
Washington, December 21, 1933

The *Richmond* has been anchored in Havana Harbor since the early part of September, during which time none of the enlisted men have been permitted to go ashore. In order to permit the men to have shore leave during the Christmas holidays, arrangements were made early in December for the *Richmond* to proceed to Panama for the holiday period and for the *Wyoming*, which has recently been stationed at Guantanamo, to take the place of the *Richmond* at Havana during the latter's absence. The replacement is purely a routine matter, determined upon many weeks ago and has no connection whatever with any recent developments in Cuba. Similar replacement of the *Richmond* by the *Wyoming* took place once before for similar reasons.

(signed) William Phillips

--◊◊◊--0--◊◊◊--

WILLIAM PHILLIPS, US UNDER SECRETARY OF STATE, WRITES TO
JEFFERSON THOMAS CAFFERY, PERSONAL REPRESENTATIVE OF THE PRESIDENT

Washington, December 21, 1933

Márquez Sterling requested that he be received as a private citizen of Cuba by President Roosevelt in order to present his respects to the President before returning to Cuba to assume the office of Secretary of State. The President received him informally yesterday afternoon and chatted with him for a few moments on topics in general unrelated to Cuba. The President did say it was a pity that large numbers of American tourists who would like to visit Cuba this winter feel impelled not to do so because of their fear of disorders. No publicity is being given to this visit.

(signed) William Phillips

--◊◊◊--0--◊◊◊--

JEFFERSON THOMAS CAFFERY, PERSONAL REPRESENTATIVE
OF THE PRESIDENT, WRITES TO
WILLIAM PHILLIPS, US UNDER SECRETARY OF STATE

Havana, December 26, 1933

I am endeavoring to explore situation thoroughly and hope to have some definite suggestions to make next week.
(signed) Jefferson Thomas Caffery

--◊◊◊--0--◊◊◊--

JEFFERSON THOMAS CAFFERY, PERSONAL REPRESENTATIVE
OF THE PRESIDENT, WRITES TO
WILLIAM PHILLIPS, US UNDER SECRETARY OF STATE

Havana, December 28, 1933   [Received 8:52 p.m.]

Uruguayan Minister tells me he is making another attempt to have his conciliation plan accepted. I told him I wished him every success. He will see me tonight to report developments.
(signed) Jefferson Thomas Caffery

--◊◊◊--0--◊◊◊--

JEFFERSON THOMAS CAFFERY, PERSONAL REPRESENTATIVE OF THE
PRESIDENT, WRITES TO
WILLIAM PHILLIPS, US UNDER SECRETARY OF STATE

Havana, December 29, 1933   [Received 3:53 p.m.]

The Uruguayan Minister has made no further progress thus far with his plan as far as I can ascertain. I, of course, have discussed the situation with many people. In some cases, I have requested a written memorandum of the opinion expressed to me. I asked one from the supporters of Mendieta which I received yesterday, a copy of which has apparently passed into the hands of Dr. Grau. The government, I am told, is disposed to consider favorably these latest Mendieta suggestions. I am a little skeptical about this.
(signed) Jefferson Thomas Caffery

--◊◊◊--0--◊◊◊--

AFTERMATH HIGHLIGHTS

1934

January 14. Grau is deposed. Guiteras nationalizes the American-owned Electric Bond and Share Company; it is his last governmental act.

February 8. The Cuban Revolutionary Party (Authentic) (Partido Revolucionario Cubano-PRC) (Auténtico) is organized.

January 17. Carlos Hevia becomes the new provisional President but resigns in few hours; Carlos Mendieta steps in as the new provisional President.

May 29. Cuba and the U.S. sign the Treaty on Relations, which eliminates the Platt Amendment and the Permanent Treaty of 1903, but allows the U.S. to continue using Guantánamo Bay. Cuban women win the right to vote.

1935

March. The various revolutionary groups, the Auténticos, Guiteras' Joven Cuba, the ABC and the Communists, join forces in a general strike to topple Batista. The effort fails.

May 8. While preparing to leave Cuba and organize an armed invasion, Guiteras is killed by the army.

May 29. The United States abrogates the Platt Amendment by signing the Treaty of Relations between Cuba and the United States.

Three 1933 photographs by **Fay S. Lincoln** (1894-1976), a famous, influential and widely respected photographer in the US with a forty-year career, featuring everyday life of Cuba. *From top to bottom*: the **swimming pool at the Hotel Nacional**; a scene from **Havana harbor**; a ***guajiro*** working his land in Pinar del Rio.

Appendices

Appendix 1

THE CRIMES OF MACHADO

It is not easy to find a contemporary study of **Gerardo Machado's** life (1869-1939), as a General in the 1895 Cuban War of Independence, and as President of the Republic of Cuba (1925-1933), that improves on the details and arguments of **Carleton Beals**. What follows is an excerpt of his book **The Crimes of Cuba**, written in 1933, when he was already a reputable analyst of Latin American politics and political readers.

Carleton Beals (1893-1979) was an American journalist, author, historian, and political activist with special interests in Latin America. He became famous after his interview with Nicaraguan rebel, *Augusto Sandino* in February 1928. In the 1920s he was part of the cosmopolitan group of intellectuals, artists, and journalists in Mexico City. He remained an active, prolific, and politically engaged journalist.  Beals wrote over 200 magazine articles for publications such as the *New Republic* and *Harper's Magazine,* as well as more than 45 books on history, geography, and travel. His autobiography, *Glass Houses*, was published by *J.B. Lippincott Company* in 1938. In 1931, he was awarded the *John Simon Guggenheim Memorial Foundation Fellowship* for biographies. His subjects included **Porfirio Díaz, Huey P. Long, Stephen F. Austin,** and **Leon Trotsky**. During his career, His travels took him to France, Turkey, the Soviet Union, Germany, and Cuba. In 1938 *Time Magazine* called Beals, the best-informed living writer on Latin America.

IN CHICAGO, WHOLESALE murder is carried on by underworld gangsters. In Cuba, wholesale murder is carried on by the government of Gerardo Machado against innocent citizens who dare criticize his terror. Students, professors, lawyers, Drs., labor-leaders, members of Congress, editors, businessmen, leaders in every profession and walk of life, have been shot down ruthlessly in their homes, on the street, or in jail by his hirelings.

Machado runs a sawed-off shotgun government. He is called *"the President of a thousand murders,"* a conservative estimate of the number of lives sacrificed that this twentieth-century Nero might continue to rule. As Elías Entralgo wrote in 1931,*"Double reincarnation. Vives misrules again. Tacón commands once more."*

In the *National Museum of Cuba*, may be seen, carefully preserved under glass, the toothbrush of one of the patriot generals who fought to free the island from Spain, a pathetic testimony that Cubans have taken liberty seriously. But the final balance-sheet of the promise of freedom we gave during our holy crusade against Spain, is a Cuba now ground under the heel of one of the most monstrous dictators in the history of the Americas and evidence by trade and production statistics leveled to relatively greater economic disaster than during the period of bloody Weyler.

Even though Machado was virtually put into office by campaign contribution of American corporations and could not stay in office except for our State Department approbation, he conceives of himself in more grandiose role. This present-day ruler of supposedly freed Cuba, not willing to permit his post-mortem fame to depend upon a chance toothbrush, has taken good care to perpetuate his greatness in more heroic tangible forms before the termination of his earthly career.

One major outdoor Havana sport is changing street names, not to hallow Cuba's honored dead but to sanctify patriots still buzzing at the honey-jar. Unfortunately, revised street names are easily pegged up by each newcomer; even a toothbrush is a more lasting memento. Machado has given more difficulty to his successors. To be named after himself, he picked out one of the longest, broadest avenues and along its length were set up heavy concrete cream-colored posts, *"Avenida Presidente Machado."* At its junction with the beautiful Malecón sea-front boulevard was erected a massive square monument with the carved motto: *"The Beginning of Avenida Presidente Machado."* On the pavement around its base was painted a wide circle to indicate a national military zone eternally guarded. Whoever steps across that red circle commits a military offense. To eliminate the new monument would require blasting.

Thus far the only service rendered by this monument has been as a refuge for two guardian policemen who ducked behind it to save themselves when the bullets flew in the 1932 assassination of Police-Captain Miguel Calvo y Herrera. Only temporarily did this save one tan-colored body beneath its nickel plaque. Promptly arrested, one soon after hung himself in jail his fellow cops, who would have braved bullets fearlessly, apparently wished to purge their corps of any stigma of cowardice and to erase the record that a monument to brave Machado should be stained by any such pusillanimity.

In contrast to Machado's bold monument, a modest exhedra in the wall opposite the first Malecón *glorieta* informs the curious that the broad sea-boulevard, extending from the dry-moat

The *Malecón Glorieta*, Havana, 1933.

La Punta fortress and flanked by glistening white palaces, was constructed in 1901, when General Leonard Wood was governor. The Malecón also harbors such noteworthy monuments as that to the USS Maine and to the great negro emancipator, Antonio Maceo. Why not one to the living Machado, greater than all predecessors? This is not Machado's only claim in stone and gold. One should not omit mentioning the hundreds of marble slabs with which the benevolent President has furnished the local cemetery. Who is this figure of force, murder, and strange vanities who, despite his atrocities, continues to command the respect of our government? Who is this stocky, bespectacled, prosy-looking individual, who has violated every pre-election promise, who has ridden rough-shod over the constitution, who has murdered, imprisoned and exiled opponents, and yet who continues to enjoy the praise of our statesmen and the cordial attention of our ambassadors? Why does he have to travel in a $30,000 armored car, a veritable army a fore and aft? Why is the Palace sown down with machine guns, packed with police and soldiers armed to the teeth?

Already in office seven years, his term will expire in 1935. Already he has announced that anyone aspiring to the presidency at that time will be considered an enemy of the fatherland. Enemies of the fatherland are unceremoniously bumped off or fed to the sharks. Gerardo Machado and his father, turbulent elements in the province of Santa Clara, were known as cattle raiders before the independence wars.

Gerardo Machado by participating in the armed movement against Spain, converted cattle raiding into a patriotic enterprise. Subsequently he was elected mayor of Santa Clara. One of his first acts was to burn down the Audiencia containing the records of a criminal accusation against his father.

During the José Miguel Gómez administration, he was Minister of Interior, a key political post, which gave him much experience in controlling political machinery. This department handled all light and power concessions. Machado dished these and other public utility privileges out right and left, with pecuniary benefit to himself. In some enterprises he was awarded promotion shares; he was half-owner of the *Santa Clara Light Company*.

When in 1921 the *Electric Bond and Share Company* began buying up Cuban utilities, it found that one of the most experienced men in the field, influential in many enterprises, and a dominant figure in the so-called Liberal Party, was Machado. It made one of his close friends, Mr. Henry Catlin,

A photo of Havana in 1933. On the circle, the electrical plant of *Cuban Electric Company* at Tallapiedra, Havana.

president of the *Cuban Electric Company*; Machado himself became vice-president. By the end of 1923 they were serving more than eighty communities with electricity, gas or water. With Machado's aid, both before and after his becoming President, a series of complicated reorganizations and stock-waterings were effected involving the Cuban Electric, the *Havana Electric Light and Power Company* and the *Havana Electric Railway Company*. The telephone system of Cuba came into the hands of the *Cuban Telephone Company*, a subsidiary of the *International Telephone and Telegraph Company*, like the *Electric Bond and Share*, sponsored financially by J. P. Morgan and Company. The principal docks in Havana harbor are the property of the *Port of Havana Docks Company*, managed by the Behn brothers, big shots in the ITT.

Catlin, who previously departed from another Latin American country rather unceremoniously, was also legal adviser of the *Chase National Bank* for the arrangement of loans to Cuba. The 1932 Senate Finance hearings on the sale of foreign bonds and securities reveal a payment to him for services; more important but unmentioned fees are said to have been paid.

Machado's hand-in-glove relationship with Catlin and those interests was a fundamental reason for his election. President Menocal had been an official in the large *Cuban American Sugar Corporation* and owed his political success largely to that connection. But with the shift of control, during Zayas administration, to the banks and public utilities interests especially as important sugar properties had been absorbed by the large banks, Machado became the representative of these interests, not of the Cuban people.

Catlin provided Machado with half a million for his campaign expenses; affiliated interests put up another half million. Also, from Machado, an important realty property, originally rifled from the nation through complicated transactions, was purchased by Catlin interests at many times its value. With such funds and the active backing of the electric and banking interests, Machado was easily elected.

Furthering his own financial interests, Machado promptly showed his gratitude. Through arbitrary governmental pressure, the remaining independent light and power plants were crippled and easily seized. Machado's own brother presented a bill in Congress to grant the light companies *"perpetual"* concessions, *"exempting them from all taxes, present or future."* This measure could not be pushed through, but the government remitted taxes to the light and power interests to the tune of several million dollars. The new law excluded workers insurance and all protection, abolished the most onerous taxes, and granted other extraordinary facilities. In these efforts, Catlin was always at Machado's elbow, even *"in orgies and bacchanals"* and the power of the electrical interests over the island was thoroughly cemented. Today, despite special privileges, Havana must pay 17 cents a kilowatt hour: the rest of the island from 20 to 30 cents.

Such outlandish rates led to a consumer strike in Havana, sponsored by the *Rotary Club* and the newspaper *El Mundo*. It ended briefly. Machado threatened he would accuse the leaders of blackmail, would *"tear off their heads if necessary."* Despite such threats other cities boycotted the company. The military authorities, hurrying to protect Machado's private interests, and those of Catlin and the companies, declared such movements *"seditious,"* prohibited all public gatherings to discuss the matter, forbade all press comments, and gave orders to fire on sight upon anyone who disconnected any wires. Despite such stern repressive measures, today in Cuba some twenty cities are dark, both homes and streets, because the people and the city administrations will not or cannot pay the high lighting costs.

The Biltmore Hotel in Coral Gables Florida in 1933.

Catlin and friends also bought up about seven million dollars of worthless Zayas paper at a few cents on the dollar, it being promised that these obligations would be recognized. Hard-pressed for funds, Machado delayed. Catlin kept pressing the matter, finally called up Machado by long distance from the to advise him that if his promises were not kept within thirty days, he would withdraw his friendship. Within less than a week, Machado ordered payment, as recorded in the *Gaceta Oficial*.

In short, murderous Machado has been not so much President of Cuba as good representative of the Power Trust and the banks.

How did Machado consolidate his power? What is the secret of his success? After brutally trying to squelch the activities of opposition parties, after browbeating them at the polls, after assassinating such independence heroes as Andre Masó, after murdering people wholesale during 1926 and on, Machado utilized more terrorized opponents to form a conciliatory pact of coalition control with the Conservative and Popular parties. Non-conformist heads were ejected, and proper minions substituted and by decree he forbade appointment of new party officers, making the rank and file powerless to throw out any of their renegade heads. Machado thus appropriated the party names, their headquarters, and active machinery. The Nationalist Union, which sprang up in opposition to these maneuvers, is absolutely proscribed, its members have suffered death and constant persecution. No new party can be formed. The famous Crowder election law was unconstitutionally set aside. All public assemblages were forbidden. No paper can print independent opinion. Even cultural organizations cannot function.

Machado also won over most of the existing Congressmen and Senators by large-scale corruption. This consisted in distributing the lottery collectorships among them, with the right to sell the tickets at from 30 to 50 percent above their marked price, in all an illegitimate profit, in which the President, military officers and other favorites also shared, totaling in good times nearly a million dollars graft a month, nearly $10,000,000 a year equivalent to nearly a fifth of the national budget. This device to assure perpetuation in power of the *Prince* was never dreamed of even by Machiavelli himself.

Havana Yacht Club, 1933.

Thugs, armed with guns and blackjacks, have invaded the sessions of such private organizations as the *Bar Association*, the *Federations of Drs., Dentists, Pharmacists,* the *Society of Engineers*, and the *Academies of Science and of History,* in most cases to impose pro-Machado officers. The lawyers were obliged by such methods to accept the corrupt and bitterly disliked Rafael Guas, imposed by Machado as President of the *National Chamber of Deputies*. (He finally resigned March 1933, when the lawyers jumped over the traces, protesting the sending of *Martínez Sáenz* to the Isle of Pines.)

Machado's attempts to use similar methods to control sport and social clubs met with more stubborn resistance. So, December 28, 1930, the aristocratic *Havana Yacht Club*, which dates far back to Spanish colonial times, was closed, soldiers placed at its doors, its directors accused of conspiracy. Subsequently it could reopen.

During his first two years Machado destroyed all *bonafide* labor organizations of the country, jailing and killing recklessly. This was easy because the cry *"Communism! "* could be raised, though scarcely a handful of the numerous labor leaders now languishing in jail without trial for years knew the slightest thing about Communism.

The *Chadbourne Sugar Plan* and the economic crisis, causing wholesale unemployment, were Machado's allies in lowering wages and destroying the labor movement. Unemployment has been further aggravated by the stopping of most public works and the discharge of thousands of government employees, without having received their pay for prior months. But the *Chase Bank*, with the aid of high discount extensions, has been faithfully paid. Government wage-scales were reduced 50% in 1931, a step enforced by Ambassador Guggenheim, who had promised he would thus salvage the government's economic position; and employees have suffered three cuts in all.

Business concerns and government employees are taxed to help the jobless, but little of this money ever reaches its destination. Responsible persons have estimated unemployment at 500,000 out of a population of less than 4,000,000. City laborers' wages have fallen from $3.00 to fifty cents a day; rural wages, from $1.50 to $2.50 to from three to twenty-five cents. The former rarely have six days work a week. The latter are lucky to get one month's work a year. Skilled cigar workers get a few days' work a week at $1.00 a day. Strippers make from 30 to 40 cents. Factory workers textiles, candy, chocolate, soap, drugs, etc. receive 20 to 25 cents a day. Common laborers work for food and shelter or for from 15 to 20 cents a day.

It should be remembered that the cost of living is in Havana as high as that of a city in the United States of comparable population. Undoubtedly wages would never have reached such low levels, despite the depression, had it not been for Machado's ruthless suppression of labor organizations, all of which are now illegal, as are strikes and public assemblages. No conceited action can be taken. Small groups anxious to maintain decent living conditions must meet secretly, and now have no means of influencing the large aggregate of workers.

The Army has closed all labor headquarters, leaders have been killed, deported or jailed, some of them for years without trial. The few labor organizations that exist are run by Machado's paid henchmen, and likewise have little influence. A recent labor conference in Cienfuegos was organized by the secret police.

The Cuban labor movement during the time of Gómez, Menocal and Zayas had come to occupy a recognized place in the scheme of Cuban life. Organizations ranged from Communist and Anarchist down to most conservative groups. But in 1925 Machado called the army out to crush the Camagüey railroad strike; some thirty labor leaders are said to have been killed at that time. Since then any worker who lifts his head has disappeared or been otherwise summarily dealt with.

In 1927 Chester Wright, editor of *International Labor News*, organ of the *American Federation of Labor*, and English Secretary of the *Pan-American Federation of Labor*, brought to Washington the account of 147 assassinations committed by the Machado regime. This evidence was given much publicity. The New York port-workers voted to sabotage Cuban sugar arriving in the port. Then something happened.

Machado hastened to Washington and met Green in the Belgian legation. Green thereupon issued a public statement that from this date on, the condition of Cuban workers *"would be improved."* After all a great labor leader must feel honored when a President calls upon him regardless of the fate of mere workers.

Wright presently was out of his two jobs, and despite the fact that the conditions of Cuban workers has grown steadily worse, that assassinations have continued, that men then jailed are today in jail without trial, Green never once has lifted his voice in their behalf.

All labor organization, except a few groups patronized by the government and without any following, mere paper organizations, have been driven underground. The *Confederation National Obrera Cubana (CNOC),* member of the *Latin American Trade Union Federation,* affiliated with the *Profintern*, comprised about thirty-five unions of all trades. The Havana local of the CNOC, the *Federation Obrera de Havana*, had thirty trade unions and about 8,000 members. Some of these unions were under Communist influence, others were Reformist, as the street-car motor-men; affiliated restaurant workers were under Anarchist Syndicalist influence.

About 30,000 tobacco workers were organized, the leading group being the *Federation National de Torcedores*. The *Railway Workers Brotherhood*, ever since the breaking of die organization with troops in 1925, has been a paper organization with leaders appointed by Machado. It belongs to the *Pan-American Federation of Labor*, manipulated by the *American Federation of Labor*. The *Union of Bakery Workers*, under Anarchist influence, and the *Shop-Assistants Union*, about 800 members, were unaffiliated. Two pseudo-labor organizations should be mentioned: the *Federación Cubana de Trabajo* and the *Union Federativa Nacional Obrera*. The *Federación Cubana* was a fake Machado organization claiming several thousand members, which joined the *Pan-American Federation of Labor*. It was formed by two paid Machado men, Juan Arévalo and Fabregat, who later quarreled over which should be city councilor. Arévalo then made rubber stamps for an organization called the *Union Federativa Nacional Obrera*. No trade unions are affiliated with the *Union Federativa*, but Arévalo published his *Action Socialista* full of pictures of Machado, *"the true friend of labor."* Despite his quarrel with Fabregat, neither got the councillorship, instead Machado appointed Urrubia, a government henchman of the *Railway Brotherhood*.

Arévalo and Fabregat became disgruntled. Arévalo constantly published in *Action Socialista* accusations that Fabregat was all the time in the pay of the police. Fabregat issued manifestoes and leaflets with photographic reproductions of Arevalo's letters to the police with lists of workers to be expelled or arrested, all which recommendations were executed.

Despite these revelations, Fabregat's union is still an accepted member of the *Pan-American Federation of Labor*. Despite the government's persecutions, murders, "kidnaping of workers" organization has proceeded underground, without much opportunity for expression. In 1930 a twenty-four hours' strike of 200,000 workmen in all industries was pulled off as a protest the crushing of labor. In 1932, when the tobacco trust attempted to return to a 1914 wage-scale, the cigar-workers walked out. The companies retaliated though also impelled by impossible taxes by removing their establishments to New Jersey.

1930: a 24-hour strike by 200,000 works in all industries in Cuba.

Strikes are now utterly taboo, and the least sign of protest is met with bloody repression. When the schoolteachers threatened to strike for their six months' unpaid salaries, the government announced it would use the army against them.

The chief instrument of tyranny has been the Army. As soon as he came into office, Machado weeded out all army officers not personally loyal. Officers mostly trained in American military academies were granted lavish privileges: salaries higher than American officers, good uniforms, comfortable homes, servants, the opportunity of buying most things below cost. Even the common soldier is the pet of the Machado system. Teachers are unpaid, jailed, or killed, but the Cuban barracks have become commodious clubrooms. All equipment is up-to-date and includes a modern airforce.

The army mule receives a food allowance of 38 cents a day; the public hospital patient, before all such institutions were dosed, but 12 cents. The salaries of public employees, after being cut over fifty percent and further reduced by exorbitant taxes, are from four to six months in arrears; but the army receives its pay on the dot; new munitions are bought constantly.

The army is not only favored at the expense of every other portion of the starving Cuban population, but its functions are continuously expanded. As the university, colleges and preparatory schools were progressively closed, soldiers were placed over them. In the few elementary schools remaining open, military supervisors were installed. Military supervisors were set over the provinces. By March 15, 1932, this was extended to the towns; army officers were put into the city halls, with full jurisdiction over civil authorities. To-day every department of government has its military supervisor. The meat and mill: monopolies, among others, are under complete military control. Local police have been absorbed into a national militia. Cuba is one vast armed camp.

The army's functions now include nearly all civil functions. From time to time attempts have been made to legalize these unconstitutional steps. Thus, the afternoon of February 16, 1932, not a regular session-day, in the absence of the President, Vice-Presidents, secretaries and stenographers of the Chamber, a group of deputies approved the law subjecting civilians to court-martial. Machado signed the bill the following day.

In 1932 Machado published a decree creating the new office of military majorship to dictate proclamations and regulate citizens lives in each province. The army officer in charge was given absolute sway except in so far as direct orders might be issued by Machado himself. Any citizen failing to obey the military proclamations is subject to arrest or arbitrarily imposed fines against which he has no legal appeal. To leave towns or cities, even to travel to Havana suburbs, all except tourists require special military permits.

Though legally the police should be at the disposal of the various mayors, these military majors absolutely control the local corps, which are automatically part of the national militia. This status was created in part to prevent civil courts, then still with some functions, from chastising policemen committing abuses and murders. Havana Province has as its Military Major, Colonel Federico Rasco, besides the Military Supervisor, at present Colonel Rogerio Caballero, who controls the national police force, the secret and judicial police, and the gang of convict sluggers known as *the Porra*.

Among policemen indicted by civil court was Israel Pérez, who murdered the American citizen Arthur T. Tagle at Virtudes and Prado streets right near the *Havana American Club*. Held without bail by the Judge of the First Instance, he mysteriously escaped. Machado and Congress put into effect an amnesty law for all militiamen and policemen who had committed any transgressions. Pérez, in defiance of justice and affronting the *American Embassy*, is now back on the force. What is an American citizen or two if he doesn't own property?

Another Machado decree forbids more than three persons to assemble without military permit. Though people go on with their dances and so on, the govern-ment can arrest almost anyone it wishes to. Thus, December 1932, Carlos Fernández and Carlos Martí, President and Secretary of the *Association of Commercial Employees of Havana*

Havana's American Club in 1932.

(over 40,000 members), were arrested and each sentenced to fifteen days and $50 fine for having assembled with other executive members of the organization for social purposes without the required permit.

Extensive espionage causes frequent arrest of people for inadvertently expressing their opinions in restaurants, dubs, theaters, sometimes in private homes. Immediately put under military jurisdiction, sometimes they are tried, sometimes merely held indefinitely. At one time the government discovered that a certain group of young oppositionists were accustomed to go without hats. A police-decree provided for the arrest of any one on the street without a hat; numbers of innocent persons chancing to be bareheaded were savagely beaten by the Porra.

Often people are arbitrarily sentenced to jail without hearings. Thus, Dr. Ofelia Domínguez Navarro, prominent criminal lawyer, head of the *Feminist League*, early in 1932 was taken out of her home from a sick bed on a stretcher, being advised by the military authorities she had been sentenced to forty-five days in prison, but without being told her offense. She has suffered similar sentence and imprisonment on other occasions. Her case is far from unique. The following extract from a *bando*, or proclamation order of the military commandant of Havana, posted late in 1932 on the walls of the city, indicates the military concept of law and justice.

A street in Havana in 1933.

After citing the names of Martí and Maceo, without which no Cuban manifesto would be complete, and reciting the military and police officers who had lost their lives, it states: *"And as this military commandancy has reports that in this comarca there exist various persons who take orders from this band of savage terrorists... as soon as one of these terrorist acts occur which endangers the life of any citizen, there will be arrested and shot, without previous trial, all those who form part of so terrible an organization because they are considered enemies of the Fatherland and of Humanity."* The result of this has been the police-murder of any number of law-abiding members of the community known merely to sympathize with the opposition.

All who have attempted to argue cases in behalf of prisoners before civil or military courts have been arrested and held incommunicado, as Pedro Herrera y Sotolongo, or assassinated, as Professor Gonzalo Freyre de Andrade. For a time, the Supreme Court valiantly attempted to maintain its independence and support constitutionality by handing down brave and honest decision on freedom of press, *habeas corpus*, trial of civilians in civil courts, the closing of the university, etc. Under the strain of attempting to uphold his innate convictions against the Machado terror, President of the Supreme Court, Dr. José Luis Vidaurreta committed suicide. His successor, Dr. Juan Gutiérrez Quiroz, soon resigned, March 29, 1932, after denouncing "*the usurpation of the constitutional life of the country,*" and declaring that the military authorities had appropriated the punishment in cases properly corresponding to civil jurisdiction, had refused to heed habeas corpus or to permit investigation of official crimes. This last accusation referred particularly to the fact that Major Arsenio Ortiz of the army, after having been indicted in the Circuit Court of Santiago for forty-four brutal murders, was protected by the army and promoted by Machado.

Machado then appointed his former Secretary of State, Dr. Vivanco. Though known as a dutiful henchman, within a month and a half the Supreme Court declared again that the military jurisdiction law was unconstitutional, null and void.

Machado thereupon put into effect a new but essentially similar law. Prisoners under the old law were released and re-arrested. Since then the Supreme Court has been completely a creature of Machado's will, though recently it has shown new signs of independence. The lower courts had long since been converted into Executive rubber-stamps.

Gutiérrez, in his final memorandum, March 29, declared that the Judicial power demanded that the Executive issue general orders that:

1. The courts of justice always be properly respected, and their *habeas corpus* Orders complied with.
2. All departments maintain respect and confidence in the court decisions.
3. All authorities promptly answer judicial communications and expedite cases before the court.
4. Measures be adopted to respect the lives of prisoners.
5. Prisoners are not required to make any declarations except to the proper court.
6. No fortress be used as a provisional prison and no prisoner be held incommunicado.
7. Arrested persons be no longer held indefinitely but be released or tried promptly.
8. Immediate modification of the February 17 law (military court jurisdiction)
9. Immediate modification of the *habeas corpus* law giving greater facilities to the judges and determining the manner to make the orders effective.
10. Constitutional amendment reforming the organic law of judicial powers.
11. Immediate approval of the laws reforming judicial appointments.
12. Exclusion of all civilians from military jurisdiction.

Turn back a few years. After having unified, political and military control, already having acquired considerable sums from American bankers (despite his pre-election promise not to increase Cuba's debt) Machado prepared to perpetuate himself in power. A new Presidential election was to take place in 1928, but after consultation with Kellogg and other American officials, Machado decided to obviate this necessity by throwing the constitution completely overboard and extending his term two years.

President Coolidge and his wife Grace with Machado and his wife Elvira, Havana, January 19, 1928.

Utilizing his personally controlled committees of the parties, in April, 1928, he assembled a hand-picked *Constitutional Convention*, and though according to the Cuban Constitution (Article 115) amendments can be adopted by such a body only if proposed by Congress and submitted to a plebiscite, the new body hastened to carry out Machado's minutest wish despite the objections of unconstitutionality formulated by the leading lawyers in Cuba. Most of these lawyers soon spent varying periods in jail, some without trial and without ever being told the reason for their arrest. Instead of proroguing his term two years, the constitution was altered, permitting a six-year term without reelection. Machado, made an exception, could re-elect himself.

Through this illegal maneuver and through a fake election in November in which he was the only candidate, Machado was given a new term to run from May 20, 1959, to May 20, 1935.

The 1933 Montevideo Pan-American Conference, with Roosevelt and Cordell Hull, where the Good Neighbor Policy was established. Cuba sent Márquez Sterling.

In this violation of the entire legal system of Cuba, with the good wishes of Washington, Machado has had the opposition of every literate Cuban except the army and a small clique on the government payroll and a few others directly benefiting from his tyranny.

It was well known in Cuba that this illegal creation of dictatorship followed on the heels of secret financial and political maneuvers. By the early part of 1928 the *Chase National Bank* had over $20,000,000 laid out in unpaid work certificates, which they feared to lose and which they wished to convert into a revolving $60,000,000 credit. Machado's term was coming to an end, trouble was brewing, and the enormous graft of his public works utilizing *Chase* money had aroused universal hostility. A successor might delay in cleaning up the Chase obligations; he might also have to make electoral promises which would prevent him from going ahead with the *Chase* financing.

The second factor in the creation of illegal tyranny in Cuba was the *Sixth Pan-American Congress* to be held in Havana in January. In the *Fifth Congress* in Santiago de Chile rather sharp opposition to American policies had arisen. Now American marines were battling bloodily in Nicaragua; hatred of the United States was seething in all Latin America. Even sharper criticism was expected in the new Congress. On the other hand, many countries were planning to boycott it entirely, denouncing it as an imperialistic body. Both prospects were not pleasing to Washington, which was arguing in Europe for disarmament, the rights of small nations, and nonaggression. What was to be done?

We might be pressing Nicaragua's face in the mud, but it was necessary to make a gesture of nobility. Suddenly Cuban Ambassador Orestes Ferrara at Washington began propagating the idea that in the Congress the Platt Amendment treaty would be denounced with Washington's consent as a preliminary to its abrogation, that the sugar tariff would be lowered, that the Cuban debt would be negotiated on a reduced basis. The *Sixth Pan-American Congress* would back up all these demands, provide the leverage for the State Department to go successfully before the United States Congress.

Machado hastened to Washington personally to invite Coolidge, his *"great and good friend,"* to attend. Conferences were held also with Ferrara, Kellogg and others, and high Cuban officials in the know declared privately that the agreement was then reached to permit Machado to remain in power. The two major considerations for Washington were apparently the Chase loan and the success of the Congress.

Machado dispatched Márquez Sterling, supposed to be a liberal-minded person, to the countries of South America to persuade them to attend the Pan-American Congress where Cuba would finally be freed from the Platt Amendment, our protectorate finally abolished. Cuba pleaded that she needed their help.

And so, despite Nicaragua, despite previous boycott plans, for the first time in the annals of the *Pan-American Union* all the twenty-one republics of the New World sent delegates.

But the agenda had been carefully prepared to exclude all controversy. The delegates were banqueted in such lavishness as to recall the words of Seneca, *"We have reached such refinement that we wish to walk treading precious stones."* The people in the cafes murmured: *"The crowning of General Machado as Emperor of the West Indies."*

But not a word about the Platt Amendment was raised by the Cuban delegation on express and severe orders of Machado. Márquez Sterling discomfited and out of face with the other Latin-American delegates made fruitless inquiries. Other Latin-American countries did give Mr. Hughes a bad day on the question of intervention reports of which were carefully kept out of the American press and most of the Latin-American press. Even here, Orestes Ferrara, instead of living up to the program which had persuaded the Latin-American countries all to attend, backed up Hughes and burst into a poetic eulogy of intervention *"Intervention is a word of honor, word of glory, word of triumph and word of liberty."* The sessions were hurriedly lifted until five years later in Montevideo.

Washington without exactly fooling anybody, through limiting the topics and discussions and connivance with the Cuban delegates, carefully prepared press dispatches from dutiful American correspondents, had won a surface victory, hollow though it really was. And Machado had won the right to overthrow the constitution; and the *Chase Bank*, the security of its past and forthcoming loans, the first of the latter being promptly celebrated in June of that year. Kellogg announced that he was pleased that the three parties (all under Machado's thumb by the means previously described) gave unanimous consent to the alteration of the constitution.

It was, as Marquez Sterling himself declares, *"a Coup d'État, upheld from Washington through banking influences."*

Appendix 2

US WARSHIPS IN CUBAN WATERS DURING THE 1933 CUBAN REVOLUTION

In August 1933, political turmoil was occurring in Cuba. **Fulgencio Batista** led the *"Sergeant's* Revolt" on September 4, 1933, after Cuban dictator, General **Gerardo Machado**, had been toppled and left Cuba. President **Roosevelt** sent thirty warships to protect US interests in Cuba. Due to a shortage of vessels on the east coast, the Navy requested that Coast Guard cutters assisted in the patrols in Cuban waters.

The US Navy ordered the destroyers **CLAXTON** and **TAYLOR** to sail from Key West for Havana. **CLAXTON** stayed only 24 hours in Havana and **TAYLOR** sailed directly for Guantanamo Bay

On September 30, 1933, eleven ships constituted a cordon around the island. They included USS **MISSISSIPPI**, the fight cruiser **RICHMOND**, and the destroyers BAINBRIDGE, GOFF at Havana, then at Cienfuegos (10 Oct 1933), **OVERTON** at Cienfuegos, **J. FRED TALBOTT** at Manzanillo, **FAIRFAX** at Guantánamo Bay (10 OCT 33) and **STUREVANT** at Santiago, then at Key West (10 OCT 1933).

The destroyer **McFARLAND** was en route to Cárdenas, Cuba and the Coast Guard cutters **GRESHAM** en route to Matanzas, **YAMACRAW** to Puerto Padre & **UNALGA** to Antilla, Cuba.

Four additional destroyers, **BADGER**, **BABBITT**, **TATTNALL** and **TILLMAN**, en route to Cuban waters from the Naval Operating Base at Norfolk, VA.

The following vessels deployed by the Navy during the period September-November 1933 are as follows:

USS ABEL P. UPSHUR - departed Miami for Nueva Gerona 30 Sept. departed for Miami 7 October.

USS GEORGE E. BADGER, at Nueva Gerona. 17 October, 31 October, 3 November.

USS HERNDON, at Cardenas. 22 September, at Havana. 22 September, 25-27 September, at Matanzas 22-25. September, at Nueva Gerona, 24-31 October .

USS HUNT, 9 SEP-6 NOV 33 at Manatí. 16 September, at Puerto Padre. 16-20 September at Matanzas. 9-12 October, at Nipe Bay. 26 October- 2 November

USS WELBORN C. WOOD, at Nueva Gerona 1-2 October, 17-24 October.

USS SEMMES, at Havana 16-23 September, at Nipe Bay 21-22 October, at Nueva Gerona later?

USS WAINWRIGHT, at Matanzas 2-9 October, at Havana 18-27 October.

USS WILKES, at Matanzas 25 September-2 October, at Havana 11-18 October .

USS GRESHAM, at Matanzas 6 October, at Puerto Padre 7-13 October, at Nipe Bay 13-17 October.

USS TUSCARORA, at Matanzas 15-22 September, at Havana 23-25 September.

USS UNALGA, at Puerto Padre ?, at Antilla 18 September.

USS YAMACRAW, at Havana 16-25 September, 9-17 October 7 Sep- 1 Nov.

--◊◊◊--O--◊◊◊--

Appendix 3

GERARDO MACHADO AND COMMUNISM

Cuban Communism was born and nurtured by many events, some real and some fictional, the result of ingenious propaganda. The Bolshevik revolution and its efforts to create an international movement of Marxist supporters was a real source, as was the spontaneous birth of anarcho-syndicalism in Cuba, inspired by similar worker's hopes and expectations in Europe. There is no doubt that behind the formation of the *Partido Socialista Popular* (PSP) in Cuba were the hands of several Cuban worker's leaders, intellectuals and academics that, in practice, had become agents of the Comintern. What is 100% fictional is to attribute the emergence of Communism in Cuba to an ominous subject called **Carlos Baliño**; much less to place him on the side of José Martí in the founding of the *Partido Revolucionario Cubano*, Martí's instrument in his effort to bring the independence of Cuba in 1895.[1]

---

[1] The is no contemporary evidence that **Baliño** ever met José Martí. In his many trips to get the exiles' contributions to the bylaws of the **Partido Revolucionario Cubano**, Martí always wanted to have a photograph taken as a memento of such meetings. Baliño doesn't appear in any of those photographs. There are no letters of Martí to Baliño o Baliño to Martí or any reference in his writings or speeches to the existence of Baliño. It was in 1961 that Communists in Cuba began to claim that Baliño had been, with Martí, one of the founders of the Partido. Moreover, they began to claim that Baliño had told Julio Antonio Mella, a real founder of Cuban Communism, that the purpose and ideology of the Partido Revolucionario Cubano was to introduce and nurture in Cuba the ideals of Karl Marx once independence was secured. There is absolutely no evidence that such conversation Baliño-Mella ever took place, or that they had ever meet. At any

The first recruits to form a Communist Party in Cuba happened during the student movements of the post WWI times, mostly to protest against the corruption of the Zayas government; the most successful were led by Julio Antonio Mella, who brought the notion of class struggle to the University. No doubt Mella was a tireless activist and a vibrant orator and, as a declared Marxist, he brought some stature to the -until then- the low-class (dirty workers in tatters) reputation of socialism, Marxism and Communism.[2]

In 1925, financed by the Comintern, the *Mexican Communist Party* [3] met with several left-leaning youth organizations and formed the Partido Comunista de Cuba. Almost immediately several intellectuals, professionals and workers became part of this nuclear group: **Rubén Martínez Villena** being the most notable. Also, almost immediately, Machado's police moved against them and in 1927, the party was declared illegal.

The party continued to grow underground through 1928 and 1929, gaining influence among the disaffected and trouncing the recruitment power of the anarcho-syndicalist leaders of the *Confederación Nacional Obrero de Cuba*, the *CNOC*. At the time, its mayor enrolling was among railways and tobacco workers, followed by the adhesion of some agricultural workers' groups. By the end of 1929, however, the party has a total membership of probably a few hundred dues paying members, and a recruiting and propaganda tool in the underground newspaper **El Comunista**, with a circulation of a few hundred. By 1930, due to policy disputes and leadership disagreements, the Cuban Communist Party had full control of the Confederación Nacional Obrero de Cuba (CNOC), which had 16,000 affiliates. The Confederación was then fully an anti-Machado and an anti-USA group, with a specific target of discrediting and destroying the moderate petty-Bourgeois opposition. In March of 1933, when Machado suspended the legal rights of the Communist-led CNOC, the union called for a general strike that paralyzed all transports in

---

rate, Mella was an unbalanced and disorderly agitator that had been expelled for erratic and disorderly from his High School (Escolapios de Guanabacoa), as well as from the Communist Parties in Cuba and Mexico.

[2] **Mella,** real name **Nicanor McPartland**, founded as Communist-dependent organizations, the **Cuban Anti-Imperialist League**, the **Anti-Clerical Federation**, the **Association of Cuban Revolutionary Emigres**, and the **Universidad Popular José Martí**, all from 1923 to 1929.

[3] Two of the most vocal and economic supporters of the party were the muralist **Diego Rivera** and his wife **Frida Kahlo**.

Havana but failed to move workers anywhere else. Machado's response was to arrest the CNOC leaders and suspend and harass all workers confederations. The CNOC, however, supported by smaller workers' unions, persisted in its efforts, and by 1932 Machado did not know how to stop the threat to his government. Its only alternative was to supply the United States with secret police files that tied the CNOC with the Communists International. By then, however, Washington was as concerned with the Communists confronting Machado as with the growth of discontent among students, non-Marxist labor unions and many Cuban professionals and middle-class people. In the view of the US Department of State, the good news in Cuba was that the Communists had no party discipline even though it consisted of a mere 3,000 members at the most. The bad news was that the party had established a strong hold on some important sectors such as sugar, urban transportation and tobacco, i.e., the economic base and the daily life.

Now, in 1933 Cuba, the alternatives were crystal clear: (1) Support Machado for his anti-Communist history and commitment; or (2) Seek a peaceful transition from Machado's government to a democratic administration that could stop the serious threat of Socialism a few miles from American shores. The unfortunate situation, however, was that Washington was not counting with the smarts of a superb diplomatic presence in Cuba.[4]

---

[4] **Benjamin Sumner Wells** (1863-1911) was in 1933 a major foreign adviser to President Roosevelt. He was a well-connected New Yorker, a Harvard alumnus and a good friend of the Roosevelts. A New York Times article described him as "*Tall, slender, blond and always correctly tailored, somewhat shy but with dignified firmness, with enough dignity to be Viceroy of India ...*" Time magazine described his writings as "Ponderous, lifeless, too technical, almost a constant indictment of U.S. foreign policy in the Hemisphere..." He was related to the Astors and the Roosevelts, serving at 12 years old as a page of Franklyn and Leonor wedding. Throughout his life he was a substantial contributor to all political campaigns of all the Roosevelts. His diplomacy in Cuba in the 1930s little and little became a promise to the opponents of Machado's government of a change of government and participation in the subsequent administration, if they joined his mediation process and supported an orderly transfer of power. He turned out to be a closeted bisexual. In 1940, returning with Roosevelt from a funeral in Alabama, he was reprimanded by the president for soliciting sex from two male African American **Pullman** car porters, an incident reported in 1956 in *Confidential*, the scandal magazine. He was attributed by Winston Churchill as the creator of the phase *"No Comment,"* as response to any undesired question by a reporter. In the end, he was forced out of government service by Secretary Hull when it was revealed he had solicited two men for sex in the streets of Washington.

In the photos, left to right:
Carlos Baliño (1848-1926), a **Cuban** writer born in **Guanajay, Cuba**; a card-carrying member of the Cuban Communist Party.
Julio Antonio Mella, whose real name was Nicanor McPartland, (1903-1929), a founder of the *"internationalized"* Cuban Communist Party. Assassinated in Mexico by orders of the *Comintern*.
Benjamín Sumner Welles (1892-1961) an American government official and diplomat in the Foreign Service, a major foreign policy adviser to President Franklin D. Roosevelt who served as Under Secretary of State from 1936 to 1943, during FDR's presidency.

--◊◊◊--0--◊◊◊--

Two important documents in 1933 Cuba: the issue of ***Bohemia Magazine*** celebrating the student-soldiers alliance during the revolution (Carlos Prío-Fulgencio Batista) and the ***Student's Manifesto*** (DEU), signed by, among others, Eduardo Chibás.

Cuba in 1933

Index

Numbers

1928, 11, 18, 25, 44, 45, 103, 114, 165, 168, 169, 170, 373, 383, 384
1933 Revolution, 8, 13
50% Law, 322, 350

A

ABC, 13, 22, 23, 26, 30, 34, 35, 39, 48, 68, 78, 81, 82, 91, 93, 98, 99, 112, 113, 166, 175, 176, 177, 179, 193, 194, 204, 207, 210, 216, 218, 222, 223, 226, 228, 229, 233, 245, 247, 250, 257, 273, 274, 292, 298, 307, 312, 313, 315, 316, 317, 322, 337, 342, 347, 363, 371
ABC countries, 218
Ainciart, 113, 134
Alfaro, 324, 325
Amnesty, 22, 94, 102, 105, 106, 107, 109, 110, 381
Anarchist, 14, 378, 379
Angulo, 335
Arévalo, 379
Arias, 287
Arsenio Ortiz, 21, 27, 41, 42, 60, 62, 382
Asbert, 240
Associated Press, 60, 225, 349, 364
Atarés, 112, 114, 322, 336, 337, 338, 351
Auténtico, 8, 371
Averhoff, 89, 91

B

Barberán, 68
Barceló, 139
Barquín, 222, 232
Barracks, 32, 39, 178, 180, 194, 315, 317, 329, 332, 336, 337, 353, 380
Barreras, 89, 139, 327
Belt, 155, 204
Bombs, 21, 38, 327, 353
Botet, 204
Burdett, 286, 287

C

Caffery, 51, 52, 95, 98, 149, 150, 159, 162, 164, 186, 187, 197, 198, 203, 213, 218, 222, 227, 228, 237, 239, 243, 244, 245, 272, 279, 286, 291, 295, 296, 299, 300, 341, 343, 345, 347, 348, 350, 359, 362, 366, 367, 369, 370
Candidate, 11, 18, 19, 25, 45, 46, 55, 66, 69, 78, 103, 110, 317, 324, 329, 358, 384
Carbó, 13, 21, 115, 175, 176, 184, 198, 288, 321, 342
Carrera Jústiz, 290
Carrillo, 20, 175, 336
Cartana, 155

Castellanos, 99
Castillo, 152, 155, 174
Catlin, 375, 376
Céspedes, 112, 113, 114, 149, 152, 153, 154, 155, 158, 160, 165, 166, 168, 170, 175, 176, 179, 182, 184, 192, 193, 199, 200, 202, 204, 205, 208, 210, 212, 218, 220, 225, 226, 233, 240, 245, 248, 276, 291, 298, 299, 300, 301, 315, 365
Chargé d'Affaires, 28, 196, 197, 205, 220, 222, 228, 237, 244, 273, 297, 298, 352
Chase, 16, 17, 68, 376, 378, 384, 385
Chibás, 16, 115, 222, 331
Chief of Staff, 158, 165, 174, 179, 180, 216, 220, 256, 317
Cintas, 22, 115, 117, 125, 126, 131, 135, 136, 140, 141, 142, 143
CNOC, 14, 177, 350, 379
Columbia, 73, 112, 115, 175, 180, 194, 204, 210, 272, 311, 315, 322, 327, 329, 338
Communist, 13, 14, 19, 26, 112, 118, 171, 189, 205, 208, 210, 214,

251, 260, 269, 274, 287, 290, 301, 330, 331, 334, 350, 378, 379
Congress, 12, 14, 19, 23, 25, 44, 45, 46, 48, 57, 64, 69, 74, 77, 78, 80, 95, 97, 100, 107, 109, 110, 113, 114, 117, 118, 122, 123, 124, 128, 129, 130, 137, 140, 143, 147, 149, 152, 157, 163, 166, 168, 169, 170, 324, 355, 373, 376, 381, 384, 385
Conservative Party, 12, 25, 64, 80, 99, 110, 128, 137, 142, 143
Constitution, 11, 12, 16, 17, 18, 42, 44, 45, 102, 114, 140, 176, 343, 384
Consul, 2, 178, 180, 198, 260, 273, 295
Convention, 11, 18, 25, 78, 177
Coolidge, 18, 385
Coro, 268
Cosme de la Torriente, 22, 64, 91, 93
Costales, 233
Crowder, 10, 44, 46, 152, 166, 377
Cuban Electric Company, 357, 359, 375
Cuban Telephone Company, 359, 375
Cuervo Rubio, 114, 175, 271

D

Daussá, 20, 35, 38, 175
De la Torre, 34, 68, 113, 312

Decree, 19, 20, 21, 46, 114
Despaigne, 176, 233, 234, 317
Destroyer, 191, 194, 337, 339, 386
Dihigo, 153
Directorio, 12, 13, 26, 35, 93, 225, 247, 248
Dorta Duque, 91, 363

E

El Mundo, 376
Escalona, 258
Estrada Palma, 11

F

Fabregat, 379, 380
Felipe Pazos, 20
Fernández, 348
Fernando Ortiz, 307, 311, 313, 315, 316
Ferrer, 174, 184, 199, 200, 202, 212, 225, 261, 299, 300
FEU, 11, 12, 15
Finlay, 176, 222, 232, 233, 272, 291, 292, 293, 295, 296, 298
Foreign Affairs, 197, 205, 209, 214, 222, 227, 228, 237, 244, 246, 297, 305, 352
Forestier, 14
Franco, 306, 310
Freyre, 22, 382

G

Gaceta Oficial, 377
García Bárcena, 20, 175
Generation of 1930, 12
GIBSON, 246, 297, 305
Giraudy, 317, 350
González Rubiera, 27
Granados, 261, 271, 309, 311

Guantánamo, 371, 386
Guardia Rural, 60
Guggenheim, 27, 28, 29, 30, 32, 34, 35, 373, 378
Guiteras, 16, 35, 176, 177, 178, 222, 233, 310, 330, 334, 336, 342, 353, 356, 363, 371

H

Heraldo de Cuba, 16, 89, 90
Hernández, 27, 114, 312, 322
Herrera, 66, 89, 91, 97, 112, 114, 124, 125, 129, 145, 146, 147, 148, 149, 153, 374, 382
Hevia, 13, 21, 27, 34, 175, 327, 367, 371
Hotel Nacional, 213
Hurley, 150, 171

I

Irisarri, 175, 176
Isla de Pinos, 10, 19, 113
Iturralde, 336

J

Joven Cuba, 371
Juan Gualberto, 20, 34

K

Kellogg, 383, 385

L

La Cabaña, 14, 21, 112, 272
La Semana, 115, 198, 327
Labourdette, 20, 306, 327

Laurent, 175, 180, 272
Lawton, 197
Left Wing, 13, 21, 26, 93
Liberal Party, 11, 12, 14, 22, 66, 69, 99, 110, 119, 120, 123, 125, 126, 128, 137, 139, 146, 149, 238, 240, 375
Library of Congress, 6
lynchings, 165

M

Mañach, 16, 351
Marianista Parties, 363
Márquez Sterling, 114, 296
Martínez Sáenz, 22, 30, 93, 115, 155, 177, 204
Martinez Villena, 13
Massaguer, 115
Matthews, 363, 364, 365, 366
McBain, 73, 78, 100, 102, 117, 160, 166, 171
Mediation, 23, 50, 64, 67, 69, 74, 75, 80, 81, 82, 84, 87, 89, 90, 91, 93, 94, 95, 97, 98, 99, 100, 107, 109, 110, 111, 113, 118, 119, 120, 128, 143, 153, 157, 166, 226, 233, 247, 248
Mella, 14, 19, 177
Memorandum, 115, 125, 140, 179, 186, 188, 191, 196, 203, 205, 213, 215, 217, 222, 227, 228, 229, 237, 242, 248, 278, 286, 324, 345, 347
Mendez Peñate, 64, 75, 80, 109, 163,
166, 184, 233, 325, 363
Méndez Peñate, 20, 27, 34
Mendieta, 13, 20, 21, 27, 34, 64, 75, 109, 110, 163, 166, 176, 177, 184, 189, 193, 204, 208, 210, 227, 233, 240, 250, 252, 265, 266, 268, 270, 273, 290, 292, 293, 306, 307, 312, 313, 315, 316, 317, 318, 320, 321, 323, 325, 327, 328, 329, 330, 332, 353, 356, 358, 360, 362, 370, 371
Mendoza, 196, 261, 271, 335
Menocal, 13, 21, 34, 64, 67, 75, 80, 81, 82, 84, 89, 93, 98, 102, 109, 113, 114, 163, 165, 166, 176, 177, 184, 186, 189, 208, 210, 227, 229, 233, 234, 250, 261, 268, 292, 301, 328, 342, 347, 348, 355, 365, 376, 378
Mexico, 15, 19, 139, 140, 176, 177, 179, 197, 198, 205, 217, 218, 220, 221, 229, 237, 244, 246, 273, 279, 282, 288, 297, 298, 313, 373
Miami, 27, 34, 67, 75, 80, 81, 84, 98, 154, 312, 355, 386
Miguel Mariano, 15, 21, 34, 81, 87, 91, 109, 110, 163,
177, 184, 250, 257, 264, 315, 317, 352, 356
Montevideo, 97, 105, 139, 162, 197, 218, 239, 322, 331, 334, 343, 347, 348, 349, 350, 367, 385
Montoro, 113
Mutiny, 180, 184, 189, 199, 200, 202, 205, 210, 212, 220, 223, 226, 227, 253, 256, 260, 285, 301, 307, 312, 323, 327, 329, 353

N

Nassau, 113, 150, 171

O

Obregón, 17, 154
OCRR, 84, 91, 93, 98, 99, 113, 177, 210, 230, 233, 247, 250, 257, 274, 292, 307, 342
Orestes Ferrara, 15, 22, 27, 28, 36, 39, 58, 113, 384, 385
Oscar Cintas, 35, 60, 112

P

Padilla, 20, 175, 197, 198, 238, 239, 350
País, 329, 350
Palace, 21, 125, 170, 178, 182, 184, 187, 200, 208, 216, 217, 220, 222, 256, 280, 307, 310, 327, 331, 350, 363, 366, 375
Pan American Conference, 17,

18, 350
Pentarquía, 175, 176
Platt, 10, 16, 17, 140, 176, 351, 371, 384, 385
Popular Party, 12, 25, 64, 99, 137
Porfirio Franca, 175, 176, 184, 198, 216
Porra, 21, 381, 382
Portela, 175, 184, 198, 213, 295, 296, 299, 309, 310, 327
Portell Vilá, 350
Presno, 153, 155, 360
Prío, 8, 20, 175, 327, 350
Proclamation, 182, 199, 226, 246, 307, 323, 382
procrastination, 106

Q

Querejeta, 322

R

Red Cross, 276, 335
Reed, 35, 36, 38, 39, 40, 52, 347, 348
Repression, 21, 46, 50, 107, 129, 130, 222, 380
Rodriguez, 315
Roosevelt, 23, 34, 35, 84, 89, 102, 111, 112, 113, 114, 140, 141, 146, 175, 176, 198, 215, 230, 239, 245, 257, 271, 322, 343, 344, 347, 350, 369, 386
Rotary, 261, 271, 376
Rubén de León, 20, 313, 365

S

Saavedra, 214, 215
Saladrigas, 34, 115, 155, 170, 184,

204, 245, 298, 313, 322
Sanguily, 113, 158, 165, 174, 175, 176, 240, 276, 300, 335
Santos Jiménez, 91, 155, 174, 259
Sardiñas, 81, 84
Seigle, 299, 334, 335
sergeants, 20, 114, 199, 205, 216, 220, 223, 227, 254, 269, 301, 306, 317, 329
Soviet, 205, 373
Spindola, 298
STIMSON, 27, 28, 30, 34, 35, 36, 38
Strauss, 247
Strikes, 380
Student Council, 91, 204, 252, 256, 258, 259, 260, 264, 266, 268, 270, 271, 274, 281, 285, 288, 291, 306
Student Directorate, 287, 290, 292, 293, 295, 298, 304, 309, 310, 311, 313, 318, 323, 325, 327, 328, 329, 330, 331, 339, 360
Sugar, 10, 17, 55, 60, 61, 103, 114, 165, 172, 174, 177, 203, 251, 275, 290, 304, 351, 367, 376, 379, 385

T

Torriente, 64, 67, 75, 78, 80, 98, 153, 166, 204, 233, 325, 330, 353, 358, 359, 363, 364
Treasury, 35, 61, 89, 91, 122, 152, 160, 176, 222, 233,

251, 317
Trejo, 20, 26
Trucco, 345

U

Unamuno, 20
Unión Nacionalista, 13, 26, 34, 91, 155, 183, 189, 208, 210, 227, 229, 233, 247, 257, 260, 265, 274, 310, 313, 328, 330, 342, 352, 353, 363
UNR, 210
US Navy, 386

V

Valdés Fauli, 114
Varona, 16, 20, 80, 114, 259, 322
Vázquez Bello, 22, 36
Velasco, 280
Vidaurreta, 382

W

Welles, 40, 42, 51, 68, 84, 85, 89, 93, 94, 112, 113, 114, 115, 117, 125, 128, 142, 143, 175, 177, 178, 179, 207, 215, 232, 242, 272, 273, 300, 321, 322, 341, 343, 344, 345, 348, 349, 350, 365, 366
Weyler, 374
WHITE, 28, 30
Wilson, 139, 196, 218, 324, 325

Z

Zaldo, 81, 84
Zayas, 10, 113, 115, 146, 152, 153, 233, 376, 377, 378
Zubizarreta, 118

 **Raúl Eduardo Chao** received his PhD from Johns Hopkins University and after a brief stint in industry spent 18 years in academe, as Full Professor and Department Chairman at the **Universities of Puerto Rico** and **Detroit**. In 1986 he founded a very successful management consultancy, assisting companies and government agencies to develop positive work environments and process improvement techniques as the means to secure concurrent improvements in productivity and quality. **The Systema Group** had as clients many Fortune 100 companies and Federal and State organizations, both in the US and abroad. As its Founder and Chairman, Chao wrote a dozen books and numerous articles in newspapers and reviewed journals. He and his wife Olga live in Lakeland, Florida.

www.ingramcontent.com/pod-product-compliance
Lightning Source LLC
Chambersburg PA
CBHW031249230426

43670CB00005B/96